ALSO BY LAWRENCE WRIGHT

Thirteen Days in September

Going Clear

The Looming Tower

God's Favorite

Twins

Remembering Satan

Saints and Sinners

In the New World

City Children, Country Summer

The Terror Years

The Terror Years

FROM AL-QAEDA TO
THE ISLAMIC STATE

LAWRENCE WRIGHT

ALFRED A. KNOPF   New York   2016

THIS IS A BORZOI BOOK
PUBLISHED BY ALFRED A. KNOPF

www.aaknopf.com

Knopf, Borzoi Books, and the colophon are registered
trademarks of Penguin Random House LLC.

Library of Congress Cataloging-in-Publication Data
Names: Wright, Lawrence, [date] author.
Title: The terror years : from al-Qaeda to the Islamic State /
Lawrence Wright.
Description: First edition \ New York : Knopf, 2016.
Identifiers: LCCN 2015046064 |ISBN 9780385352055 (hardback)
9780385352079 (eBook)
Subjects: LCSH: Terrorism—Middle East. | Terrorism—Religious
aspects—Islam. | Terrorism—United States—Prevention. |
Qaida (Organization) | IS (Organization) | Middle East—Politics
and government—1945– | Middle East—History—1979– |
BISAC: LITERARY COLLECTIONS / Essays. | BIOGRAPHY &
AUTOBIOGRAPHY / Composers & Musicians. |
BIOGRAPHY & AUTOBIOGRAPHY / Religious.
Classification: LCC HV6433.M5 .W75 2016 | DDC 363.3250956—dc23
LC record available at http://lccn.loc.gov/2015046064

Jacket image: ISIS militants firing from the back of a vehicle
near the Iraqi city of Tikrit. AFP Photo.
Jacket design by Chip Kidd

Manufactured in the United States of America
First Edition

IN MEMORY OF

James Foley

Steven Sotloff

Peter Kassig

Kayla Mueller

and the world they might have made

CONTENTS

PROLOGUE

My experience in the Middle East began as a kind of accident of history. I was a conscientious objector during the Vietnam War, and I had to spend two years doing alternative service in a low-paying job, at least fifty miles from home, that was nominally in the national interest. Such jobs typically consisted of changing bedpans in hospitals, but this was during the Nixon recession, and even those jobs were hard to come by. I didn't mind being away from home; at the time, I wanted to get as far away from America as possible. I went to the United Nations, in New York, thinking that there would be a position that might satisfy these requirements. The person who met me had apparently encountered others in my situation. He said that while working at the UN did not qualify as alternative service, he had a list of American institutions abroad that should serve. One of them had an office across the street. It was the American University in Cairo.

I didn't know, when I walked across United Nations Plaza, that the United States and Egypt had no diplomatic relations, and that there were scarcely any Americans in the whole country, outside of the diminished faculty at AUC. I'm not sure I even knew what language they spoke in Egypt. But thirty minutes after I entered the office, I was asked if I could leave that very night. No, I couldn't. My clothes were in Boston, along with my girlfriend; I hadn't told my parents what I was doing; I also had to consult with my draft board. In that case, could I leave tomorrow? Forty-eight hours later I taught my first class, to young Egyptians whose English language ability wasn't quite good enough to gain admission to the university.

That stint in Egypt would shape my career in decisive ways. In 1998 I was the cowriter of a movie, *The Siege,* starring Denzel Washington, Bruce Willis, Annette Bening, and Tony Shalhoub, which was about a hypothetical attack by an Arab terrorist on New York City. The question the movie posed was: What would happen if terrorism came to America, in the same way that it was already being experienced in France and England? How would we react? What kind of country would we become? *The Siege* was a box-office failure, in part because of protests by Arabs and Muslims resentful of being stereotyped as terrorists. After 9/11, it was the most rented movie in America. It came to be seen as a kind of creepy prophecy.

For the next five years, I was immersed in researching *The Looming Tower: Al-Qaeda and the Road to 9/11.* There are three pieces included here as consolidated portraits that would later be incorporated in different form into that book. "The Man Behind Bin Laden" took me back to Egypt in order to learn about Ayman al-Zawahiri, then the number-two man in al-Qaeda, who would become its leader upon the death of bin Laden. It was strange to find the country I had been so fond of now roiled by the conflicting emotions of pride, shame, and denial that the attacks on New York and Washington had engendered. It was also disconcerting to revisit places once dear to me now stained with such starkly different connotations: the classrooms of the American University where I had taught were haunted by the ghost of Mohamed Atta, who had studied English there; and the Maadi Sporting Club, where I had played in tennis tournaments, had also hosted young Ayman al-Zawahiri at the outdoor cinema on summer evenings.

"The Counterterrorist" began days after 9/11, as I was desperately trying to find a way to understand how and why this had happened. I began going through obituaries that were then streaming online. On the *Washington Post* site, I found one for John O'Neill, the former head of counterterrorism in the New York office of the FBI—the same office I had written about in *The Siege.* The obit made it seem as if O'Neill was a bit of a disgrace—he had lost his job shortly before 9/11 because he had taken classified information out of the office. He then became head of security at the World Trade Center and died on that day. At the time, I thought his death was ironic: instead of getting bin Laden, bin Laden got him. I now think of O'Neill's death as a Greek tragedy. He willingly placed himself at what he expected would be Ground Zero in the tragedy he saw approaching.

A related piece, included here, is "The Agent," my profile of Ali Soufan, John O'Neill's talented protégé, who was the case agent of the USS *Cole* bombing by al-Qaeda in October 2000. Soufan also played an unwitting role in my research for *The Siege.* I had heard about a skillful undercover operative in the New York office of the bureau, a Muslim American who was born in Beirut and spoke fluent Arabic. I based the Tony Shalhoub character on him, although Soufan and I wouldn't actually meet until several years later. In this piece, I raise questions about the failure of the CIA to cooperate with Soufan's investigation into the murder of seventeen American sailors. Had the agency responded to Soufan's requests for information—leads that would have exposed the presence of al-Qaeda in America twenty months before 9/11—it is very likely that those attacks would never have happened. To this day, the CIA has failed to hold anyone accountable for this catastrophic negligence.

I knew that Osama bin Laden was going to be one of my central characters in *The Looming Tower,* but for more than a year the Saudis refused to give me a visa as a journalist. Finally, I got a job as the mentor to young reporters at the *Saudi Gazette,* an English-language daily in Jeddah, bin Laden's hometown. Normally, when I am researching a piece, I am in a hotel, making calls, trying to set up appointments. In this case, I lived in a middle-class Saudi flat, and I went to work every day. I was nominally teaching the craft of journalism, but my students were teaching me far more about their country than I could ever have learned on my own. It was a chastening lesson about the blinders that reporters wear when they drop from the sky into another culture. My experience is chronicled here in "The Kingdom of Silence."

Silence was a theme that drew me to another country, Syria, in 2006. The Middle East is a quarrelsome, voluble region—paradise for reporters, except when it is a lethal trap—but Syria was oddly mute. At a remove, it seemed progressive and secular compared with its Arab neighbors, but also elusive and enigmatic. How could I hope to decipher such a reticent culture? I reflected on how much the world understands America by our movies. Syria had a small but intriguing film industry, and I decided to watch Syrian movies and interview the filmmakers in order to glimpse the nation's closely guarded inner world. The piece is called "Captured on Film." What I found was a people who had been beaten into silence. The civil war was hard to imagine back then, but the desperation and simmering fury were already evident, both in the filmmakers and in their art.

Al-Qaeda and its progeny are not only terror organizations but also religious cults—deviant, isolated, and hostile to opposing views. Since 9/11, al-Qaeda has presented an extraordinary opportunity to observe a belief system that is evolving under pressure and adapting to challenges. I've traced some of the consequential but often bewildering theological arguments that govern this movement in "The Master Plan," "The Rebellion Within," and "The Terror Web."

For decades, the Israeli-Palestinian dispute has provided moral justification for terrorism, with devastating consequences for the region. In 2006, a young Israeli soldier, Gilad Shalit, was captured by Hamas, which demanded a thousand Palestinian prisoners in exchange. Before that deal was finally struck, Israel invaded, and thirteen Israelis and fourteen hundred Gazans were killed. The disparity in the value of human lives struck me as being one of the confounding factors that contributes to violence on both sides. I call the piece "Captives," because it reflects the condition of both Gilad Shalit and the people who were holding him.

The war on terror has shaken the American intelligence community and compromised our democracy. From 2007 to 2009, the man in the middle of this maelstrom was Mike McConnell, the director of national intelligence and overseer of America's sprawling spy world. My profile of McConnell is included here as "The Spymaster." He and I had different views on privacy. My phone had been monitored while writing for *The New Yorker* and working on *The Looming Tower.* McConnell was unapologetic; such intrusions were insignificant and accidental, he believed. We also strongly differed on the value of what was then called "enhanced interrogation techniques." During the course of one of our interviews, McConnell told me that he had been "tortured." He meant that while he was undergoing survival training in the navy, he had been subjected to physical abuse that was supposed to prepare him to deal with the possibility of being held captive. Later, while the article was being fact-checked, McConnell denied that he had made such a statement. When I reminded him that the interview had been taped, he asked me to drop that statement because he said it would cost him his job. It wasn't my goal to have McConnell fired, and he had been unusually generous in granting me access. But I did wonder if I made a mistake in omitting that portion of the conversation from the *New Yorker* profile that followed, since I believe it was pertinent to the national conversation we were having about torture at the time. McConnell is now retired from government, and I've restored his remarks.

This book can be seen as a primer on the evolution of the jihadist movement from its early years to the present, and the parallel actions of the West to attempt to contain it. America's involvement in the Middle East since 9/11 has been a long series of failures. Our own actions have been responsible for much of the unfolding catastrophe. The 2003 invasion of Iraq by U.S. and coalition partners stands as one of the greatest blunders in American history. The Islamic State, also known as ISIL or ISIS, rose out of the chaos, throwing the region into turmoil that hasn't been equaled since the fall of the Ottoman Empire. The fecklessness of U.S. foreign policy was made shatteringly clear to me while I was researching a piece about young American reporters and aid workers who had been captured in Syria ("Five Hostages"). Their families were largely left to themselves to try to negotiate their children's release. The heroic efforts of David Bradley, the publisher of *The Atlantic,* on their behalf cast a light on the failure of the U.S. government to render any real assistance. It's a tragic reflection of American power neutralized in a world it fails to understand.

All of these pieces appeared originally in *The New Yorker,* although I have taken the liberty of editing and updating them for this book. (They also include material that was drawn from my two one-man plays, *My Trip to al-Qaeda* and *The Human Scale.*) My relationship with that magazine has gone on now for almost a quarter century, and my debt to that organization and to my longtime editor, Daniel Zalewski, is bottomless.

The Terror Years

The Man Behind bin Laden

I n March 2002, a band of horsemen journeyed through the province of Paktika, in Afghanistan, near the Pakistan border. Predator drones were circling the skies and American troops were sweeping through the mountains. The war had begun six months earlier, and by now the fighting had narrowed down to the ragged eastern edge of the country. For twelve days, American and Coalition forces had been bombing the nearby Shah-e-Kot Valley and systematically destroying the cave complexes in the al-Qaeda stronghold. Regional warlords had been bought off, the borders supposedly sealed. And yet the horsemen were riding unhindered toward Pakistan.

They came to the village of a local militia commander named Gula Jan, whose long beard and black turban might have signaled that he was a Taliban sympathizer. "I saw a heavy, older man, an Arab, who wore dark glasses and had a white turban," Jan said four days later. "He was dressed like an Afghan, but he had a beautiful coat, and he was with two other Arabs who had masks on." The man in the beautiful coat dismounted and began talking in a polite and humorous manner. He asked Jan and an Afghan companion about the location of American and Northern Alliance troops. "We are afraid we will encounter them," he said. "Show us the right way."

While the men were talking, Jan slipped away to examine a poster that had been dropped into the area by American airplanes. It showed a photograph of a man in a white turban and glasses. His face was broad and meaty, with a strong, prominent nose and full lips. His untrimmed beard was gray at the temples and ran in milky streaks below his chin. On his high forehead, framed by the swaths of his turban, was a darkened callus formed by many hours of prayerful prostration. His eyes reflected the sort of decisiveness one might expect in a medical man, but they also showed a measure of serenity that seemed oddly out of place. Jan was looking at a wanted poster for Dr. Ayman al-Zawahiri, who had a price of $25 million on his head.

Jan returned to the conversation. The man he now believed to be Zawahiri said to him, "May God bless you and keep you from the enemies of Islam. Try not to tell them where we came from and where we are going."

There was a telephone number on the wanted poster, but Gula Jan did not have a phone. Zawahiri and the masked Arabs disappeared into the mountains.

IN JUNE OF 2001, two terrorist organizations, al-Qaeda and the Egyptian Islamist group al-Jihad, formally merged into one. The name of the new entity—Qaeda al-Jihad—reflects the long and interdependent history of these two groups. Although Osama bin Laden, the founder of al-Qaeda, was the public face of Islamic terrorism, the members of al-Jihad and its guiding figure, Ayman al-Zawahiri, provided the backbone of the larger organization's leadership and was responsible for much of the planning of the terrorist operations against the United States, from the assault on American soldiers in Somalia in 1993, and the bombings of the American embassies in East Africa in 1998 and of the USS *Cole* in Yemen in 2000, to the attacks on the World Trade Center and the Pentagon on September 11.

Bin Laden and Zawahiri were bound to discover each other among the radical Islamists who were drawn to Afghanistan after the Soviet invasion in 1979. Bin Laden, who was in his early twenties, was already an international businessman; Zawahiri, six years older, was a surgeon from a notable Egyptian family. They saw in each other a solution to their dilemma. "Bin Laden had followers, but they weren't organized," recalls Essam Deraz, an Egyptian filmmaker who made several documentaries about the Soviet-Afghan War. "The people with Zawahiri had extraordinary capabilities—doctors, engineers, soldiers. They had experience in secret work. They knew how to organize themselves and create cells. And they became the leaders."

The goal of al-Jihad was to overthrow the civil government of Egypt and impose a theocracy that might eventually become a model for the entire Arab world; however, years of guerrilla warfare had left the group shattered and bankrupt. For Zawahiri, bin Laden was a savior—rich and generous, with nearly limitless resources, but also pliable and politically unformed. "Bin Laden had an Islamic frame of reference, but he didn't have anything against the Arab regimes," Montasser al-Zayat, a lawyer for many of the Islamists, told me. "When Ayman met bin Laden, he created a revolution inside him."

FIVE MILES SOUTH of the chaos of Cairo is a quiet middle-class suburb called Maadi. A consortium of Egyptian Jewish financiers, intending to create a kind of English village amid the mango and guava plantations and Bedouin settlements on the eastern bank of the Nile, began selling lots in the first decade of the twentieth century. The developers regulated everything, from the height of the garden fences to the color of the shutters on the grand villas that lined the streets. They planted eucalyptus trees to repel flies and mosquitoes, and gardens to perfume the air with the fragrance of roses and jasmine and bougainvillea. Many of the early settlers were British military officers and civil servants, whose wives started garden clubs and literary salons; they were followed by Jewish families, who by the end of the Second World War made up nearly a third of Maadi's population. After the war, Maadi evolved into a community of expatriate Europeans, American businessmen and missionaries, and a certain type of Egyptian—typically one who spoke French at dinner and followed the cricket matches.

The center of this cosmopolitan community was the Maadi Sporting Club. Founded at a time when Egypt was occupied by the British, the club was unusual for admitting not only Jews but Egyptians. Community business was often conducted on the all-sand eighteen-hole golf course, with the Giza Pyramids and the palmy Nile as a backdrop. As high tea was served to the British in the lounge, Nubian waiters bearing icy glasses of Nescafé glided among the pashas and princesses sunbathing at the pool. High-stepping flamingos waded through the lilies in the garden pond. The Maadi Club became an ideal expression of the founders' vision of Egypt—sophisticated, safe, secular, and ethnically diverse, though still married to British notions of class.

The careful regulations could not withstand the pressure of Cairo's burgeoning population, and in the late 1960s another Maadi took root. "We called its residents the 'Road 9 crowd,'" Samir Raafat, a journalist who has written a history of the suburb, told me. "It was very much 'them' and 'us.'" Road 9 runs beside train tracks that separate the tony side of Maadi from the *baladi* district—the native part of town. Here donkey carts clop along unpaved streets past peanut vendors and yam salesmen hawking their wares and fly-studded carcasses hanging in butcher shops. There is also, on this side of town, a narrow slice of the middle class, composed mainly of teachers and low-level bureaucrats who were drawn to the suburb by the cleaner air and the dream of crossing the tracks and being welcomed into the club.

In 1960, Dr. Rabie al-Zawahiri and his wife, Umayma, moved from Heliopolis to Maadi. Rabie and Umayma belonged to two of the most prominent families in Egypt. The Zawahiri (pronounced za-*wah*-iri) clan was creating a medical dynasty. Rabie was a professor of pharmacology at Ain Shams University in Cairo. His brother was a highly regarded dermatologist and an expert on venereal diseases. The tradition they established continued into the next generation; a 1995 obituary in a Cairo newspaper for one of their relatives, Kashif al-Zawahiri, mentioned forty-six members of the family, thirty-one of whom were doctors or chemists or pharmacists; among the others were an ambassador, a judge, and a member of parliament.

The Zawahiri name, however, was associated above all with religion. In 1929, Rabie's uncle Mohammed al-Ahmadi al-Zawahiri became the Grand Imam of al-Azhar, the thousand-year-old university in the heart of Old Cairo, which is still the center of Islamic learning in the Middle East. The leader of that institution enjoys a kind of papal status in the Muslim world, and Imam Mohammed is still remembered as one of the university's great modernizers. Rabie's father and grandfather were al-Azhar scholars as well.

Umayma Azzam, Rabie's wife, was from a clan that was equally distinguished but wealthier and also a little notorious. Her father, Dr. Abd al-Wahab Azzam, was the president of Cairo University and the founder and director of King Saud University, in Riyadh. He had also served at various times as the Egyptian ambassador to Pakistan, Yemen, and Saudi Arabia. Another relative was secretary-general of the Arab League. "From the first parliament, more than a hundred and fifty years ago, there have been Azzams in government," Umayma's uncle Mahfouz Azzam, who is an attorney in Maadi, told me. "And we were always in the opposition." Mahfouz was a fervent Egyptian nationalist in his youth. "I was in prison when I was fifteen years old," he said proudly. "They condemned me for making what they called a 'coup d'état.'" In 1945, Mahfouz was arrested again, in a roundup of militants after the assassination of Prime Minister Ahmad Mahir. "I myself was going to do what Ayman has done," he said.

Despite their pedigrees, Rabie and Umayma settled into an apartment on Street 100, on the *baladi* side of the tracks. Later, they rented a duplex at No. 10, Street 154, near the train station. High society held no interest for them. At a time when public displays of religious zeal were rare—and in Maadi almost unheard of—the couple was religious but not overtly pious. Umayma went about unveiled. There were more churches than mosques in the neighborhood, and a thriving synagogue.

Children quickly filled the Zawahiri home. The first, Ayman and a twin sister, Umnya, were born on June 19, 1951. The twins were extremely bright, and were at the top of their classes all the way through medical school. A younger sister, Heba, also became a doctor. The two other children, Mohammed and Hussein, trained as architects.

Obese, bald, and slightly cross-eyed, Rabie al-Zawahiri had a reputation as being eccentric and absentminded, and yet he was beloved by his students and by the neighborhood children. He spent most of his time in the laboratory or in his private medical clinic. Professor

Zawahiri's research occasionally took him to Czechoslovakia, at a
time when few Egyptians traveled, because of currency restrictions.
He always returned laden with toys for the children. He sometimes
found time to take them to the movies at the Maadi Sporting Club,
which were open for nonmembers. Young Ayman loved the cartoons
and Disney films, which played three nights a week on an outdoor
screen. In the summer, the family went to a beach in Alexandria. Life
on a professor's salary was constricted, especially with five ambitious
children to educate. The Zawahiris never owned a car until Ayman
was out of medical school. To economize, the family kept hens behind
the house for fresh eggs, and the professor bought oranges and man-
goes by the crate, which he pressed upon the children as a natural
source of vitamin C.

Umayma Azzam was a wonderful cook, famous for her *kunafa*—a
pastry of shredded phyllo filled with cheese and nuts and drenched in
orange-blossom syrup. She inherited several substantial plots of farm-
land in Giza and the Fayyum Oasis from her father, which provided
her with a modest income. Ayman and his mother shared a love of
literature. "She always memorized the poems that Ayman sent her,"
Mahfouz Azzam told me. Although Ayman maintained the Zawahiri
medical tradition, he was actually closer in temperament to his mother's side of the family. "The Zawahiris are professors and scientists,
and they hate to speak of politics," Azzam said. "Ayman told me that
his love of medicine was probably inherited. But politics was also in
his genes."

FOR ANYONE LIVING in Maadi in the fifties and sixties, there was
one defining social standard: membership in the Maadi Sporting
Club. "The whole activity of Maadi revolved around the club," Samir
Raafat, the historian of the suburb, told me one afternoon as he drove
me around the neighborhood. "If you were not a member, why even
live in Maadi?" The Zawahiris never joined, which meant that Ayman
would be curtained off from the center of power and status. "He
wasn't mainstream Maadi; he was totally marginal Maadi," Raafat
said. "The Zawahiris were a conservative family. You would never
see them in the club, holding hands, playing bridge. We called them

saidis. Literally, the word refers to someone from a district in Upper Egypt, but we use it to mean something like 'hick.'"

At one end of Maadi, surrounded by green playing fields and tennis courts, is Victoria College, a private British-built preparatory school for boys. The students attended classes in coats and ties. One of its best-known graduates was a talented cricket player named Michel Chalhub; after he became a film actor, he took the name Omar Sharif. Edward Said, the Palestinian scholar and author, attended the school, along with Jordan's future king, Hussein.

Zawahiri, however, attended the state secondary school, a modest low-slung building behind a green gate, on the opposite side of the suburb. "It was the hoodlum school, the other end of the social spectrum," Raafat told me. The students of the two schools existed in different worlds, never meeting each other even in sports. Whereas Victoria College measured itself by European standards, the state school had its back to the West. Inside the green gate, the schoolyard was run by bullies and the classrooms by tyrants. A physically vulnerable young boy such as Ayman had to create strategies to survive.

Ayman's childhood pictures show him with a round face, a wary gaze, and a flat and unsmiling mouth. He was a bookworm and hated contact sports—he thought they were "inhumane," according to his uncle Mahfouz. From an early age, he was devout, and he often attended prayers at the Hussein Sidki Mosque, an unimposing annex of a large apartment building; the mosque was named after a famous actor who renounced his profession because it was ungodly. No doubt Ayman's interest in religion seemed natural in a family with so many distinguished religious scholars, but it added to his image of being soft and otherworldly.

Although Ayman was an excellent student, he often seemed to be daydreaming in class. "He was a mysterious character, closed and introverted," Zaki Mohammed Zaki, a Cairo journalist who was a classmate of his, told me. "He was extremely intelligent, and all the teachers respected him. He had a very systematic way of thinking, like that of an older guy. He could understand in five minutes what it would take other students an hour to understand. I would call him a genius."

Once, to the family's surprise, Ayman skipped a test, and the principal sent a note to his father. The next morning, Professor Zawahiri met with the principal and told him, "From now on, you will have the honor of being the headmaster of Ayman al-Zawahiri. In the future, you will be proud." Indeed, that incident was never repeated.

Ayman often showed a playful side at home. "When he laughed, he would shake all over—*yanni*, it was from the heart," Mahfouz says. But at school he held himself apart. "There were a lot of activities in the high school, but he wanted to remain isolated," Zaki told me. "It was as if mingling with the other boys would get him too distracted. When he saw us playing rough, he'd walk away. I felt he had a big puzzle inside him—something he wanted to protect."

IN 1950, the year before Ayman al-Zawahiri was born, Sayyid Qutb, a well-known literary critic in Cairo, returned home after spending two years at Colorado State College of Education in Greeley. He had left Cairo as a secular writer who enjoyed a sinecure in the Ministry of Education. One of his early discoveries was a young writer named Naguib Mahfouz, who would win the 1988 Nobel Prize in Literature. "Qutb was our friend," Mahfouz recalled. "When I was growing up, he was the first critic to recognize me." Mahfouz, who was stabbed and nearly killed by an Islamic fundamentalist in 1994, said that before Qutb went to America he was at odds with many of the sheikhs, who he thought were "out of date." Qutb saw himself then as part of the modern age, and he wore his religion lightly. His great passion was Egyptian nationalism, and, perhaps because of his strident opposition to the British occupation, the Ministry of Education decided that he would be safer in America.

Qutb had studied American literature and popular culture, and he idealized the United States, which seemed to him and other Egyptian nationalists to be a friendly neutral power and a democratic ideal. In Colorado, however, Qutb encountered a postwar America unlike the one he had found in books and Hollywood films. "It is astonishing to realize, despite his advanced education and his perfectionism, how primitive the American really is in his views on life," Qutb wrote upon his return to Egypt. "His behavior reminds us of the era of the caveman. He is primitive in the way he lusts after power, ignoring

ideals and manners and principles." Qutb was impressed by the number of churches in America—there were more than twenty in Greeley
alone—and yet the Americans he met seemed completely uninterested
in spiritual matters. He was appalled to witness a dance in a church
recreation hall, during which the minister, setting the mood for the
couples, dimmed the lights and played "Baby, It's Cold Outside." "It is
difficult to differentiate between a church and any other place that is
set up for entertainment, or what they call in their language, 'fun,'"
he wrote. The American was primitive in his art as well. "Jazz is his
preferred music, and it is created by Negroes to satisfy their love of
noise and to whet their sexual desires," he concluded. He even complained about his haircuts: "Whenever I go to a barber I return home
and redo my hair with my own hands."

In what he saw as the spiritual wasteland of America, Qutb re-
created himself as a militant Muslim, and he returned to Egypt with
the vision of an Islam that would throw off the vulgar influences of
the West. Islamic society had to be purified, and the only mechanism
powerful enough to cleanse it was the ancient and bloody instrument
of jihad. "Qutb was the most prominent theoretician of the fundamentalist movements," Zawahiri wrote in a brief memoir entitled
"Knights under the Prophet's Banner," in December 2001. "Qutb said,
'Brother push ahead, for your path is soaked in blood. Do not turn
your head right or left but look only up to Heaven.'"

Qutb, a dark-skinned Egyptian, also brought home a new and
abiding anger about race. "The white man in Europe or America is
our number-one enemy," he declared. "The white man crushes us
underfoot while we teach our children about his civilization. . . . We
are endowing our children with amazement and respect for the master who tramples our honor and enslaves us. Let us instead plant the
seeds of hatred, disgust, and revenge in the souls of these children.
Let us teach these children from the time their nails are soft that the
white man is the enemy of humanity, and that they should destroy
him at the first opportunity."

It is clear that Qutb was not just writing about America. His
polemic was directed at Egyptians who wanted to bend Islam around
the modern world. Modern values—secularism, rationality, tolerance, democracy, subjectivity, individualism, mixing of the sexes,

materialism—had infected Islam through the agency of Western colonialism. His extraordinary project was to take apart the entire political and philosophical structure of modernity and return Islam to its unpolluted origins.

Egypt was already in the midst of a revolution. The Society of Muslim Brothers, the oldest and most influential fundamentalist group in Egypt, instigated an uprising against the British, whose lingering occupation of the Suez Canal Zone enraged the nationalists. In January 1952, in response to the British massacre of fifty Egyptian policemen, mobs organized by the Muslim Brothers in Cairo set fire to movie theaters, casinos, department stores, nightclubs, and automobile showrooms, which, in their view, represented an Egypt that had tied its future to the West. At least thirty people were killed, seven hundred and fifty buildings were destroyed, and twelve thousand people were made homeless. The dream of a cosmopolitan metropolis ended, and the foreign community began its exodus. In July of that year, a military junta, dominated by an army colonel, Gamal Abdel Nasser, packed King Farouk onto his yacht and seized control of the government without firing a shot. According to several fellow conspirators who later wrote about the event, Nasser secretly promised the Brothers that he would impose Sharia—the rule of Islamic law—on the country.

A power struggle developed immediately between the leaders of the revolution, who had the army behind them, and the Muslim Brothers, who had a large presence in the mosques. Neither faction had the popular authority to rule, but, as Nasser imposed martial law and eliminated political parties, the contest narrowed to a choice between a military society and a religious one, either of which would have been rejected by the majority of Egyptians, had they been allowed to decide.

Nasser threw Qutb into prison for the first time in 1954. Three months later, he let him out and allowed him to become the head of the Muslim Brothers' magazine, *Al-Ikwan al-Muslimoun*. Presumably, he hoped that his display of mercy would enhance his standing with the Islamists and keep them from turning against the socialist and increasingly secular aims of the new government. One of the writers Qutb published was Zawahiri's uncle Mahfouz Azzam, who was then a young lawyer. Azzam had known Qutb nearly all his life. "Sayyid Qutb was my teacher," he told me. "He taught me Arabic grammar in 1936 and 1937. He came daily to our house. He held seminars and gave us books for discussion. The first book he asked me to write a report on was *What Did the World Lose with the Decline of the Muslims?*"

It quickly became obvious to Nasser that Qutb and his corps of young Islamists had a different agenda for Egyptian society from his, and he shut down the magazine after its first few issues. But the religious faction was not so easily controlled. The struggle for Egypt's future reached a climax on the night of October 26, 1954, as Nasser spoke before an immense crowd in Alexandria. The entire country was listening to the radio as a member of the Muslim Brothers stepped forward and fired eight shots at the Egyptian president, wounding a guard but missing Nasser. Nasser responded by having six conspirators executed immediately and arresting more than a thousand others, including Qutb. He had crushed the Brothers, once and for all, he thought.

Stories about Sayyid Qutb's suffering in prison have formed a kind of Passion play for Islamic fundamentalists. Qutb had a high fever when he was arrested, but the state-security officers handcuffed him and took him to prison. He fainted several times on the way. For several hours, he was kept in a cell with vicious dogs, and then, during long periods of interrogation, he was beaten. His trial was overseen by three judges, one of whom was a future president of Egypt, Anwar Sadat. In the courtroom, Qutb ripped off his shirt to display the marks of torture. The judges sentenced him to life in prison, but when Qutb's health deteriorated further, they reduced the sentence to fifteen years. He suffered chronic bouts of angina, and it is likely that he contracted tuberculosis in the prison hospital.

ONE LINE OF THINKING proposes that America's tragedy on September 11 was born in the prisons of Egypt. Human-rights advocates in Cairo argue that torture created an appetite for revenge, first in Sayyid Qutb and later in his acolytes, including Ayman al-Zawahiri. The main target of their wrath was the secular Egyptian government, but a powerful current of anger was directed toward the West, which they saw as an enabling force behind the repressive regime. They held the West responsible for corrupting and humiliating Islamic society. Indeed, the theme of humiliation, which is the essence of torture, is important to understanding the Islamists' rage against the West. Egypt's prisons became a factory for producing militants whose need for retribution—they called it "justice"—was all-consuming.

The hardening of Qutb's views can be traced in his prison writings. Through friends, he managed to smuggle out, bit by bit, a manifesto titled *Milestones* (*Ma'alim fi al-Tariq*). The manuscript circulated underground for years. It was finally published in Cairo in 1964 and was quickly banned; anyone caught with a copy could be charged with sedition. Its ringing apocalyptic tone may be compared with Rousseau's *The Social Contract* and Lenin's *What Is to Be Done?*—with similar bloody consequences.

Qutb begins, "Mankind today is on the brink of a precipice. Humanity is threatened not only by nuclear annihilation but by the absence of values. The West has lost its vitality, and Marxism has failed. At this crucial and bewildering juncture, the turn of Islam and the Muslim community has arrived."

Qutb divides the world into two camps—Islam and *jahiliyya*. The latter, in traditional Islamic discourse, refers to a period of ignorance that existed throughout the world before the Prophet Muhammad began receiving his divine revelations, in the seventh century. For Qutb, the entire modern world, including so-called Muslim societies, is *jahiliyya*. This was his most revolutionary statement—one that placed nominally Islamic governments in the crosshairs of jihad. "The Muslim community has long ago vanished from existence," he contends. "It is crushed under the weight of those false laws and customs which are not even remotely related to Islamic teachings." Humanity cannot be saved unless Muslims recapture the glory of their earliest and purest expression. He writes: "We need to initiate the movement of Islamic revival in some Muslim country," in order to fashion an example that will eventually lead Islam to its destiny of world dominion. "There should be a vanguard which sets out with this determination and then keeps walking on the path." These words would echo in the ears of young Muslims who were looking for a role to play in history.

Qutb was hanged after dawn prayers on August 29, 1966. "The Nasserite regime thought that the Islamic movement received a deadly blow with the execution of Sayyid Qutb and his comrades," Zawahiri observes in his memoir. "But the apparent surface calm concealed an immediate interaction with Sayyid Qutb's ideas and the formation of the nucleus of the modern Islamic jihad movement in Egypt." The same year Qutb was hanged, Zawahiri helped to form an underground militant cell dedicated to replacing the secular Egyptian government with an Islamic one. He was fifteen years old.

"WE WERE a group of students from Maadi High School and other schools," Zawahiri testified about his days as a young radical, when he was put on trial in 1981 for conspiring in the assassination of President Sadat. The members of his cell usually met in one another's homes; sometimes they got together at a mosque and then went to a park or to a quiet spot on the tree-lined Corniche along the Nile. In the beginning, there were five members, and before long Zawahiri became the emir, or leader. "Our means didn't match our aspirations," he conceded in his testimony. But he never seemed to question his decision to become a revolutionary. "Bin Laden had a turning point in his life," Zawahiri's cousin Omar Azzam pointed out, "but Ayman and his brother Mohammed were like people in school moving naturally from one grade to another. You cannot say those boys were naughty guys or playboys, then turned one hundred and eighty degrees. To be honest, if Ayman and Mohammed repeated their lives, they would live them the same way."

Under the monarchy, before Nasser's assumption of power, the affluent residents of Maadi had been insulated from the whims of the government. In revolutionary Egypt, they suddenly found themselves vulnerable. "The kids noticed that their parents were frightened and afraid of expressing their opinions," Zawahiri's former schoolmate Zaki told me. "It was a climate that encouraged underground work." Clandestine groups like Zawahiri's were forming all over Egypt. Made up mainly of restless or alienated students, they were small and disorganized and largely unaware of one another. Then came the 1967 war with Israel. The speed and the decisiveness of Israel's victory in the Six-Day War humiliated Muslims who had believed that God favored their cause. They lost not only their armies and territory but also faith in their leaders, in their countries, and in themselves. For many Muslims, it was as though they had been defeated by a force far larger than the tiny country of Israel, by something unfathomable—modernity itself. The profound appeal of Islamic fundamentalism in Egypt and elsewhere was born in this shocking debacle. A newly strident voice was heard in the mosques, one that answered despair with a simple formulation: Islam is the solution.

The clandestine Islamist groups were galvanized by the war, and their primary target was Nasser's secular regime. In the terminology of jihad, the priority was to defeat the "near enemy"—that is, impure Muslim society. The "distant enemy"—the West—could wait until Islam had reformed itself. For the Islamists, this meant, at a minimum, imposing Sharia on the Egyptian legal system. Zawahiri also wanted to restore the caliphate, the rule of Islamic clerics, which had formally ended in 1924, after the dissolution of the Ottoman Empire, but had not exercised real power since the thirteenth century. Once the caliphate was reestablished, Zawahiri believed, Egypt would become a rallying point for the rest of the Islamic world. He later wrote, "Then, history would make a new turn, God willing, in the opposite direction against the empire of the United States and the world's Jewish government."

Nasser died of a heart attack in 1970. His successor, Sadat, desperately needed to establish his political legitimacy, and he quickly set about trying to make peace with the Islamists. Saad Eddin Ibrahim, a dissident sociologist at the American University in Cairo and an advocate of democratic reforms, who spent seven years in prison, told me, "Sadat was looking around for allies. He remembers the Muslim Brothers. Where are they? In prison. He offers the Brothers a deal: in return for their political support, he'll allow them to preach and to advocate, as long as they don't use violence. What Sadat didn't know was that the Islamists were split. Some of them had been inspired by Qutb. The younger, more radical ones thought that the older ones had gone soft."

Sadat emptied the prisons, miscalculating the peril that the Islamists posed to his regime.

———

THE MUSLIM BROTHERS, who were forbidden to act as a genuine political party, began colonizing professional and student unions. By 1973, a new band of young fundamentalists had appeared on campuses, first in the southern part of the country, then in Cairo. They called themselves al-Gama'a al-Islamiyya—the Islamic Group. Encouraged by Sadat's acquiescent government, which covertly provided them with arms so that they could defend themselves against any attacks by Marxists and Nasserites, the Islamic Group radicalized most of Egypt's universities. Soon it became fashionable for male students to grow beards and female students to wear the veil. Zawahiri kept his underground life a secret, even from his family, but he would later claim that his group had grown to forty members by 1974, when he was attending medical school at Cairo University.

Zawahiri was tall and slender, and he wore a mustache that paralleled the flat lines of his mouth. His face was thin, and his hairline was in retreat. He dressed in Western clothes, usually a coat and tie. He did not completely hide his political feelings, however. He once gave a campus tour to an American newsman, Abdallah Schleifer. A gangly, wiry-haired man who wore a goatee, a throwback to his beatnik phase in the late fifties, Schleifer was a challenging figure in Zawahiri's life. He was brought up in a non-observant Jewish family on Long Island. He went through a Marxist period and then, during a trip to Morocco in 1962, he encountered the Sufi tradition of Islam. One meaning of the word "Islam" is "to surrender," and that is what happened to Schleifer. He converted, changed his name from Marc to Abdallah, and spent the rest of his professional life in the Middle East. In 1974, when Schleifer first came to Cairo, as the bureau chief for NBC News, Zawahiri's uncle Mahfouz Azzam became a kind of sponsor for him. "Converts often get adopted, and Mahfouz was fascinating," Schleifer told me. "To him, it was sort of a gas that an American had taken to Islam. I had the feeling I was under the protection of the whole Azzam family."

Through Mahfouz, Schleifer met Zawahiri, who agreed to show him around the campus to get a better understanding of the scene. "He was scrawny and his eyeglasses were extremely prominent," Schleifer said. "He looked like a left-wing City College intellectual of thirty years earlier." During the tour, Zawahiri proudly pointed out students who were painting posters for political demonstrations, and he boasted that the Islamist movement had found its greatest recruiting success in the university's two most elite faculties—the medical and engineering schools. "Aren't you impressed by that?" he said. Schleifer patronized him. He observed that in the sixties those same faculties had been strongholds of the Marxist youth. The Islamist movement, he observed, was merely the latest trend in student rebellions. "Listen, Ayman, I'm an ex-Marxist," Schleifer said. "When you talk, I feel like I'm back in the Party. I don't feel as if I'm with a traditional Muslim." Zawahiri listened politely. "We parted on a friendly note," Schleifer said. "But I think he was puzzled."

Schleifer encountered Zawahiri again at a celebration of the Eid festival, one of the holiest days in the Muslim calendar. "I heard they were going to have outdoor prayer in the Farouk Mosque in Maadi," he recalled. "So I thought, Great, I'll go pray in their lovely garden. And who do I see but Ayman and one of his brothers. They were very intense. They laid out plastic prayer mats and set up a microphone." What was supposed to be a meditative day of chanting the Quran turned into a contest between the congregation and the Zawahiri brothers with their microphone. "I realized that they were introducing the Salafist formula, which does not recognize any Islamic traditions after the time of the Prophet. It was chaotic. Afterward, I went over to Zawahiri and said, 'Ayman, this is wrong.' He started to explain. I said, 'I'm not going to argue with you. I'm a Sufi and you're a Salafist. But you are making *fitna*'"—a term for stirring up trouble, which is proscribed by the Quran—"'and if you want to do that you should do it in your own mosque.'" Zawahiri meekly responded, "You're right, Abdallah."

ZAWAHIRI GRADUATED FROM medical school in 1974, then spent three years as a surgeon in the Egyptian Army, posted at a base outside Cairo. He was now in his late twenties, and it was time for him to marry. He had never had a girlfriend. "Our custom is to have friends or relations suggest a spouse," his cousin Omar told me. "If they find acceptance, they are allowed to meet once or twice, then start the engagement. It's not a love story." One of the possible brides suggested to Ayman was Azza Nowair, the daughter of a prominent Cairo family. Both her parents were lawyers. In another time, she might have become a professional woman herself or a socialite going to parties at the Sporting Club, but at Cairo University she adopted the *hijab*, the headscarf that has become a badge of conservatism among Muslim women. Azza's decision to veil herself was a shocking disavowal of her class. "Before that, she had worn the latest fashions," her older brother, Essam, told me. "We didn't want her to be so religious. She started to pray a lot and read the Quran. And, little by little, she changed completely." Soon, Azza went further and put on the *niqab*, the veil that covers a woman's face below the eyes. According to her brother, Azza spent whole nights in spiritual meditation. When he woke in the morning, he would find her sitting on the prayer mat with the Quran in her hands, fast asleep.

The *niqab* imposed a formidable barrier for a marriageable young woman. Because of Azza's wealthy, distinguished family, she had many suitors, but they all insisted that she drop the veil. Azza refused. "She wanted someone who would accept her as she was," her brother told me. "Ayman was looking for that type of person."

At the first meeting between Azza and Ayman, according to custom Azza lifted her veil for a few minutes. "He saw her face and then he left," Essam said. The young couple talked briefly on one other occasion after that, but it was little more than a formality. Ayman never saw his fiancée's face again until after the marriage ceremony. He had made a favorable impression on the Nowair family, who were a little dazzled by his distinguished ancestry. "He was polite and agreeable," Essam said. "He was very religious, and he didn't greet women. He wouldn't even look at a woman if she was wearing a short skirt." He apparently never talked about politics with Azza's family, and it's not clear how much he revealed about his activism to her. She once confided to Omar Azzam that her greatest desire was to become a martyr.

Their wedding was held in February 1978, at the Continental-Savoy Hotel, which had slipped from colonial grandeur into dowdy respectability. According to the wishes of the bride and groom, there was no music, and photographs were forbidden. "It was pseudo-traditional," Schleifer recalled. "Lots of cups of coffee and no one cracking jokes."

"MY CONNECTION WITH Afghanistan began in the summer of 1980 by a twist of fate," Zawahiri writes in his memoir. The director of a Muslim Brothers clinic in Cairo asked if Zawahiri would like to accompany him to Pakistan to tend to the Afghan refugees. Thousands were fleeing across the border as a result of the Soviet invasion, which had begun a few months earlier. Although he had recently gotten married, Zawahiri writes that he "immediately agreed." He had been preoccupied with the problem of finding a secure base for jihad, which seemed practically impossible in Egypt. "The River Nile runs in its narrow valley between two deserts that have no vegetation or water," he laments. "Such a terrain made guerrilla warfare in Egypt impossible and, as a result, forced the inhabitants of this valley to submit to the central government and to be exploited as workers and compelled them to be recruited into its army." Perhaps Pakistan or Afghanistan would prove a more suitable location for raising an army of radical Islamists who could eventually return to take over Egypt.

Zawahiri traveled to Peshawar with an anesthesiologist and a plastic surgeon. "We were the first three Arabs to arrive there to participate in relief work," he writes. He spent four months in Pakistan, working for the Red Crescent Society, the Islamic arm of the Red Cross.

Peshawar sits at the eastern end of the Khyber Pass, the historic concourse of invading armies since the days of Alexander the Great and Genghis Khan. After the British abandoned the area, in 1947, Peshawar again became a quiet farming town, and the gates to the city were closed at midnight. When Zawahiri arrived, however, it was teeming with arms merchants and opium dealers. Young men from other Muslim countries were beginning to hear the call of jihad, and they came to Peshawar, often with nothing more than a phone number in their pockets, and sometimes without even that. Their goal was to become *shaheed*—a martyr—and they asked only to be pointed in the direction of the war. Osama bin Laden was one of the first to arrive. He spent much of his time shuttling between Peshawar and Saudi Arabia, raising money for the cause.

The city also had to cope with the influx of uprooted and starving Afghans. By the end of 1980, there were 1.4 million Afghan refugees in Pakistan—a number that nearly doubled the following year—and almost all of them came through Peshawar, seeking shelter in nearby camps. Many of the refugees were casualties of Soviet land mines or of the intensive bombing of towns and cities. The conditions in the clinics and hospitals were appalling. Zawahiri reported that he sometimes had to use honey to sterilize wounds.

Through connections with local tribesmen, Zawahiri made several trips across the border into Afghanistan. He was one of the first outsiders to witness the courage of the Afghan freedom fighters, who called themselves the "mujahideen"—the holy warriors. They were defending themselves on foot or on horseback with First World War carbines. American Stinger missiles would not be delivered until 1986, and Eastern-bloc weapons that the CIA had smuggled in were not yet in the hands of the fighters. But the mujahideen already sensed that they were becoming pawns in the superpowers' game.

That fall, Zawahiri returned to Cairo full of stories about the "miracles" that were taking place in the jihad against the Soviets. He had grown a beard and was affecting a Pakistani outfit—a long tunic over loose trousers. When a delegation of mujahideen leaders came to Cairo, Zawahiri took his uncle Mahfouz to the venerable Shepheard Hotel to meet them. Zawahiri presented an idea that had come from Abdallah Schleifer. As the NBC bureau chief, Schleifer had been frustrated by the inability of Western news organizations to get close to the war. He said to Zawahiri, "Send me three bright young Afghans, and I'll train them to use film, and they can start telling their story."

When Schleifer called on Zawahiri to discuss the proposal, he was surprised by his manner. "He started off by saying that the Americans were the real enemy and had to be confronted," Schleifer told me. "I said, 'I don't understand. You just came back from Afghanistan, where you're cooperating with the Americans. Now you're saying America is the enemy?'"

"Sure, we're taking American help to fight the Russians," Zawahiri replied. "But they're equally evil."

"How can you make such a comparison?" Schleifer said. "There is more freedom to practice Islam in America than here in Egypt. And in Afghanistan the Soviets closed down fifty thousand mosques!"

Schleifer recalled, "The conversation ended on a bad note. In our previous debates, it was always eye to eye, and you could break the tension with a joke. Now I felt that he wasn't talking to me; he was addressing a mass rally of a hundred thousand people. It was all rhetoric." Nothing came of Schleifer's offer.

Zawahiri returned to Peshawar for another tour of duty with the Red Crescent Society in March of 1981. This time, he cut his stay short and returned to Cairo after two months. He wrote in his memoir that he regarded the Afghan jihad as "a training course of the utmost importance to prepare the Muslim mujahideen to wage their awaited battle against the superpower that now has sole dominance over the globe, namely, the United States."

ISLAMIC MILITANCY HAD BECOME a devastating force throughout the Middle East. Ayatollah Ruhollah Khomeini had returned to Iran from Paris in 1979 and led the first successful Islamist takeover of a major country. When Mohammad Reza Pahlavi, the exiled shah, sought treatment for cancer in the United States, the ayatollah incited student mobs to attack the American Embassy in Tehran. They held fifty-two Americans hostage, and the United States severed all diplomatic ties with Iran.

For Muslims everywhere, Khomeini reframed the debate with the West. Instead of conceding the future of Islam to a secular, democratic model, he imposed a stunning reversal. His sermons summoned up the unyielding force of the Islam of a previous millennium in language that foreshadowed bin Laden's revolutionary diatribes. The specific target of his anger against the West was freedom. "Yes, we are reactionaries, and you are enlightened intellectuals: you intellectuals do not want us to go back fourteen hundred years," he said, immediately after the revolution. "You, who want freedom, freedom for everything, the freedom of parties, you who want all the freedoms, you intellectuals: freedom that will corrupt our youth, freedom that will pave the way for the oppressor, freedom that will drag our nation to the bottom." As early as the 1940s, Khomeini had signaled his readiness to use terror to humiliate the perceived enemies of Islam, providing theological cover in addition to material support: "People cannot be made obedient except with the sword! The sword is the key to Paradise, which can be opened only for holy warriors!"

This defiant turn against democratic values had been implicit in the writings of Qutb and other early Islamists, and it now shaped the Islamist agenda. The overnight transformation of a relatively wealthy, powerful modern country such as Iran into a rigid theocracy proved that the Islamists' dream was eminently achievable, and it quickened their desire to act.

In Egypt, President Sadat called Khomeini a "lunatic madman . . . who has turned Islam into a mockery." Sadat invited the ailing shah to take up residence in Egypt, and he died there the following year.

In April of 1979, Egyptians voted to approve the peace treaty with Israel, which had been celebrated with a three-way handshake between President Jimmy Carter, Sadat, and the Israeli prime minister, Menachem Begin, on the White House lawn a few months earlier. The referendum was such a charade—99.9 percent of the voters reportedly approved it—that it underscored how dangerous Sadat's decision to make peace was. In response to a series of demonstrations orchestrated by the Islamists, Sadat banned all religious student associations. Reversing his position of tolerating these groups, he now declared, "Those who wish to practice Islam can go to the mosques, and those who wish to engage in politics may do so through legal institutions." The Islamists insisted that their religion did not permit such distinctions; Islam was a total system that encompassed all of life, including law and government. Sadat went as far as to ban the *niqab* at universities. Many who said that he had signed his death warrant when he made peace with Israel now also characterized him as a heretic. Under Islamic law, that was an open invitation to assassination.

Zawahiri envisioned not merely the removal of the head of state but a complete overthrow of the existing order. Stealthily, he had been recruiting officers from the Egyptian military, waiting for the moment when his group had accumulated enough strength in men and weapons to act. His chief strategist was Aboud al-Zumar, a military hero of the 1973 war with Israel. Zumar's plan was to kill the most powerful Egyptian leaders and capture the headquarters of the army and the state security, the telephone-exchange building, and the radio-and-television building. From there, news of the Islamic revolution would be broadcast, unleashing—he expected—a popular uprising against secular authority all over the country. It was, Zawahiri later testified, "an elaborate artistic plan."

One of the members of Zawahiri's cell was a daring tank commander named Isam al-Qamari. Zawahiri, in his memoir, characterizes Qamari as "a noble person in the true sense of the word. . . . Most of the sufferings and sacrifices that he endured willingly and calmly were the result of his honorable character." Although Zawahiri was the senior member of the Maadi cell, he often deferred to Qamari, who had a natural sense of command—a quality that Zawahiri notably lacked. Indeed, Qamari saw that there was "something missing" in Zawahiri, and once cautioned him, "No matter what group you belong to, you cannot be its leader."

Qamari began smuggling weapons and ammunition from army strongholds and storing them in Zawahiri's medical clinic in Maadi. In February of 1981, as the weapons were being transferred, police arrested a man carrying a bag loaded with guns, along with maps that showed the location of all the tank emplacements in Cairo. Qamari, realizing that he would soon be implicated, dropped out of sight, but several of his officers were arrested. Zawahiri inexplicably stayed put.

The evidence gathered in these arrests alerted government officials to a new threat from the Islamist underground. That September, Sadat ordered a roundup of more than fifteen hundred people, including many prominent Egyptians—not only Islamists but also intellectuals with no religious leanings, Marxists, Coptic Christians, student leaders, and various journalists and writers. The dragnet missed Zawahiri but captured most of the other leaders of his group. However, a military cell within the scattered ranks of al-Jihad had already set in motion a hastily conceived plan: a young army recruit, Lieutenant Khaled Islambouli, had offered to kill Sadat during an appearance at a military parade the following month.

———

ZAWAHIRI LATER TESTIFIED that he did not learn of the plan until nine o'clock on the morning of October 6, 1981, a few hours before it was scheduled to take place. One of the members of his cell, a pharmacist, brought him the news at his clinic. "In fact, I was astonished and shaken," Zawahiri told interrogators. In his opinion, the action had not been properly thought through. The pharmacist proposed that they do something to help the plan succeed. "But I told him, 'What can we do?'" Zawahiri told the interrogators. He said that he felt it was hopeless to try to aid the conspirators. "Do they want us to shoot up the streets and let the police detain us? We are not going to do anything." Zawahiri went back to his patient. When he learned, a few hours later, that the military exhibition was still in progress, he assumed that the operation had failed and that everyone connected with it had been arrested.

The parade commemorated the eighth anniversary of the 1973 war. Surrounded by dignitaries, including several American diplomats, President Sadat was saluting the troops when a military vehicle veered toward the reviewing stand. Lieutenant Islambouli and three other conspirators leaped out and tossed grenades into the stand. "I have killed the Pharaoh!" Islambouli cried, after emptying the cartridge of his machine gun into the president, who stood defiantly at attention until his body was riddled with bullets.

It is still unclear why Zawahiri did not leave Egypt when the new government, headed by Hosni Mubarak, rounded up seven hundred suspected conspirators. In any event, at the end of October Zawahiri packed his belongings for another trip to Pakistan. He went to the house of some relatives to say good-bye. His brother Hussein was driving him to the airport when the police stopped them on the Nile Corniche. "They took Ayman to the Maadi police station, and he was surrounded by guards," Omar Azzam recalled. "The chief of police slapped him in the face—and Ayman slapped him back!" Omar and his father, Mahfouz, recall this incident with amazement, not only because of the recklessness of Zawahiri's response but also because until that moment they had never seen him resort to violence. After his arrest and imprisonment, Zawahiri became known as the man who struck back.

IN THE TWELFTH CENTURY, the great Kurdish conqueror Saladin built the Citadel, a fortress on a hill above Cairo, using the labor of captured Crusaders. For seven hundred years, the fortress served as the seat of government; the structure also contained several mosques and a prison. "When the security forces brought people here, they took off their clothes, handcuffed them, blindfolded them, then started beating them with sticks and slapping them on the face," the Islamist attorney Montasser al-Zayat, who was imprisoned with Zawahiri, told me. "Ayman was beaten all the time—every day," Zayat said. "They sensed that he had a lot of significant information."

Jolly and devious, Zayat is an appealingly slippery figure. He has a large belly, and he always wears a coat and tie, even in the Cairo heat. In the fundamentalist style, he keeps his hair cropped close and his beard long and untrimmed. For years, he has been the main source for information about Zawahiri and the Islamist movement, in both the Egyptian and the Western press. As we walked through the old prison, which is now part of the Police Museum, Zayat talked about his time there and recalled hearing the voices of tourists, who were always just outside the prison walls. He pointed to the stone cell where Zawahiri was held—an enclosure of perhaps four feet by eight. "I didn't know him before we were brought here, but we were able to talk through a hole between our cells," Zayat said. "We discussed why the operations failed. He told me that he hadn't wanted the assassination to take place. He thought they should have waited and plucked the regime from the roots through a military coup. He was not that bloodthirsty."

Zayat believed that the traumatic experiences suffered by Zawahiri during his three years in prison transformed him from a relative moderate in the Islamist underground into a violent extremist. He and other witnesses point to what happened to Zawahiri's relationship with Isam al-Qamari, who had been his close friend and a man he greatly admired. Immediately after Zawahiri's arrest, officials in the

Interior Ministry began grilling him about Qamari's whereabouts. In their relentless search for Qamari, they threw the Zawahiri family out of their house, then tore up the floors and pulled down the wallpaper looking for evidence. They also waited by the phone to see if Qamari would call. "They waited for two weeks," Omar Azzam told me. Finally, a call came. The caller identified himself as "Dr. Isam," and asked to meet Zawahiri. A police officer, pretending to be a family member, told "Dr. Isam" that Zawahiri was not there. The caller suggested, "Have Ayman pray the *magreb*"—the sunset prayer—"with me," at a mosque they both knew.

Under interrogation, Zawahiri admitted that "Dr. Isam" was actually Qamari, and he also confirmed that Qamari had supplied him with weapons. Qamari was still unaware that Zawahiri was in custody when he called the Zawahiri home and made a date for the two of them to meet at the Zawya Mosque in Embaba. The police arrested Qamari when he arrived at the mosque. In Zawahiri's memoir, the closest he comes to confessing this betrayal is an oblique reference to the "humiliation" of imprisonment: "The toughest thing about captivity is forcing the mujahid, under the force of torture, to confess about his colleagues, to destroy his movement with his own hands, and offer his and his colleagues' secrets to the enemy." Qamari was given a ten-year sentence. "He received the news with his unique calmness and self-composure," Zawahiri recalls. "He even tried to comfort me, and said, 'I pity you for the burdens you will carry.'" Perversely, after Zawahiri testified against Qamari and thirteen others, the authorities placed the two of them in the same cell. Qamari was later killed in a shoot-out with the police after escaping from prison.

ZAWAHIRI WAS defendant No. 113 of more than three hundred militants accused of aiding in the assassination of Sadat, and of various other crimes as well—in Zawahiri's case, possession of a gun. Nearly every notable Islamist in Egypt was implicated in the plot. The defendants, some of whom were adolescents, were kept in a zoolike cage that ran across one side of a vast improvised courtroom set up in the Exhibition Grounds in Cairo, where fairs and conventions are often

held. International news organizations covered the trial, and Zawahiri, who had the best command of English among the defendants,
was designated as their spokesman.

Video footage that was shot during the opening day of the trial,
December 4, 1982, shows the three hundred defendants, illuminated
by the lights of TV cameras, chanting, praying, and calling out desperately to family members. Finally, the camera settles on Zawahiri,
who stands apart from the chaos with a look of solemn, focused inten-
sity. Thirty-one years old, he is wearing a white robe and has a gray
scarf thrown over his shoulder.

At a signal, the other prisoners fall silent, and Zawahiri cries out,
"Now we want to speak to the whole world! Who are we? Who are
we? Why they bring us here, and what we want to say? About the first
question, we are Muslims! We are Muslims who believe in their religion! We are Muslims who believe in their religion, both in ideology
and practice, and hence we tried our best to establish an Islamic state
and an Islamic society!"

The other defendants chant, in Arabic, "There is no god but God!"

Zawahiri continues, in a fiercely repetitive cadence, "We are not
sorry, we are not sorry for what we have done for our religion, and we
have sacrificed, and we stand ready to make more sacrifices!"

The others shout, "There is no god but God!"

Zawahiri continues, "We are here—the real Islamic front and the
real Islamic opposition against Zionism, Communism, and imperial-
ism!" He pauses, then: "And now, as an answer to the second question, Why did they bring us here? They bring us here for two reasons!
First, they are trying to abolish the outstanding Islamic movement . . .
and, secondly, to complete the conspiracy of evacuating the area in
preparation for the Zionist infiltration."

The others cry out, "We will not sacrifice the blood of the Muslims
for the Americans and the Jews!"

The prisoners pull off their shoes and raise their robes to expose
the marks of torture. Zawahiri talks about the torture that took place
in the "dirty Egyptian jails . . . where we suffered the severest inhu-
man treatment. There they kicked us, they beat us, they whipped us
with electric cables, they shocked us with electricity! They shocked us
with electricity! And they used the wild dogs! And they used the wild

dogs! And they hung us over the edges of the doors"—here he bends over to demonstrate—"with our hands tied at the back! They arrested the wives, the mothers, the fathers, the sisters, and the sons!"

The defendants chant, "The army of Muhammad will return, and we will defeat the Jews!"

The camera captures one particularly wild-eyed defendant in a green caftan as he extends his arms through the bars of the cage, screams, and then faints into the arms of a fellow prisoner. Zawahiri calls out the names of several prisoners who, he says, died as a result of torture. "So where is democracy?" he shouts. "Where is freedom? Where is human rights? Where is justice? Where is justice? We will never forget! We will never forget!"

Zawahiri's reference to dogs has a special significance in Muslim culture, where dogs occupy a lowly place, next to pigs in their filthy natures. I spoke to an Arab American FBI agent who has spent a lot of time in Egypt. He told me that the Egyptian police bragged of a technique they used of stripping a prisoner naked, tying him backward over a chair, and letting the dogs fuck him.

Zawahiri's allegations of torture were supported by the testimony of an intelligence officer, who said that he had seen Zawahiri, "his head shaved, his dignity completely humiliated, undergoing all sorts of torture." The officer went on to say that he had been part of Zawahiri's interrogation when another prisoner was brought in. The officers demanded that Zawahiri confess to complicity in the assassination plot in front of his fellow conspirator. When the other prisoner said, "How can you expect him to confess when he knows that the penalty is death?" Zawahiri replied, "The death penalty is more merciful than torture."

ZAWAHIRI WAS CONVICTED of dealing in weapons and received a three-year sentence, which he had nearly finished serving by the time the trial ended. Released in 1984, Zawahiri emerged a hardened radical whose beliefs had been hammered into brilliant resolve. Saad Eddin Ibrahim, the American University sociologist, spoke with Zawahiri after his release, and conjectured that he emerged with an overwhelming desire for revenge. "Torture does have that effect on people," he told me. "Many who turn fanatic have suffered harsh treatment in prison. It also makes them extremely suspicious." Torture had other, unanticipated effects on these extremely religious men. Many of them said that after being tortured they had had visions of being welcomed by saints into Paradise and of the just Islamic society that had been made possible by their martyrdom.

Ibrahim had done a study of political prisoners in Egypt in the 1970s. According to his research, most of the Islamist recruits were young men from villages who had come to one of the cities for schooling. The majority were the sons of middle-level government bureaucrats. They were ambitious and tended to be drawn to the fields of science and engineering, which accept only the most qualified students. They were not the alienated, marginalized youth that a sociologist might have expected. Instead, Ibrahim wrote, they were "model young Egyptians." Ibrahim attributed the recruiting success of the militant Islamist groups to their emphasis on brotherhood, sharing, and spiritual support, which provided a "soft landing" for the rural migrants to the city.

Zawahiri, who had read the study in prison, heatedly disagreed. "You have trivialized our movement by your mundane analysis," he told Ibrahim. "May God have mercy on you."

Zawahiri decided to leave Egypt, worried, perhaps, about the political consequences of his testimony in the case against the intelligence unit. According to his sister Heba, who is a professor of oncology at the National Cancer Institute at Cairo University, he thought of applying for a surgery fellowship in England. Instead, he arranged to work at a medical clinic in Jeddah, Saudi Arabia. At the Cairo airport, he ran into his friend Abdallah Schleifer. "Where are you going?" Schleifer asked.

"Saudi," said Zawahiri, who appeared relaxed and happy.

The two men embraced. "Listen, Ayman," Schleifer said. "Stay out of politics."

"I will," Zawahiri promised. "I will!"

ZAWAHIRI ARRIVED IN Jeddah in 1985. At thirty-four, he was a formidable figure. He had been a committed revolutionary and a member of an Islamist underground cell for more than half his life. His political skills had been honed by prison debates, and he had discovered in himself a capacity—and a hunger—for leadership. He was pious, determined, and embittered.

Osama bin Laden, who was based in Jeddah, was twenty-eight and had lived a life of boundless wealth and pleasure. His family's company, the multinational and broadly diversified Saudi Binladin Group, was one of the largest companies in the Middle East. Osama was a wan and gangly young man—estimated to be six feet five inches—and was by no means perceived to be the charismatic leader he would eventually become. He lacked the underground experience that Zawahiri had and, apart from his religious devotion, had few settled beliefs. But he had been radicalized by the Soviet invasion of Afghanistan in 1979, and he had already raised hundreds of millions of dollars for the mujahideen resistance.

"You have the desert-rooted streak of bin Laden coming together with the more modern Zawahiri," Saad Eddin Ibrahim observed. "But they were both politically disenfranchised, despite their backgrounds. There was something that resonated between these two youngsters on the neutral ground of faraway Afghanistan. There they tried to build the heavenly kingdom that they could not build in their home countries."

In the mid-eighties, the dominant Arab in the war against the Soviets was Sheikh Abdullah Azzam, a Palestinian theologian who had a doctorate in Islamic law from al-Azhar University. (He is not related to the Azzam family of Zawahiri's mother.) Azzam got a job leading prayers at King Abdul Aziz University, in Jeddah, where bin Laden was a student. As soon as Azzam heard about the Soviet invasion of Afghanistan, he moved to Pakistan. He became the gatekeeper of jihad and its main fund-raiser. His formula for victory was "Jihad and the rifle alone: no negotiations, no conferences, and no dialogues."

Many of the qualities that people now attribute to bin Laden were seen earlier in Abdullah Azzam, who became his mentor. Azzam was the embodiment of the holy warrior, which, in the Muslim world, is as popular a heroic stereotype as the samurai in Japan or the cowboy in America. His long beard was vividly black in the middle and white on either side, and whenever he talked about the war his gaze seemed to focus on some glorious interior vision. "I reached Afghanistan and could not believe my eyes," Azzam says in a recruitment video, produced in 1988, as he holds an AK-47 rifle in his lap. "I traveled to acquaint people with jihad for years. . . . We were trying to satisfy the thirst for martyrdom. We are still in love with this." Azzam was a frequent speaker at Muslim rallies, even in the United States, where he came to raise money. When bin Laden first came to Peshawar, he stayed at Azzam's guesthouse. Together, they set up the Maktab al-Khadamat, or Services Bureau, to recruit and train resistance fighters.

Peshawar had changed in the five years since Zawahiri had last been there. The city was congested and rife with corruption. As many as two million refugees had flooded into the North-West Frontier Province, turning Peshawar, the capital, into the prime staging area for the resistance. The United States was contributing approximately $250 million a year to the war, and the Pakistani intelligence service was distributing arms to the numerous Afghan warlords, who all maintained offices in Peshawar. A new stream of American and Pakistani military advisers had arrived to train the mujahideen. Aid workers and freelance mullahs and intelligence agents from around the world had set up shop. "Peshawar was transformed into this place where whoever had no place to go went," Osama Rushdi, one of the young Egyptian jihadis, remembered. "It was an environment in which a person could go from a bad place to a worse place, and eventually into despair."

Across the Khyber Pass was the war. The young Arabs who came to Peshawar prayed that their crossing would lead them to martyrdom and then to Paradise. Many were political fugitives from their own countries, and, as stateless people, they naturally turned against the very idea of a state. They saw themselves as a great borderless posse whose mission was to defend the entire Muslim people.

This army of so-called Afghan Arabs soon became legendary throughout the Islamic world. Some experts have estimated that as many as fifty thousand Arabs passed through Afghanistan during the war against the Soviets. However, Abdullah Anas, an Algerian mujahid who married one of Abdullah Azzam's daughters, says that there were never more than three thousand Arabs in Afghanistan, and that most of them were drivers, secretaries, and cooks, not warriors. The war was fought almost entirely by the Afghans, not the Arabs, he told me. According to Hani al-Sibai, an alleged leader of al-Jihad (he denies it) now living in exile, there were only some five hundred Egyptians. "They were known as the thinkers and the brains," Sibai said. "The Islamist movement started with them."

ZAWAHIRI'S BROTHER MOHAMMED, who had loyally followed him since childhood, joined him in Peshawar. The brothers had a strong family resemblance, though Mohammed was slightly taller and thinner than Ayman. Another colleague from the underground days in Cairo, a physician named Sayyid Imam, arrived, and in 1987, according to Egyptian intelligence, the three men reorganized al-Jihad. Zawahiri's wife, Azza, set up house in Peshawar. Azza's mother, Nabila Galal, visited her daughter in Pakistan three times, the last time in 1990. "They were an unusually close family and always moved together as one unit," she told a reporter for the Egyptian magazine *Akher Saa* in December 2001. While Zawahiri was in prison after the assassination of Sadat, Nabila took care of Azza and her first child, Fatima, who was born in 1981. She visited Azza again a few years later, in Saudi Arabia, to attend the birth of Umayma, who was named after Zawahiri's mother. "One day, I got a letter from Azza, and I felt intense pain as I read the words," Nabila recalled. "She wrote that she was to travel to Pakistan with her husband. I wished that she would not go there, but I knew that nobody can prevent fate. She was well aware of the rights her husband held over her and her duty toward him, which is why she was to follow him to the ends of the earth." In Pakistan, Azza gave birth to another daughter, Nabila, in 1986. A fourth daughter, Khadiga, arrived the following year, and in 1988 the Zawahiris' only son, Mohammed, was born. Nearly ten years later, in 1997, another daughter, Aisha, arrived. "Azza and her family lived a good life in Peshawar," her brother Essam told me. "They had a two-story villa with three or four bedrooms upstairs. One of the rooms was always available for visitors—and they had a lot of visitors. If they had money left over, they gave it to the needy. They were happy with very little."

Unlike the other leaders of the mujahideen, Zawahiri did not pledge himself to Sheikh Abdullah Azzam when he arrived in Afghanistan; from the start, he concentrated his efforts on getting close to bin Laden. He soon succeeded in placing trusted members of al-Jihad in key positions around the wealthy young Saudi. According to the Islamist attorney Montasser al-Zayat, "Zawahiri completely controlled bin Laden. The largest share of bin Laden's financial support went to Zawahiri and the Jihad organization, while he supported the Islamic Group only with tiny morsels."

Zawahiri must have recognized—perhaps even before bin Laden himself did—that the future of the Islamic movement lay with "this heaven-sent man," as Abdullah Azzam called bin Laden. Azzam soon felt the gravitational force of Zawahiri's influence over his protégé. "I don't know what some people are doing here in Peshawar," Azzam complained to his son-in-law Abdullah Anas. "They are talking against the mujahideen. They have only one point, to create *fitna*"—discord— "between me and these volunteers." He singled out Zawahiri as one of the troublemakers.

An Egyptian filmmaker, Essam Deraz, who worked in Afghanistan between 1986 and 1988, received special permission to visit the mujahideen's main base camp in a complex of caves in the Hindu Kush mountains known as Masaada (the Lion's Den). "It was snowing when we arrived at the Lion's Den," Deraz told me. "The Arabs hated anybody with cameras, because of their concern for security, so they stopped me from entering the cave. I was with my crew, and we were standing outside in the snow until I couldn't move my legs. Finally, one of the Arabs said that I could come in but my crew must stay out. I said, 'Either we all come in or we all stay out.' They disappeared and came back with Dr. Abdel Mu'iz." (The name was Zawahiri's nom de guerre. In Arabic, Abdel means "slave," and Mu'iz, one of the ninety-nine names of God, means "bestower of honor.") The man who called himself Dr. Abdel Mu'iz insisted that Deraz and his crew come into the cave, where he served them tea and bread. "He was very polite and very refined," Deraz said. "I could tell that he was from a good background by the way he apologized for keeping us outside." That night, Deraz slept on the floor of the cave, next to Zawahiri.

Deraz observed that bin Laden had become dependent on Zawahiri's medical care. "Bin Laden had low blood pressure, and sometimes he would get dizzy and have to lie down," Deraz told me. "Ayman came from Peshawar to treat him. He would give him a checkup and then leave to go fight." Deraz recalls that during one of the most intense battles of the war, he and the two men were huddled in a cave near Jalalabad with a group of fighters. "The bombing was very heavy," Deraz said. "Bin Laden had his arm stretched out, and Zawahiri was preparing to give him glucose. Whenever the doctor was about to insert the needle, there was a bombing and we would all hit the ground. When the bombing stopped for a while, Zawahiri would set up the glucose stand again, but as soon as he picked up the bottle there would be another bombing. So one person said, 'Don't you see? Every time you pick up the bottle, we are bombed.' And another said, 'In Islam, it is forbidden to be pessimistic,' but then it happened again. So the pessimistic one got up very slowly and threw the glucose bottle out of the cave. We all laughed. Even bin Laden was laughing."

Bin Laden sometimes came to lecture at the hospital where Zawahiri worked. Although the two men had different goals, they had much in common. They were both very modern men, members of the educated and technological class. They were both from families that were well known throughout the Arab world. They were soft-spoken, devout, and politically stifled by the regimes in their own countries. Each man filled a need in the other. Zawahiri wanted money and contacts, which bin Laden had in abundance. Bin Laden, an idealist given to causes, sought direction; Zawahiri, a seasoned propagandist, supplied it. The Egyptian had little interest in Afghanistan except as a staging area for the revolution in his own country. Bin Laden's main interest was in expelling the infidel invader from a Muslim land, but he also nursed an ill-formed longing to punish America and the West for what he believed were crimes against Islam. The dynamic of the two men's relationship made Zawahiri and bin Laden into people they would never have been individually; moreover, the organization they would create, al-Qaeda, would be a vector of these two forces, one Egyptian and one Saudi. Each would have to compromise in order to accommodate the goals of the other; as a result, al-Qaeda would take a unique path, that of global jihad.

Bin Laden's final break with Abdullah Azzam came in a dispute over the scope of jihad. Bin Laden envisioned an all-Arab legion, which eventually could be used to wage jihad in Saudi Arabia and

Egypt. Sheikh Abdullah strongly opposed making war against fellow Muslims. Zawahiri undermined Azzam's position by spreading rumors that he was a spy. "Zawahiri said he believed that Abdullah Azzam was working for the Americans," Osama Rushdi told me. "Sheikh Abdullah was killed that same night." On November 24, 1989, Azzam and two of his sons were blown up by a car bomb as they were driving to a mosque in Peshawar. Although no one has claimed credit for the killings, many have been blamed, including Zawahiri himself, and even bin Laden. The next day, Zawahiri was at Azzam's funeral, praising the martyred sheikh, as did his many other jubilant enemies.

IN 1989, after ten years of warfare, the Soviets gave up and pulled their forces out of Afghanistan. More than a million Afghans—8 percent of the country's population—had been killed, and hundreds of thousands had been maimed. Out of some thirteen million Afghans who survived the war, almost half were refugees. And yet the war against the Soviets was only the beginning of the Afghan tragedy.

After the Soviet pullout, many of the Afghan Arabs returned home or went to other countries, carrying the torch of Islamic revolution. In the Balkans, ethnic hostility among Muslims, Croats, and Serbs prompted Bosnia-Herzegovina to vote to secede from Yugoslavia; that set off a three-year war in which 150,000 people died. In November of 1991, the largely Muslim region of Chechnya declared its independence from Russia—an act that soon led to war. In 1992, civil war broke out in Algeria when the government canceled elections to prevent the Islamist party from taking power, a conflict that took as many as 200,000 lives. In Egypt, the Islamic Group launched a campaign against tourism and Western culture in general, burning and bombing theaters, bookstores, and banks, and killing Christians. "We believe in the principle of establishing Sharia, even if this means the death of all mankind," one of the Islamic Group's leaders later explained. And the war in Afghanistan continued—only now it was Muslims fighting Muslims for political control.

Bin Laden had returned to Saudi Arabia, ostensibly to work in the family business. In 1990, however, Saddam Hussein ordered the Iraqi invasion of Kuwait. Bin Laden, who had achieved mythic status in his country because of his role in the Soviet-Afghan War, went to the royal family and offered to defend the Saudi oil fields with his mujahideen companions. The rulers decided to put their faith in an American-led coalition instead, reportedly promising bin Laden that the foreigners would leave as soon as the war was over. But American forces were still in Saudi Arabia a year after the Gulf War ended, and bin Laden felt betrayed. He returned to Afghanistan and began speaking out against the Saudi regime. He also started funding the activities of Saudi dissidents in London. Then, in 1992, bin Laden abruptly left Kabul for Sudan, in despair over the infighting among the various factions of the mujahideen and convinced that the Saudis were scheming to kill him. He arrived in Khartoum with his three wives and fifteen children. He went into business, investing heavily in Sudanese construction projects, including an airport and the country's main highway; he also bought up the entire crop of Sudanese cotton, and he occasionally picked up the tab for the country's oil imports. In those early days in Khartoum, bin Laden felt secure enough to walk to the mosque five times a day without his bodyguards.

Zawahiri's relatives expected him to return to Egypt; throughout the Soviet-Afghan War and for several years afterward, he continued to pay rent on his clinic in Maadi. But he felt that it was not safe for him to return. Eventually, he followed bin Laden to Sudan. There he set about reorganizing al-Jihad. He gave a Sudanese mujahid named Jamal al-Fadl $250,000 to buy a farm north of the Sudan capital, where members of his organization could receive military training.

Despite Zawahiri's close ties to bin Laden, money for al-Jihad was always in short supply. Many of Zawahiri's followers had families, and they all needed food and housing. A few turned to theft and shakedowns to support themselves. Zawahiri strongly disapproved of this; when members of al-Jihad robbed a German military attaché in Yemen, he investigated the incident and expelled those responsible. But the money problem remained. In the early 1990s, Zawahiri sent several of his followers to Albania to work for Muslim charities. They were expected to send 10 percent of their paychecks to al-Jihad, but it was a meager contribution. Zawahiri bristled at bin Laden's lack of support. "The young men are willing to give up their souls, while the wealthy remain with money," he wrote in the Islamist magazine

Kalimat Haq. Bin Laden, for his part, was continually frustrated by the conflict between the two principal Egyptian organizations and was increasingly unwilling to fund either of them.

Zawahiri decided to look for money in the world center of venture capitalism—Silicon Valley. He had been to America once before, in 1989, when he paid a recruiting visit to the mujahideen's Services Bureau branch office in Brooklyn. He returned in the spring of 1993, this time to Santa Clara, California, where he met Dr. Ali Zaki, a gynecologist and a prominent civic leader in San Jose. "He came as a representative of the Red Crescent of Kuwait," Zaki said. "I was also a physician, so they asked me to accompany him while he was here." Zaki escorted Zawahiri to mosques in Sacramento and Stockton. The two doctors spent most of their time discussing medical problems that Zawahiri encountered in Afghanistan. "We talked about the children and the farmers who were injured and were missing limbs because of all the Russian mines," Zaki recalled. "He was a well-balanced, highly educated physician." But financially the trip was not a success. Zaki estimated that, at most, the donations produced by these visits to the California mosques amounted to several hundred dollars.

Immediately after this dispiriting trip, Zawahiri began working more closely with bin Laden, and most of the Egyptian members of al-Jihad went on the al-Qaeda payroll. These men were not mercenaries; they were highly motivated idealists, many of whom had turned their backs on middle-class careers. Their wages were modest—about a hundred dollars a month for the average fighter, two hundred for a skilled worker. They faced a difficult choice: whether to maintain their allegiance to a bootstrap organization that was always struggling financially or to join forces with a wealthy Saudi who had long-standing ties to the oil billionaires in the Persian Gulf. Moreover, the two organizations had different goals: al-Jihad's efforts were still concentrated on Egypt; bin Laden, the businessman, sought to merge all Islamic terrorist groups into a single multinational corporation, with departments devoted to everything from personnel to policymaking. Despite al-Jihad's financial precariousness, many of its members were suspicious of bin Laden and had no desire to divert their efforts outside Egypt. Zawahiri viewed the alliance as a marriage of convenience. One of his chief assistants, Ahmed al-Najjar, later testified in

Cairo that Zawahiri had confided to him that "joining with bin Laden [was] the only solution to keeping the Jihad organization alive."

SUDAN SEEMED an ideal spot from which to launch attacks on Egypt. The active cooperation of Sudan's intelligence agency and its military forces provided a safe harbor for the militants. The long, trackless, and almost entirely unguarded border between the two countries facilitated secret movements; and ancient caravan trails provided convenient routes for smuggling weapons and explosives into Egypt on the backs of camels. Iran supplied many of the weapons, and the Iranian-backed terrorist organization Hezbollah provided training in the use of explosives.

Al-Jihad began its assault on Egypt with an attempt on the life of the interior minister, who was leading the crackdown on Islamic militants. In August of 1993, a bomb-laden motorcycle exploded next to the minister's car, killing the bomber and his accomplice. "The minister escaped death, but his arm was broken," Zawahiri writes in his memoir. "A pile of files that he kept next to him saved his life from the shrapnel." The following November, Zawahiri's men tried to kill Egypt's prime minister with a car bomb as he was being driven past a girls' school in Cairo. The bomb missed its target, but the explosion injured twenty-one people and killed a twelve-year-old schoolgirl, Shayma Abdel-Halim, who was crushed by a door blown loose in the blast. Her death outraged Egyptians, who had seen more than 240 people killed by terrorists in the previous two years. As Shayma's coffin was borne through the streets of Cairo, people cried, "Terrorism is the enemy of God!"

Zawahiri was shaken by the popular outrage. "The unintended death of this innocent child pained us all, but we were helpless and we had to fight the government, which was against God's Sharia and supported God's enemies," he notes in his memoir. He offered what amounted to blood money to the girl's family. The Egyptian government arrested hundreds of his followers; six were eventually given a sentence of death. Zawahiri writes, "This meant that they wanted my daughter, who was two at the time, and the daughters of other colleagues, to be orphans. Who cried or cared for our daughters?"

Zawahiri was a pioneer in the use of suicide bombers, which became a signature of al-Jihad assassinations. The strategy broke powerful religious taboos against suicide and the murder of innocents. (For these reasons, the Islamic Group preferred to work with guns and knives.) Although Hezbollah employed truck bombers to attack the American Embassy and the U.S. Marine barracks in Beirut in 1983, such martyrdom operations had not yet worked their way into the modern vocabulary of terror. In Palestine, suicide bombings were virtually unknown until the mid-nineties, when the Oslo accords began to unravel. Another of Zawahiri's innovations was to tape the bomber's vows of martyrdom on the eve of the mission.

Obsessed with secrecy, Zawahiri imposed a blind-cell structure on the Jihad organization, so that members in one group would not know the activities or personnel in another. Thus, a security breach in one cell should not compromise other units, and certainly not the entire organization. However, in 1993, Egyptian authorities arrested al-Jihad's membership director, Ismail Nassir. "He had a computer containing the entire database," Osama Rushdi, a former member of the Islamic Group, told me. "Where the member lived, which home he might be hiding in, even what names he uses with false passports." Supplied with this information, the Egyptian security forces pulled in a thousand suspects and placed more than three hundred of them on trial in military courts on charges of attempting to overthrow the government. The evidence was thin, but the judicial standards weren't very rigorous. "It was all staged," Hisham Kassem, the publisher of the *Cairo Times* and the president of the Egyptian Organization for Human Rights, told me. "The ones you think are dangerous, you hang. The rest, you give them life sentences."

BOTH AL-JIHAD AND the Islamic Group had been decimated by defections and arrests. The Islamic Group's leader, Sheikh Omar Abdel Rahman, had emigrated to the United States, and was arrested following the 1993 World Trade Center bombing. He and nine followers were convicted in 1996 of conspiring to destroy New York landmarks, including the Lincoln and Holland Tunnels, the Federal Building, and the United Nations headquarters. In April of 1995, Zawahiri chaired a meeting in Khartoum attended by the remaining members of the two organizations, along with representatives of other terrorist groups. They agreed on a spectacular act: the assassination of the Egyptian president, Hosni Mubarak. It was a dangerous bet for the Islamists. The attack was carried out in June in Addis Ababa, Ethiopia, where Mubarak was on a state visit. There was a shoot-out between Mubarak's bodyguards and the assassins; two Ethiopian policemen were killed, but Mubarak escaped unharmed.

The Egyptian government responded with a furious determination to finish off al-Jihad. "The security forces used exemplary punishment," Hisham Kassem told me. "They torched houses in a village because a member of Jihad had come from there. A mother would be stripped naked in front of a guy, who was told, 'Next time we'll rape her if your younger brother is not here.'" A recently instituted anti-terrorism law had made it a crime even to express sympathy for terrorist movements. Five new prisons were being built to house the thousands of suspects that were rounded up, many of whom were never charged.

Zawahiri's response to the crackdown was to blow up the Egyptian Embassy in Islamabad, Pakistan. On November 19, 1995, two cars filled with explosives crashed through the embassy gates, killing the bombers and sixteen other people. Sixty were wounded. This act of mass murder was al-Jihad's first success under Zawahiri's administration. "The bomb left the embassy's ruined building as an eloquent and clear message," Zawahiri boasts in his memoir.

AFTER THE BOMBING OF the embassy in Pakistan, Egyptian intelligence agents devised a fiendish plan. They lured a thirteen-year-old Egyptian boy, the son of a senior member of al-Jihad in Sudan, into an apartment with the promise of juice and videos. The boy was drugged and sodomized; when he woke, he was confronted with photographs of the homosexual activity and threatened with the prospect of having them shown to his father. For the child, the consequences of such a disclosure were overwhelming. "It could even be that the father would kill him," a source close to Zawahiri admitted.

Egyptian intelligence forced the child to recruit another boy whose father was the treasurer for al-Qaeda. That boy endured the same humiliating initiation of drugs and sexual abuse and was forced to turn against his own family. The agents taught the boys how to plant microphones in their own homes and photograph documents. A number of arrests followed because of the information provided by the boy spies.

The Egyptian agents then decided to use the boys to kill Zawahiri. They gave one of them a suitcase filled with explosives, which he was to leave near a place where Zawahiri was expected to be. The plan failed when Sudanese intelligence agents and al-Jihad security spotted the boy in the company of Egyptian Embassy personnel. They arrested him while he was holding the suitcase.

"The Sudanese captured the other boy and put them both in jail," Hani al-Sibai, who has become a kind of historian of the Islamist movement, told me. "Most of the Islamic groups were in Sudan, so the rumors about the story were huge. The Jihad organization considered the whole thing a scandal for them." Zawahiri went to the Sudanese authorities and asked that the boys be temporarily released from jail so that he could interrogate them. He promised to return them safely. The Sudanese, who were now addicted to bin Laden's financial generosity, agreed. Zawahiri convened an Islamic court, put the boys on trial for treason, convicted them, and had them shot. In a characteristic gesture, he made a tape of their confessions and had it distributed as a warning to others who might betray the organization.

The Sudanese, furious at Zawahiri's duplicity, and also under intense pressure from the United States and Saudi Arabia to stop harboring terrorists, decided to expel Zawahiri and bin Laden and their followers. The Sudanese did not even give them time to pack. "All we did was to apply God's Sharia," Zawahiri complained. "If we fail to apply it to ourselves, then how can we apply it to others?"

In Zawahiri's hands, al-Jihad had splintered into angry and homeless gangs. There were fewer than a hundred members left in the organization, now scattered throughout the region. "These are bad times," Zawahiri admitted in Yemen, where he had taken refuge. He confided to some of his colleagues that he was developing an ulcer.

ZAWAHIRI'S NEXT MOVEMENTS are unclear. He was tracked by Egyptian intelligence agents in Switzerland and Sarajevo, and he allegedly sought asylum in Bulgaria. An Egyptian newspaper reported that Zawahiri had gone to live in luxury in a Swiss villa near the French border, and that he had $30 million in a secret account. Zawahiri did claim on several occasions to have lived in Switzerland, but the Swiss say they have no evidence that he was ever in the country, much less that he was granted asylum. He turned up briefly in Holland, which does not have an extradition treaty with Egypt. He had talks there about establishing a satellite television channel, backed by wealthy Arabs, that would provide a fundamentalist alternative to the Al Jazeera network, which had recently been launched in Qatar. Zawahiri's plan was to broadcast ten hours a day to Europe and the Middle East, using only male presenters. Nothing came of the idea.

A memo that Zawahiri later wrote to his colleagues—it was recovered from an al-Qaeda computer obtained by a *Wall Street Journal* reporter after the fall of the Taliban—reveals that in December of 1996 he was on his way to Chechnya to establish a new home base for the remnants of al-Jihad. "Conditions there were excellent," he wrote in the memo. The Russians had begun to withdraw from Chechnya earlier that year after achieving a cease-fire with the rebellious region. To the Islamists, Chechnya offered an opportunity to create an Islamic republic in the Caucasus, from which they could wage jihad throughout Central Asia.

Soon after Zawahiri and two of his top lieutenants, Ahmad Salama Mabruk and Mahmud Hisham al-Hennawi, crossed into the Russian province of Dagestan, they were arrested for entering the country illegally. The Russians discovered, among other documents, false identity papers, including a Sudanese passport that Zawahiri sometimes used. Zawahiri's passport indicated that he had been to Yemen four times, Malaysia three times, Singapore twice, and China (probably Taiwan) once—all within the previous twenty months. The Russians were never able to discover their real identities. At the trial, in April 1997, Zawahiri insisted that he had come to Russia "to find out the price for leather, medicine, and other goods." He said he was unaware that he was crossing the border illegally. The judge sentenced the three men to six months in jail. They had nearly completed the term by the time of the trial, and the following month they were released.

Once again, his disgruntled followers chastised him for his carelessness. An e-mail from colleagues in Yemen referred to the Russia adventure as "a disaster that almost destroyed the group." This fiasco had a profound consequence. With even more defectors from his membership and no real sources of income, Zawahiri had no choice but to rejoin bin Laden, who had moved his base to Kandahar. Pakistani intelligence had persuaded the Taliban to return the al-Qaeda camps in Khost and elsewhere to bin Laden's control in order to train militants to fight in Kashmir. Despite the still dire financial circumstances, Zawahiri believed that his fortunes were better served with bin Laden than without him.

Bin Laden had had enough of the fighting between the Egyptian factions. He told members of al-Jihad that their ineffectual operations in Egypt were too expensive, and that it was time for them to "turn their guns" on the United States and Israel.

On August 23, 1996, bin Laden issued an edict entitled "Declaration of War against the Americans Occupying the Land of the Two Holy Places." "Everyone agrees that the shadow of a stick cannot be straightened as long as the stick is crooked," he writes. "Hence, it is imperative to focus on attacking the main enemy." He argues that the West deliberately divided the Muslim world into "states and ministates," which could be easily controlled. He declares, "There is no higher priority, after faith, than pushing back the American-Israeli alliance." He calls upon all Muslims to participate in jihad in order to liberate Saudi Arabia and restore the dignity of the Islamic community. "In view of the enemy's strength, fast and light forces must be used and must operate in absolute secrecy."

ZAWAHIRI FORMALLY SEALED his new alliance with bin Laden on February 23, 1998, when his name appeared as one of the signatories on a document published in the London newspaper *Al-Quds al-Arabi*. The document announced the formation of the International Islamic Front for Jihad on the Jews and Crusaders. "In compliance with God's order," the text read, "we issue the following fatwa to all Muslims: the ruling to kill the Americans and their allies—civilian and military—is an individual duty for every Muslim who can do it in any country in which it is possible to do it." Included in the alliance were jihad groups in Afghanistan, Sudan, Saudi Arabia, Somalia, Yemen, Eritrea, Djibouti, Kenya, Pakistan, Bosnia, Croatia, Algeria, Tunisia, Lebanon, the Philippines, Tajikistan, Chechnya, Bangladesh, Kashmir, Azerbaijan, and Palestine.

The document gave the West its first glimpse of the worldwide conspiracy that was beginning to form. Since the early nineties, Egyptian authorities had felt stymied in their efforts to stamp out Islamic fundamentalists by the protection that Western governments afforded fugitives. The Egyptians complained that more than five hundred terrorists had found refuge in England, France, Germany, Austria, Denmark, Belgium, Holland, and the United States, among other countries, on the grounds that they would be subjected to political persecution and perhaps torture if they were sent home. Many European governments refused to return a suspect to face a trial in which he might receive the death penalty.

But the formation of the Islamic Front and its call for a fatwa against Americans and their allies prompted a new vigilance in the West. The CIA, which had sporadically tried to keep track of al-Jihad over the years, acted quickly. In July of 1998, American agents kidnapped Ahmad Salama Mabruk and another member of Jihad outside a restaurant in Baku, Azerbaijan. Mabruk's laptop computer turned out to contain vital information about Jihad members in Europe. The same summer, the CIA moved against an al-Jihad cell in Tirana, Albania; the cell, with sixteen members, had been created by Zawahiri's brother Mohammed in the early nineties. Albanian agents, under CIA supervision, kidnapped five members of the cell, blindfolded them, interrogated them for several days, and then sent the Egyptian members to Cairo. They were put on trial with more than a hundred other suspected terrorists. Their lawyer, Hafez Abu-Saada, maintains that they were tortured. The ordeal produced twenty thousand pages of confessions, and both Zawahiri brothers were given death sentences in absentia.

On August 6, a month after the breakup of the Albanian cell, Zawahiri sent the following declaration to a London-based Arabic paper: "We are interested in briefly telling the Americans that their message has been received and that the response, which we hope they will read carefully, is being prepared, because, with God's help, we will write it in the language that they understand." The following day, simultaneous suicide bombings destroyed the American embassies in Kenya and Tanzania; 223 people died, and more than five thousand were injured.

AMERICAN INTELLIGENCE OFFICIALS were stunned by the extent of the devastation in East Africa, and they were amazed by the skill with which the bombings were carried out. The level of planning and coordination indicated that the bombers had a new degree of sophistication, as well as a willingness to raise the stakes in terms of innocent lives. On August 20, President Clinton ordered an attack on bin Laden's training camps in Afghanistan, and also on a pharmaceutical plant in Sudan that was thought to be manufacturing a precursor to the lethal nerve gas VX.

American warships in the region fired seventy-nine Tomahawk cruise missiles into Afghanistan and Sudan. A subsequent investigation established that the plant in Sudan was making Ibuprofen and veterinary medicines, not poison gas; the strike killed a night watchman. In Afghanistan, the attack failed to hit its main targets—bin Laden, Zawahiri, and the other al-Qaeda leaders.)

The strikes, which, in the big-chested parlance of military planners, were dubbed Operation Infinite Reach, cost American taxpayers $79 million, but they merely exposed the inadequacy of American intelligence. President Clinton later explained that one of the strikes had been aimed at a "gathering of key terrorist leaders," but the meeting in question had occurred a month earlier. According to Russian intelligence sources cited in *Al-Majallah,* an Arabic magazine in London, bin Laden sold the Tomahawk missiles that failed to explode to China for more than $10 million, which he then used to finance operations in Chechnya.

The failure of Operation Infinite Reach established bin Laden as a legendary figure not just in the Muslim world but wherever America, with the clamor of its narcissistic culture and the presence of its military forces, had made itself unwelcome. When bin Laden's voice came crackling across a radio transmission—"By the grace of God, I am alive!"—the forces of anti-Americanism had found their champion. Those who had objected to the slaughter of innocents in the embassies in East Africa, many of whom were Muslims, were cowed by the popular response to this man whose defiance of America now seemed blessed by divine favor.

The day after the strikes, Zawahiri called a reporter in Karachi, with a message: "Tell the Americans that we aren't afraid of bombardment, threats, and acts of aggression. We suffered and survived the Soviet bombings for ten years in Afghanistan and we are ready for more sacrifices. The war has only just begun; the Americans should now await the answer."

The Counterterrorist

The legend of John P. O'Neill begins with a story by Richard A. Clarke, the chairman of the Counterterrorism Security Group in the White House from from 1992 until 2003. On a Sunday morning in February 1995, Clarke went to his office to review intelligence cables that had come in over the weekend. One of the cables reported that Ramzi Yousef, the suspected mastermind behind the first World Trade Center bombing, two years earlier, had been spotted in Pakistan. Clarke immediately called the FBI. A man whose voice was unfamiliar to him answered the phone. "O'Neill," he growled.

"Who the hell are you?" Clarke said.

"I'm John O'Neill," the man replied. "Who the hell are you?"

O'Neill had just been appointed chief of the FBI's counterterrorism section, in Washington. He was forty-two years old, and had been transferred from the bureau's Chicago office. After driving all night, he had gone directly to headquarters that Sunday morning without dropping off his bags. When he heard Clarke's report about Yousef, O'Neill entered the FBI's Strategic Information Operations Center (SIOC) and telephoned Thomas Pickard, the head of the bureau's National Security Division in New York. Pickard then called Mary Jo White, the U.S. Attorney for the Southern District of New York, who had indicted Yousef in the bombing case.

One of O'Neill's new responsibilities was to put together a rendition team, composed of agents who were working on the case, a State Department representative, a medical doctor, a hostage-rescue team, and a fingerprint expert whose job was to make sure that the suspect was, in fact, Ramzi Yousef. Under ordinary circumstances, the host country would be asked to detain the suspect until extradition paperwork had been signed and the FBI could place the man in custody. There was no time for that. Yousef was reportedly preparing to board a bus for Peshawar. Unless he was apprehended, he would soon cross the Khyber Pass into Afghanistan, where he would be out of reach. There was only one FBI agent in Pakistan at the time, as well as several agents from the Drug Enforcement Administration and the State Department's Bureau of Diplomatic Security. "Our ambassador had to get in his car and go ripping across town to get the head of the local military intelligence," Clarke recalled. "The chief gave him his own personal aides, and this ragtag bunch of American law enforcement officials and a couple of Pakistani soldiers set off to catch Yousef before he got on the bus."

O'Neill had joined the bureau in the J. Edgar Hoover era, and throughout his career he had something of the old-time G-man about him. He wore a thick pinky ring and carried a nine-millimeter automatic strapped to his ankle. He talked tough, in a New Jersey accent that many loved to imitate. He was darkly handsome, with winking black eyes and slicked-back hair. He favored fine cigars and Chivas Regal and water with a twist. His manner was blunt and dominating, but his nails were buffed and he was always immaculately, even fussily, dressed. One of his colleagues in Washington took note of O'Neill's "nightclub wardrobe"—black double-breasted suits, semitransparent black socks, and shiny loafers supple as ballet slippers.

In SIOC, O'Neill walked around with a phone at each ear, coordinating the rendition team on one line and arranging for an air force transport on the other. Because Pakistan would not permit an American military aircraft to land on its soil, O'Neill ordered the air force to paint its jet in civilian colors—immediately! He also demanded that the flight home be refueled in midair, so that Yousef would not be able to claim asylum if the aircraft had to land in another country. O'Neill was operating well outside his authority, but he was reckless and domineering by nature. (The Pentagon later sent him a bill for $12 million for the midair refueling and the paint job. The bill went unpaid.)

At 9:30 a.m. Pakistani time on February 7, the agents entered the Su-Casa Guest House in Islamabad and knocked on the door of room 16. A sleepy Yousef was immediately thrown to the floor and handcuffed. Moments later, the news reached the jubilant agents at FBI headquarters.

During the three days he was in SIOC, John O'Neill turned forty-three years old. He finally took his luggage to his new apartment. It was Tuesday, his first official day on the job.

In Washington, O'Neill became part of a close-knit group of counterterrorism experts that formed around Richard Clarke. In the web of federal agencies concerned with terrorism, Clarke was the spider. Everything that touched the web eventually came to his attention. The members of this inner circle, which was known as the Counterterrorism Security Group (CSG), were drawn mainly from the CIA, the National Security Council, and the upper tiers of the Defense Department, the Justice Department, and the State Department. They met every week in the White House Situation Room.

Clarke immediately spotted in O'Neill an obsessiveness about the dangers of terrorism that mirrored his own. "Prior to September 11, a lot of people who were working full-time on terrorism thought it was no more than a nuisance," Clarke told me. "They didn't understand that al-Qaeda was enormously powerful and insidious and that it was not going to stop until it really hurt us. John and some other senior officials knew that. The impatience really grew in us as we dealt with the dolts who didn't understand."

Osama bin Laden had been linked to terrorism since the first World Trade Center bombing, in 1993. His name had turned up on a list of donors to an Islamic charity that helped finance the bombing, and defendants in the case referred to a "Sheikh Osama" in a recorded conversation. "We started looking at who was involved in these events, and it seemed like an odd group of people getting together," Clarke recalled. "They clearly had money. We'd see CIA reports that referred to 'financier Osama bin Laden,' and we'd ask ourselves, 'Who the hell is he?' The more we drilled down, the more we realized that he was not just a financier—he was the leader. John said, 'We've got to get this guy. He's building a network. Everything leads back to him.' Gradually, the CIA came along with us."

O'Neill worked with Clarke to establish clear lines of responsibility among the intelligence agencies, and in 1995 their efforts resulted in a presidential directive giving the FBI the lead authority both in investigating and in preventing acts of terrorism wherever Americans or American interests were threatened. After the April 1995 bombing in Oklahoma City, O'Neill formed a separate section for domestic terrorism, but he concentrated on redesigning and expanding the foreign-terrorism branch. He organized a swap of deputies between his office and the CIA's counterterrorism center, despite resistance from both agencies.

What distinguished O'Neill early in his new posting was his recognition of the fact that the nature of terrorism had changed; it had gone global. In the recent past, terror in America had been largely a domestic product, produced by underground associations such as the Ku Klux Klan, the Black Panthers, or the Jewish Defense League. O'Neill's realization, shared by few, was that the radical Islamists had a wider dramatic vision that included murder on a massive scale, and that the man behind this worldwide network was a reclusive Saudi dissident, then in the Sudan, who dreamed of demolishing America and the West. Early in O'Neill's career as the bureau's counterterrorism chief, his interest in bin Laden became such an obsession that his colleagues began to question his judgment.

O'Neill was separated from bin Laden by many layers of culture and belief, but he devoted himself to trying to understand this new enemy in the darkened mirror of human nature. They were quite different men, but O'Neill and bin Laden were well-matched opponents: ambitious, relentless, and each eager to destroy the other and all he represented.

ON JUNE 25, 1996, O'Neill arranged a retreat for FBI and CIA agents at the bureau's training center in Quantico, Virginia. There were hot dogs and hamburgers, and O'Neill let the CIA guys on the firing range, because they rarely got to shoot. O'Neill played a round of golf on the Quantico course. Suddenly everyone's beeper went off.

An explosion in Saudi Arabia, at the Khobar Towers, a military-housing complex in Dhahran, had killed nineteen American soldiers and injured more than five hundred other people, including Saudis. O'Neill dispatched a team of nearly a hundred agents, support personnel, and members of various police agencies the very next day. A few weeks later, O'Neill and the FBI director, Louis Freeh, joined them.

It was evening when the two men arrived in Dhahran. The disaster site was a vast crater illuminated by lights on high stanchions; nearby lay charred automobiles and upended Humvees. Looming above the debris were the ruins of the housing complex. This was the largest bomb that the FBI had ever investigated, even more powerful than the explosives that had killed 168 people in Oklahoma City in 1995. O'Neill walked through the rubble, greeting exhausted agents who were sifting the sand for evidence. Under a tarp nearby, investigators were gradually reconstructing fragments of the truck that had carried the bomb.

Freeh was initially optimistic that the Saudis would cooperate in the investigation, but O'Neill became increasingly frustrated, and eventually a rift seems to have developed between the two men. "John started telling Louis things Louis didn't want to hear," Clarke said. "John told me that after one of the many trips he and Freeh took to the Mideast to get better cooperation from the Saudis, they boarded the Gulfstream to come home and Freeh says, 'Wasn't that a great trip? I think they're really going to help us.' And John says, 'You've got to be kidding. They didn't give us anything. They were just shining sunshine up your ass.' For the next twelve hours, Freeh didn't say another word to him."

Freeh denies that this conversation took place. "Of course, John and I discussed the results of every trip at that time," he wrote to me in an e-mail. "However, John never made that statement to me. . . . John and I had an excellent relationship based on trust and friendship."

Recognizing O'Neill's talents and his passion, Freeh sent him back to Saudi Arabia repeatedly. Intelligence agencies across the world are jealous and insular organizations, not inclined to share information, which O'Neill appreciated. He was used to cadging what he could through charm and persistence, but the Saudis were immune to his wooing. Their own investigation pointed to a branch of Iran-backed

Hezbollah inside the kingdom, and they worried about the possible American reaction. "Maybe you have no options," one of the Saudis told O'Neill. "If it is a military response, what are you going to bomb? Are you going to nuke them? Flatten their military facilities? Destroy their oil refineries? And to achieve what? We are next door to them. You are six thousand miles away."

In the new era of the globalized FBI, O'Neill learned, it was one thing to solve a case, another to achieve justice.

O'NEILL LONGED TO get out of Washington so that he could "go operational" and supervise cases again. In January 1997, he became special agent in charge of the National Security Division in New York. His office was in the northeast corner of 26 Federal Plaza, overlooking the Chrysler and Empire State Buildings through one window and the Brooklyn Bridge through the other. O'Neill made sure there was no other FBI office like it. He cleaned out the prison-made government-issued furniture and brought in a lavender couch. On his flame mahogany coffee table there was a book about tulips—*The Story of a Flower That Has Made Men Mad*—and he filled the room with plants and cut flowers. Instead of the usual family photographs, there were French Impressionist prints on the walls.

When he arrived, he dumped four boxes of Rolodex cards on the desk of his new secretary, Lorraine di Taranto. Then he handed her a list of everyone he wanted to meet—"the mayor, the police commissioner, the deputy police commissioners, the heads of the federal agencies, religious and ethnic leaders," di Taranto recalled. Within six months, O'Neill had met everyone on the list. He stood with John Cardinal O'Connor, the archbishop of New York, on St. Patrick's Day. He prayed with imams in Brooklyn. Sports figures and politicians and movie stars called him their friend. "John, you've got this town wired," one of his buddies said after a late night when it seemed that everyone had bowed in O'Neill's direction. O'Neill replied, "What's the point of being sheriff if you can't act like one?"

In New York, O'Neill created a special al-Qaeda desk, and when the bombings of the American embassies in Kenya and Tanzania occurred, in August 1998, he was sure that bin Laden was behind them. "He was pissed, he was beside himself," Robert M. Blitzer, who was head of the FBI's domestic-terrorism section at the time, remembered. "He was calling me every day. He wanted control of that investigation." O'Neill finally persuaded Freeh to let the New York office handle the case, and he eventually dispatched nearly five hundred investigators to Africa.

The level of coordination required to pull off the simultaneous bombings stunned the counterterrorist community. As many as five American embassies had been targeted—luck and better intelligence had saved the others. It was discouraging to learn that nearly a year before, a member of al-Qaeda had walked into the American Embassy in Nairobi and told the CIA of the bombing plot. The agency had dismissed this intelligence as unreliable. "The guy was a bullshit artist, completely off the map," an intelligence source said. But his warnings about the impending attacks proved accurate.

O'Neill never assumed that killing bin Laden alone would be sufficient. In speeches, he identified five tools to combat terrorism: diplomacy, military action, covert operations, economic sanctions, and law enforcement. So far, the tool that had worked most effectively against al-Qaeda was the last one—the slow, difficult work of gathering evidence, getting indictments, hunting down the perpetrators, and gaining convictions.

O'Neill was worried that terrorists had established a beachhead in America. He was particularly concerned that as the millennium approached, al-Qaeda would seize the moment to dramatize its war with America. The intelligence to support that hypothesis was frustratingly absent, however. Then, on December 14, 1999, a border guard in Port Angeles, Washington, stopped an Algerian man, Ahmed Ressam, who then bolted from his car. He was captured as he tried to hijack another automobile. In the trunk of his car were four timers, more than a hundred pounds of urea, and fourteen pounds of sulfate—the makings of an Oklahoma City–type bomb. It turned out that Ressam's target was Los Angeles International Airport. The following day, Jordanian authorities arrested thirteen suspected terrorists who were believed to be planning to blow up a Radisson Hotel in Amman and a number of tourist sites frequented by Westerners.

The Jordanians also discovered an al-Qaeda training manual on a CD-ROM.

What followed was the most comprehensive investigation ever conducted before September 11. O'Neill supervised the operation in New York. Authorities had found several phone numbers on Ressam when he was arrested. There was also a name, Ghani, which the agents connected to Abdel Ghani Meskini, an Algerian, who lived in Brooklyn and who had traveled to Seattle to meet with Ressam. O'Neill personally oversaw the stakeout of Meskini's residence and spent much of his time at the Brooklyn command post. On December 30, O'Neill arrested Meskini on conspiracy charges and a number of other suspected terrorists on immigration violations. (Meskini and Ressam eventually became cooperating witnesses and both assisted the FBI's investigation of the September 11 attacks.)

O'Neill was proud of the efforts of the FBI and the New York Joint Terrorism Task Force to avert catastrophe. At midnight on New Year's Eve, O'Neill stood with two million people in Times Square. He called Clarke in the White House to let him know that he was standing directly under the giant crystal ball. "If they're going to do anything in New York, they're going to do it here," he told Clarke. "So I'm here."

WHEN THE POST of chief of the New York office opened up, in early 2000, O'Neill lobbied fiercely for it. There was only one other candidate who was seriously considered: Barry Mawn, a former special agent in charge of the Boston office. Mawn had more experience and O'Neill had more enemies. The two men met at a seminar just after Mawn got the job. "I got a knock on the door, and there was John holding two beers," Mawn recalled. O'Neill promised complete loyalty in return for Mawn's support of his work on counterterrorism. "It turns out that supporting him was a full-time job," Mawn said.

The World Trade Center had become a symbol of America's success in fighting terrorism, and in September 2000, the New York Joint Terrorism Task Force celebrated its twentieth anniversary in the Windows on the World restaurant. Representatives of seventeen law enforcement agencies, including agents from the FBI and the CIA, New York City and Port Authority policemen, U.S. Marshals, and members of the Secret Service, attended the event. Mary Jo White praised the task force for a "close to absolutely perfect record of successful investigations and convictions." White had served eight years as the U.S. Attorney for the Southern District, and she had convicted twenty-five Islamic terrorists, including Yousef, six other World Trade Center bombers, the blind cleric Sheikh Omar Abdel Rahman, and nine of Rahman's followers, who had planned to blow up the Lincoln and Holland Tunnels, the United Nations headquarters, and the FBI offices.

O'Neill seemed at ease that night. Few of his colleagues knew of a troubling incident that had occurred two months earlier at an FBI preretirement conference in Orlando. During a meeting, O'Neill got a page. He left the room to return the call, and when he came back, a few minutes later, the other agents had left for lunch. His briefcase, which contained classified material, was missing. O'Neill immediately called the local police, and they found the briefcase a couple of hours later, in another hotel. A Montblanc pen had been stolen, along with a silver cigar cutter and a lighter. The papers were intact; fingerprint analysis soon established that they had not been touched.

"He phoned me and said, 'I gotta tell you something,'" Barry Mawn recalled. O'Neill told Mawn that the briefcase contained some classified e-mails and one highly sensitive document, the Annual Field Office Report, which is an overview of every counterterrorism and counterespionage case in New York.

Mawn said that as O'Neill's supervisor, he would have recommended an oral reprimand or, at worst, a letter of censure. Despite their competition for the top job in New York, Mawn had become one of O'Neill's staunchest defenders. "He demanded perfection, which was a large part of why the New York office was so terrific," Mawn said. "But underneath his manner, deep down, he was very insecure." Mawn felt guilty because he was the one who had been pressuring O'Neill to complete the report.

Even though none of the information in the briefcase had been compromised, the Justice Department ordered a criminal inquiry—the first step in O'Neill's downfall.

On October 12, 2000, a small boat filled with C4 explosives motored alongside a U.S. destroyer, the *Cole*, which was fueling up off the coast of Yemen. The two men aboard then blew themselves to pieces. Seventeen American sailors died, and thirty-nine others were seriously wounded.

Within hours of the attack, Barry Mawn called headquarters and demanded that the New York office gain control of the investigation, with O'Neill to be the on-scene commander. O'Neill was overjoyed. It would be his best chance to break up the criminal enterprise of al-Qaeda and perhaps his last opportunity to redeem his career. "This is it for me," he told a friend in Washington.

O'Neill had learned many lessons since his first day on the job in Washington five years before, when he coordinated the Ramzi Yousef rendition. One of those lessons was to stockpile supplies on skids at Andrews Air Force Base so that a rapid-response team would be ready to go at any moment. In a little more than twenty-four hours after the explosion, O'Neill and his team were in the air.

They had to stop first in Germany to await clearance from the Yemen authorities, who were still claiming that the explosion had been an accident. Coincidentally, many of the injured sailors were also in Germany, having been flown to the Landstuhl Regional Medical Center, the largest American hospital outside the United States. O'Neill took his investigators directly to the ward where the sailors were being treated. While the bomb technicians swept the victims' hair and clothing for residue, O'Neill went through the room with a naval investigator, talking to the wounded sailors. They were young men and women, most them not yet out of their teens, some of them missing limbs, some horribly burned. Three of the sailors were too badly wounded to be interviewed, and yet one of them, Petty Officer Kathy Lopez, who was completely swathed in bandages, insistently motioned that she wanted to say something. A nurse put her ear to the sailor's lips to hear the whispered words. She said, "Get them."

O'NEILL KNEW THAT Yemen was going to be an extremely difficult place in which to conduct an investigation. The country was filled with spies and jihadis and was reeling from a 1994 civil war. "Yemen is a country of eighteen million citizens and fifty million machine guns," O'Neill reported. On the day the investigators arrived in Yemen, O'Neill warned them, "This may be the most hostile environment the FBI has ever operated in."

The American ambassador to Yemen, Barbara Bodine, saw things differently. In her eyes, Yemen was the poor and guileless cousin of the swaggering petro-monarchies of the Persian Gulf. Unlike other countries in the region, Yemen was a constitutional democracy— however fragile—in which women were allowed to vote. Bodine had had extensive experience in Arab countries. During the Iraqi invasion and occupation of Kuwait, she had been the deputy chief of mission in Kuwait City, and she had stayed through the 137-day siege of the American Embassy by Iraqi troops until all the Americans were evacuated.

Bodine contends that she and O'Neill had agreed that he would bring in a team of no more than fifty. She was furious when three hundred investigators, support staff, and marines arrived, many carrying automatic weapons. "Try to imagine if a military plane from another country landed in Des Moines, and three hundred heavily armed people took over," she said. She pleaded with O'Neill to consider the delicate diplomatic environment he was entering. She quoted him as responding, "We don't care about the environment. We're just here to investigate a crime."

"There was the FBI way, and that was it," Bodine recalled. "O'Neill wasn't unique. He was simply extreme."

O'Neill spent much of his time coaxing the Yemeni authorities to cooperate. To build a case that would hold up in American courts, he wanted his agents present during interrogations by local authorities, in part to ensure that none of the suspects were tortured. He also wanted to gather eyewitness testimony from residents who had seen the explosion. Both the Yemeni authorities and Bodine resisted these requests. "You want a bunch of six-foot-two Irish Americans to go door-to-door?" Bodine asked. "And, excuse me, but how many of your guys speak Arabic?"

When O'Neill expressed his frustration to Washington, President Clinton sent a note to the Yemeni president, Ali Abdullah Saleh. It had little effect. O'Neill's people were never given the authority they needed for a proper investigation. Much of their time was spent on board the *Cole*, interviewing sailors, or lounging around the sweltering hotel. Some of O'Neill's requests for evidence mystified the Yemenis. They couldn't understand, for instance, why he was demanding a hat worn by one of the conspirators—he wanted to examine it for DNA evidence. Even the harbor sludge, which contained residue from the bomb, was off limits until the bureau paid the Yemeni government a million dollars to dredge it.

Relations between Bodine and O'Neill deteriorated to the point that Barry Mawn flew to Yemen to assess the situation. Bodine told him that O'Neill was insulting and not getting along with the Yemenis. Mawn then talked to members of the FBI team and American military officers, and he observed O'Neill's interactions with Yemeni authorities. He told O'Neill that he was doing "an outstanding job." On Mawn's return, he reported favorably on O'Neill to Freeh, adding that Bodine was his "only detractor."

An ambassador, however, has authority over which Americans are allowed to stay in a foreign country. A month after the investigation began, Assistant Director Dale Watson told the *Washington Post*, "Sustained cooperation" with the Yemenis "has enabled the FBI to further reduce its in-country presence. . . . The FBI will soon be able to bring home the FBI's senior on-scene commander, John O'Neill." It was a very public surrender.

O'Neill came home feeling that he was fighting the counterterrorism battle without support from his own government. He had made some progress in gaining access to evidence, but so far the investigation had been a failure. Concerned about continuing threats against the remaining FBI investigators, he tried to return to Yemen in January of 2001. Bodine denied his application to reenter the country.

After O'Neill's departure, the remaining agents, feeling increasingly vulnerable, retreated to the American Embassy in Sana'a, the capital of Yemen. In June, the Yemeni authorities arrested eight men who they said were part of a plot to blow up the embassy. New threats against the FBI followed, and Freeh, acting upon O'Neill's recommendation, withdrew the team entirely. Its members were, he told me, "the highest target during this period." Bodine calls the total pullout "unconscionable." In her opinion, there was never a specific, credible threat against the bureau. The American Embassy, Bodine points out, stayed open. But within days American military forces in the Middle East were put on top alert.

FEW PEOPLE IN the bureau knew that O'Neill had a wife and two children (John Jr. and his younger sister, Carol) in New Jersey, who did not join him when he moved to Chicago in 1991. There he met Valerie James, a fashion sales director, who was divorced and was raising two children. She was tall and beautiful, with a level gaze and a sultry voice. She saw O'Neill at a bar and bought him a drink because "he had the most compelling eyes." Within a year, he had asked Valerie's father for her hand.

While he was courting Valerie, O'Neill had a girlfriend in Washington, Mary Lynn Stevens, who worked at the Pentagon Federal Credit Union. He had asked her for an "exclusive" relationship two years before, when she visited him in Chicago. Mary Lynn happened to hear a message from Valerie on O'Neill's answering machine. When she confronted him, O'Neill dropped to his knees and begged forgiveness, promising he would never see Valerie again. When O'Neill transferred to headquarters, in Washington, he also began seeing Anna DiBattista, a stylish blonde who worked in the defense industry. Often he spent part of the night with Mary Lynn and the rest of it with Anna. "I never made him breakfast," Mary Lynn recalls. Then, when he moved to New York, Valerie James joined him. In 1999, Anna said she might move to New York to take a new job, which would complicate O'Neill's life considerably, and yet he pleaded for her to come. "We can get married!" he said. But when she arrived, he said she couldn't move in with him right away because there were "linguists" staying in his apartment.

His friends in Chicago and New York knew Valerie, and his friends in Washington knew Anna or Mary Lynn. If someone happened to see him in the company of the "wrong" woman, O'Neill pledged the person to secrecy. All three women were under the impression that he intended to marry them. He was also obsessed with a beautiful, high-powered woman in the Justice Department who was married, a fact that caused him endless despair. On holidays, O'Neill went home to New Jersey to visit his parents and to see his children. He never got a divorce.

The stress of O'Neill's tangled personal life began to affect his professional behavior. One night he left his PalmPilot in Yankee Stadium; it was filled with his police contacts all around the world. On another occasion, he left his cell phone in a cab. In the summer of 1999, he and Valerie James were driving to the Jersey shore when his Buick broke down near the Meadowlands. His bureau car was parked nearby, at a secret office location, and so O'Neill switched cars. One of the most frequently violated rules in the bureau is the use of an official vehicle for personal reasons, and O'Neill's infraction might have been overlooked had he not let Valerie enter the building to use the bathroom. She had no idea what it was. Still, when the FBI learned about the violation, apparently from a spiteful agent who had been caught using the site as an auto-repair shop, O'Neill was reprimanded and docked fifteen days' pay.

That was a penalty O'Neill could scarcely afford. He had always been a showy host, grabbing every tab, even going so far as to tear another agent's money in half when he offered to split the bill. These lavish gestures mounted up. O'Neill was also paying the mortgage on his wife's house and dipping into his retirement funds and borrowing money from wealthy friends, who held promissory notes that he had to disclose. Anyone with that much liability would normally come under scrutiny as a security risk.

He was insecure, deceptive, and potentially compromised. He was also driven, resourceful, and brilliant. For better or worse, this was the man that America depended on to stop Osama bin Laden.

Richard Clarke says that in March 2001 he asked the national security adviser, Condoleezza Rice, for a job change; he wanted to concentrate on cybersecurity. Rice asked who could possibly replace him. "Well, there's only one person who would fit that bill," Clarke replied. For months, Clarke sought to persuade O'Neill to become his successor.

O'Neill viewed Clarke's job as in many ways a perfect fit for him, but throughout the summer, he refused to commit himself. He was financially pressed, and the White House position paid no more than he was making at the FBI. He talked about Clarke's offer with a number of friends but became alarmed when he thought that headquarters might hear of it. "He called me in a worked-up state," Clarke recalled. "He said, 'People in the CIA and elsewhere know you are considering recommending me for your job. You have to tell them it's not true.'" Clarke dutifully called a friend in the agency.

The professional and personal pressures were mounting. Although the Justice Department dropped its inquiry into the briefcase incident, the bureau started conducting an internal investigation of its own. O'Neill was aware that the *Times* was preparing a story about the affair, and he learned that the reporters had personal information that probably came from the bureau's investigative files, including the episode of letting Valerie James into the off-site facility, and the amount of his personal debt. Someone in the bureau or the Justice Department leaked this information to the reporters, along with highly sensitive details about the budget that O'Neill had been preparing. The very material that had caused the Justice Department to investigate O'Neill had been freely given to reporters in order to sabotage his career.

O'Neill began reading the Bible intensely and going to Mass every morning. He was on the edge of an emotional breakdown. One morning, when Valerie was getting dressed for work, O'Neill began reading aloud from a children's book, *The Soul Bird*. It's about a bird that perches on one foot inside our soul, O'Neill read. The bird feels everything we feel. It runs around in pain when someone hurts us, then swells with joy when we are embraced. As he read, O'Neill began to weep, suddenly bursting into sobs, unable to finish. He was completely broken.

Meanwhile, intelligence had been streaming in concerning a likely al-Qaeda attack. "It all came together in the third week in June," Clarke said. "The CIA's view was that a major terrorist attack was coming in the next several weeks." On July 5, Clarke summoned all the domestic security agencies—the Federal Aviation Administration, the Coast Guard, Customs, the Immigration and Naturalization Service, and the FBI—and told them to increase their security in light of an impending attack.

In July, O'Neill heard of a job opening in the private sector that would pay more than twice his government salary—that of chief of security for the World Trade Center. O'Neill had finally realized there was no future for him in the FBI. He had always harbored two aspirations—to become a deputy director of the bureau in Washington or to take over the New York office. Those dreams would never be realized. Nor would he ever catch Osama bin Laden.

On August 19, the *Times* ran an article about the briefcase incident and O'Neill's forthcoming retirement, which was to take place three days later. There was a little gathering for coffee as he packed up his office. Some of O'Neill's friends congratulated him on his new post at the World Trade Center, saying, "At least now you'll be safe. They already tried to bomb it." O'Neill replied, "They'll try again. They'll never stop trying to get those two buildings." He instinctively placed himself in the bull's-eye. And perhaps in this decision there was a certain acceptance of his fate.

On the day he started at the World Trade Center—August 23—the CIA sent a cable to the FBI disclosing that two suspected al-Qaeda terrorists were already in the country. The agency had known this for more than a year and a half. The bureau tried to track them down, but the addresses the future hijackers had given when they entered the country proved to be false, and the men were never located.

WHEN O'NEILL WAS growing up in Atlantic City, he was an altar boy at St. Nicholas of Tolentine Church. On September 28, a week after his body was found in the rubble of the World Trade Center, a thousand mourners gathered at St. Nicholas to say farewell. Many of them were agents and policemen and members of foreign intelligence services who had followed O'Neill into the war against terrorism long before it became a rallying cry for the nation. The hierarchy of the FBI attended, including the now retired director Louis Freeh. Richard Clarke, who had not shed a tear since September 11, suddenly broke down when the bagpipes played and the casket passed by.

O'Neill's last weeks were happy ones. The moment he left the FBI, his spirits had lifted. He talked about getting a new Mercedes to replace his old Buick. He told Anna that they could now afford to get married. On the last Saturday night of his life, he attended a wedding with Valerie, and they danced nearly every number. He told a friend within Valerie's hearing, "I'm gonna get her a ring."

On September 10, O'Neill called Robert Tucker, a friend and

security-company executive, and arranged to get together that evening to talk about security issues at the World Trade Center. Tucker met O'Neill in the lobby of the north tower, and the two men rode the elevator up to O'Neill's new office, on the thirty-fourth floor. "He was incredibly proud of what he was doing," Tucker told me. Then they went to a bar at the top of the tower for a drink. Afterward, they headed uptown to Elaine's, where their friend Jerry Hauer joined them. Around midnight, the three men dropped in on the China Club, a legendary nightspot in midtown. "John made the statement that he thought something big was going to happen," Hauer recalled.

Valerie James waited up for O'Neill. He didn't come in until 2:30 a.m. "The next morning, I was frosty," she recalled. "He came into my bathroom and put his arms around me. He said, 'Please forgive me.'" He offered to drive her to work, and dropped her off at 8:13 a.m. in the flower district, where she had an appointment, and headed to the Trade Center.

At 8:46 a.m., when American Airlines Flight 11 crashed into the north tower, John P. O'Neill Jr. was on a train to New York, to install some computer equipment and visit his father's new office. From the window of the train he saw smoke coming from the Trade Center. He called his father on his cell phone. O'Neill said he was okay. He was on his way out to assess the damage.

Valerie James was arranging flowers in her office when "the phones started ringing off the hook." A second airliner had just hit the south tower. At 9:17, O'Neill called. He said, "Honey, I want you to know I'm okay. My God, Val, it's terrible. There are body parts everywhere. Are you crying?" he asked. She was. Then he said, "Val, I think my employers are dead. I can't lose this job."

"They're going to need you more than ever," she told him.

At 9:25, Anna DiBattista, who was driving to Philadelphia on business, received a call from O'Neill. "The connection was good at the beginning," she recalled. "He was safe and outside. He said he was okay. I said, 'Are you sure you're out of the building?' He told me he loved me. I knew he was going to go back in."

Wesley Wong, an FBI agent who had known O'Neill for more than twenty years, raced over to the north tower to help set up a command center. "John arrived on the scene," Wong recalled. "He asked me if there was any information I could divulge. I knew he was now basically an outsider. One of the questions he asked was 'Is it true the Pentagon has been hit?' I said, 'Gee, John, I don't know. Let me try to find out.' At one point, he was on his cell phone and he was having trouble with the reception and started walking away. I said, 'I'll catch up with you later.'"

Wong last saw O'Neill walking toward the tunnel leading to the second tower.

The Agent

O n October 12, 2000, in the deepwater port of Aden, Yemen, the USS *Cole*, a guided-missile destroyer weighing eighty-three hundred tons, was docked at a fueling buoy. The *Cole,* which cost $1 billion to build, was one of the most "survivable" ships in the U.S. Navy, with seventy tons of armor, a hull that could withstand an explosion of fifty-one thousand pounds per square inch, and stealth technology designed to make the ship less visible to radar. As the *Cole* filled its tank, a fiberglass fishing boat containing plastic explosives approached. Two men brought the skiff to a halt amidships, smiled and waved, then stood at attention. The symbolism of this moment was exactly what Osama bin Laden had hoped for when he approved a plan to attack an American naval vessel. "The destroyer represented the West," bin Laden said later. "The small boat represented Muhammad."

The shock wave from the blast shattered windows onshore. Two miles away, people thought there had been an earthquake. The blast opened a hole, forty feet by forty feet, in the port side of the ship, tearing apart sailors belowdecks who were waiting for lunch. The fireball that rose from the waterline swallowed a sailor who had leaned over the rail to see what the men in the skiff were up to. Seventeen sailors perished, and thirty-nine were wounded. Some had to swim through the blast hole to escape the flames. The great man-of-war looked like a gutted animal.

Shortly after the attack, Special Agent Ali Soufan, a twenty-nine-year-old Lebanese American, was driving across the Brooklyn Bridge when he received a page from the New York office of the FBI. He was told to report to work at once. At the time, Soufan was the only FBI agent in the city who spoke Arabic, and one of only eight in the country. He had joined the New York office in the fall of 1997. The following February, when bin Laden issued a fatwa declaring war on America, Soufan wrote a trenchant report on Islamic fundamentalism that caught the attention of John O'Neill, then head of the New York office of the FBI's National Security Division. Soufan's language skills, his relentlessness, and his roots in the Middle East made him invaluable in helping the FBI understand al-Qaeda, an organization that few Americans were even aware of before the 1998 bombings of the American embassies in East Africa. Despite Soufan's youth and his relatively short tenure, O'Neill placed him in charge of the *Cole* investigation. As it turned out, Soufan became America's best chance to stop the attacks of September 11.

Soufan speaks rapidly, and there is still a hint of Lebanon in his voice. He has an open face and an engaging smile, although there are circles under his eyes from too many long nights. He is a Muslim, but he doesn't follow any particular school of Islam; instead, he is drawn to mystical thought, especially that of Kahlil Gibran, the Lebanese American poet. He is also fascinated by the Kabbalah, because "it appeared at a time when the political environment for the Jews was so harsh that they used this philosophy to escape their anguish." When he wants to relax, he watches reruns of *Seinfeld*—he's seen every episode three or four times—or Bugs Bunny cartoons. One of his favorite writers is Karen Armstrong, whose biographies of Muhammad and the Buddha knit together history and religion in a way that makes sense to him.

Soufan grew up in Lebanon during the calamitous civil war, when cities were destroyed and terrorists were empowered by lawlessness and chaos. His father was a journalist in Beirut, and as a child Ali helped out at the business magazine his father produced, often car-

rying galleys to the printshop. In 1987, when Soufan was sixteen, the
family moved to the United States. Soufan's most vivid initial impression of his adopted country was that it was safe. "Also, it allowed me
to dream," he said.

In return, America embraced Soufan. He never suffered from prejudice because he was Muslim or an Arab. His experience was completely opposite to that of the alienated Muslims in the West who had
turned to Islamism as a way of finding an identity. He won many academic awards in high school, then attended Mansfield University, in
central Pennsylvania, where he was elected president of the student
government. In 1997, he received a master's degree in international
relations from Villanova University, outside Philadelphia. He planned
to continue his studies in a PhD program at Cambridge University,
but he had developed a fascination with the U.S. Constitution—in
particular with its guarantees of freedom of speech, religion, and
assembly, and the right to a speedy trial—and like many natural-
ized citizens, he had a feeling of indebtedness for the new life he had
been given. "People who are born into this system may take it for
granted," he said. "You don't know how important these rights are
if you haven't lived in a country where you can be arrested or killed
and not even know why." Although he was poised for an academic
career, he decided—"almost as a joke"—to send his résumé to the FBI.
He thought it was inconceivable that the bureau would hire someone
with his background, but he was intrigued by the mystique, and obviously something inside him longed to be saved from the classroom.
In July 1997, as he was packing to go to Cambridge, a letter arrived
instructing him to report to the FBI Academy, in Quantico, Virginia,
in two weeks.

Upon graduation, Soufan went to the New York bureau. He was
soon assigned to the I-40 squad, which concentrated mainly on the
Islamist paramilitary group Hamas, but, in 1998, on the day after the
East African embassy bombings, O'Neill drafted him into I-49, which
had become the lead unit in the FBI's investigation of al-Qaeda.

O'Neill could be brutal not only to those under him but to superiors who he felt were not fully committed to an investigation. Soufan proved to be a tireless ally, willing to work nights and holidays.
The fact that a novice like Soufan had direct access to O'Neill aroused

some resentment among the other agents, but the bureau had nobody else with his skills and dedication.

Yemen was filled with active al-Qaeda cells and with sympathizers at very high levels of government. On television, Yemeni politicians called for jihad against America. When the advance team of agents landed in Aden, the day after the attack, Soufan looked out at a detachment of the Yemen Special Forces, who wore yellow uniforms with old Russian helmets; each soldier was aiming an AK-47 at the U.S. plane. A jittery twelve-man hostage-rescue team, which had been sent along to protect the FBI agents, responded by brandishing their M4s and handguns. Soufan realized that everyone might die on the tarmac if he didn't do something quickly. He opened the plane's door. One Yemeni soldier was holding a walkie-talkie. Soufan walked directly toward him, carrying a bottle of water as the guns followed him. It was 110 degrees outside.

"You look thirsty," Soufan said, in Arabic, to the officer with the walkie-talkie. He handed him the bottle.

"Is it American water?" the officer asked.

Soufan assured him that it was, adding that he had American water for the other soldiers as well. The Yemenis considered the water such a precious commodity that some would not drink it. With this simple act of friendship, the soldiers lowered their weapons.

Soufan divided the agents on the ground into four teams. The first three were responsible for forensics, intelligence, and security; the last was devoted to exchanging information with Yemeni authorities. Just getting permission from the Yemeni government to go to the crime scene—the wounded warship in the Aden harbor—required lengthy negotiations with hostile officials. Security was a great concern, considering that automatic weapons were ubiquitous in the country, and Barbara Bodine, the American ambassador, refused to allow the agents to carry heavy arms for fear of offending the Yemeni authorities.

When Soufan and the investigators visited the ship, clumps of flesh were strewn belowdecks, amid the tangled mass of wire and metal. FBI divers, hoping to make DNA identifications of the victims and the bombers, netted body parts floating in the waters around the ship. Looking through the huge blast hole, Soufan could see the mountainous, ancient city of Aden, rising above the curved harbor like a classical amphitheater. He figured that somewhere in the city a camera had been set up to record the explosion, since terrorists regularly documented their work. Although the bombers were likely dead, a cameraman might still be at large.

When O'Neill finally arrived in Aden with the rest of the FBI investigators, he was puzzled, as he disembarked, to see the Yemeni soldiers saluting. "I told them you were a general," Soufan explained to him.

Yemen is a status-conscious society, and because Soufan had promoted O'Neill to "general," his counterpart was General Ghalib Qamish, the head of Yemeni intelligence. Every night, when the Yemeni authorities did business, Soufan and O'Neill spent hours pushing for access to witnesses, evidence, and crime scenes. Initially, the Yemenis told them that since both of the bombers were dead, there was nothing to investigate. But who gave them money? Soufan asked. Who provided the explosives? The boat? He gently prodded the Yemenis to help him.

O'Neill kept Soufan constantly at his side. Once, when he was talking to an obstructionist colonel in Yemen intelligence, O'Neill exclaimed in frustration, "Christ, this is like pulling teeth!" The colonel's personal translator repeated the remark in Arabic, and the officer leaped up, visibly angry. "What'd I say?" O'Neill asked Soufan. Soufan replied that the translator had told the colonel, "If you don't answer my questions, I'm going to pull out your teeth!"

A few days after the bombing, the Yemenis brought in two known associates of bin Laden's for questioning: Jamal Badawi and Fahd al-Quso. They admitted to the Yemeni authorities that they had recently traveled to Afghanistan and had met there with a one-legged jihadi named Khallad. Badawi said that he had bought a boat for Khallad, who, he explained, had wanted to go into the fishing business. The Yemenis determined that this was the boat used in the Cole bombing.

When Soufan learned that the men had mentioned Khallad, he was startled: he had heard the unusual name from a source he had recruited previously, in Afghanistan. The source had told him that he had met a fighter in Kandahar with a metal leg who was one of bin Laden's top lieutenants. When Soufan asked to speak to Quso and

Badawi, the Yemenis told him that the men had sworn on a Quran that they were innocent of any crime. For them, that settled the matter.

Soufan and O'Neill knew that General Qamish represented their best hope of gaining any cooperation. He was a small, gaunt man whose face reminded Soufan of Gandhi's. Despite the tensions between the two sides, Qamish had begun calling his American colleagues Brother John and Brother Ali. O'Neill and Soufan spent long hours asking Qamish for passport photographs of suspected plotters, especially Khallad. They pointed out that the sooner they could interrogate suspects linked to the *Cole* bombing, the sooner they might obtain intelligence that could destroy al-Qaeda, while Qamish took the position that the FBI was not needed on this case. Then one night Qamish simply announced, "I have your photos for you." Soufan immediately sent Khallad's photo to the CIA. He also faxed it to an FBI agent in Islamabad, Pakistan; the agent showed it to Soufan's source in Afghanistan, who identified the man as Khallad, the al-Qaeda lieutenant. It was the first tentative link connecting al-Qaeda to the *Cole* attack.

Another break came that same evening, when a twelve-year-old boy named Hani went to the local police. He said that he had been fishing on a pier when the bombers placed their skiff in the water. One of the men had paid the boy a hundred Yemeni riyals—about sixty cents—to watch his Nissan truck and boat trailer, but he never returned. When the police heard Hani's story, they locked him in jail to make sure he didn't disappear, and arrested his father as well. "If this is how they treat their cooperating witnesses," O'Neill observed, "imagine how they treat the more difficult ones."

After repeated requests, the Americans got permission to interview the boy and to examine the launch site. Hani was scared, but he provided a description of the bombers: one was heavy, and the other was "handsome." He said that the bombers had invited him and his family to take a ride in the boat, which was white, with red carpeting on the floor. When Soufan heard this, he deduced that the bombers had been trying to determine how much weight the skiff could carry.

The abandoned truck and trailer were still at the launch site. It was a major mistake on the part of al-Qaeda not to have retrieved them. By checking registration records, investigators connected the truck and trailer to a house in a neighborhood of al-Burayqah. When Soufan went to the house, which was surrounded by a wall and a gate, he had an eerie feeling: this residence had a striking resemblance to the house in Nairobi where the bomb for the 1998 embassy attack had been made. Inside, in the master bedroom, there was a prayer rug oriented to the north, toward Mecca. The bathroom sink was full of body hair; the bombers had shaved and performed ritual ablutions before going to their deaths. Soufan's men collected a razor and hair samples, which might provide the FBI with the DNA evidence necessary to establish the identity of the killers.

Investigators found another house in Aden that had been rented by the terrorists; it was registered to "Abda Hussein Mohammad." The name was dimly familiar to Soufan. At one point during the Nairobi investigation, a witness had mentioned an al-Qaeda operative named Nasheri who had proposed attacking an American vessel in Aden. Soufan did some research and discovered that Nasheri's full name was Abdul Rahim Mohammad Hussein Abda al-Nasheri. The middle names were the same, just reversed. Soufan's hunch paid off when American agents discovered a car in Aden that was registered to Nasheri. The connections between al-Qaeda and the *Cole* attack were mounting up.

A couple of weeks after the bombing, Yemeni authorities placed Badawi and Quso, the two al-Qaeda operatives, under arrest, apparently as a precaution. Soufan continued to press General Qamish to let him interrogate the men directly, and finally, after several weeks, Qamish relented.

Soufan spent hours preparing for the encounters, with the goal of finding some common ground with the suspects. Often, the bond centered on religion. Soufan was more familiar with the Quran and the sayings of the Prophet than the two operatives, and was able to shake their rationalizations about the crimes. In the interrogation of Badawi, Soufan learned that the skiff had been purchased in Saudi Arabia. Soufan questioned Quso over the course of several days. Quso was small, wiry, and insolent, with a wispy beard that he kept tugging on. Before Soufan could even begin, a local intelligence official came into the room and kissed Quso on both cheeks—a blatant signal that Quso was protected. Whenever it seemed that Quso was on the verge of making an important disclosure, the Yemeni colonel would insist that the session stop for meals or prayers.

Eventually, however, Soufan wore Quso down. He said he had been in Afghanistan and boasted that he had fought beside bin Laden, who inspired him with his speeches about expelling the infidels from the Arabian Peninsula—in particular, American troops stationed in Saudi Arabia.

Soufan asked if Quso ever planned to get married. A shy, embarrassed smile appeared. "Well, then, help yourself out," Soufan urged him. "Tell me something."

Quso admitted that he was supposed to film the *Cole* bombing but had overslept. He also disclosed that several months before the attack he and one of the bombers had delivered $36,000 to Khallad, the one-legged al-Qaeda lieutenant, in Bangkok. The money, Quso added, was meant only to buy Khallad a new prosthesis.

Soufan was suspicious of this explanation. Why had al-Qaeda sent money out of Yemen just before the *Cole* bombing took place? Money always flowed toward an operation, not away from it. He wondered if al-Qaeda had a bigger plot in the works.

In November 2000, a month after the *Cole* bombing, Soufan sent the CIA the first of several official queries. On Soufan's behalf, the director of the FBI sent a letter to the director of the CIA, formally requesting information about Khallad, and whether there might have been an al-Qaeda meeting somewhere in Southeast Asia before the bombing. The agency said that it had nothing. Soufan trusted this response; he thought that he had a good working relationship with the agency.

Quso had told Soufan that when he went to Bangkok to meet Khallad they had stayed in the Washington Hotel. FBI agents went through phone records to verify his story. They found calls between the hotel and Quso's house, in Yemen. They also noticed that there were calls to both places from a pay phone in Kuala Lumpur, Malaysia. In April 2001, Soufan sent another official teletype to the CIA, along with the passport photo of Khallad. He asked whether the telephone numbers had any significance, and whether there was any connection between the numbers and Khallad. Again, the CIA said that it could not help him.

IN FACT, the CIA knew a lot about Khallad and his ties to al-Qaeda. The FBI and the CIA have long quarreled over bureaucratic turf, and their mandates place them at odds. The ultimate goal of the bureau in gathering intelligence is to gain convictions for crimes; for the agency, intelligence itself is the object. If the agency had responded candidly to Soufan's requests, it would have revealed its knowledge of an al-Qaeda cell that was already forming inside the United States. But the agency kept this intelligence to itself, an action that by itself amounted to obstruction of justice in the death of seventeen American sailors. Much more tragic consequences were on the horizon.

As the FBI had become more involved in international law enforcement, it was increasingly encroaching on territory that the CIA jealously protected. At the same time, the agency often benefited from the bureau's investigations. In 1998, for instance, FBI investigators found an essential clue—a phone number in Yemen that functioned as a virtual switchboard for the terror network. The bombers in East Africa called that number before and after the attacks; so did Osama bin Laden. The number belonged to a jihadi named Ahmed al-Hada. By combing through the records of all the calls made to and from that number, FBI investigators constructed a map of al-Qaeda's global organization. The phone line was monitored as soon as it was discovered. But the CIA, as the primary organization for gathering foreign intelligence, had jurisdiction over conversations on the Hada phone, and did not provide the FBI with the information it was getting about al-Qaeda's plans.

A conversation on the Hada phone at the end of 1999 mentioned a forthcoming meeting of al-Qaeda operatives in Malaysia. The CIA learned the name of one participant, Khaled al-Mihdhar, and the first name of another: Nawaf. Both men were Saudi citizens. The CIA did not pass this intelligence to the FBI.

However, the CIA did share the information with Saudi authorities, who told the agency that Mihdhar and a man named Nawaf al-

Hazmi were members of al-Qaeda. On the basis of this intelligence, the CIA broke into a hotel room in Dubai where Mihdhar was spending the night, en route to Malaysia. The operatives photocopied Mihdhar's passport and faxed it to Alec Station, the CIA unit devoted to tracking bin Laden. Inside the passport was the critical information that Mihdhar had a U.S. visa. The agency did not alert the FBI or the State Department so that Mihdhar's name would be put on a terror watch list, which would have prevented him from entering the United States.

The CIA asked Malaysian authorities to provide surveillance of the meeting in Kuala Lumpur—the same meeting that the agency had denied knowing about in response to Soufan's official request. The gathering took place on January 5, 2000, at a condominium overlooking a golf course designed by Jack Nicklaus. The condo was owned by a Malaysian businessman who had ties to al-Qaeda. The pay phone that Soufan had queried the agency about was directly in front of the condo. Khallad used it to place calls to Quso in Yemen. Although the CIA later denied that it knew anything about the phone, the number was recorded in the Malaysians' surveillance log, which was given to the agency. Special Branch, the Malaysian secret service, also photographed about a dozen al-Qaeda associates outside the condo and visiting nearby Internet cafés. These pictures were turned over to the CIA. The meeting was not wiretapped; had it been, the agency might have uncovered the plots that culminated in the bombing of the *Cole* and the September 11, 2001, attacks. On January 8, Special Branch notified the CIA that three of the men who had been at the meeting—Mihdhar, Hazmi, and Khallad—were traveling together to Bangkok. There, Khallad met with Quso and one of the suicide bombers of the *Cole*. Quso gave Khallad the $36,000, which was most likely used to buy tickets to Los Angeles for Mihdhar and Hazmi and provide them with living expenses in the United States. Both men ended up on planes involved in the September 11 attacks.

In March, the CIA learned that Hazmi had flown to Los Angeles two months earlier, on January 15. If the agency checked the flight manifest, it would have noticed that Mihdhar was traveling with him. Once again, the agency neglected to inform the FBI or the State Department that at least one al-Qaeda operative was in the country.

Although the CIA was legally bound to share this kind of information with the bureau, it was ferociously protective of sensitive intelligence. The agency feared that FBI prosecutions resulting from such intelligence might compromise its relationships with foreign services, although there were safeguards to protect confidential information. The CIA was particularly wary of O'Neill, who demanded control of any case that touched on an FBI investigation. Many CIA officials disliked him and feared that he could not be trusted with sensitive intelligence. "O'Neill was duplicitous," Michael Scheuer, the former CIA official who founded Alec Station, told me. "He had no concerns outside of making the bureau look good." (In testimony before a congressional committee on April 17, 2007, Scheuer was questioned about his relationship with O'Neill, and he responded, "The only good thing that happened to America on 9/11 September was that the building fell on him, sir.")

The CIA may also have been protecting an overseas operation and was afraid that the FBI would expose it. Moreover, Mihdhar and Hazmi might have seemed like attractive recruitment possibilities— the CIA was desperate for a source inside al-Qaeda, having failed to penetrate the inner circle or even to place someone in the training camps, even though they were basically open to anyone who showed up. However, once Mihdhar and Hazmi entered the United States they were within the province of the FBI. The CIA has no legal authority to operate inside the country. Because of Mihdhar and Hazmi's connection to bin Laden, who had a federal indictment against him, the FBI had all the authority it needed to use every investigative technique to penetrate and disrupt the al-Qaeda cell. Instead, the hijackers were free to develop their plot until it was too late to stop them.

IN YEMEN, the security situation deteriorated rapidly. Soufan and the other FBI agents were quartered at the Aden Hotel, crammed in with other U.S. military and government employees, including marine guards, billeted three and four to a room; several dozen slept on bedrolls in the hotel ballroom. Gunfire frequently erupted outside the hotel.

It wasn't clear that the Yemeni government troops who were guarding the hotel from machine-gun nests would truly protect the Americans. "We were prisoners," an agent recalled. One night, shots were fired on the street nearby while O'Neill was running a meeting inside the hotel. The marines and the hostage-rescue team adopted defensive positions. Soufan ventured out, unarmed, to talk to the Yemeni troops.

"Hey, Ali!" O'Neill called out. "Be careful!" He raced down the steps of the hotel to make sure Soufan was wearing his flak jacket. Frustration, stress, and danger, along with the enforced intimacy of their situation, had brought the two men even closer. O'Neill had begun to describe Soufan as his "secret weapon." Speaking to the Yemenis, he called him simply "my son."

Snipers covered Soufan as he approached a Yemeni officer, who assured him that everything was okay.

"If everything is okay, why are there no cars on the street?" Soufan asked.

The officer said that there must be a wedding nearby. Soufan looked around and saw that the hotel was surrounded by a large number of men in traditional dress—some in jeeps, all carrying guns. They were civilians, not soldiers. They could be intelligence officers, or a tribal group bent on revenge. In either case, they easily outnumbered the Americans. Soufan was reminded of the 1993 uprising in Somalia, which ended with eighteen American soldiers dead and one of the bodies being dragged through the streets of Mogadishu. He noted that the Aden Hotel backed up to the harbor, and the Americans were essentially trapped.

After Soufan went inside and offered his assessment of the situation, O'Neill ordered the marines to deploy two armored vehicles to block the street in front of the hotel. The night passed without further incident, but the next day O'Neill moved the investigators to the USS *Duluth*, stationed ten miles away, in the Bay of Aden.

That proved to be a dangerous mistake. The next morning, when O'Neill and Soufan were flying back to town, their helicopter suddenly lurched into violent evasive maneuvers. The pilot reported that an SA-7 missile had locked in on them. O'Neill decided to send most of the investigators home; those who remained returned to the deserted hotel.

Just before Thanksgiving, the FBI pulled O'Neill out of Yemen, apparently as a concession to Ambassador Bodine, who felt that the conspicous FBI presence was straining diplomatic relations between America and Yemen. Soufan stayed on, but the threats in Aden became so acute that he and the other agents moved to the American Embassy in Sana'a, Yemen's capital. The investigation was losing its momentum.

In the late spring of 2001, Tom Wilshire, a CIA liaison at FBI headquarters, in Washington, was studying the relationship between Khaled al-Mihdhar, the Saudi al-Qaeda operative, and Khallad, the one-legged jihadi. Because of the similarity of the names, the CIA had thought that they might be the same person, but thanks to Ali Soufan's investigations in Yemen, the agency now knew that they were not, and that Khallad had orchestrated the *Cole* attack. "O.K. This is important," Wilshire said of Khallad, in an e-mail to his supervisors at the CIA Counterterrorism Center on July 13. "This is a major-league killer." Wilshire already knew that Hazmi, the other Saudi operative, had arrived in the United States and that Mihdhar was possibly with him. "Something bad [is] definitely up," Wilshire wrote to a colleague. He asked permission to disclose this vital information to the FBI. His superiors at the CIA never responded to his request.

Wilshire asked an FBI analyst to review the material on the Malaysia meeting, but he did not reveal that some of the participants might be in the United States. More important, he conveyed none of the urgency reflected in his e-mail; he told the analyst that she should examine the material in her free time. She didn't get around to it until the end of July.

Wilshire did want to know, however, what the FBI knew. He provided Dina Corsi, another FBI analyst, with three surveillance photos from the Malaysia meeting to several agents on the I-49 squad, the group responsible for counterterrorism. The pictures showed Mihdhar and Hazmi and a man who the CIA believed resembled Quso, the failed *Cole* cameraman. Wilshire told Corsi that one of the men was named Khaled al-Mihdhar, but he did not explain why the pictures had been taken, and he did not mention that Mihdhar had a U.S. visa.

On June 11, Clark Shannon, a CIA supervisor, went with Corsi to New York to meet with FBI case agents on the *Cole* investigation; Soufan was still in Yemen. The meeting started in midmorning, with the New York agents briefing Shannon and Corsi for three or four hours on the progress of their investigation. Corsi then displayed the three Malaysia photographs for her FBI colleagues. They were high-quality surveillance photos. One, shot from a low angle, showed Mihdhar and Hazmi standing beside a tree. Shannon wanted to know if the agents recognized anyone. The I-49 agents asked who was in the pictures, and when and where they had been taken. "Were there any other photographs of this meeting?" one of the FBI agents demanded. Shannon refused to say. Corsi promised that "in the days and weeks to come" she would try to get permission to pass that information along. The meeting became heated. The FBI agents sensed that these photographs pertained directly to crimes they were trying to solve, but they couldn't elicit any further information from Shannon. Corsi finally dropped the name Khaled al-Mihdhar. Steve Bongardt, Soufan's top assistant in the *Cole* investigation, asked Shannon to provide a date of birth or a passport number to go with Mihdhar's name. A name by itself was not sufficient to prevent his entry into the United States. Bongardt had just returned from Pakistan with a list of thirty names of suspected al-Qaeda associates and their dates of birth, which he had given to the State Department. That was standard procedure—the first thing most investigators would do. But Shannon declined to provide the additional information. Top CIA officials had not authorized him to disclose the vital details of Mihdhar's U.S. visa, his association with Hazmi, and their affiliation with Khallad and al-Qaeda. (The CIA's own inspector general would discover that as many as fifty to sixty individuals in the agency had read cables relating the presence of al-Qaeda operatives in America.)

There was a fourth photograph of the Malaysia meeting that Shannon did not produce. That was a picture of Khallad, the one-legged operative. Thanks to Soufan's interrogation of Quso, the *Cole* investigators had an active file on Khallad and were preparing to indict him. Knowledge of that fourth photo would likely have prompted O'Neill to demand that the CIA turn over all information relating to Khallad and his associates. The al-Qaeda summit meeting in Kuala Lumpur would have been revealed, as would the names of the al-Qaeda operatives already in America. By withholding the picture of Khallad attending the meeting with the future hijackers, the CIA may have allowed the September 11 plot to proceed.

That summer, Mihdhar returned to Yemen and then went to Saudi Arabia, where he presumably helped the remaining hijackers secure entry into the United States. He also received yet another American visa from the consulate in Jeddah, Saudi Arabia. Since the CIA had not given his name to the State Department to post on its watch list, Mihdhar arrived in New York on the Fourth of July.

The June 11 meeting was the culmination of a strange trend in the U.S. government toward hiding information from the people who most needed it. In this regard, the FBI was as guilty as the CIA. A federal law at the time prohibited the sharing of information arising from grand-jury testimony, but the FBI took it as a nearly absolute bar to revealing any investigative evidence and, as a result, repeatedly turned down requests for information from other intelligence agencies. In 1995, the Justice Department established a policy known as "the Wall," which regulated the exchange of foreign intelligence information between agents and criminal investigators. Managers at FBI headquarters turned it into a straitjacket for their own investigators. Intelligence agents in the bureau were warned that sharing such information with criminal agents could mean the end of their careers. The Wall even separated people who were on the same squad. The FBI also began withholding intelligence from the White House. Every morning on the classified computers of the National Security Council there were at least a hundred reports, from the CIA, the NSA, and other intelligence branches, but the FBI never disseminated information.

The CIA frequently decided to shield intelligence from the FBI on the grounds that it would compromise "sensitive sources and methods." The NSA also jealously withheld intelligence, collecting crucial information about Mihdhar, for instance, that it did not provide to the FBI. Mihdhar, it turned out, was the son-in-law of Ahmed al-Hada, the al-Qaeda loyalist in Yemen whose phone number operated as the network's switchboard. In San Diego, Midhar made at least eight calls to the Hada phone to talk to his wife, who was about to give birth. Those calls were not shared with the FBI, even though the calls made to and from that phone provided the basis for the bureau's worldwide map of al-Qaeda. In the I-49 squad's office, there was a link chart drawing connections between Hada's phone and other phones around the globe. Had a line been drawn from Hada's Yemen home to Mihdhar's San Diego apartment—eight times—al-Qaeda's presence in America would have been glaringly obvious.*

After September 11, the CIA claimed that it had divulged Mihdhar's identity to the FBI in a timely manner; indeed, both George Tenet, the agency's director, and Cofer Black, the head of its Counterterrorism Center, testified to Congress that this was the case. Later, the 9/11 Commission concluded that the statements of both were false. The CIA was unable to produce any evidence proving that the information had been passed to the bureau.

The I-49 squad responded to the secrecy in aggressive and creative ways. When the CIA refused to share intercepts of bin Laden's satellite phone, the squad came up with a plan to build two antennae to capture the signal—one on Palau, in the Pacific, and another on Diego Garcia, in the Indian Ocean. The squad also constructed an ingenious satellite telephone booth in Kandahar, hoping to provide a convenient facility for jihadis wanting to call home. The agents listened in on the calls, and they received videos of callers through a camera hidden in the booth. Millions of dollars and thousands of hours of labor were consumed in replicating information that other U.S. officials already had but refused to share. According to Soufan, the I-49 agents were so used to being denied access to intelligence that they bought a CD containing the Pink Floyd song "Another Brick in the Wall." He recalled, "Whenever we got the speech about 'sensitive sources and methods,' we'd just hold up the phone to the CD player and push Play."

JUST DAYS BEFORE the June 11 meeting took place in the New York office, new threats in Yemen created a security crisis for the Americans. Yemeni authorities arrested eight men who they said were part

---

* Michael Scheuer, the former head of Alec Station, told journalist James Bamford that the NSA also failed to distribute this information to the CIA as well, forcing the agency to build its own collection capability. "Missed Calls," *Foreign Policy*, July 21, 2015.

of a plot to blow up the American Embassy, where Soufan and other investigators had taken refuge. Louis Freeh, the director of the FBI, acting on O'Neill's recommendation, withdrew the team entirely.

By then, Soufan had a much clearer idea of the relationship between Khallad and the *Cole* conspirators. In July 2001, he sent a third formal request to the CIA asking for information about a possible al-Qaeda meeting in Malaysia, and about Khallad's trip to Bangkok to meet with Quso and the *Cole* suicide bomber. Yet again, the agency did not respond.

On August 22, John O'Neill was packing boxes in his office, on his last day at the FBI. He had decided to retire from the bureau after the *Times* reported that his briefcase, containing sensitive documents, was stolen while he was attending an FBI conference in Florida. Although the briefcase was quickly recovered, and it was determined that none of the sensitive material had been touched, it had ruined his prospects at the bureau.

That day, Soufan came by O'Neill's office to say good-bye. He was returning to Yemen later that afternoon; O'Neill's last act as an FBI agent was to sign the paperwork that would send Soufan's team back into the country. They were determined to arrest the killers of the American sailors, despite the risks of working in such a hostile environment.

The two men walked to a nearby diner. O'Neill ordered a ham-and-cheese sandwich. "You don't want to change your infidel ways?" Soufan kidded him, indicating the ham. "You're gonna go to hell."

O'Neill urged Soufan to visit him at the World Trade Center, where he had taken a job as head of security. "I'm going to be just down the road," he said.

Soufan confided that he and his longtime girlfriend had decided to get married. O'Neill gave his blessing. "She has put up with you all this time," he joked. "She must be a good woman."

The week that O'Neill retired from the bureau, the FBI analyst at Alec Station who had been reviewing intelligence on the Malaysia meeting realized that Mihdhar and Hazmi were in the United States. She passed the information to Dina Corsi, at FBI headquarters. Corsi, alarmed, sent an e-mail to the supervisor of the I-49 squad, ordering the unit to locate the al-Qaeda operatives. But, she added, because of the Wall no criminal investigators could be involved in the search. As it turned out, there was only one intelligence agent available, and he was new. An FBI agent forwarded Corsi's message to Steve Bongardt, Soufan's top assistant. He called her. "Dina, you got to be kidding me!" he said. "Mihdhar is in the country?" He complained that the Wall was a bureaucratic fiction that was preventing investigators from doing their work. In a conversation the next day, he said, "If this guy is in the country, it's not because he's going to fucking Disneyland!" Later, he wrote in an e-mail, "Someday somebody will die—and, Wall or not, the public will not understand why we were not more effective." The rookie agent's attempt to find Mihdhar and Hazmi proved fruitless.

Three weeks later, on September 11, 2001, Soufan was at the embassy in Sana'a. He spoke on the phone with his fiancée, who told him that the Twin Towers had been attacked. He turned on a television and watched as the second plane hit. He called O'Neill's cell phone repeatedly, but there was no answer.

The FBI ordered Soufan and the rest of his team in Yemen to evacuate. The morning of September 12, the CIA's chief of station in Aden escorted the agents to the airport in Sana'a. The CIA official was sitting in the lounge with Soufan when he got a call on his cell phone from FBI headquarters. He told Soufan, "They want to talk to you."

Dina Corsi spoke to Soufan, and ordered him to stay in Yemen. He was upset. He wanted to return to New York and investigate the attack on America. "This is about that—what happened yesterday," she told him. "Quso is our only lead." She wouldn't tell him any more. Soufan got his luggage off the plane, but he was puzzled. What did Quso, the sleeping *Cole* cameraman, have to do with September 11?

Robert McFadden, a naval investigator who speaks Arabic, and a couple of SWAT guys stayed behind to help Soufan along with a small team of FBI agents. The order from headquarters was to identify the September 11 hijackers "by any means necessary," a directive that Soufan had never seen before. When he returned to the embassy, a fax containing photographs of twenty suspects came over a secure line. Then the CIA chief drew Soufan aside and handed him a manila envelope. Inside were three surveillance photographs and a complete report about the Malaysia meeting—the very material that he had asked for so many times. The Wall had come down. When Soufan realized that the CIA had known for more than a year and a half that two of the hijackers were in the country, he ran into the bathroom and threw up.

Soufan went to General Qamish's office and demanded to see Quso again. "What does this have to do with the *Cole*?" Qamish wanted to know. "I'm not talking about the *Cole*," said Soufan. "Brother John is missing." He started to say something else, but he was unable to continue. General Qamish's eyes also filled with tears.

"Qamish instantly made a decision," McFadden recalls. "He said, 'You tell me what you want, and I'll make it happen.'" Qamish said that Quso was in Aden, and there was one last flight that evening from there to the capital. He called his subordinates on the phone and began shouting, "I want Quso flown in here tonight!" Then the general called the airport and demanded to be patched through to the pilot. "You will not take off until my prisoner is aboard," he ordered.

At midnight, in a room not far from Qamish's office, Soufan met with Quso, who was in a petulant frame of mind. "Just because something happens in New York or Washington, you don't need to talk to me," he said. Soufan showed him the three surveillance photographs of the Malaysia meeting, which included the Saudi hijackers Mihdhar and Hazmi. Quso thought he remembered seeing them in al-Qaeda camps, but he wasn't certain. "Why are you asking about them?" he wanted to know. He denied being in any of the photos.

Finally, the next day, the CIA passed along the fourth photograph of the Malaysia meeting—the picture of Khallad, the mastermind of the *Cole* operation. The two plots, Soufan instantly realized, were linked, and if the CIA had not withheld information from him he likely would have drawn the connection months before September 11. He met again with Quso, who identified the figure in the picture as Khallad—the first confirmation of al-Qaeda's responsibility for the September 11 attacks.

Soufan interrogated Quso for three nights, while during the day he wrote reports and did research, sleeping little more than an hour at a time. "He was sick as a dog, but he was getting really good information," his fellow agent Carlos Fernandez recalled. On the fourth night, Soufan collapsed from exhaustion. "We wanted to medevac him out of there," Fernandez said. "We took him to the emergency room. The kid could barely stand. But he refused to leave, and the next day he was right back at it. None of us had ever seen anything like that." His coworkers began referring to Soufan as "an American hero."

Soufan was intensely aware that the information he was getting was critical, and that perhaps no one else could extract the truth from Quso. Finally, after hours of extended questioning, Quso was shown a photograph of Marwan al-Shehhi, the hijacker who piloted United Airlines Flight 175, which crashed into the second tower. Quso identified him, and said that he had met Shehhi in a guesthouse in Kandahar. He remembered that Shehhi had been ill during Ramadan and that the emir—or chief—of the guesthouse had taken care of him. The emir's name was Abu Jandal.

As it happened, Abu Jandal was also in Yemeni custody, and the Americans arranged to interview him. He was a large, powerful man with a dark beard. "What are these infidels doing here?" he demanded. He took a plastic chair and turned it around, sitting with his arms crossed and his back to the interrogators. After some coaxing, Soufan got Abu Jandal to face him, but he refused to look him in the eye. Abu Jandal did want to talk, however; he delivered a lengthy, rapid-fire rant against America.

Soufan realized that the prisoner was trained in counter-interrogation techniques, since he easily agreed to things that Soufan already knew—that he had fought in Bosnia, Somalia, and Afghanistan, for instance—and denied everything else. Abu Jandal portrayed himself as a good Muslim who had considered jihad but had become disillusioned. He thought of himself not as a killer but as a revolutionary who was trying to rid the world of evil, which he believed came mainly from the United States, a country he knew practically nothing about.

As the nights passed, Abu Jandal warmed to Soufan. He was in his early thirties, older than most jihadis. He had grown up in Jeddah, Saudi Arabia—bin Laden's hometown—and he was well read in religion. He seemed to enjoy drinking tea and lecturing the Americans on the radical Islamist view of history; sociability was his weak spot.

Soufan flattered him and engaged him in theological debate.

Listening to Abu Jandal's diatribes, Soufan picked up several useful details: that he had grown tired of fighting; that he was troubled by the fact that bin Laden had sworn loyalty to Mullah Omar, the leader of the Taliban, in Afghanistan; and that he worried about his two children, one of whom had a bone disease. Soufan also noted that Abu Jandal declined some pastries because he was a diabetic.

The next night, Soufan brought some sugarless wafers, a courtesy that Abu Jandal acknowledged. Soufan also brought him a history of America, in Arabic. Abu Jandal was confounded by Soufan: a moderate Muslim who could argue about Islam with him, who was in the FBI, and who loved America. He quickly read the history that Soufan gave him and was amazed to learn of the American Revolution and its struggle against tyranny.

Soufan, meanwhile, was trying to determine the boundaries of Abu Jandal's moral landscape. He inquired about the proper way to wage jihad. Abu Jandal eagerly talked about how a warrior should treat his adversary in battle. The Quran and other Islamic texts discuss the ethics of conduct in warfare. Where do they sanction suicide bombing? Soufan asked him. Abu Jandal said that the enemy had an advantage in weapons, but the suicide bombers evened the score. "These are our missiles," he said. What about women and children? Soufan asked. Aren't they supposed to be protected? Soufan pointed to the bombings of the American embassies in East Africa. He recalled a woman on a bus in front of the Nairobi embassy, who, after the bomb exploded, was found clutching her baby, trying to protect him from the flames. Both had been incinerated. What sin had the mother committed? What about the soul of her child? "God will give them their rewards in the Hereafter," Abu Jandal said. Besides, he added, "can you imagine how many joined bin Laden after the embassy bombings? Hundreds came and asked to be martyrs." Soufan countered that many of the East African victims—perhaps most of them—were Muslims. Several times, Abu Jandal quoted clerical authorities or chapters from the Quran, but he found that Soufan was more than a match for him on theological matters. Abu Jandal finally asserted that because the embassy bombings were on a Friday, when the victims should have been in the mosque, they were not real Muslims.

On the fifth night, Soufan slammed a news magazine on the table between them. The magazine had photographs of the airplanes crashing into the Twin Towers—graphic shots of people trapped in the buildings and jumping a hundred stories. "Bin Laden did this," Soufan told him. Abu Jandal had heard about the attacks, but he didn't know many details. He studied the pictures in amazement. He said that they looked like a "Hollywood production," but the scale of the atrocity visibly shook him.

McFadden and two Yemeni investigators joined Soufan and Abu Jandal in the small interrogation room. Everyone sensed that Soufan was closing in. American and allied troops were preparing to go to war in Afghanistan, but they desperately needed more information about the structure of al-Qaeda, the locations of hideouts, and the plans for escape—all of which American intelligence officials hoped Abu Jandal could supply.

Coincidentally, a local Yemeni paper was on a shelf under the coffee table. Soufan showed it to Abu Jandal. The headline read, "Two Hundred Yemeni Souls Perish in New York Attack." (At the time, the death-toll estimates were in the tens of thousands.) Abu Jandal read the headline and drew a breath. "God help us," he muttered. Soufan asked what kind of Muslim would do such a thing. Abu Jandal insisted that the Israelis must have committed the attacks on New York and Washington. "The Sheikh is not that crazy," he said of bin Laden.

Soufan then took out a book of mug shots containing photographs of known al-Qaeda members and of the hijackers. He asked Abu Jandal to identify them. The Yemeni flipped through them quickly and closed the book.

Soufan opened the book again and told him to take his time. "Some of them I have in custody," he said, hoping that Abu Jandal wouldn't realize that the hijackers were all dead. Abu Jandal paused for a half-second on the photograph of Shehhi, the pilot of United Airlines Flight 175, before he started to turn the page. "You're not done with this one," Soufan said. "Ramadan, 1999. He's sick. You're his emir, and you take care of him." Abu Jandal looked at Soufan in shock. "When I ask you a question, I already know the answer," said Soufan. "If you're smart, you'll tell me the truth."

Abu Jandal conceded that he knew Shehhi and gave his al-Qaeda nom de guerre, Abdullah al-Sharqi. He did the same with Khaled al-Mihdhar and five others, including Mohamed Atta, the lead hijacker. But he still insisted that bin Laden would never commit such an action. It was the Israelis, he maintained.

"I know for sure that the people who did this were al-Qaeda guys," said Soufan. He took seven photographs out of the book and laid them on the table.

"How do you know?" Abu Jandal asked. "Who told you?"

"You did," said Soufan. "These *are* the hijackers. You just identified them."

Abu Jandal turned pale. He covered his face with his hands. "Give me a moment," he pleaded. Soufan walked out of the room. When he came back, he asked Abu Jandal what he thought now. "I think the Sheikh went crazy," he said. And then he told Soufan everything he knew.

Postscript

Ali Soufan played an important role in debunking the CIA's assertions about the usefulness and effectiveness of torture. I interviewed him for my 2010 documentary, *My Trip to al-Qaeda* (directed by Alex Gibney), when he was still undercover, and he spoke about how he refused to participate in what the agency termed "enhanced interrogation techniques." In fact, he considered placing the interrogators under arrest before the FBI decided that it could no longer be a part of such procedures.

Soufan retired from the FBI in 2005 and is the founder of the Soufan Group, an international security and intelligence organization.

The Kingdom of Silence

T his is a newspaper?" I asked the cabdriver in Jeddah, Saudi Arabia, as he pulled up in front of the lavish new headquarters of *Okaz*, the most popular paper in the kingdom. I had expected the usual dingy firetrap that characterizes newspaper offices all over the world, but this building loomed over the humble neighborhood like a royal palace. Workmen were still laying marble tiles on the steps as I entered a towering atrium. Envious reporters for other newspapers call *Okaz*'s new headquarters the Taj Mahal. Saudi men solemnly passed by, wearing crisp white robes and red checked headscarves. I felt out of place and underdressed.

Newspapers are a surprisingly good business in a country where the truth is so carefully guarded. Members of the royal family, al-Saud, are obsessively concerned about their image; they own or control most of the Saudi press, which dominates the Arab world. Within the kingdom, there are more than a dozen papers on the newsstands every morning. The most authoritative of them, and the most progressive, *Al-Hayat* and *Asharq al-Awsat,* are owned by Saudi princes but published in London. They are constrained by the same taboos that cripple all Saudi publications, however: nothing provocative can be said about Islam, the government, or the royal family. Another paper, *Al-Watan,* partly owned by Prince Bandar bin Khalid, models itself on *USA Today.* But *Okaz* remains the national favorite. On the coffee table in the lobby was a copy of that morning's edition, January 28, 2003. It was like an Arabic version of the *New York Post,* filled with Hollywood gossip, and stories of djinns who haunt the sand dunes. Although ostensibly independent, *Okaz* is closely identified with Prince Naif bin Abdul Aziz al-Saud, the minister of interior, who also controls the secret police and the media.

Up a flight of stairs, in a modest wing by itself, is the *Saudi Gazette,* an English-language daily published by *Okaz,* which had hired me for three months to help train young Saudi reporters. The job offered me a way of getting into the kingdom after more than a year of fruitless attempts to get a visa as a journalist. Working at the *Gazette* would also give me a vantage on the Saudi press, which had struggled for a decade to liberate itself from the bonds of government control. In 1990, just before the Gulf War, the media was forced to wait a week before reporting on Saddam Hussein's invasion of Kuwait; meantime, satellite news coverage leaped borders, as did the Internet. The press gained a measure of freedom. Suddenly, there were stories about crime, drug use, divorce, even the presence of AIDS in the kingdom. For the first time, Saudis were taking a critical look at their country and its problems. But after September 11 the media retreated; as a result, it largely missed the biggest story in the kingdom's modern history, blinding itself to the danger within its own society.

Walking around the *Gazette,* I soon found Dr. Mohammad Shou-kany, the deputy editor in chief, sitting in a dim office overlooking the newsroom. There was a television in one corner, and a Mexican soap opera was playing on mute. Like most Saudi men, he wore a white *thobe,* a shirtlike gown that reached his ankles. His headscarf, called a *gutra,* was folded on the couch, but he wore the white skullcap that goes under it, which gave him a pastoral air. He was a stocky man, with a round face and a narrow salt-and-pepper mustache. At heart, he was an academic, not a newsman, and he taught courses in English literature at King Abdul Aziz University, in Jeddah. As we talked, it seemed to me that his eyes were almost retractable, receding into slit-ted boredom when the subject was not of interest to him, then bulg-ing with excitement when he was fully engaged—as when he told me about his great passion, Joseph Conrad. "Some of the characters in his early stories come from the Hadhramaut, which is where the bin Ladens come from," Shoukany said. "Also, in *Lord Jim* there is one of the earliest mentions in literature of a Wahhabi preacher. Conrad is definitely a man of our time!"

Shoukany assumed that I had come to the country with a set of stereotypes about Saudis. "All we ask is that you judge us on our own terms," Shoukany said.

He led me through the newsroom, where two dozen editors and typesetters, most of them Indian expatriates, were working on Apple G4s. I could see layouts for the next morning's paper on the screens. The readership of the *Gazette* is drawn largely from the millions of foreign workers, like these editors, who do much of the essential labor in the kingdom, from driving cabs to manning the oil fields. World and national news is at the front of the paper, with separate pages for the Indian subcontinent and the Philippines, where most of the expats come from. There is also a culture section, a sports page (primarily soccer and cricket), business news, and editorials. Most of the international news comes from wire services. On Friday, Islam's holy day, there is a page on Islamic teachings.

In a side room, at a long library table, four translators from Sudan were scanning the daily Arabic press for usable stories. One of them wore a white turban and another had tribal scars on his cheeks. A Yemeni and a couple of Bangladeshi teaboys in brown uniforms patrolled the floor. Beyond the main newsroom, behind a long wall of glass, the local reporters were waiting to meet me.

I sensed the lethargy as soon as I entered the room. Cigarette smoke combined with a fluorescent pall to create a dense, subterranean atmosphere. Three young Saudi reporters greeted me with expressions that appeared welcoming but puzzled.

We sat down, and I asked them to tell me about themselves. There were two reporters named Hasan—Hasan Baswaid and Hasan Hatrash—but they were strikingly different. Baswaid, thirty-four, was tall and broad-shouldered, with sideburns and curly black hair, and omnipresent earphones for his mobile phone, which rang every few minutes, playing the theme from *Mission: Impossible*. He wore jeans and a partly buttoned, untucked white shirt. His handsome face belonged on the cover of a romance novel. Hatrash, twenty-eight, was slight and short; he wore traditional Saudi clothes, a trim black goatee, and black glasses that tended to be at half-mast on his nose. Under his headscarf, however, there was a snaky mass of dreadlocks. At heart, Hatrash said, he was a musician, but that was a hopeless career choice in such a puritanical society. Both men had been working at the *Gazette* for several years; the third reporter, Mamdouh al-Harthy, had joined the staff only about an hour before I arrived.

"How do you like working here?" I asked them.

The two Hasans shrugged and looked away. "Maybe we can talk about this later, mon," Hatrash said. It was several weeks before I learned why he had a West Indian accent: he had honed his English by listening to Bob Marley songs.

The serendipitous assignment of training young reporters, I may as well confess, thrilled me. I suspected that behind the closed gates of Saudi society there was a social revolution in the making. With some guidance, I thought, these journalists could help inspire change. Confronted with the demoralized reporters in my charge, however, I didn't know where to begin. My duties were vague. I was to "mentor" the reporters by hanging around the office for part of each day, and teach them some elementary techniques of investigative journalism. "Don't expect too much," Shoukany had warned me. "You can assign them stories, do whatever you want. You have complete freedom." I wondered what he meant by that.

MY FIRST BIG TASK was to help the local reporters cover the 2003 hajj, which began in February. Each year, at the end of the Islamic calendar, more than two million pilgrims arrive in Jeddah on their way to Mecca, forty miles to the east. It is the largest annual human gathering in the world—and also the biggest event for the local press to cover. Competition for stories is fierce. The *Gazette* was sending four reporters—most of the male staff—to cover it; Hasan Hatrash would lead the team.

In the past, the hajj has been the scene of numerous tragedies: stampedes, fires, air crashes, bombings, bloody riots, and epidemics. The pilgrims, coming from all over the world, invariably bring with them assorted viruses and bacteria, and by the time this hajj started, on February 9, there had already been outbreaks of influenza and meningitis in the kingdom. Hatrash wasn't worried, though. He told me that he ensured his immunity by eating small green native lemons. "They protect me against everything," he said.

The expectation of war in Iraq made this hajj especially tense. If the war began before the pilgrims got home, they could be stranded for months. The Saudi government's ambiguous attitude toward the Iraq crisis—officially condemning it, but allowing American forces to use Saudi bases as a staging area for search-and-rescue missions—left the kingdom open to political demonstrations by Muslims who opposed the war. The government, remembering disasters of the past, was determined to squelch any such dissent.

One of the most significant moments in modern Saudi history came at the end of the 1979 hajj. Several hundred Islamist radicals, many of them students, took over the Grand Mosque in Mecca, using the holiest spot in Islam as a forum for challenging the authority of the royal family. King Khalid obtained a fatwa from the clergy permitting government troops to retake the mosque. Two weeks of savage, hand-to-hand combat in the underground chambers of the holy site left 127 Saudi soldiers dead and more than 450 injured. French commandos provided the Saudis with an unspecified "nonlethal" gas. When that failed to flush out the terrorists, Saudi forces drilled holes into the chambers and dropped hand grenades through. Amazingly, 170 rebels survived; 63 of them were beheaded, in the largest mass execution in Saudi history.

This year, as many as half the pilgrims would be women—the highest percentage ever—but, curiously, the *Gazette* was not sending any female reporters to cover the event. According to Shoukany, I was supposed to have three women under my supervision, but after a week at the paper I still had not met them. By then, I had spotted a sign on the first floor, behind the stairwell, marked Ladies Section. I had no idea who, if anyone, was behind the door. Shoukany assured me that female reporters were allowed to attend meetings in the conference room, and yet they missed the first session I called, at four o'clock on a Wednesday afternoon. "I learned they go home early," Shoukany said apologetically.

The following day, with the meeting set for an hour earlier, three black-shrouded figures slipped into the *Gazette* conference room. Once they were seated, the male reporters followed, arraying themselves on the opposite side of the table. I sat awkwardly at the head. The women were all in black abayas and hijabs—the obligatory robes and headscarves—and one of them veiled her face as well, with only a pair of cat-eye glasses peeking out from the mask of black cloth. Hanging from her chair was an alligator purse with a long gold chain.

The self-effacement of an entire sex, and consequently of sexuality itself, was the most unnerving feature of Saudi life. I could go through an entire day without seeing any women, except perhaps some beggars sitting on the curb outside a prince's house. Almost all public space, from the outdoor terrace at the Italian restaurant to the sidewalk tables at Starbucks, belonged to men. The restaurants had separate entrances for "families" and "bachelors," and I could hear women scurrying past, hidden by screens, as they went upstairs or to a rear room. The only places I was sure to see women were at the mall or the grocery store, and even there they seemed spookily out of place. Many of them wore black gloves, and their faces were covered entirely, like canary cages—not even a pair of plummy, heavy-lidded Arabian eyes apparent. Sometimes I couldn't tell what direction they were facing. It felt to me as if the women had died, and only their shades remained.

The reporter with the alligator purse was named Najla Fathi. It was a surprise to learn that Najla and her female colleagues were far better educated than the men on the staff, most of whom had not finished college. Najla, for instance, had obtained a master's degree in political science from the University of Louisville, in 1995. "And I haven't been outside the Arab world since!" she declared. Her tone suggested anger or defiance, or even an attempt at humor, but it was maddeningly difficult to read her intentions without access to her facial expressions. She was a riddle to me.

I wanted to get the *Gazette* reporters like Najla started on investigative stories while Hatrash and his team were covering the hajj. There was one piece I was particularly keen on. In March 2002, a fire had broken out in the Thirty-first Girls' Middle School, in Mecca, a dilapidated four-story building that held 835 students and 55 teachers. According to initial reports, the fire had begun in the kitchen at about eight in the morning, creating panic. The only exit was locked; an elderly guard had wandered away with the key. Fifteen girls were trampled to death; more than fifty others were injured, some having jumped from the windows. According to eyewitnesses, a number of people had rushed to put out the blaze, but they were turned away by a representative of the Commission for the Promotion of Virtue and Prevention of Vice—the country's religious police—because the girls were not wearing their abayas. (The director of the commission denied these accounts.)

Female education, which was introduced in 1960, was born in controversy. Although females now outnumber males at the university level, only 6 percent of women in the overall population are employed, a statistic that has led religious conservatives to argue that education is "wasted on girls." After the fire, the head of the General Presidency for Girls' Education announced that it had been "God's will." He said this at a press conference at which he awarded each reporter in the room an expensive lambskin briefcase. I was told that he was later photographed surveying the ruins of the school in his ministerial robes; the pictures captured him stepping absentmindedly on the abayas that had been left behind.

But it was the detail about the religious police blocking the rescue of the girls that sent the country into a paroxysm of introspection. Ever since the 1979 attack on the Grand Mosque, the *muttawa'a*, as these government-subsidized vigilantes are informally called, have become a far more invasive presence in the country. The lesson the royal family had drawn from that traumatic attack was that it could protect itself from religious extremists only by empowering them. The *muttawa'a* prowl restaurants and shopping malls and amusement parks, making sure that businesses have closed for prayer time and chastising women whose attire fails to meet their standards of modesty. They have been known to shoot up satellite dishes and break into private homes. The *muttawa'a* are usually trailed by official policemen, who are at their command.

The Saudi press made history by writing about the fire without first asking the Ministry of Information for permission. For several weeks, the government stood aside and simply let the press be free. "When will we ever be ashamed of our attitude towards women?"

the editor of *Al Riyadh* asked his readers. "We ascribe all of society's ills to them. . . . Does the Committee for the Promotion of Virtue and Prevention of Vice care about our wives, sisters, mothers and daughters more than we do?" The *Gazette,* which rarely criticized the government, demanded an investigation of the religious police and prosecution of those responsible for the deaths of the girls. By Saudi standards, the coverage was so relentless that even reformists were troubled. Eventually, the interior minister summoned the editors in chief of all the newspapers in the country and told them that the stories must stop. They immediately did.

For Saudi journalists, the drama over the girls' school was both liberating and disconcerting. It confirmed that the Saudi press could play a dissenting role. But some said that ultimately the story had proved to be a setback; the government sharply reduced the zone of freedom because it had been so alarmed by the popular fury the story had unleashed.

Near the end of the Thursday meeting, I suggested assigning a one-year-anniversary story about the event. I wanted a woman reporter to write it. "The question is, after a year, have things really changed?" I asked.

"Of course they have," Najla said impatiently, leaning on the table with what must have been her chin resting on her fist. "Everybody knows this. The head of the General Presidency for Girls' Education was fired. They merged that department into the Ministry of Education. These are huge changes."

"To me, they seem like symbolic changes," I said. "The girls died because they were locked inside a ramshackle, overcrowded building with no fire escapes. Is the government actually building safe schools for girls? Are the teachers conducting fire drills? Are girls still locked inside?"

One of the women, Sabahat Siddiqi, shyly spoke up. "I will do this story, if you will tell me how," she said. I suggested that Sabahat talk to civil-defense authorities to see if they had improved fire safety, and to the minister of education to determine if the government had followed through on its pledge to build safe schools. I advised her to go to Mecca and talk to the families of the girls who died. She should visit girls' schools in Jeddah and talk to women educators to see whether they were satisfied with the government's response. Sabahat nodded and earnestly took notes, but Najla laughed. "That's not the way things work here," she warned me.

WHILE HATRASH AND his hajj team were in Mecca, I took time to drive around Jeddah. I rented a Hyundai, with 57,000 kilometers on it and dents on every panel, including the roof. The traffic was frightening. "We have the highest number of accidents in the world, and we don't even have alcohol!" Hatrash had told me. He attributed the accident rate to the high level of stress in Saudi society, which also contributes to extraordinary rates of diabetes and high blood pressure in the kingdom. Every time a signal turned green, there would be drivers in the far-right lane turning left across six lanes and drivers in the left-hand lane going straight, and then we would all speed like dragsters to the next light.

Jeddah is an ancient city that displays almost no evidence of the past. In the Old Quarter, houses made of coral brick with latticed balconies are crumbling from neglect. Buildings that fell decades ago are still rubble. Outside this small historical district, one enters what could be a seedy suburb of Houston, with familiar American franchises lining potholed boulevards. Despite the wealth of the bin Laden clan, Osama bin Laden grew up in a working-class neighborhood called al-Amariyya, where laundry dries on the balconies and shopkeepers chat on the stoops. Later, he moved with his mother and his stepfather to a new neighborhood; they lived in a modest white villa on Jabal al-Arab Street, with a filigree iron gate and a small courtyard. In 1984, when Osama took a second wife, he bought a run-down apartment house off Macaroni Street—so named because of an old pasta factory nearby.

At night, teenagers cruise Palestine Street, one of Jeddah's main thoroughfares, which begins in the desert hills on the east side of town and ends at the Red Sea. On the beach, families picnic and go for camel rides and sport about in fanciful neon-lit donkey carts. Between the beach and a spit of land that holds the king's summer royal palace, a majestic fountain spouts 853 feet into the air, making it the tallest in the world. (Jeddah also boasts the world's largest Chuck E. Cheese's pizza parlor.) Everything of value that Saudi Arabia produces—i.e., oil—comes out of the Eastern Province, on the other side of the country, where supertankers ply the Persian Gulf on their way to refueling the industrial world. The Jeddah Islamic Seaport, on the other hand, is devoted almost entirely to imports—food, clothing, appliances, furniture, and electronics, which fill the stores in this highly consuming but notoriously unproductive society.

The kingdom of Saudi Arabia was founded in its modern incarnation in 1932, by Abdul Aziz ibn Abdul Rahman al-Saud. The first oil boom hit in the early fifties, and soon desert nomads were docking their yachts in Monaco and renting entire floors of the Ritz. By 1981, per capita income was more than $28,000, about equal to that of the United States at the time. Saudi Arabia seemed to be on the way to becoming the richest nation in history, the global landlord. Oil prices have fluctuated since then, but when I arrived in the kingdom, oil was at $30 a barrel, and the Saudi per-capita income was less than $7,000, around that of Mexico. (Statistics in the kingdom are rarely more than guesses. An employee at the Jeddah Chamber of Commerce and Industry cheerfully told me, "At the chamber, we cook our own figures.")

The oil wealth of the country runs first through royal pockets. Various businessmen and economists speculate that the Saud family skims off as much as 30 or 40 percent. "We build forty-million-dollar palaces for even minor princes," an architect told me. Those closest to the crown are staggeringly wealthy. "Abdul Aziz bin Fahd, a son of King Fahd, is in his early thirties, and his wealth alone could solve the entire unemployment problem of Saudi Arabia," Mohsen al-Awajy, a lawyer and a spokesman for Wahhabi dissidents, told me. "There are billions upon billions in his account. Nobody can challenge him. Nobody can ask the royal family why."

The royal family includes everyone related to the founder, King Abdul Aziz, and his brother or his cousins. That's about thirty thousand people, according to Princess Reem al-Faisal, a photographer in Jeddah. "Titles in Europe were often connected to political positions," she observed. "Here, anybody from al-Saud is called a prince. It is more like the Irish clans. You can say we are like the O'Briens. There are thousands of us."

Still, with Saudi Arabia containing one-fourth of the world's known oil reserves, the government has no need to tax its citizens. Education and health care are free. But there is little evidence of public wealth or philanthropy. As I explored the kingdom, I noticed few parks or playgrounds or museums. There are not enough universities or private schools to serve the population, practically no research institutions, few public arts groups, and no human-rights organization. Muslims are supposed to give 2.5 percent of their savings and investments each year to the poor, an offering called the *zakat*. Much of it is given out directly as Ramadan gifts to the needy, or else poured into Islamic charities. "The government does not like to be outdone in spending money," a Jeddah businessman told me. "That might provide for a cult of personality not tied to the royal family. The only thing you can do in this country with your money is to build a mosque, and we have enough mosques, for crying out loud! God forbid you should open an orphanage."

The fact that there are no secular charities or nongovernmental institutions or, of course, political parties—civil society, in other words—means that there is no moderate, stabilizing middle ground between the government and the clerics. This situation has inevitably elevated the power of religious conservatives. Although many of the country's own citizens struggle to make do, the Saudi government sends about $2 billion a year in aid to other Islamic countries, building mosques and madrassas, underwriting religious universities, distributing books and tracts, funding charities—and supporting jihad. These donations, approved by the small inner circle of elderly princes who run the government, are made with an eye toward placating the country's religious extremists; they also ensure that the Wahhabi strain of Sunni Islam, the official dogma of the kingdom, will be the Muslim voice heard above all others.

Life in the kingdom changed after the 1979 attack on the Grand Mosque. The newly empowered Wahhabi clerics waged war on art and the pleasures of the intellect. Music was the first victim. Umm Kulthum and Fairouz, the songbirds of the Arab world, disappeared from the Saudi television stations. A magnificent concert hall in Riyadh was completed in 1989, but no performance has ever been held there. The Islamic courts have even banned the music played when a telephone call is placed on hold. There had been some movie theaters, but they were all shut down.

Meantime, religion has steadily increased its dominance of the Saudi school curriculum, so students have correspondingly less exposure to science, art, and languages. Dr. Nahed Taher is a senior strategic economist at the largest bank in the Middle East, the National Bank of Commerce, the first woman to occupy that position. She pointed out that the population of the country has been growing at twice the rate of the economy for the past twenty years. The unemployment problem is aggravated by an educational system that produces more and more unqualified graduates. "Forty-five percent of our graduates have degrees in Islamic studies or literature," she observed. "Also fifty-five percent of our graduates are females, but they make up only five percent of the labor force."

"My kid is in the fifth grade," Omar Bagour, a columnist for *Al-Madina* and a professor of economics at King Abdul Aziz University, told me. "Out of twelve subjects, seven are pure religion. You tell me a system of this nature is going to bring into the labor force a highly qualified Saudi? Bullshit."

The religious establishment, however, wants education to become even more Islamic. "Educational systems of atheist nations and civilizations cannot be like the systems of a believing nation," Saalih Ibn Humayd, a Saudi cleric, warned. "This country represents the power of Islam. . . . Any attempt to change this status will be vehemently opposed."

The religious establishment makes sure that millions of Islamic books are translated into other languages each year, but very few books are translated into Arabic. "Censorship of books is more rigid now than forty years back," Mohammad Salahuddin, a columnist for *Al-Madina*, told me one night at dinner. "Back then, I could buy a copy of *Das Kapital* in Mecca. Now you cannot dream of finding such books."

Although there are several popular Saudi painters in the kingdom, the Wahhabi ban on the representation of human beings or animals makes for geometric abstractions and unpeopled landscapes, a studied avoidance of the real. There was even a cultural war over the Starbucks logo—a mermaid. The religious police complained about the emblem when the company opened its first store, in Riyadh, in 2000; under pressure, Starbucks changed its logo. Government authorities

eventually overruled the complaint, deciding that mermaids are neither human nor animal but mythological. By the time I got to Jeddah
the mermaid was back on the company's signs.

One evening in Riyadh, I went to the National Museum after
evening prayers. It is a spectacular building, made of Arabian limestone and designed by the Canadian firm Moriyama & Teshima to
resemble the gently bending wall of a desert wadi. I walked through
the vast exhibition halls, alone except for one Saudi couple and their
young daughter. I could hear their footsteps echoing just behind me,
and their voices, hushed in the emptiness. The display cases told the
history of the Arabian Peninsula, from the dinosaurs and the early
petroglyphs to the triumphant arrival of Islam. Eerily absent from the
exhibit were representations of the people who lived there. I suppose
that was why there were so few visitors in the museum; it was a story
with no characters.

In one of the grand halls, I noticed an odd cul-de-sac under a stairwell, where I found a painting of a human face—the only one in the
museum. It was a wall drawing from the village of Al Fao, from the
second or third century A.D., depicting a man with a garland around
his curly hair. It looked like a Roman Christian icon; at that time Jews
and Christians were making inroads among the polytheists of the
peninsula. The man had wide, round eyes, like the figures in the fres-
coes of Pompeii. It was a tribute to the importance of this miniature
portrait that it was displayed at all; still, that it was hidden under the
stairs, almost as if it were pornography, made me admire as never
before the power of the human form.

ONE DAY IN JEDDAH, I went across town to see Jamal Khashoggi,
who was then the deputy editor of the *Arab News,* the main English-
language competitor of the *Saudi Gazette.* We met in his office. He is
a tall man with a trim beard and a pale, moon-shaped face. He had
covered the Afghan jihad sympathetically, and had been a friend of bin
Laden's, but he had rejected the Islamist movement when it turned
toward terror. After September 11, he was practically the only Saudi
journalist who addressed the cultural failures within Saudi society
that had contributed to the tragedy. "Despite the enormity of what

happened, we are still in denial," he wrote a year after the event. "We still cling to unlikely conspiracy theories and eye the truth with suspicion. The most pressing issue now is to ensure that our children can never be influenced by extremist ideas—like those fifteen Saudis who were misled into hijacking four planes on that fine September day, piloting them, and us, straight into the jaws of hell."

After tea had been served, Khashoggi and I began talking about the term "schizophrenic," which many Saudis use to characterize the quality of their lives. Khashoggi said it referred to the split between what he called "virtual" Saudi Arabia and "real" Saudi Arabia. "The virtual Saudi Arabia actually exists in its rules and in the minds of the people," he told me. "For instance, in virtual Saudi Arabia there is no satellite television. In principle, and by law, you are not allowed to own a satellite dish. But in reality we are the biggest consumers of satellite television in the Middle East. Not only that, Saudi businessmen are also the biggest investors in satellites. In principle, and by law, Saudi Arabia is not supposed to have interest-based banking, but in fact 90 percent of our banking system is interest-based. And it goes on and on. The solution for Saudi problems is to bring the virtual world and the real world together."

I asked Khashoggi what role the press could play in the country's efforts to change. "I don't think the press *can* play a role," he told me. "I don't see a single paper calling for reform. The papers are not structured in a way to make that possible." (Every editor in chief is ultimately approved by the minister of interior, who is also in charge of the country's secret police.) Khashoggi pointed to a broad petition for reform that had been put forward in February 2003 by 104 Saudi intellectuals. Crown Prince Abdullah, the de facto ruler of the country, had received the signers warmly, but not a single newspaper had published their list of demands. The limits of press freedom were always changing, Khashoggi explained. "We are pushing the boundaries but at the same time being cautious," he said. "Now it's accepted that we can get on the toes of the mayor but not those of the governor."

Later, I met with Hussein Shobokshi, a columnist for *Okaz* and a wealthy building contractor, who embodies the progressive, often American-educated business community. (He graduated from the

University of Tulsa.) Shobokshi was a member of the board of trustees of the private female college in Jeddah. He is a good-looking man, with large, sleepy eyes and a wry sense of humor. His father was head of *Okaz* and the founder of the *Saudi Gazette,* and Hussein is a major stockholder. He told me that there had been some progress in press freedom in the past decade: "Now we don't get locked up because of what we say; we get locked up because of what we do."

The girls' school story, Shobokshi said, was "a very important dialogue between the government and the press. But there is no new cause célèbre."

"If you were trying to point young reporters to one story that could shake the country, what would it be?" I asked him.

"Sewage," he said emphatically.

Twenty years ago, Shobokshi told me, Jeddah had been provided with the money to build a modern sewage system that would accommodate the fast-growing city. The government official in charge of the project, however, took the money and built himself a mansion in San Francisco and a palace in Jeddah that is equipped with a discotheque and a bowling alley. As a result, Shobokshi said, the streets in Jeddah are constantly filled with tanker trucks to drain the city's cesspools. Worse, sewage has got mixed into Jeddah's groundwater, and this has contaminated drinking water in many parts of the city. "We have new diseases of the eye and skin that didn't exist here ten years ago," Shobokshi said. "Lung and breast cancers are forty percent above the national rate. Hepatitis is so high that it has to be classified as an epidemic. Marine biologists tell me that certain fishes have become extinct because of the overflow. Swimming will be history."

Shobokshi said that he had traveled to Delft University of Technology, in Holland, for advice. "I gave them all the figures. They told me, 'Hussein, you've got a time bomb.' The sewage right now is dumped in a huge lake above the city. The walls of this lake are made of sand. And Jeddah is on a geological fault! They said that if there's an earthquake of five on the Richter scale, it will take six hours for the entire city of Jeddah to be flooded with sewage water one and a half meters deep."

"What happened to the guy who stole the money?"

"The government investigated and it was ruled that he should pay a penalty and go to jail," Shobokshi said. "But then he was pardoned because his brother is the private secretary to the king."

Shobokshi confided that he was initiating what he called "the first-ever class-action lawsuit in the kingdom." He was gathering five thousand signatures and had hired ten young lawyers to prepare the case. Nobody had yet written about the suit in the press, and he agreed that if the *Saudi Gazette* published a series of stories about the sewage crisis he would give the paper a scoop about the lawsuit. He had me hooked, and he knew it. "This is history with a capital 'H,'" he said.

I WAS HANDED the draft of an article by Mamdouh al-Harthy, the new reporter. He was from a prominent Bedouin tribe, but instead of a *thobe* he usually dressed in upscale casual Western clothes—jeans, oversized T-shirt, and sunglasses—with the name of the designer prominently displayed on every item. "Chicks notice such things," he advised me. When we went to the mall together, he stopped in his tracks like a bird dog and watched a pair of girls, entirely swathed in black, descending an escalator. "Check 'em out!" he said, without irony.

Mamdouh was a child of the souk. His father owned an elegant shop downtown that sold dates and candies. He had a merchant's facility with languages, speaking Urdu and Turkish, and his English was so colloquial that I never thought to worry about his writing ability. He had been working on a story about the hajj travel industry. His first draft began, "Hundreds of airplanes flaying hajjis to Saudi Arabia to performed hajj .most of those planes go back with no single passenger such as the Turkish airlines .other airlines claimed they r full occupied." I read through the brief piece, wondering what he could possibly mean by "the income is very pen fetal."

"What do you think, chief?" Mamdouh asked.

"I want you to write this for me in Arabic," I said.

"No problemo," he said, but he sounded a little puzzled.

When he finished, I took his Arabic draft to one of the Sudanese translators.

"It's excellent Arabic," he told me.

I went back to Mamdouh. "How far did you go in school?" I asked. "I've got a B.A. in English literature."

That stopped me. "Okay, now you're in charge of your own education," I told him. "Stop watching girls. Read a book in English. Watch BBC. Rent American movies. Whatever you do, do it in English. In the meantime, write your articles in Arabic first, then translate them."

"Okay, chief," he said, but he sounded discouraged.

All the reporters had problems writing in English—that was what the Indian editors were there for. The editors could sometimes salvage pieces that were inscrutable to me. Every other week, it seemed, a new reporter came on board, often someone just out of high school. They weren't really expected to produce. Some reporters went weeks without writing a single story, and when they did write one it might be about an event that had taken place ten days before. Many mornings, the paper didn't carry any local news at all. I began to wonder if it was an accident that the local reporters were ill equipped to handle the job.

I was heartened, therefore, to read some engaging stories from the *Gazette* team in Mecca. "The tent city of Mina, on the outskirts of Makkah [Mecca], is all ready to welcome the pilgrims," the *Gazette* reported on the eve of the hajj. Five hospitals with more than seven hundred beds were set up. Thirty thousand butchers staffing five slaughterhouses were on hand to dispatch hundreds of thousands of sacrificial animals. According to a story filed by Hasan Hatrash, four thousand Boy Scouts would have new software available to help pilgrims locate their cots among the forty-four thousand air-conditioned tents that filled the valley like a whitecapped sea. "Scouts until recently used to serve in excess of ten thousand lost pilgrims a day," Hatrash wrote.

The second morning of the hajj, immediately after the dawn prayer, the pilgrims proceeded to Mount Arafat, twelve miles outside Mecca. There, nearly fourteen hundred years earlier, the Prophet gave his last sermon. The second day is supposed to be a day of repentance and self-examination, but the air was charged with politics. "Don't you see how the enemies are gathering and are preparing to wage war on you?" the Grand Mufti, Sheikh Abdul Aziz bin Abdullah Aal al-Sheikh, said in his noon sermon. Many pilgrims told the *Gazette* team that they hoped Iraq would be "victorious" in the coming conflict. "America wants to control the Arab world and its wealth. We are all soldiers for Iraq," a Syrian hajji said.

Later that day, Hatrash called me. He was furious because many of the stories that he and his team were writing weren't getting into the paper—"and Najla Fathi gets a big story about a conference five days old!" It was true that Najla's story, about a cultural symposium in Mecca, was a little stale, but it was the only piece we had in the paper reflecting the participation of women in the hajj. Hatrash also had a piece about the first baby born during that year's pilgrimage, on Mount Arafat, but another story, about a hajji who had a heart attack and was brought back to life, didn't run.

"You sound terrible," I observed.

"It's the flu, mon," he said.

"I thought the lemons were supposed to protect you."

Hatrash admitted that he'd neglected to buy any. I worried that he was too ill to supervise the other reporters; some of them were also getting the flu. "Now we will have to expect that they will bring it back to us," Dr. Shoukany said unsympathetically. "For the next two weeks, everyone will be sick."

The *Gazette* story the next morning was headlined "Faithful Stone the Devil, Make Sacrifices." After spending the night praying under the stars, the pilgrims had returned to Mina, each collecting seven pebbles along the way. Then they threw the pebbles at three stone pillars, called the Jamarat, which represents the place where Satan tried to tempt the Prophet Muhammad. The Stoning of the Devil, which lasts for three days, is the climax of the hajj; it is also the most dangerous period, as people jostle to the front to throw their rocks, and sometimes shoes or umbrellas, crying, *"Allahu Akbar!"*

Mazhar Siddiqi, Sabahat's father and the national affairs editor at the *Gazette*, was upset by the quotes from a couple of pilgrims who said that they were imagining George Bush when they hurled the pebbles at the devil. "What is behind this?" he asked me. "Saudi Arabia never has been a place that would talk against other countries. It has always been known for its neutrality." The subhead of the stoning story was "14 pilgrims killed in stampede." Around ten thirty on the first morning of stoning, a group of hajjis leaving the Jamarat ran into another group just arriving; there was some shoving that quickly turned to panic. Fourteen deaths were sufficiently routine that they didn't merit a separate article.

"Something else we missed," Mazhar said grumpily the morning the pilgrimage ended. "It was the safest hajj in memory." This was despite three stampedes, and thirty-two pilgrims who died in traffic accidents, and five without valid permits who were run over as they tried to evade a checkpoint, and one Pakistani who was swallowed up by the sand while taking a nap. Altogether more than four hundred deaths were reported, most attributable to natural causes. Hundreds more pilgrims suffered from heatstroke or food poisoning, but fortunately there were no epidemics. Of course, when the *Gazette* team came back to Jeddah, everyone in the office got sick.

I KEPT PRESSING Sabahat Siddiqi to produce a draft about the aftermath of the girls' school tragedy. Sabahat, who is Pakistani, reads Arabic poorly, and so Najla agreed to study the news clips and assemble some notes for her. Najla began by reading bound volumes of *Okaz* in our library. Then she called *Al-Madina*, which was only a few blocks away. She was told that she could request pages for fifty riyals each (about fourteen dollars), but as a woman she could not enter the information center, nor would library clerks bring the clippings to her in the ladies' section.

"The public library should have all the clippings on microfilm," I suggested.

"Women aren't allowed in the public library, except one day a week," Najla informed me. And since there was a limit on how much she would be allowed to copy—no more than a few pages at a time—it would take her weeks to gather all the material.

I told her I would call the editor of *Al-Madina* and ask him to help her. Also, I was sure there was a library at the women's college that she could use. The important thing was to get the facts about what occurred when the fire started, and what the government had promised to do afterward.

"There's another problem," she said. "There are some people who don't like knowing about depressing things, and one of those people is me." She paused. "What makes me upset is that, in my reading, I see that maybe some people are covering up."

She wouldn't tell me what she had learned. After a few weeks, I asked her why she hadn't gone to Mecca to interview the families or visited local schools to see if fire codes had been enacted. "Things are getting better," she insisted. She refused to dig any deeper.

Her reluctance puzzled me. Perhaps she was afraid of the authorities; one of the editors had told me that the women believed I was forcing them to do stories that were critical of the government. But Najla was one of our most ambitious reporters. Perhaps she felt protective of her society and didn't want to expose its shortcomings, although she had not hesitated to express criticism in conversation. In any case, her caution was so deeply embedded that I could not break through. Without her aid, Sabahat could not continue, and the story died. The first anniversary of the school fire came and went, largely unremarked in the Saudi press.

In frustration, I made some inquiries on my own. When I had first heard of the tragedy, I imagined that the girls were trampled as they fell in a stairwell or crushed against the locked gate. Then I spoke to Dr. Khaled Abou El Fadl, a law professor at UCLA and a member of the board of Human Rights Watch. He told me that he had received a call from a businessman in Mecca who claimed to be the father of one of the dead girls. "He was at work, a ten-minute drive from the school," Abou El Fadl told me. "He got a call and rushed over, and there he encountered police and firemen. He pushed his way through, and then he noticed the *muttawa'a*." A few minutes later, the father said, his daughter ran to the gate with a group of girls. The girls pleaded for someone to let them out. "She was screaming, 'Break the lock! Break the lock!' " Abou El Fadl continued. "The smoke was overwhelming; it was very hot. One of the girls was screaming that her clothes were sticking to her skin."

Seventeen fire engines had responded to the alarm, along with members of the civil defense squad. Between them and the desperate students stood the *muttawa'a*. None of the representatives of Saudi society standing outside the gate of the girls' school—the police, the firemen, the parents, the bystanders—were able to summon the collective will to ignore the *muttawa'a* and save the girls. The man who called Abou El Fadl said he was afraid of challenging the religious police. They sent his daughter back into the school to get her abaya. She burned to death. "He said, 'I want the criminals tried. They murdered my daughter. Help me bring justice,'" Abou El Fadl told me. But that was the last he heard from the man.

No one was prosecuted for the deaths. The chief of police in Mecca told the Associated Press at the time that he had arrived to find a *muttawa'a*—he mentions only one—quarreling with a police officer. "I immediately instructed him to leave, and he did," he said. The government said that there would be a follow-up investigation, but nothing came of it.

Great stories often arise from what might be called representative tragedies—those that expose warring social forces that are at the heart of people's everyday concerns. The fire in the girls' school had that epochal quality. It posed questions about the roles of women and religion that went to the heart of the Saudi dilemma. Was it true that a single *muttawa'a* had blocked the town from saving the girls? Didn't he effectively murder them? What did it say about the misplaced power of religion that a father would send his daughter back into a burning building to retrieve her abaya? Would he rather have her dead than disgraced? Why was the initial investigation covered up? Why did the government stop the press from pursuing the story? Why did the press so meekly obey?

MEN IN WHITE, women in black: the basic Saudi wardrobe expresses a polarity between the sexes that is absolute. The men look monkish in their gownlike *thobes,* made of cotton or silk, and the black bands around their headscarves reminded me of halos. They are as nearly covered up as the women (except those who, like Najla, choose to conceal their face). At first, I was frustrated by how little information I could gain about a man from looking at his white clothes, but soon I learned to read the accessories—the pen, the watch, the shoes— each of which was freighted with status. Nearly every Saudi man has facial hair. A long, full beard marks a man as pious. An untrimmed beard, a *thobe* that is a couple of inches shorter than usual, and the absence of a headband to hold the scarf in place: this is the costume of fundamentalists and the *muttawa'a*. Some Saudi men wear socks and shoes, but many prefer flat sandals made of ostrich or crocodile skin. Headscarves have a red-check or white-on-white pattern, but even these seemingly identical garments are full of nuance to the Saudi eye, which picks up the Valentino or Christian Dior name sewn into the weave. Heavy platinum Rolexes or TAG Heuers complete their wardrobes. (Islam allows only women to wear gold.)

The strict separation of the sexes is a comparatively recent phenomenon, as Abdullah al-Shehri, a professor of linguistics at King Abdul Aziz University, explained during a long conversation in a Starbucks. "There is a religious term, *khalwah,* which means a man and a woman who are unrelated and are behind a closed door," Abdullah said. "There is another term, *ikhtilat.* This is an invented term. It's heard only in Saudi Arabia, and is never mentioned in any religious text. It means 'mixing of more than two men and women.' There is confusion between these two terms in the Saudi mind. The Prophet said whenever a man and a woman are in *khalwah* Satan will join them. But *ikhtilat* is part of the Saudi tribal culture. Before I was born, in the thirties and forties men and women used to celebrate weddings together. Now bride and groom have separate wedding celebrations."

"Traditions say that eating alone with your female relatives is shameful," Raid Qusti, a journalist, wrote in a daring column for the crosstown *Arab News.* "Where in our religion does it say that sitting with your own family is forbidden?" Qusti complained that many Saudi men thought it was taboo to utter a woman's name in public. "Ask any Saudi male in the street what the names of his wife or daughters are, and you will either have embarrassed him or insulted him. Islamic? Not in any way." There are some parts of the country where a woman never unveils—her husband and children see her face only when she dies. "Women will always be the core issue that will hinder any social progress in Saudi Arabia," Qusti wrote. "We limit their roles in public, ban them from public participation in decision making, we doubt them and confine them because we think they are the source of all seduction and evil in the world. And then we say proudly: 'We are Muslims.'"

A middle-aged Saudi told me, "I am worried about the next generation. They don't see any real women at all. You don't see each other's wives, daughters, sisters. Everything is masculine. And yet they are bombarded by images. They can easily see porn. They live in the imagination of sex all the time. We don't grow naturally, to be loved, not to be loved—we don't undergo these changes. Two-thirds of the marriages here are basically loveless. Many men cheat—there's a lot going on underground."

Some Saudi men openly joke about their behavior when they leave the country. "We're all sex maniacs, by the way," one said to me. He regularly flies to Morocco for female companionship. "There's a part of me that I share with all men, where women are concerned. And there's a part I share with Arab men. But there's a big part that only Saudi guys have in common."

The absence of socialization between men and women struck me as a potent factor in terrorist fantasies. The hijackers who killed themselves on September 11 were propelled in part by the notion of being rewarded in the afterlife with the company of virgins. Such abstractions don't seem quite so strange in a country where images of women piped through a satellite dish seem more vivid than actual Saudi women—whom the male reporters at the *Gazette* liked to call BMOs, or "black moving objects."

In Dr. Shoukany's office there was a doll wearing an abaya. I knew how much he hated the garment. He told me that he had once accused a woman friend of loving her abaya, when she should spurn it. Naturally, he attacked it on a literary level. "In the past, females were an object of shame in Arabia," he had told her. "Fathers would bury their daughters alive. The abaya is a symbolic representation of this kind of female burial." As a teasing rejoinder, his friend gave him the doll.

The year before I arrived in the kingdom, there had been a brief attempt at introducing blue abayas. The religious police rampaged through the garment stores pulling all the non-black versions off the shelves. Then, in Jeddah, which considers itself the most liberal Saudi city, a new abaya suddenly appeared—black, but diaphanous and form-fitting—gaining the fervent endorsement of the *Gazette*'s young male reporters, but those disappeared from the stores as quickly as they appeared.

The abaya obliterates fashion and curtains off women's bodies, but the gowns themselves are various and full of meaning to those who can read the signs. "Some go from the head, some from the shoulder, some are open, some are closed," Najla explained to me. (We were speaking on the phone, as usual, since individual meetings between the two of us would have been taboo.) Sabahat's gown, she pointed out, buttoned up the front and had an attractive embroidered trim. There are others that look a bit like opera capes, with stylish hoods. Najla wears a closed abaya that is like a cotton poncho and is called a *baltu*. "My *baltu* is my personal design," Najla said. Every year, she goes to a tailor to have a new one made. "I always try to make it more conservative," she said. "A few years ago, I saw some abayas with a covering for the hands. I added that." She used to cover her entire face as well, but her glasses made that impractical, so she wears the *niqab*, a covering that goes over her nose and under the gold rims of her cat-eye glasses. "By the way, some people think we make faces under the veil—and we do," she confided.

"Why do you cover your face at all?" I asked.

"In the world of male prejudice, why not?" she said. Another time, she told me, "I just don't like people staring at me."

She began wearing the abaya when she was about fourteen. She gave it up when she came to the United States to study, although she continued to wear the headscarf, with a long-sleeved shirt and long pants. When Najla returned home, she adopted the full veil. "There's not any other girl in my family who has done what I did," she said. "They uncover their faces, they shake men's hands. I don't."

Before going to America, she studied biology at King Faisal University, in Dammam, living in a dorm, her window facing a high wall so that no one could see in. "After *maghreb*, the sunset prayers, I'd get really sad," she recalled. "I couldn't live there any longer. I was spending time learning English just to get my family to agree to let me go to America to get my degree. I didn't want to come back to Jeddah, because I was afraid they would make me marry someone I didn't like."

Hearing Najla's stories, I pictured her parents clenching their teeth as they dealt with this strong-willed daughter. "After three years in King Faisal, I said to my family, 'No more!' I quit school and came home. They said, 'Get married.' I said, 'No.'" Her brothers were in America and she wanted to go, too. Najla's parents agreed to let her finish her bachelor's degree in Kentucky. "My first interest was in politics," she continued. "I spoke to my dad. He said, 'You won't go into politics—I won't spend a penny on you!' " Reluctantly, she began studying microbiology.

After she got her bachelor's degree, Najla wanted to remain in the States for more study, but her family ordered her home to get married. "It was to someone I really didn't want," she said. She had never had a date in her life. The marriage ended quickly. "I had a divorce. I forced him to do that."

Divorce is a drastic step in a country where women's lives are so circumscribed, and yet more than 20 percent of Saudi marriages end in divorce within a single year. Without a man in their home, divorced women are shunned in Saudi society. As a consequence, they tend to form their own community; there is even a road in Riyadh called the Street of Divorcées. Saudi marriages suffer from all the usual afflictions—infidelity, incompatibility, household violence—but the biggest problem is polygamy. In Islam, a man is allowed up to four wives at a time, and many Saudi husbands continually change partners, a practice that causes constant heartache.

Having ended her marriage, Najla continued to push for independence. "I got out of microbiology," she said. "I thought, It's my life. I'm going to do what I want. I'm going to be a politician, no matter what other people think." She went back to Kentucky and got a master's degree in political science.

I asked her what she understood politics to mean in a country with no political system. She said that she was referring to something like social work. "It's a term I use," she said. Speaking of her *Gazette* work, she said, "This job might not be at the level of what I understand a 'politician' is." She added, "As a journalist, there are so many ways you can push society forward. But is it effective?" Another time, she admitted, "I no longer know what I want."

Najla travels quite freely, although she needs her father's written permission to leave town. Her family has a driver, but Najla doesn't like him, so within Jeddah she usually goes by cab. Either way, she thinks that it is improper to be confined in the same vehicle with a man. At the very least, she believes, there should be a partition between the woman and the driver. The best solution, she says, is allowing women to drive. "We have to pay for drivers," she said. "This is a burden on women."

Until 1990, there was no law forbidding women to drive—the social prohibition was sufficient. That year, more than two hundred thousand American troops—including women GIs who drove trucks and jeeps—arrived in the kingdom to repel the Iraqi invasion of Kuwait. Fifty Saudi women decided that it was the right time to challenge tradition. They met in front of a Safeway in Riyadh and ordered their drivers out of their cars, then took a thirty-minute spin through the capital. The police detained them, but there was no legal reason to arrest them. The interior minister immediately banned the practice. The Grand Mufti at the time, Abdul-Aziz bin Baz, helpfully added a fatwa calling female driving a source of depravity. The female drivers' passports were seized, and those who were employed lost their jobs. Several of them had been professors at the women's college of King Saud University, and the king himself suspended them after their own female students protested that they did not want to be taught by "infidels."

On a warm Saturday morning, I went to the beach with Hasan Hatrash, Hasan Baswaid, and Mamdouh al-Harthy. They took me to a secluded compound north of town, run by the Sheraton. It was designated for Westerners, but everyone there was Arab; it was one of the few places in Jeddah where men and women could mix freely. Hatrash brought his guitar, and a keyboard for me. We spent the day jamming, playing blues and reggae tunes beside the Red Sea. At one point, Hatrash launched into "Redemption Song," by Bob Marley. "Emancipate yourselves from mental slavery," he sang. "None but ourselves can free our minds."

Then we had a barbecue with a mixed group of their friends. After dinner, someone brought out an oud, the Arabian lute. Hatrash picked up a drum, Hasan Baswaid took over the keyboard, and the music took a sinuous turn. We sat there till late at night, men and women together, enjoying the light breeze wafting across the water from Africa—a fleeting vision of what Saudi Arabia could be like without the enforced piety that holds the sexes apart.

ONE AFTERNOON, I was in the al-Mamlaka mall, in Riyadh, waiting with other shoppers for the stores to open after sunset prayers. A group of Filipino guys who were hanging out in front of Planet Hollywood abruptly rushed away, like a flock of ducks taking flight. Behind them came a *muttawa'a*. He was a squat man with a wide, red face and a black beard down to his chest. Over his shortened *thobe* he wore a sheer black *mashlah,* a ceremonial robe, with gold piping on the sleeves. As he walked, he leaned backward into his authority, his thumbs stuck in the lapels of his *mashlah*. On either side of him, and a step behind, were two Saudi policemen; they were comical bookends, tall and skinny, with berets and stringy fundamentalist beards. I decided to follow them around the mall, which has four stories, the top floor for women only. We circumnavigated the complex as the *muttawa'a* shooed the men to a nearby mosque, reprimanded women whose attire failed to conform to his standards, peeked in store windows at decapitated mannequins to make sure that no surreptitious shopping was taking place, and looked in restaurants to make certain that they were closed for prayers.

Later, I asked Prince Alwaleed bin Talal bin Abdulaziz Al Saud, the mall's owner, who is one of the richest men in the world, about the bullying *muttawa'a*. "I personally talked to the boss of that chap, who was a bit on the rough side," he told me. "If you talk to their leaders, they are logical, pragmatic people. I said, 'Your guys are scaring the heck out of people.' He gave them orders to change."

The religious police often seem intent on making themselves ridiculous: they will randomly black out faces in advertisements in the malls so that a men's store will feature a headless photograph of a man in a Hugo Boss suit, while posters in a nearby Gap are untouched. A number of Saudis told me that many of the *muttawa'a* are ex-convicts who would be unemployable except for the fact that in prison they memorized the Quran. They receive a bounty from the government for every arrest they make: reportedly, three hundred dollars for every Saudi, and half that for a foreigner. One Jeddah resident described them as "an occupying force." He told me that they had recently burst in on the graduation ceremony of his daughter's French elementary school and ordered the children to stop singing "Alouette."

One evening in Riyadh, I was climbing into a cab when I noticed something highly unusual: a woman standing on the corner with her head uncovered. She was remarkably beautiful, and looked directly at me. I could see the fear in her eyes. I almost asked if I could give her a lift, but that would have been an unthinkable breach of custom: as an unmarried couple in the same car, we could both be taken to jail. So I said nothing. My cab had to make a U-turn, and when we came back past the corner I saw the woman running. She now had the hood of her abaya over her hair. She ran to a shop and tried to open the door, but it was closed for prayers. Then I saw that she was being trailed by a Suburban with the emblem of the Commission for the Promotion of Virtue and Prevention of Vice on the door. The woman went from door to door, banging on the glass. Every instinct in me cried out to help her, yet I could think of nothing that would not make the situation worse. I rode on, feeling guilty and helpless, as the *muttawa'a* closed in.

At times, the main target of the religious police seemed to be not virtue but love. Boys and girls are kept strictly separate throughout their education, and the *muttawa'a* patrol public places, trying to keep romance at bay. The week before Valentine's Day, the *muttawa'a* began going through card and flower shops, attacking anything that had hearts on it or was red, the color of romance; florists hid their roses as if they were contraband. Flirting takes place in opportunistic bursts, at stoplights or in the mall, where telephone numbers are furtively exchanged. Some young people adopt riskier strategies. To see his girlfriend in public, Mamdouh, the Bedouin reporter, dressed up in an abaya. "I do it all the time," he confessed.

Hasan Baswaid told me that the best way to get around the *muttawa'a* and meet girls was through the Internet. He had met a nice girl in a chat room, and he began talking with her on the telephone. Finally, they arranged to meet in a café, each bringing a sister as an escort. They enjoyed the date, and within three months Baswaid decided to propose. The girl accepted, and there was a small engagement party, which included meeting with her relatives to haggle over the dowry. "After that, she is my wife," he told me the day of the meeting.

The next morning, Baswaid returned to the office a married man—although he and his wife couldn't live together until after a wedding ceremony, which would be held a few weeks later. We met that day in the *Okaz* cafeteria. He was already a little nostalgic for his bachelor days. We began talking about parties, and he recalled a rather wild event he had attended a few years earlier. Except for the feast days at the end of Ramadan and the hajj, all holidays, including birthdays, are nominally banned in the kingdom. One year, however, he visited his cousin in Dubai, and his cousin's wife, who is American, held a Halloween masquerade.

"She wanted me to dress up like a woman," he confessed.

"And did you?"

He laughed, a little embarrassed. "I went to the party for about fifteen minutes, then said I had to leave. I went upstairs with my cousin's wife. She owns a beauty salon." The relative put Nair on Baswaid's legs and shaved his arms and mustache and even his eyebrows. "At the time, I wore my hair really long. So she curled it. She gave me some panty hose and a dress with socks in the bra. And then I went downstairs." The disguise was surprisingly convincing, and he began to flirt—even plopping himself on a good friend's lap. Soon, of course, the guests figured out who he really was. His buddy was mad, but the women were intrigued by his role-playing. "They were, like, kissing me. They even let me come into the women's bathroom!" He had a great time, he said. "But I hated myself in the morning. I woke up with no eyebrows."

"WHAT DOES YOUR FAMILY think about you being here?" Hasan Hatrash asked me one afternoon. We were sitting on the floor of the *Gazette* newsroom having lunch—a large platter of grilled chicken and rice, which we ate with our fingers.

"They're all terrified," I admitted.

"How did we get into this situation where everybody thinks we're terrorists!" he said miserably.

The West's fear of the Arab world was mirrored by many Saudis I talked to. Young people who had been studying in the West were afraid to return there. Businessmen confessed that they would feel humiliated if they tried to travel to the United States and were fingerprinted upon entering the country. These were men who had once enjoyed the nearly universal access that a Saudi passport vouchsafed them. For most of the country's business and intellectual leaders, and for many of the royals, the Western world had been a refuge from the intellectual and sensual sterility of the kingdom. I suspected that many had nurtured a secret escape plan in case the extremists gained complete control—they would retreat to second homes in Santa Barbara or Miami. But now such places seemed hostile to them. These elite men who had prided themselves on living in two worlds felt trapped in their own stern culture, and they were suffocating.

I went with Dr. Shoukany one evening to hear an Arab American political consultant, Hady Amr, speak about Saudi-U.S. relations. "Be rational when you talk to Americans," he advised. "It's okay to be passionate, but don't raise your voices or wave your hands." That seemed to be a needless admonition; the men in the audience were subdued, almost numb. After the lecture, Shoukany drove me back to my apartment. He reflected on what America had meant to him. He had grown up in a small village in Asir, the southern province where several of the hijackers were from. Like most boys in that part of the country at the time, Shoukany was a shepherd, and he curled his hair and decorated it with flowers. He did not see an automobile until he was ten years old. "Most men my age, they will tell you the same story," he said. For Shoukany, America was just a rumor on the other side of the horizon, and yet he and thousands of young men like him went there to study, often gravitating to sheltered university towns. As a matter of fact, Shoukany went to the University of Texas, in Austin, where I live. Young intellectuals like Shoukany became repositories of Western science and art, and they returned to fill the faculties of the new Saudi universities. For some of these men, the return to their own country was a kind of exile. They had traveled too far, and they would never be entirely at home anywhere.

Immediately after September 11, Shoukany told me, he had called to check on an old Saudi friend who had stayed in the United States. His friend said that he had been well treated, but he was filled with anxiety nonetheless. "The people are fine," he said. "I think it's me. There's still some desert wildness inside me."

I was surprised how open these naturally reticent Saudis were about their state of mind. One morning, several of the *Gazette* reporters admitted to me that they were depressed. "Last night, I didn't even sleep," Hasan Hatrash told me. "I just sat on the beach. Till four in the morning. When I do sleep, it's like I'm dead for three days."

I worried about them, especially Hatrash. He was always forgetting to eat, and during meetings he jiggled his leg nervously. In many respects, he was our best reporter, but music was his passion. There wasn't a place for him in a society that smothered art and other pleasures. The fact that he was in his late twenties, lived at home, and couldn't meet women—and couldn't afford to marry one if he did—also weighed on him.

In the *Gazette,* Baswaid reported on a survey of more than two thousand students in Jeddah, aged thirteen to twenty-five, that was conducted by a researcher at King Abdul Aziz University. Sixty-five percent of the boys and 72 percent of the girls showed symptoms of depression. Drug use was nearly 5 percent for both sexes, as was the rate of alcoholism, even though alcohol was strictly forbidden. "Five percent alcoholism among intermediate and high school students in an Islamic country is jarring to our ears," a professor at the university told Baswaid. What struck me was the rate of attempted suicide, which is strictly forbidden in Islam; 7 percent of the girls admitted that they had attempted to kill themselves (more than twice the rate of the boys).

One afternoon, I went to the gym near my apartment and started doing yoga exercises. A Saudi man saw me doing a headstand; he walked over, bent down, and cranked his head sideways.

"Is that good for depression?" he asked.

"It might be," I said.

"Can you show me how to do it?"

I helped him up against a wall, and after a while he learned to hold the position. When I went back to the locker room, it was prayer time, and four men happened to be praying on the floor directly facing my locker. I waited for them to finish. One of them asked me afterward if I would start a yoga class. "Maybe it will help relieve the stress," he said.

Such polite entreaties caught me off guard. Before arriving in Saudi Arabia, I had expected loud confrontations that went on into the night, as I had experienced in Cairo in the spring of 2002. I found neither open anger nor the natural exuberance, humor, and mischief that are so much a part of the Egyptian character. Instead, there was quiet despair, an ominous emotional flatness.

"Don't you guys ever tell jokes?" I asked one Saudi friend.

"Of course," he said. "We're very funny."

"So tell me a Saudi joke."

He thought for a moment and finally offered this: A Somali, an Egyptian, and a Saudi are asked, "What is your opinion of eating meat?" The Somali said, "What is eating?" The Egyptian said, "What is meat?" And the Saudi said, "What's an opinion?"

IN MARCH, a soft-spoken retired chemistry professor invited me to have lunch at his house, in Riyadh. The place was impressive; it had marble floors and two large public rooms with the chairs pushed against the wall, in the Islamic style. I learned that his wife and daughters would be joining us—an extraordinarily kind and progressive gesture for such a conservative man.

The presentation of a Saudi family is a careful ritual. The protocol begins with the entry of the youngest son, who in this case was an officer in the Saudi Air Force and a veteran of the Gulf War. After we chatted for a few minutes, the older son, a banker, joined us. Then the father came in, and accepted a kiss on the top of his head from his older son. They invited me to the kitchen to eat, rather than the dining room, which was an honor. The professor's wife appeared and sat down at the head of a long table, and we began to eat from eight huge platters of food. Then, one by one, his four grown daughters and daughters-in-law came to the table. They were all intelligent, well educated, and hospitable, and the conversation was so agreeable that I was unprepared for the argument that followed.

The professor began talking about the black boxes in the hijacked planes that had struck the World Trade Center. He questioned the Americans' claim that they had not survived. Then he spoke about the unsolved anthrax poisonings that followed the attack, suggesting that it was the U.S. government that had carried them out, to scare people.

"What kind of country do you think we are?" I said heatedly. "Do you think we are really so wicked that we would poison our own citizens?"

"You have gotten angry in my house," the professor said, offended.

The conversation inevitably turned toward the notion that Mossad or the CIA had engineered the 9/11 hijackings. The logic is based on two assumptions: that these organizations were scheming for an excuse to attack the Arab world and that Arabs are too incompetent to have pulled off the attacks. I had had the same discussion countless times.

"Let's ask your son," I suggested, when the professor said that none of the hijackers had sufficient training to handle a commercial airliner. "Let's ask the pilot how hard it is."

The officer looked at his father and said, "To ram a skyscraper on a cloudless day? I should think it would be the easiest thing in the world."

The room was quiet—the family stunned, I think, that the younger son would openly contradict his father. "Do you accept his testimony?" I gently asked the father, but he only turned away.

I had the sense that the generations were engaged in a struggle over the future of the country, but it was not at all clear that the young had a better vision of what needed to be done. I went one evening to a *diwaniyya,* a weekly men's dinner that is a kind of literary and political salon. We sat on the floor until past midnight, eating from platters of lamb and rice. Most of the men were professionals: lawyers, editors, and doctors. "We were educated in America, and I see the world going against everything I have built," said Dr. Mujahid al-Sawwaf, a lawyer in Jeddah and a former professor at Umm al-Qura University, in Mecca. "We were always for liberalism, but some of the terrorists were my students."

"My daughter is for bin Laden," another man admitted. "When I go to wake her up, I see pictures of Palestinian girl martyrs on her wall. It scares me to death. If we go into her room at night, she'll be listening to Britney Spears, but as soon as we close the door she's listening to martyr songs."

The other men nodded. "They come to us and say, 'Dad, why didn't you fight in 1948 and 1967?' They see us as cowards," a dentist said.

"One of the children said to me, 'Uncle, is it true that when you went to the West you became a puppet like our leadership?' Our kids don't want to study in America, as we did."

"Bin Laden changed our life. He proved that mighty America is vulnerable. To us, we're afraid of our future, but the youth think America is on the verge of collapsing and it's time for us to fight it."

"We are afraid of our children."

ON A BRIGHT APRIL MORNING, I drove up to Taif, a lovely mountain town in the great Sarawat range. It looks out over a sheer cliff toward the Red Sea. Behind Taif is the vast Saudi desert, stretching all the way to the Persian Gulf; in front is the Hijaz, a narrow strip of coastal land that includes Jeddah, as well as the holy cities of Mecca and Medina. Taif is only fifty-five miles up the mountain from Mecca, but the kingdom was not fully consolidated until a road was built, connecting the two halves. It had been such a formidable engineering problem that no reputable company would undertake the challenge, until a one-eyed illiterate contractor named Mohammed bin Laden submitted a bid.

There's a story that Osama often told about his father. When it came time to lay out the road, Mohammed pushed a donkey over the edge of the escarpment and followed him down the long, looping path, marking the route of the future highway. When the road was completed, in 1962, the kingdom was united, and Mohammed bin Laden became a national hero.

Taif was important to 9/11 for two reasons. One is that the Prophet Muhammad laid siege to the city in the year 630. The Muslim army received permission from their leader to use a catapult to breach the city's defenses, even though women and children would be harmed. Al-Qaeda would later use this precedent to justify the killing of innocents on 9/11, comparing the use of airplanes to that of the catapult fourteen centuries before.

The other reason is that one of Taif's citizens was Hani Hanjour, one of the four hijacker pilots, who crashed into the Pentagon that day, killing 125 people in the building and the 64 passengers and crew on American Airlines Flight 77.

I picked up a reporter from a Saudi business paper, and we parked outside the imposing two-story marble house where Hanjour grew up; like most of the hijackers, he was a product of the middle class. His father was a provisioner for a nearby military base.

Sometime after midnight Yasser Hanjour came outside and got into the backseat. Slight and meek, he looked like a clone of his sad-eyed older brother. As he saw it, his brother's story was a simple one. Hani had never wanted to be anything other than a pilot. He had trained in America, where he had suddenly become very religious. When he returned from his first trip there, he applied for a job at Saudi Arabian Airlines but was turned down. He disappeared into his room for six months.

"Why was he so depressed?" I asked.

"You know the reason," the business reporter interjected impatiently. "This joblessness." Yasser shrugged and agreed.

There was a sameness to the stories of the hijacker pilots. They had become Muslim extremists in Europe and America—presumably as a way of holding on to their sense of who they were in the engulfing West. Their own cultures offered them no way to be powerful in the world. Traditionally, the Saudi government absorbed nearly all the university graduates, but after the oil shock of the mid-eighties the government, saddled with debt, could no longer hire as before. Unemployment and idleness became central facts of life for young Saudi men (as they had always been for Saudi women). Bin Laden gave young men with no control over their lives an identity, and a wanton chance to make history. "Death is better than life in humiliation!" bin Laden said.

That was a constant theme of bin Laden's speeches. One of the critical documents in understanding his motivation is his "Declaration of War Against the Americans Occupying the Land of the Two Holy Places," written in 1996, in which he cites the sources of Arabs' shame. Although the "Declaration" calls on Muslims everywhere to fight "Jews and Crusaders," the heart of its argument is a populist attack on the mismanagement of the Saudi economy. "Everybody talks about the deterioration of the economy, about inflation, and about the ever-increasing debts," he writes. "More than three hundred and forty billion Saudi riyals are owed by the government to the people—in addition to the daily accumulated interest, let alone the foreign debt! People wonder whether we are the largest oil exporting country?! They even believe that this situation is a curse put on them by Allah for not objecting to the oppressive and illegitimate behavior and measures of the ruling regime." In a country where discontent with the ruling family is widespread but rarely expressed directly, where resentment against the power and influence of the West is nearly universal, and where unemployment is creating a class of well-educated but idle young men, bin Laden's words resonated so strongly in part because no one else would say them.

"Our society is confused," Abdullah al-Shehri, the linguistics professor, told me during another Starbucks seminar. He was from the same tribe as three of the fifteen Saudi hijackers, but that scarcely sets him apart in a country whose inhabitants are so intimately bound together. "It bothers me a lot when I see things about our society that are negative or backward, which in the West are blamed on religion. You can easily look at Muslim history, at the Umayyads and the Abbasids, and see how powerful Islamic culture was then. What has changed is the mentality and the culture. Islam is a religion of tolerance, but now there is a sense of frustration and defeat that makes people hate others. For some, hate becomes their only weapon. If you can't beat them, hate them."

"FROM NOW ON, you should be Mr. Sewage," I said to Hasan Hatrash, who was not quite persuaded. "It will make your career. This is a 'Holy shit!' story, I guarantee you."

He laughed. "Yeah, I see your point, mon," he said.

The sewage story would require Hatrash, who had never finished college, to learn about geology, epidemiology, sewage treatment, dams, city building codes, and legal procedures. He was intimidated, but he was also a quick study. His self-taught English was so fluent that he could pass for an American (or a Jamaican). He also spoke passable Japanese and German. He began to explore the story cautiously, not entirely trusting my enthusiasm. What was the point of writing an exposé in a country where it couldn't be published?

I took him to interview Hussein Shobokshi, the contractor who had originally told me about the sewage scandal. He received us in a dark office whose walls were covered with beautiful examples of Arabic calligraphy. I pulled out my legal pad and my tape recorder; Hatrash took a folded sheet of notebook paper from the pocket of his *thobe*. I asked Shobokshi why he was bothering to sue Jeddah's former director of sewage. Saudi courts have always been protective of government officials.

"Hyundai won a case against the Ministry of Public Works," Shobokshi told us. "So that got me thinking: maybe the judicial system is willing to raise the bar a bit. We began collecting testimonials. It's been my crusade."

Shobokshi started cataloging the costs of the sewage crisis: real estate prices had dropped by 70 percent in some districts; the beaches were polluted and marine life was dying; sewage was eating into the city's limestone bedrock. He gave us references for medical sources and environmental studies, including one commissioned by the Jeddah Chamber of Commerce and Industry that he said warned of a hepatitis epidemic. "We will see people dying, and buildings will collapse. It will certainly get worse before it gets better."

When we left Shobokshi's office, Hatrash was excited. He began talking about all the sources he was going to interview. I asked to see his notes. I could see some figures—more than 60 percent of the palm trees were dying, for instance—scribbled on the folded paper, but the texture of Shobokshi's conversation was missing. I gave him a little lecture about the importance of capturing quotes and then sent him off to pursue the story.

MEANWHILE, I went to speak with Ramesh Balan, the managing editor of the *Gazette*. A non-Muslim from southern India, he darted around the newsroom like a hummingbird, and he talked faster than he moved. If you could hold him in place for a moment, you would observe a dashing, graying man in his mid-forties. One day he emerged from his office and cried, "Look at this!" He was waving a copy of the *Arab News*. The headline reported the arrest of eight al-Qaeda suspects involved in a January shoot-out in Riyadh. "Local coverage, here on the front page!" he said jealously. "I'm going to retaliate."

Ramesh handed me a bunch of letters to the editor and said that perhaps they would inspire an assignment. In the pile was a handwritten letter from a Saudi soldier. "Please help us," it said. The writer complained that all the soldiers in his unit had just seen their salaries cut in half.

I called Hasan Baswaid over to my desk. "Do you know anybody in the military?" I asked.

Baswaid nodded. He had more connections than anyone else in the office. I handed him the soldier's letter. "Why don't you call around and see if other soldiers are having their salaries cut? This could be a big story."

Baswaid quickly set the letter back on my desk. He put his hands together as if they were in handcuffs. "This could put you in the calaboose," he said with a sheepish grin. A little while later, however, he came by my desk and told me of a rumor that had washed over the city: the bin Ladens were changing their name.

"They're going to call themselves 'A'wadh,'" he said. It was Osama bin Laden's grandfather's name. Their motivation for making the change was understandable—if it was true.

"Hasan, get this story and your byline will be on the front page of every paper in the world."

Baswaid shrugged and gave me a look.

"Let me worry about getting it published," I said. "Do you think you can get someone to confirm it?"

Baswaid became very sober. "I know Osama's son Abdullah a little," he said.

"Can you talk to him?"

"Maybe."

Baswaid started making calls on his mobile phone. Meanwhile, I went to visit Ramesh again. He was smarting from a confrontation with Dr. Ahmed al-Yusuf, the *Gazette*'s editor in chief, a man I saw only rarely. Ramesh said that he had wanted to run a big story about Libya withdrawing its ambassador to the kingdom after a clash between Muammar Qaddafi and Crown Prince Abdullah at an Arab League meeting. Dr. Yusuf ordered that the story be played down. "He doesn't know what real press freedom is!" Ramesh said. He took a few deep breaths. "I'm about to have a nervous breakdown!"

I told him about Hasan Baswaid's story. "Will you print it?" I asked.

"If they don't print it, I'll quit!" he exclaimed. He suddenly seemed exhilarated. Ramesh then offered me an exciting piece of information: the sewage workers in Jeddah were on strike. We both felt a little giddy. We could envision the *Gazette* front page with the bin Laden name change, a city sewage strike, and a reference to the withdrawal of the Libyan ambassador—what a news day!

I sent Hasan Hatrash off to the municipal yard where the sewage trucks typically gathered. "The drivers aren't on strike," he reported. "They are afraid, because the police are impounding their trucks." As a result, the drivers were staying home, letting the waste build up.

"Why in the world would they do that?"

Hatrash said he would find out, but it was already after 10:00 p.m., and the paper's deadline was only an hour away. Meanwhile, Baswaid was standing at my desk expectantly. "I found Abdullah bin Laden," he told me. "He's having dinner right now at the Italian restaurant."

The restaurant was in a strip shopping center off Medina Road, about twenty minutes away—less, given Baswaid's driving, which I decided to think of as a kind of video game. There was a small patio in front of the restaurant, and four young men were seated at a table, laughing. Baswaid and I entered with studied casual chatter, planning to make it all seem natural. Abdullah and two of his friends wore *thobes;* the other friend was in jeans and wore a rasta hat. All were in their middle twenties.

We sat down at a table next to theirs, and Abdullah bin Laden took no apparent notice. He was tall and clean-shaven and his head was uncovered. His hair was close-cropped, almost stubbly; his nose was long and flat, like his father's. The mild eyes were the same.

Baswaid got up and went inside the restaurant, then returned to the patio with a pack of cigarettes. He pretended to have just recognized Abdullah, and walked over, smiling. A few pleasantries were exchanged, then Abdullah turned to be introduced to me. In the Saudi style, he brushed my hand and touched his heart.

Baswaid asked the question. Abdullah denied the rumor. "It's my name, and I am very proud of it. There is no way to change it," he said. He didn't sound plaintive or embarrassed.

"Should we do a story anyway?" Baswaid asked as we watched the young men getting into an SUV with darkened windows. I suggested that Baswaid continue to ask around, to find out, for instance, if the Saudi Binladin Group, the family construction company, was changing its name. There was still a possibility that the family would seek the change on their passports, but more reporting would be required before the story could run.

The next morning, the *Gazette*'s front page did carry Hasan Hatrash's story, headlined "Jeddah Sewage Disposal Stops." The drivers were perplexed, he reported. "We don't know why the cops are harassing us," one said. Homeowners were already complaining of overflowing septic tanks that were flooding the city streets. In a single skillful anecdote, Hasan caught the sense of a disaster in the making:

> Irfan Khan, an Indian, who had just got back from work to find his ground-floor apartment in a total mess from overflowing toilets, was livid with rage. "Come, look at my carpets, my kitchen—how will I ever live here now!" he raved.
>
> "Get back in!" he broke off to yell at two children wanting to try out the stepping-stones dotting a cesspool on the street. "Now there'll be mosquitoes and disease—and already there is a Dengue fever scare in the city!"

By the time the article appeared, the impact of the sewage problem was obvious throughout Jeddah. In many places, the streets were wet; hideous lakes were forming out of gurgling spouts. Nevertheless, no other newspaper had taken notice of the crisis.

Hatrash then learned that the police were confiscating the trucks because the drivers hadn't paid a new disposal fee at the sewage pond. He tracked down the idle drivers, then came back and wrote a story that began, "Police have impounded trucks in the past week because of a failure to remit a new disposal fee."

"How much is the fee?" I asked.

"Five riyals." About a dollar.

"This whole city is drowning in shit because of five riyals? Hasan, paint the picture! Sewage collection has stopped. Toilets are overflowing. The streets are turning into lakes of excrement. And why?"

"All because of a measly five riyals!"

Hatrash went back to work. The story was terrific. The police had been pressured by the mayor's office to confiscate the trucks of the drivers who refused to pay the new fee. But the drivers were being forced to pay out of their own pockets, and many of them scarcely had enough to cover their gas. Sewage from the streets was streaming into people's houses, and although homeowners were willing to pay any amount for service, the drivers were afraid of losing their trucks. The health department warned about the danger of hepatitis, but the mayor's office refused comment, saying simply that the problem would "end soon."

For the first time, the *Gazette* was looking like a real newspaper. The headline of Hassan's next article was "Municipality Caves In— Sewage Disposal Resumes in Jeddah." Strangely, we were again the only paper to carry the story.

Within a week, the drivers were idled once more, over the same dispute. "I just learned something interesting," Hatrash told me one morning. I was gleefully reading his latest piece, titled "Problem Over, Says Mayor, as Jeddah Sinks in Sewage." There was a full page of photographs showing impassable puddles in the streets and flooded front yards. "I have a source who tells me that the decision to impose the new fee came from the governor, Prince Abdul Aziz bin Majid," he continued. "The prince sent a letter ordering this new plan to be implemented. They wanted the five-riyal toll to pay for the new sewage dam." The twenty-five-million-riyal dam, which would back up the existing one, was to be built by the Saudi Binladin Group.

Hatrash said he had spoken to a geologist who pointed out that the new concrete dam was potentially worse than the old sand one, because it would expand the reservoir and add significant pressure to the earthquake fault that ran directly below it. One great tremor would let loose a torrent of sludge that could turn Jeddah into a modern Pompeii.

"Let's make a story out of it," I said.

"It would be such a relief to tell the truth," Hatrash said.

That didn't happen. Once the rumors about the prince's involvement began to circulate, the story died. We soon learned that not only was the prince behind the five-riyal toll but he was fronting a new company that proposed to build a sewer system for the city, which would cost the kingdom twenty billion riyals. None of this informa-

tion, however, ended up in the *Gazette*. The editor in chief would not
print it. Meanwhile, the truck contractors were forced to pay the fee,
and the immediate crisis passed—but the prince paid no political price
for endangering the health of the citizens and despoiling the city.

A FEW WEEKS LATER, the *Gazette* received a tantalizing letter—a
plea from a group of Indian cabdrivers. Fifty of them had been
brought to the kingdom seven years before with the promise of office
jobs in private companies and a guaranteed monthly wage of six hundred riyals. (They included a copy of the contract with their letter.)
Upon their arrival, the employer seized their passports and their residence permits, and told them that they actually would be "limousine
drivers"—that is, cabbies—and that rather than receiving a wage, they
would be required to pay daily rent on their cabs. Some of the men
didn't even have a driver's license, but they were all thrown out onto
the chaotic streets of Jeddah. The men were crowded into a hovel,
stranded, hungry—virtual prisoners. After enduring a series of indig-
nities, including beatings, fifteen of the men had gone on strike.

There is no clear figure on how many expats (as all foreign workers are called) are in the kingdom—four million, nine million, nobody
knows—but very few people know how many Saudis there are, either.
"Since King Faisal's census in the sixties, the actual population figure
has been a state secret," a source close to the Interior Ministry told me.
"The king saw the figure was low, and he immediately doubled it."
According to CIA statistics, the native population is about nineteen
million, but the actual number of Saudis may be as few as ten million.
Certainly one has the feeling, in the cities at least, that there are as
many expats as Saudis.

Expats hold seven out of ten jobs in the kingdom, and 90 percent
of all private-sector positions. For decades, the Saudi government has
been attempting to replace foreigners with native workers, but it has
run into resistance from employers who don't want to hire their own
people. "Saudis aren't qualified," Prince Sultan bin Salman bin Abdul
Aziz, the secretary-general for tourism, told me. "Showing up for a
job is not a priority for them. Even the culture of working as a team is
not there." Increasingly, the unemployed natives tend to view the Ban-

gladeshi houseboys, the Lebanese waiters, and the Egyptian barbers with resentment rather than gratitude. "We hate it!" a Saudi friend exclaimed when I asked how he felt when he had to speak English or Urdu just to order coffee. Entry-level service jobs, however, are forms of employment that Saudis refuse to accept.

The expat readership of the *Gazette* would, I thought, see the Indian-cabbie story in a sympathetic light. I arranged for three of the drivers who had signed the letter to come to the *Gazette* offices to talk to Faisal Bajaber, a smart Indian reporter who had just graduated from high school. The cabdrivers were led by Nainan Philopose, a small, intense man in a dirty shirt, who arrived carrying a thick file of documents. He had the bearing of a man who is not easily intimidated. His wife was desperately ill in India, he told us. He had planned to visit her, but, when he sought his passport from his employer, company goons had dragged him to a detention center for illegal aliens. The owner of the limousine company beat him in front of several immigration officers. Philopose and some other men had complained to the Indian Embassy about their treatment, to no effect. Because they were expats, they had no real legal standing in the country. Their employer had made them sign documents in Arabic that they couldn't read, as well as some blank sheets of paper. One of the drivers told Faisal that the owner of the company had his own jail, where he locked up drivers who defied him.

I watched Faisal interviewing the drivers in Urdu. Although he had lived nearly his entire life in the kingdom, Faisal was not allowed to attend the public universities, because he didn't have Saudi citizenship. Yet he spoke five languages, and his English was nearly flawless. He asked detailed questions and took careful notes. He had the makings of an excellent journalist.

Faisal presented the story at a reporters' meeting. Dr. Shoukany listened sleepily until he heard that the owner of the limousine company had a private jail. Then he nearly jumped out of his chair. "He's not a prince, is he?" he asked. "No? Well, we'll go after him!"

After several weeks, Faisal produced a draft. The owner of the limousine company had dodged him, saying only that the drivers were lying. Now the drivers and the owner were headed for labor court, where such disputes are nearly always resolved in favor of the Saudi employers. Faisal called me to say that there was a problem with the story.

I went into Ramesh's office to find Faisal and Dr. Yusuf, the editor in chief, who was reading the draft. The reporters were frightened of him. He was a slight man with shrewd eyes and a nervous giggle, but he had an unguarded temper and he didn't mind humiliating his employees. Yusuf wasn't really a newsman—he was a former professor of advertising—but I tried to appeal to his sense of community. There really was no reason for the *Gazette* to exist if it didn't address the kinds of concerns detailed in the cabdriver story.

Yusuf waved the draft dismissively and observed that Faisal hadn't talked to the Indian Embassy. That seemed a small, if valid, point. Faisal had a letter registering a complaint by the embassy on behalf of the drivers. Yusuf also noted that the court hearing was the following morning. "We don't want to put pressure on the government," he said.

"What's wrong with that?" I asked.

Yusuf explained that the cabdrivers would pay the price for any quixotic effort on our part to champion their case. Then he handed the story back to Faisal. I protested a bit, but walked out compliantly. Maybe Dr. Yusuf was right. I didn't want the penniless cabdrivers to be punished because of my principles. I recalled the story of Abd al-Karim Mara'i al-Naqshabandi, a Syrian expat worker who had been sentenced to death for allegedly practicing witchcraft against his employer, a nephew of King Fahd. The evidence against him was absurd. Human rights workers leaped on the case when they discovered that Naqshabandi's employer had wanted him to falsely testify against another employee and, when he refused, made the witchcraft charge. Naqshabandi became a cause célèbre, but he was peremptorily beheaded—a grisly message to outsiders who meddled in Saudi affairs.

The next day, the cabdrivers went to labor court. Faisal told me that the Arabic document that they had signed when they first arrived in the kingdom released the owner from any financial liability. The owner also produced other documents, apparently made up from the blank sheets of paper the drivers had signed, which said that they owed him several thousand riyals each.

"What will happen to them now?" I asked.

"They're going to prison," he told me.

Faisal's story on the drivers never appeared.

HASAN HATRASH WAS WALKING in circles in front of the *Okaz* building when I arrived. He looked shaken. "Oh, my God," he told me. "I found a dead body."

"Where?"

"Right here, in the garden!" He led me around the side of the building, next to the parking lot. "It's not a body, actually, but bones, human bones, a jawbone anyway, and I think there are other bones around it."

Between the side street and the parking lot was a median strip that recently had been planted with sprigs of oleander. There was some debris—a matchbook, some nails, shards of a coffee cup—and a human jawbone jutting out of the soil.

"You see I dug around it a bit," Hatrash told me. "There are other bones under there."

"Huh."

We watched a fly land on the bone and then move on. I suggested we call the police.

"You can call them, but they won't come," he said. "It's better if you find one and get him to call on his radio."

We got in my car and drove around looking for a policeman, which took a surprisingly long time. The cop then had us follow him to the local substation. It was in the bottom floor of an apartment house, a dim room with gray linoleum tiles and broken-bottom leather chairs with foam spilling out of the arms. Two young detectives sat behind desks taking reports. On the wall above them there was a Quranic injunction: "Whoever fears God, a way will be opened for him." One of the detectives, wearing a khaki uniform and sandals, came over to the newspaper office to view the jawbone. He warily agreed that it looked human, but he didn't seem to know what to do with it. He drove off without marking it as a crime scene. The next morning the jawbone was gone, but we never heard from the officer again.

I had expected more of a police state. The nature and scope of the repression were hard to calculate. I did encounter frequent roadblocks, mainly designed to trap illegal residents. American intelligence officials told me to expect that the Saudis would monitor my phone calls and e-mails—and even break into my apartment and clone my computer. So I was on guard.

"See that building?" a lawyer said to me under his breath as we drove down Tahlia Street. He indicated with his eyes a large two-story structure at the corner of Medina Road. "That's the political jail." There was nothing notable about it except for the absence of shops or signs on the ground floor. I didn't see any obvious security forces around it. The lawyer said that he had had clients detained there in the past.

"Who's in there now?" I asked.

"Who knows?"

In contrast with Egypt, where nearly everyone knew somebody who had been illegally arrested, and often tortured, in Saudi Arabia few people could say that they knew someone who had been detained for political reasons. Jeddah residents were always looking over their shoulders, but had only vague rumors to report when I pressed them. I did meet a man who had been tortured by the Saudi secret police ten years before. "They tickled me here," he said, showing me his hands, which were scarred by knife wounds. They thought he had helped a dissident escape the country. "If I knew how to do that, I would escape myself!" he had told them.

"You are being watched," a *Gazette* editor once told me. He spoke to me in a stairwell, where he assumed we wouldn't be overheard.

"How do you know?"

"A man came this morning from the secret police to see Dr. Yusuf. After this, Dr. Yusuf called me in to ask about you."

I asked what Dr. Yusuf wanted to know. "How you were doing, what you were up to," the editor said.

That didn't sound so sinister. Dr. Yusuf repeatedly asked about my welfare and kindly expressed concern for my safety, especially since, during my stay, several Westerners were assassinated. No one from the Ministry of Information came to see me, no minders were assigned, and if anyone could follow me in Jeddah traffic he represented a force beyond reckoning.

But suspicion darkened the atmosphere in Saudi Arabia, even among people who worked together every day. I asked Mahmoud Shukri, a seventeen-year-old reporter, where his friends were going to school. "We don't tell each other things like that," he said. When he asked my advice about college plans, we had to meet outside the office, to avoid being overheard. "If you let people know what you are up to, they might be envious," he explained. Telephone numbers were especially hard to obtain. One of the more experienced *Gazette* reporters kept an old ledger with handwritten numbers he had compiled over the years; it was perhaps the most valuable document in the entire office, given the reluctance of many Saudis to be listed.

By now, I had begun to look at Saudi society as a collection of opposing forces: the liberals against the religious conservatives, the royal family versus democratic reformers, the unemployed against the expats, the old against the young, men against women. The question was whether the anger that results from all this conflict would be directed outward, at the West, or inward, at the Saudi regime.

I went to the Ministry of Interior, in Riyadh, hoping to gain permission to talk to members of Saudi intelligence who had investigated the September 11 hijackers. The ministry is one of the largest branches of the Saudi government, with half a million employees. Its building is a giant inverted pyramid, which looms like a Death Star on the edge of downtown Riyadh. I was told that the architect was a poet, and that the building was a structural catastrophe. It certainly projects an air of menace. Inside the marble atrium, black tubular elevator columns rise through the interior balconies. The summit of this upside-down building is a dome with an eight-pointed star.

My appointment was with Dr. Sa'id al-Harthi, who was an adviser to the interior minister and the chairman of the board of *Okaz*—and therefore at the top of the *Gazette* masthead. All lines of power in the Saudi press converge in this building. I had been promised an interview with Prince Naif, the interior minister, and had prepared a long list of questions about the hijackers. A year after September 11, the prince had asserted that Zionists were behind the plot. "I cannot still believe that nineteen youths, including Saudis, carried out the September eleventh attacks with the support of bin Laden," he said. "It's impossible." Then, in February, Saudi police rounded up more than ninety al-Qaeda suspects; nevertheless, Prince Naif maintained that there was no terrorist threat in Saudi Arabia. It seemed like a bizarre blindness on the part of the man charged with protecting the kingdom, and I was eager to hear his explanation.

Dr. Harthi had other ideas, however. He wanted to talk only about the *Gazette*. He asked me what I thought could help sales. "The circulation has shrunk to nearly nothing," he said. He had a copy of the paper on his desk and glanced at it without actually reading it. "I think the name is the problem," he continued. "'*Saudi Gazette*' sounds like a government publication."

I told him that it would sell more copies if it were a better paper—if it covered local news and took more-courageous editorial stands.

"I don't think that Prince Naif would really be that helpful to you," Dr. Harthi said. It took a moment for me to realize that he had abruptly canceled my appointment.

A few hours after I visited the ministry, a house blew up in central Riyadh. Later that night, I was having a *sheesha*—flavored tobacco in a water pipe—with one of Naif's assistants and asked about it. "Some guy, he had a lot of explosives in his house, and it blew up," he said unconcernedly. It seemed far more ominous to me.

I WANTED TO SEE how the law worked in the kingdom, so in April I asked Hasan Baswaid to do a story on a new legal code, put into effect in May 2002, which guarantees defendants the right to consult with an attorney. It also contains a prohibition against torture. The kingdom had been struggling to conform to international legal standards in order to succeed in its bid to join the World Trade Organization. There are only about seven hundred judges in the entire country, all of whom are trained exclusively in Sharia, or Islamic law.

Baswaid landed an interview with Khalid Abu Rashid, a prominent attorney, and I went along. I asked if the new code was creating a class of Western-style criminal-defense attorneys. "Here our cases are very simple, not complicated like in America," Rashid told us. "We have been mainly concerned with financial crimes. Other types of crimes, like murder, are very rare here, and they are mainly revenge killings among tribes." Those score-settlings seldom get to court, he

explained. Crimes such as robbery, he said, "always happen with foreigners, and when they're captured they immediately confess—not
just about the new crime, but about all the rest. They do not ask for
lawyers."

On the table in Rashid's office were homemade *maamoul*—date-
filled pastries—and fresh dates from his native province. He wore a
silver watch with diamonds that caught the light. "The judicial system
is fixed because it depends on Sharia," he said. "For example, the idea
that a killer should be killed in return, this will not change. What can
change are the procedures that must be followed before you can kill
someone."

When we left, I made a joke about how eager people in Saudi Arabia
were to confess. The justice system often demanded the incontestable
proof that only confessions can provide. A Western-style prosecuto-
rial quid pro quo didn't seem to be operating here: people frequently
confessed to crimes that guaranteed them the death penalty. Torture,
I supposed, was the unmentioned motivator.

In February, for instance, after Saudi security forces arrested the
eight purported members of al-Qaeda in connection with the Riyadh
shooting, all the suspects confessed to murder. "The voluntary surrender of culprits to police and their confessions reaffirm their desire
to return to the right path and correct their mistakes," a member of
the Interior Ministry told *Asharq al-Awsat*. Similarly, Saudi authorities
charged seven British citizens with a series of bombings in Riyadh
in 2000 and 2001 that were alleged to have been part of a mob war
among bootleggers. Six of them confessed on Saudi television. *The
Guardian* of London published a story arguing that all the men were
tortured into making the statements, or else the confessions were fab-
ricated; the bombings, the paper insinuated, were actually targeted
assassinations by Islamists against Westerners who consumed alcohol. Soon afterward, more bombs went off—yet all the accused men
remained in jail. After considerable pressure by the British government, the men were released. One of those arrested, Ron Jones, later
said that he had been beaten on the soles of his feet. Another detainee
said, "They threatened to plant drugs in my house to get my wife and
child beheaded."

There is a stark difference between the way the Saudi government treats its own citizens and the way it treats foreign workers. "There is a huge population that is not thought of as human at all," Khaled Abou El Fadl, the UCLA law professor, told me. "If you exclude Iraq, then Saudi Arabia would be one of the worst offenders in the Arab world. In Saudi Arabia, there is a well-established practice of 'disappearances,' people who have been missing for ten or fifteen years."

In Saudi Arabia, the death penalty is usually carried out in public. The senior public executioner was a man named Ahmad Rezkallah, who had been chopping off the heads of murderers, rapists, and drug smugglers in the public square for twenty-three years. He killed more than three hundred people in that time, seventy of them women, who were dispatched with two shots to the head. "Most of the women I executed were strong and calm," he told *Al-Majalla*, an Arabic-language magazine published in London. "Women in general have nerves of steel." His technique with the men is to poke the condemned person in the back with the tip of his sword, which causes the head to jerk upward. Then off it comes.

The practice of public execution gives the Saudi legal system a medieval reputation in the West. The Saudi method appears to succeed as deterrence—crime is very low. In Texas, where I live, executions are common but clemency is as rare as a snowstorm, and the governor holds himself aloof from the process of pardons and paroles. In Mecca province, the governor himself chairs a committee of reconciliation that asks the families of victims to spare the life of the convicted man or woman. Before killing the condemned person, the executioner once again publicly begs the family of the victim to show mercy. "I go and ask the family of the victim to give the criminal another chance," the executioner told *Al-Majalla*. "It has worked many times and the family has forgiven the criminal at the last minute. There is clapping and cheering. The scenes of happiness are indescribable." Sometimes wronged family members insist on carrying out the execution themselves, which is permitted in Saudi Arabia. They usually make a mess of it.

WHEN AMERICAN SOLDIERS had crossed into Iraq in March 2003, many Saudis were furious. "The U.S. is dying to slaughter the Iraqi people!" Prince Amr Mohammad Al Faisal, an architect in Jeddah, said to me on the eve of the invasion. "They're thirsty for it! They can't wait!" But many who denounced the invasion in front of their friends privately confessed to me that at least a part of them welcomed it. "This entire region is in a fossilized state," Prince Amr conceded. "What is happening in Iraq is going to shake up the whole business. My guess is it will lead to greater nationalism. There will be more robust participation in decision making, although not necessarily a democracy like in the West."

"We need a push," one reporter told me. "Maybe this is it."

The night before the war began, I went to dinner with Ihsan Bu-Hulaiga, an economist and a member of the Shoura Council, the king's consultative body. Outside the Chinese restaurant, a sandstorm darkened the streets and blurred the lights of the passing traffic. Ihsan and I had spoken several times before, and I had begun to regard him as a friend. A pale man with blue eyes and a blond goatee, he was part of the minority Shi'a community, but he said he didn't feel persecuted; on the contrary, he was grateful for the many advances that have lifted the country from the poverty of his childhood. "When I was a kid, I lived in a small mud house in Hofuf, a village in the Eastern Province," he told me. "It wasn't only my family—everyone lived in a very humble house, even King Abdul Aziz! We didn't have streets to speak of, just narrow, unpaved roads." Directly beneath the sand of Hofuf, however, was the largest oil field in the world.

The kingdom then had a new problem: what to do with the money. In 1970, it inaugurated its first five-year development plan. "At the time, we had very little infrastructure," said Ihsan. "We built schools, highways, hospitals. We sent people abroad to study, and we invited people from abroad to work. I can't claim that the oil revenues were used in the most efficient way, but in comparison to other developing countries, we've done very well."

The sandstorm had grown more intense while we were in the restaurant. When we came out, the wind was sharp and grating, and the air above the streetlights was an ominous shade of orange. The same storm was creating havoc a few hundred miles away among the American and British forces in Kuwait preparing to cross the border into Iraq. "This is God standing in the way of your guys," Ihsan teased, but he was also angry and full of dread. "Yesterday there was an official announcement from the royal court about prayer. The ruler has asked the people to go outside the city into the emptiness to pray." It was called *istisqa'*, which is ordinarily a rain-seeking prayer. "Muslims feel when there has been no rain for a long time, God is angry at them," Ihsan continued, "so they go into the desert and beseech him to forgive them. This year it is because of Iraq. The people try to be as humble as possible. Certain people wear their clothes inside out, just to show their humility. It's very close to panicking, this prayer."

The next day the weather cleared, and American bombers began their assault on Baghdad.

WAR IS SUPPOSED TO BE great for newspapers. Khaled al-Maeena, the editor of *Arab News,* boasted that newsstand sales were already up 27 percent on the first morning of the war. He had one reporter embedded with the U.S. Marines and two in Kuwait trying to sneak across the border into Iraq. At the *Gazette,* no one spoke of sales, since there were scarcely any, and none of our reporters were anywhere near combat. When I came into the office, the Indian editors were crowded around the television set, but they were watching the World Cup cricket matches. It wasn't their war.

I was a little anxious about going outside. People had been warning me constantly of the explosion of anger that would definitely accompany the invasion if it really happened. For weeks, Saudis had been telling themselves that the war talk was just a very showy bluff, and that all the chest-pounding proclamations from the Pentagon about "shock and awe" were only meant to terrify Saddam into surrendering power. There was some discussion about offering him sanctuary in the kingdom, but Prince Naif squelched that. Saudi Arabia already had plenty of political refugees, he said. (Idi Amin, the former man-eating dictator of Uganda, was one of Jeddah's most infamous citizens.) I had hoped they were right. There were peace marches all over the globe, even in other Arab countries, but not in Saudi Arabia. My own wife and children were marching in Austin, Boston, and Florence, Italy. "How do you think we feel about this?" one Saudi said to me during that long, tense prelude. "The whole world is free to comment on this, except for us—and we are the people who will be affected!"

I spent most of the war in my flat watching the war on Al Jazeera and Fox, two rather similar news organizations. Each was wedded to a particular narrative. On Fox, the story was "Operation Iraqi Freedom," the American liberation of the oppressed Iraqi people, told from the blinkered viewpoint of the embedded reporters. The implicit goal of the war was dancing in the streets, the visual that would go with the liberation motif. On Al Jazeera it was the continuing humiliation of the Arabs. "Iraqi Hiroshima" was the logo behind the newscasters. There were countless shots of surrendering Iraqi troops, hands behind their heads, shuffling past the American conquerors; charred corpses in the street; women in abayas being frisked by a female marine. These were images of a subjugated nation, not a liberated one.

One sequence, which I first saw on CNN, was a video of a pair of U.S. Marines knocking on the door of a house they intend to search. A military analyst—a very hip retired American general with a flat-top and the sleeves of his sport coat rolled up—proudly demonstrates to the TV audience the proper way in which the soldiers evacuate the home. Notice their stance on either side of the door, the general remarks, as the father is made to bring out his wife and children. Notice the placement of the soldiers' hands on the outside of the trigger guard, the general says, ignoring the face of a little girl whose lips are trembling and whose eyes are so wide with fright they look as if they could explode. Notice the way the soldiers have taken control of the situation, the general says, as the family is made to kneel at the feet of the Americans.

This scene was captured by Al Jazeera and repeated endlessly, obsessively, ritualistically, because it expressed so poignantly the theme of the war, from the Arab perspective.

My own paper, the *Gazette*, published a photo on the front page of an Iraqi child with his head blown off. The Arabic press and many of the satellite channels framed the bombing of Baghdad as "America's war on children." The Saudi public was understandably inflamed. One Jeddah merchant waved a copy of *Al-Watan* in my face and pointed at a photograph of an Iraqi boy being treated for hideous burns. "Do you think he will grow up and think that America is a great nation?" the man demanded. He showed me another newspaper with a picture of two dead Iraqi soldiers in a foxhole, their heads missing, with a white flag of surrender beside them. Standing over the foxhole were two American soldiers.

I'm not opposed to this kind of journalism. I hate war and think it should be seen for what it is. The dead and wounded Iraqi children should be a part of our conscience.

The *Gazette*'s editorial slant was clear from the beginning. "Wounded U.S. Soldiers in Shock and Awe" read a headline a week after the war began. Like every other paper in the kingdom, the *Gazette* gloated when the Iraqi troops made a stab at resistance. There was a front-page story about the imam of the Grand Mosque calling for an end to the "unjust" war. "Muslims across the Kingdom prayed for Baghdad's victory against the U.S., British 'aggressors,'" the story read.

One steamy evening, I went to a *sheesha* bar with Dr. Khaled M. Batarfi, a columnist for *Al-Madina*. As a child, Khaled had been Osama bin Laden's friend and next-door neighbor. Khaled was constantly laboring for peace and was on a mission to help Saudis and Westerners understand each other. I had become quite fond of him. We began discussing what we thought would be the long-term effect of the war on Saudi Arabia. In Khaled's opinion, America's aggression showed that it was intending to remake the Middle East in its image. "But what you really want is to divide the kingdom into several states so you can take our oil, and we will have no power to resist you," he said.

Many Saudis believed that the invasion of Iraq was the opening act of a drama that would end with their main ally and protector consuming them. "The whole world is undoubtedly seeing the American cowboys as having come for only one aim: killing, destruction, and bloodshed," Khaled's newspaper declared in an editorial that morning. The relentless theme of the Saudi media was that the sole objectives of American power were oil and murder.

The next morning, at the *Gazette* office, Ramesh came into the local reporters' room with a mischievous look on his face. "Well, we're all pro-American now," he said.

"What do you mean?"

He told me that all the editors in chief in the kingdom had been ordered to drop their anti-American line.

At lunch that day, I asked Khaled Batarfi if *Al-Madina* was really going to change its editorials. He gave me a resigned nod. "The editors were told, 'No more pictures of dead babies. Also, don't call it an invasion.'"

Indeed, by the next morning the entire Saudi press had moderated its position on the war. It was a strange experience for me, with all my preaching about the need for a free press. The newspapers suddenly appeared more sober and responsible, and I felt a sullied sense of relief.

In the days after the war, however, reports began to appear about young Saudis who had responded to the calls for jihad against the Anglo-American coalition. "Volunteers Achieve Martyrdom" was how it was reported in the *Gazette*. One of my reporters, who had lost a friend in Iraq, invited me to meet some other young members of his tribe. They were Bedouins, and inside the middle-class apartment in south Jeddah where his brother lived there was a room that replicated a desert tent—the ceiling draped with fabric, and bolsters on the rug to lean against as we sipped tea. Inside the tent were four men in their twenties. The death of a friend was nothing new, they told me; they had already lost a number of young male relatives in Afghanistan, and another one in Iraq.

I asked them how they thought Saudi Arabia would be different ten years from now. The youngest of them, who had a wispy beard, said, "I think the Americans will invade Saudi Arabia, and a quarter of the population will be in American jails." Another told me that he prayed the Saudi government would evolve into a pure Islamic state, following the Taliban model.

The oldest Bedouin was a delicate man with long, fine fingers and a pointed goatee that gave him a noble and stylized appearance. His round wire-rimmed glasses caught whatever dim light there was inside the pavilion, making it hard to read his eyes. I was intrigued by him, perhaps because of his intellectualism and his romantic, revolutionary air. The man who was killed was his cousin. I asked him what force had drawn his relative to Iraq. "It's when you have this power inside you—and in this closed country you can't get it out—that you go to such places," he told me.

His cousin couldn't find a job, he continued, and he didn't have the connections to get into the military. He himself had experienced the same problems. "Since the first Gulf crisis, I graduated with a good major, and the government promised me a lot of things," he went on. "I have the ambition to have a PhD or a great job, and I suddenly found that the government put a new rule. They stopped any new government employment! The price of electricity and gas doubled, and the phone, and even rice and sugar. But they said be patient, we have to pay the price of the war. They promised it was just for a short period. It's been thirteen years now! I graduated seven years ago and still have no job." He said he often thought about becoming a martyr himself, like his cousin, who must have gone directly to Paradise. "Paradise is better than this miserable life!"

I asked him what he had studied in school.

"Library science."

With all their talk about martyrdom, there was another dark thought in their minds. "It might be government policy to send these guys to Iraq, instead of having them here, acting up," the oldest one said.

"Who are you talking about?" I asked. "Who is sending them?"

"Somebody who wants to make moral points around the world. They want to have these guys get killed instead of staying in the country and helping it out."

The others nodded. They saw a conspiracy between the clergy and the government—a plot to eliminate them, the unemployed Saudis. "It's been a holocaust for young people, what's happened in Iraq and Afghanistan," the librarian said.

These young men recognized the pointlessness of jihad, at least the way it was being promoted by the bloodthirsty clerics—who were, after all, government employees. There had to be a reason that the government would allow such dangerous talk, and in the minds of these young men the reason was that they were expendable. And a part of them said yes to that. They wanted out, and the only exit was Paradise.

———

I MET MY REPORTERS for the final time in the *Gazette* conference room. I had a deep sense of disappointment about how little I had accomplished. Many of the stories my reporters had labored over never got published. There were a few good pieces, such as a profile Najla had written of the American consul general in Jeddah, Gina Abercrombie-Winstanley, but Dr. Yusuf was angry that the piece had not been cleared with him.

I handed out a few mementos, including Texas Longhorn key chains for the women, for the day when they finally could drive.

There was a brief farewell party for me, with punch and pastries. Dr. Yusuf gave me a watch. The party was delayed a bit by my insistence that the women be allowed to attend. Najla handed me a card that everyone had signed. I said good-bye without once seeing her face.

Hasan Hatrash wasn't there. I found him in the cafeteria, his shoulders hunched, drinking tea and picking at a half-eaten piece of chocolate cake. He looked shattered. "I just got out of the hospital," he told me. "The doctor told me I shouldn't drive, but I wanted to come here and see you." He said he had low blood pressure, but that wasn't the real problem. "I told the doctor, when I sleep I can't wake up. I can't even put my thoughts together! He said that's depression." He seemed to me like many other young Saudis, whose lives are so unrealized and unexpressed. I wanted to give him some final word of advice, but I could think of nothing useful to say.

On May 12, a few weeks after I left the kingdom, al-Qaeda bombed three Riyadh housing compounds, killing thirty-four. A subsequent bombing in November killed eighteen. Throughout the fall and into winter, there were frequent raids and shoot-outs with suspected terrorists, and Saudi authorities claimed to have prevented several other catastrophic attacks, including at least one directed at the royal family. Reformers seized upon this volatile moment to campaign for certain progressive changes, such as an independent judiciary and popular elections. The government began a very difficult process of trying to bridle the radical voices in the mosques and cull certain hateful passages from the textbooks used in Saudi classrooms. The press was allowed to cover these events more freely than in the past; then again, the coverage served the government's interest in quelling Western critics of the regime.

When I read some of these more candid reports, my optimism about the Saudi press resurfaced. In March, Jamal Khashoggi was hired to be the editor in chief of *Al-Watan*—a sign, perhaps, that the government was going to allow the press more freedom. And, indeed, Khashoggi published searching articles about the legacy of Wahhabism and cartoons ridiculing the religious police and the corrupt clergy who encouraged the suicide of Muslim youth. "Those who committed yesterday's crime are not only the suicide terrorists, but also everyone who instigated or justified the attacks, everyone who called them *mujahideen,* even everyone who kept silent," Khashoggi wrote after the May bombings. But days later Khashoggi was fired. Soon afterward, Hussein Shobokshi, the businessman who had been planning the class-action suit about Jeddah's sewage problem, wrote a column in *Okaz* in which he fantasized about a future Saudi Arabia. The story is powerful because it seems so ordinary, but so unreachable. He writes about returning from a business trip in Riyadh, where he has received a prize on behalf of the kingdom from an international human-rights conference. His daughter, a lawyer, picks him up at the airport and drives him to the office. On the way, they talk about voting in the municipal elections the next morning. He tells her to hurry, because he doesn't want to miss the broadcast of the finance minister proposing a national budget. After the article appeared in *Okaz,* the government ordered the paper to stop publishing Shobokshi's column.

Soon after I returned home, Najla wrote me a note saying that she had been fired. She asked for my help in finding a job. Then I heard from Mamdouh al-Harthy, who said that he had quit the *Gazette* and wanted to go to journalism school in the West. And Hasan Hatrash wrote to say that he'd gone to Malaysia for a vacation. In Kuala Lumpur, he was invited to sit in with a band. "I had the time of my life, and the number of chicks who wanted to talk to me was more than I could handle," he reported. "The good news is, they invited me to play with them in their second gig at a bigger club on Sunday. Wow! Finally, I'm living!"

The Terror Web

For much of Spain's modern history, the organization that has defined its experience with terror is ETA, which stands for Euskadi ta Azkatasuna (Basque Homeland and Liberty). ETA, which was founded in 1959, has a clear political goal: it wants to set up a separate nation, comprising the Basque provinces in northern Spain and parts of southern France. Although ETA has killed some eight hundred people, it has developed a reputation for targeting, almost exclusively, politicians, security officials, and journalists. Over the years, the terrorists and the Spanish police have come to a rough understanding about the rules of engagement. "They don't commit attacks on the working class, and they always call us before an explosion, telling us where the bomb is situated," an intelligence official in the Spanish National Police told me. "If they place a bomb in a backpack on a train, there will be a cassette tape saying, 'This bag is going to explode. Please leave the train.'" And so on March 11, 2004, when the first reports arrived of mass casualties resulting from explosions on commuter trains, Spanish intelligence officials assumed that ETA had made an appalling mistake.

At 7:37 a.m., as a train was about to enter Madrid's Atocha station, three bombs blasted open the steel cars, sending body parts through the windows of nearby apartments. The station is in Madrid's center, a few blocks from the Prado Museum. Within seconds, four bombs exploded on another train, 550 yards from the station. The bombs killed nearly a hundred people. Had the explosions occurred when the trains were inside the station, the fatalities might have tallied in the thousands; a quarter of a million people pass through Atocha every workday. The trains at that hour were filled with students and young office workers who live in public housing and in modest apartment complexes east of the city. Many were immigrants, who had been drawn by the Spanish economic boom.

As emergency crews rushed to the scene, two more bombs demolished a train at the El Pozo del Tío Raimundo station, three miles away. By then, José María Aznar, the prime minister, had learned of the attacks, which were taking place at the end of an uneventful political campaign. The conservative Popular Party, which Aznar headed, was leading the Socialists by four and a half points in the polls, despite the overwhelming opposition of the Spanish population to the country's participation in the war in Iraq, which Aznar had backed. It was Thursday morning; the election would take place on Sunday.

At 7:42, one minute after the El Pozo bomb, a final bomb went off, on a train at the suburban Santa Eugenia station. Emergency workers arrived to find mangled bodies littering the tracks. The Spanish had never seen anything like this—the worst ETA atrocity, in 1987, had killed 21 shoppers in a Barcelona grocery store. At Santa Eugenia, there were so many wounded that rescue crews ripped up the benches in the waiting area to use as stretchers. In all, there were 191 fatalities and 1,600 injuries. It was the most devastating act of terrorism in European history, except for the 1988 bombing of Pan Am Flight 103 over Lockerbie, Scotland.

Aznar, who survived an ETA car bomb in 1995, had made the elimination of the group his top priority. His security forces had decimated ETA's ranks, but they were aware that remnants of the organization were attempting to stage a retaliatory attack in Madrid. The previous Christmas Eve, police had arrested two ETA commanders who had planted backpack bombs on trains, and in February the Civil Guard intercepted an ETA van that was headed to the capital carrying eleven hundred pounds of explosives. Authorities had planned a major strike against ETA for March 12, the last official day of campaigning. Such a blow might have boosted Aznar's party at the polls. ETA, however, had seemingly struck first.

At 10:50 a.m., police in Alcalá de Henares received a call from a witness who pointed them to a boxy white Renault van that had been left that morning at the train station. "At the beginning, we didn't pay too much attention to it," an investigator told me. "Then we saw that the license plate didn't correspond to the van." That clue, though, struck a false note. When ETA operatives steal a car, they match it with license plates from the same model car. It had been years since ETA had made such an elementary mistake.

The lack of warning, the many casualties, the proletarian background of many of the victims, and ETA's quick disavowal of the crime all suggested that there was reason to question the assignment of blame. Moreover, the telephones of known ETA collaborators were bugged. "The bad guys were calling each other, saying, 'Was it us? It's craziness!'" a senior intelligence official said.

That afternoon, detectives looked more carefully at the white van. They collected fingerprints, and under the passenger seat they found a plastic bag with seven detonators matching the type used in the bombings. There were cigarette butts, a woman's wig, and a Plácido Domingo cassette. In the tape player was a different recording—it bore Arabic inscriptions and turned out to be Quranic recitations for religious novices. By that time, police had learned that the explosive used in the bombings was Goma-2, which ETA no longer used. "We told the government that there was something odd, that it was possibly not ETA," the intelligence official told me.

That evening, however, Prime Minister Aznar called the editors of Spain's newspapers. "ETA is behind the attacks," he assured them. Then he called José Luis Rodríguez Zapatero, his Socialist opponent, to tell him about the van with the Arabic tape; at the same time, he insisted that "there is no doubt who did the attacks."

The case broke open in the middle of the night, when a young police officer, sorting through belongings recovered from the trains, opened a sports bag and discovered twenty-two pounds of Goma-2, surrounded by nails and screws. Two wires ran from a blue mobile phone to a detonator. It wasn't clear why the bomb had failed to explode.

Police officers realized that a chip inside the phone would contain a record of recently dialed numbers. By tracing these calls, they were quickly able to map out a network of young Arab immigrants, many of whom were known to Spanish intelligence. Data stored on the chip revealed that a calling plan had been set up at a small telephone and copy shop in Lavapiés, a working-class neighborhood near the Atocha station. The store was owned by Jamal Zougam, a Moroccan who had previously been under surveillance because of alleged connections to al-Qaeda.

Information began leaking to the public about the direction of the investigation. By Friday afternoon, demonstrators were standing in front of the Atocha station, holding signs that linked the tragedy to the war in Iraq. It was clear that the election would swing on the question of whether Islamists or ETA terrorists were responsible for the bombings. That day, the interior minister, Ángel Acebes, insisted publicly that ETA was the prime suspect—even though the police were now certain that ETA was not directly involved.

At twilight, some eleven million Spaniards assembled around the country to protest the violence. In rainy Madrid, the umbrellas stretched for miles down the Paseo del Prado. The anger and grief of the marchers were compounded by confusion about the investigation. "I walked with a million people in Madrid's streets," Diego López Garrido, a Socialist deputy in the Spanish congress, told me. "Many people were saying, 'Who is the author of these attacks?' And they wondered, 'Why is the government lying to us?'"

THE DAY OF THE BOMBINGS, analysts at the Forsvarets Forsknings-institutt, a Norwegian think tank near Oslo, retrieved a document that they had noticed on an Islamist website the previous December. At the time, the document had not made a big impression, but now, in light of the events in Madrid, it read like a terrorist road map. Titled "Jihadi Iraq: Hopes and Dangers," it had been prepared by a previously unknown entity called the Media Committee for the Victory of the Iraqi People (Mujahideen Services Center).

The document, which is forty-two pages long and appears to be the work of several anonymous authors, begins with the proposition that although coalition forces in Iraq, led by America, could not be defeated by a guerrilla insurgency, individual partners of the coalition could be muscled out, leaving America more vulnerable and discouraged as casualties increased and the expenses became insupportable. Three countries—Britain, Spain, and Poland—formed the European backbone of the coalition. Poland appeared to be the most resolute, because the populace largely agreed with the government's decision to enter Iraq. In Britain, the war was generally deplored. "Before the war, in February, about a million people went out on a huge march filling the streets of London," the document notes. "This was the biggest march of political protest in the history of Britain." But the authors suggest that the British would not withdraw unless the casualty count sharply increased.

Spain, however, presented a striking opportunity. The war was almost universally unpopular. Aznar had plunged his country into Iraq without seeking a consensus, unlike other coalition leaders. "If the disparity between the government and the people were at the same percentage rate in Britain, then the Blair government would fall," the author of this section observes. The reason Aznar had not yet been ousted, the author claims, was that Spain is an immature democracy and does not have a firm tradition of holding its rulers accountable. Right-wing Spanish voters also tended to be more loyal and organized than their leftist counterparts. Moreover, there had been fewer than a dozen Spanish casualties in Iraq. "In order to force the Spanish government to withdraw from Iraq, the resistance should deal painful blows to its forces," the writer proposes. "It is necessary to make utmost use of the upcoming general election in Spain in March next year. We think that the Spanish government could not tolerate more than two, maximum three blows, after which it will have to withdraw as a result of popular pressure. If its troops still remain in Iraq after these blows, the victory of the Socialist Party is almost secured, and the withdrawal of the Spanish forces will be on its electoral program." Once Spain pulled out of Iraq, the author theorizes, the pressure on Tony Blair, the British prime minister, to do the same might be unbearable—"and hence the domino tiles would fall quickly."

The document specifies that the attacks would be aimed at Spanish forces within Iraq—there is no call for action in Spain. Nonetheless, the authors' reading of the Western political calendar struck the Norwegian researchers as particularly keen. "The relation between the text and the bombings is unclear," Thomas Hegghammer, a researcher at Forsvarets Forskningsinstitutt, told me. "But, without the text, we would still be asking, 'Is this a coincidence?'"

That day, Hegghammer forwarded a copy of the document to Haizam Amirah Fernández, a colleague at Madrid's Real Instituto Elcano. Amirah was shocked. Until now, the announced goals of al-Qaeda had been mainly parochial, directed at purging the Islamic world, especially Saudi Arabia, of Western influences; overturning the established Arabic governments and restoring the clerical rule of the ancient caliphate; and purifying Islam by returning it to the idealized time of the Prophet. In an audiotape aired on the Arabic satellite channel Al Jazeera in February 2003, Osama bin Laden had identified Jordan, Morocco, Nigeria, Pakistan, Saudi Arabia, and Yemen as "the most qualified regions for liberation." (Iraq was notably absent from his list.) And yet he offered no political platform—no plan, for instance, for governing Saudi Arabia on the morning after the revolution. As for the rest of the world, bin Laden's goals seemed to be motivated mainly by revenge. In 1998, he had decreed that it was the "duty of every Muslim" to kill Americans and their allies. The spectacular violence that characterized al-Qaeda's attacks was not a means to a goal—it *was* the goal. Success was to be measured by body count, not by political change.

The Internet document suggested that a new intelligence was at work, a rationality not seen in al-Qaeda documents before. The Mujahideen Services Center, whatever that was, appeared to operate as a kind of Islamist think tank. "The person who put together those chapters had a clear strategic vision, realistic and well thought out," Amirah says. He told Hegghammer, "This is political science applied to jihad."

Although the document was posted on the Internet in December 2003, the authors note that a draft had been written in September. In October, assassins shot a Spanish military attaché in Iraq, José Antonio Bernal Gómez, near his residence; in November, seven Spanish intelligence agents were ambushed and murdered south of Baghdad. Photographs of the killers standing on the agents' bodies circulated on

Islamist websites. Another Internet document soon appeared, titled "Message to the Spanish People," which threatened more attacks. "Return to your country and live peacefully," it demands, or else "the battalions of the Iraqi resistance and its supporters outside of Iraq are able to increase the dosage and will eclipse your memory of the rotten spies."

Variations in the Arabic transcriptions of English words in the "Jihadi Iraq" document suggested to Amirah that writers of different nationalities had drafted it. For instance, in some cases the "T" in Tony Blair's name was transcribed with the Arabic *ta,* but in the section about Spain the author used the *dha,* which was more typical of the Moroccan dialect. Also characteristic of Morocco was the use of Arabic numerals (the style used in the West) in place of the numbering system that was common from Egypt to the Persian Gulf. Those clues, plus certain particularly Moroccan political concerns expressed in the document, such as the independence movement in Western Sahara, suggested that at least some of the authors were diaspora Moroccans, probably living in Spain.

The link between the Internet document and the bombings soon became clearer. There was a reference early in the document to Abu Dujana, a companion of the Prophet who was known for his ferocity in battle. His name had been invoked by other jihadis, notably in the suicide bombings at the JW Marriott Hotel in Jakarta in August 2003. On Saturday evening, a television station in Madrid received a call from a man speaking Spanish with a Moroccan accent, who said that a videotape had been placed in a trash bin near the city's main mosque. "We declare our responsibility for what has occurred in Madrid, exactly two and a half years after the attacks on New York and Washington," a masked speaker on the videotape said. He identified himself as Abu Dujan al-Afghani, "the military spokesman for al-Qaeda in Europe." He continued, "It is a response to your collaboration with the criminal Bush and his allies. You love life and we love death, which gives an example of what the Prophet Muhammad said. If you don't stop your injustices, more and more blood will flow."

Until this tape appeared, even those investigators who were arguing that the train bombings were perpetrated by Islamic terrorists, not ETA, had been troubled by the fact that there were no "martyrs" in the attacks. It was a trademark of al-Qaeda to sacrifice its killers, thus providing a scanty moral cover for what would otherwise be seen simply as mass murder. When the investigators saw that the man calling himself Abu Dujan al-Afghani was dressed in white funeral robes, however, they realized that suicide was on the horizon.

THE AL-QAEDA CELL in Spain was old and well established. Mohamed Atta, the commander of the September 11 attacks, came to Spain twice in 2001. The second time was in July, for a meeting in the coastal resort of Salou, which appears to have been arranged as a final go-ahead for the attacks. After September 11, Spanish police estimated that there were three hundred Islamic radicals in the country who might be affiliated with al-Qaeda. Even before then, members of the Spanish cell had been monitored by police agencies, as was evident from the abundant use of wiretaps and surveillance information in indictments that were issued in November 2001, when eleven suspects were charged with being al-Qaeda members—the first of several terrorist roundups. And yet, according to Spanish police officials, at the time of the Madrid attacks there was not a single Arabic-speaking intelligence agent in the country. Al-Qaeda was simply not seen as a threat to Spain. "We never believed we were a real target," a senior police official admitted. "That's the reality."

At four o'clock on Saturday afternoon, sixty hours after the attacks and the day before the elections, Interior Minister Acebes announced the arrest of Jamal Zougam and two other Moroccans. Still, he continued to point at ETA. But by now the Socialists were publicly accusing the government of lying about the investigation in order to stay in power.

Polls opened the next morning at nine. Thirty-five million people voted, more than 77 percent of the electorate, 8 percent more than expected. Many were young, first-time voters, and their votes put the Socialists over the top. As José Luis Rodríguez Zapatero declared victory, he again condemned the war in Iraq and reiterated his intention to withdraw troops.

Four days later, the Abu Hafs al-Masri Brigades, a group claiming affiliation with al-Qaeda, sent a message to the London newspaper *Al-Quds al-Arabi*, avowing responsibility for the train bombings. "Whose turn will it be next?" the authors taunt. "Is it Japan, America, Italy, Britain, Saudi Arabia, or Australia?" The message also addresses the speculation that the terrorists would try to replicate their political success in Spain by disrupting the U.S. elections in November. "We are very keen that Bush does not lose the upcoming elections," the authors write. Bush's "idiocy and religious fanaticism" are useful, the authors contend, for they stir the Islamic world to action.

On April 2, two weeks after the election, a security guard for the AVE, Spain's high-speed train line, discovered a blue plastic bag beside the tracks forty miles south of Madrid. Inside the bag were twenty-six pounds of Goma-2. Four hundred and fifty feet of cable had been draped across the security fence and attached, incorrectly, to the detonator. Had the bomb gone off when the AVE passed by—at 180 miles per hour, carrying 1,200 passengers—the results could have been far more catastrophic than those of March 11. Spanish citizens asked themselves: If the bombings of March 11 had accomplished the goals set by al-Qaeda, what was the point of April 2?

UNTIL THE MADRID ATTACKS, the al-Qaeda operations—in Dhahran, Nairobi, Dar es Salaam, Aden, New York, Washington, Jerba, Karachi, Bali, Mombasa, Riyadh, Casablanca, Jakarta, and Istanbul—had been political failures. The massacres committed in the name of jihad had achieved little except anger, grief, and the deaths of thousands. Soon after September 11, al-Qaeda lost its base in Afghanistan and, along with that, its singular role in the coordination of international terror. New groups, such as the bombers in Madrid, were acting in the name of al-Qaeda, and although they may well have had the blessings of its leaders, they did not have the training, resources, or international contacts that had bolstered the previous generation of terrorists. Some operations, such as the 2003 attack on Western compounds in Riyadh, which killed mainly Muslims, were such fiascoes that it appeared that al-Qaeda was no longer able to exercise control.

"Al-Qaeda was always a social movement," Marc Sageman, a psychiatrist, a former CIA case officer, and the author of *Understanding Terror Networks,* told me. He pointed out that the latest converts to the cause didn't spend time in Afghanistan, and they approach jihad differently. "These local guys are reckless and less well trained, but they are willing to kill themselves, whereas the previous leaders were not," Sageman said. Moreover, as the Spanish attacks showed, the new generation was more interested in committing violence for the sake of immediate political gain.

The kind of short-term tactical thinking displayed in the "Jihadi Iraq" document and the March 11 bombings is decidedly out of step with al-Qaeda's traditional worldview, in which history is seen as an endless struggle between believers and infidels—the mind-set of fundamentalists of all religions. That war is eternal, and is never finally won until the longed-for Day of Judgment. In this contest, the first goal is to provoke conflict. Bold, violent deeds draw the lines and arouse ancient resentments, and are useful even if they have unsought consequences. Polarization is to be encouraged, radical simplicity being essential for religious warfare. An al-Qaeda statement posted on the Internet after the March 11 bombings declared, "Being targeted by an enemy is what will wake us from our slumber." Seen in this light, terrorism plays a sacramental role, dramatizing a religious conflict by giving it an apocalyptic backdrop. And Madrid was just another step in the relentless march of radical Islam against the modern, secular world. Had the Madrid cell rested on its accomplishment after March 11, al-Qaeda would properly be seen as an organization now being guided by political strategists—as an entity closer in spirit to ETA, with clear tactical objectives.

April 2 throws doubt on that perspective. There was little to be gained politically from striking an opponent who was complying with the stated demand; after all, the government had capitulated and withdrawn troops from Iraq. If the point was merely humiliation or revenge, then April 2 makes more sense; the terrorists wanted more blood, even if a second attack backfired politically. (The Socialists would hardly have been able to continue following the terrorist agenda with a thousand new corpses along the tracks.) April 2 is comprehensible only if the real goal of the bombers was not Iraq but Spain, where the Islamic empire began its retreat five hundred years ago.

IN THE WEEKS AFTER the March 11 attacks, Spanish police combed the immigrant neighborhoods outside Madrid, carrying photographs of suspects. "We didn't have them perfectly located, but we knew they were in Leganés," a police official told me. Leganés is a bland suburb of uniform five-story redbrick apartment complexes. The wide streets are lined with evenly spaced adolescent oaks. In the mornings, the sidewalks teem with commuters rushing for the trains; then the place is vacant, except for grandmothers and strollers. In the evenings, the commuters return and close their doors.

At three o'clock on the afternoon of April 3, the day after the discovery of the bomb on the AVE tracks, police approached an apartment building on Calle de Carmen Martín Gaite. They saw a young Moroccan man with a baseball cap on backward who was taking out trash. He yelled something in Arabic, then ran away at an impressive pace. (He turned out to be a track champion; the police could not catch him.) A moment later, voices cried out, *"Allahu Akhbar!,"* and machine-gun fire from the second floor of the apartment house raked the street, scattering the cops. Over the next few hours, the police tactical unit, Grupo Especial de Operaciones, evacuated the residents of nearby apartments. Tanks and helicopters moved in, and the siege of Leganés began.

Inside the apartment were seven young men. Most of them were Moroccan immigrants who had come to Europe seeking economic opportunity. They had gone through a period of becoming "Westernized"—that is to say, they had been drinkers, drug dealers, womanizers. They hung out in cybercafes. They folded into the ethnic mix of urban Madrid. But they also lived in the European underground of Islamic radicalism, whose members were recruited more often in prison than in the training camps of Afghanistan.

Their leader was Sarhane Ben Abdelmajid Fakhet, who was thirty-five years old and had a round, fleshy face and a patchy beard. He was a real estate agent who had come to Madrid eight years earlier on a scholarship to study economics. His boss told the Spanish press that Fakhet was "a wonderful salesman," who held the record for the number of apartments sold in a month. Yet he did not talk to his coworkers or make friends with other Spaniards; he remained sequestered in his Muslim world.

"He was very soft and well educated," Moneir Mahmoud Aly el-Messery, the imam at the principal mosque in Madrid, told me. The mosque—a massive marble structure, built with Saudi money—was the center of Muslim cultural life in the Spanish capital. It overlooked the M-30, one of the freeways that ring Madrid. When Fakhet was a student, he worked in a restaurant attached to the mosque, and he sometimes came to Messery's weekly religion class. In the beginning, the imam noticed that Fakhet spoke familiarly to women as well as to men. "Then, for three or four years, I sensed that he had some extremist thoughts," Messery recalled. After class, Fakhet would ask provocative questions, such as whether the imam thought that the leaders of the Arab countries were true believers, or if Islam authorized the use of force to spread the religion. He married a sixteen-year-old Moroccan girl who veiled her face and dressed entirely in black, including gloves. His performance at work declined, and he eventually stopped showing up altogether. He began attending meetings with a small group of fellow Muslims at a barbershop in Madrid, where the men would drink holy water from Mecca. Police believed that this ritual was aimed at absolving the men of the sin of suicide, which is condemned by Islam.

Soon after the attacks of September 11, the imam had a dream about Fakhet. "Sarhane was in his kitchen, cooking on the stove," he recalled. "I saw what he was cooking was a big pot of worms. He tried to give me a plate of the food to eat. I said no. I said, 'Please clean the kitchen!'" Days later, the imam confronted Fakhet with the dream. "This is a message from God!" the imam said to him. "The kitchen is the thought, and the thought is dirty." Fakhet didn't respond. "He's a very cold person," the imam told me.

Fakhet was not the only young man in the M-30 mosque who had taken a turn toward extremism. Amer Azizi, a thirty-six-year-old Moroccan who was a veteran of jihad in Bosnia and Afghanistan, had been indicted in Spain for helping to plan the September 11 attacks. (He was accused of setting up the July 2001 meeting between Mohamed Atta and other conspirators in Salou.) Among people who frequented the mosque, Azizi had a reputation as a drug addict, although he attended some classes on Islam along with Fakhet. In June 2000, when the Arab countries' ambassadors to Spain came to the mosque to mourn the death of the Syrian dictator Hafez al-Assad, Azizi insulted them, yelling, "Why do you come to pray for an infidel?" Police eventually charged him with being a senior member of al-Qaeda and the leader of the Moroccan Islamic Combat Group, which was responsible for five bombings in Casablanca in May 2003. He fled Spain just before his indictment.

Another of Fakhet's friends was Jamal Ahmidan, a drug dealer who police say financed the March 11 bombings with seventy pounds of hashish. Messery blamed an Islamist cleric in London, Abu Qatada, a radical Palestinian from Jordan who emigrated to Britain as a refugee in 1994. After September 11, police in Hamburg found eighteen tapes of Abu Qatada's sermons in Mohamed Atta's apartment there. British authorities arrested him in October 2002, but he continued to wield great authority among Islamists around the world. The imam told me, "It was as if there were black hands behind a curtain pushing these young men."

AT SIX O'CLOCK in the evening on April 3, three hours after the start of the Leganés siege, a handwritten fax in Arabic, signed by Abu Dujan al-Afghani, arrived at *ABC,* a conservative daily in Madrid. Referring to the bomb found beside the AVE tracks the day before, the author argues that it failed to explode because "our objective was only to warn you and show you that we have the power and capacity, with the permission of Allah, to attack you when and how we want." The letter demanded that Spain withdraw its troops from both Iraq and Afghanistan by the following Sunday. Otherwise, "we will turn Spain into an inferno and make your blood flow like rivers." On the surface, the fax represented another turn toward tactical political thinking; more likely, it was an attempt to salvage a bungled operation.

Outside the Leganés apartment, the police attempted to negotiate, but the cornered terrorists cried out, "We will die killing!" Phone calls that they made to relatives during the siege confirmed their intentions. They also attempted to call Abu Qatada in London's Belmarsh Prison, apparently seeking a fatwa that would morally sanction their suicide.

Instead of turning off the electricity and waiting them out, the police decided to storm the apartment. They ordered the terrorists to come out "naked and with your hands up." One of the occupants responded, "Come in and we'll talk." At 9:05 p.m., the police blew the lock on the door and fired tear gas into the room. Almost immediately, an explosion shattered the apartment, killing the terrorists and a police officer. The blast was so intense that it took days before the authorities could determine how many people had been in the apartment. The body of Jamal Ahmidan was hurled through the walls and into a swimming pool.

In the ruins, police found twenty-two pounds of Goma-2 and two hundred copper detonators that were similar to those used in the train bombings. They also found the shredded remains of a videotape. The fragments were painstakingly reassembled, to the point where police could view the final statement of Fakhet and two other members of the cell, which called itself "the brigade situated in al-Andalus." Unless Spanish troops left Iraq within a week, the men had declared, "we will continue our jihad until martyrdom in the land of Tariq ibn Ziyad."

Al-Andalus is the Arabic name for the portion of Spain that fell to Muslim armies after the invasion by the Berber general Tariq ibn Ziyad in 711. It includes not only the southern region of Andalusia, but most of the Iberian Peninsula. For eight hundred years, al-Andalus remained in Islamic hands. "You know of the Spanish crusade against Muslims, and that not much time has passed since the expulsion from al-Andalus and the tribunals of the Inquisition," Fakhet says on the tape. He is referring to 1492, when King Ferdinand of Aragon and Queen Isabella of Castile completed the reconquest of Spain, forcing Jews and Muslims to convert to Catholicism or leave the Iberian Peninsula. "Blood for blood!" Fakhet shouts. "Destruction for destruction!"

Were these the true goals of al-Qaeda? Were the besieged terrorists in Leganés simply struggling to get Spain out of Iraq, or were they also battling to regain the lost colonies of Islam? In other words, were these terrorists who might respond to negotiation or appeasement, or were they soldiers in a religious fight to the finish that had merely been paused for five hundred years?

———

WASHINGTON IRVING, America's first international best-selling author, moved to Spain in 1826, at the invitation of the U.S. ambassador, Alexander Hill Everett. Irving had a genius for taking legends and folktales and spinning them into popular literature. He had already written many of the stories that would lend him literary immortality, including "Rip Van Winkle" and "The Legend of Sleepy Hollow." Everett enticed him to write a history of Christopher Columbus's voyages to the New World, based on archival manuscripts that had become public.

Three years later, Irving took a trip from Seville to Granada. When he arrived at the ruins of the great Moorish fortress, the Alhambra, Irving was enchanted by the "light, elegant, and voluptuous" architecture—the geometric mosaics, the interplay of streams and fountains, the grand courtyards so thoughtfully blended with the landscape. Captivated by fables of a bygone empire, Irving took up residence in the unfurnished palace of Sultan Boabdil, the last of the Moorish rulers.

Writing in these dilapidated quarters, with "nothing but bats and owls flitting about," Irving began his imaginative narration. "As conquerors, their heroism was only equaled by their moderation," he writes of the Islamic princes. "They loved the land given them as they supposed by Allah, and strove to embellish it with every thing that could administer to the happiness of man. Laying the foundations of their power in a system of wise and equitable laws, diligently cultivating the arts and sciences, and promoting agriculture, manufactures, and commerce, they gradually formed an empire unrivaled for its prosperity by any of the empires of Christendom." These sentiments were unusual at a time when Islam was both obscure and disparaged in the West, but Irving was the herald of a new romanticism. After his best-selling book *Tales of the Alhambra* appeared in 1832, Moorish Spain became an object of veneration by painters, poets, and musicians, who now saw in the splendid ruins a vanished Camelot. "Such is the Alhambra," Irving writes. "A Moslem pile in the midst of a Christian land, an Oriental palace amidst the Gothic edifices of the West, an elegant memento of a brave, intelligent, and graceful people who conquered, ruled and passed away."

Irving's nostalgic portrait of the Alhambra was translated into

Arabic, and his stories found their way into textbooks, which would have been taught to the future leaders of al-Qaeda. Less than a month after 9/11, Osama bin Laden and his chief lieutenant, Dr. Ayman al-Zawahiri, had appeared on Al Jazeera. "We will not accept that the tragedy of al-Andalus will be repeated in Palestine," Zawahiri said, drawing an analogy between the expulsion of the Moors from Iberia and the present-day plight of the Palestinians. Two months before the Madrid bombings, bin Laden issued a "Message to the Muslim People," which was broadcast on Al Jazeera. He lamented the decline of the Islamic world compared with Spain: "It is enough to know that the economy of all Arab countries is weaker than the economy of one country that had once been part of our world when we used to truly adhere to Islam. That country is the lost al-Andalus."

It is a paradox that bin Laden would glorify a civilization with values so starkly at odds with those he represents. His use of the archaic name al-Andalus left most Spaniards nonplussed. "We took it as a folkloric thing," Ramón Pérez-Maura, an editor at *ABC,* told me. "We probably actually laughed."

The Muslims who were expelled from fifteenth-century Spain took refuge mainly in Morocco, Algeria, and Tunisia. Some families, it is said, still have the keys to their houses in Córdoba and Seville. But the legacy of al-Andalus persisted long after the diaspora. Up until the Victorian era, Spain was considered to be more a part of the Orient than of Europe. The language, the food, and the architecture were all deeply influenced by the Islamic experience—a rival history that Catholic Spain, despite its splendor, could never bury. "In modern Arabic literature, al-Andalus is seen as the lost paradise," Manuela Marín, a professor at the Consejo Superior de Investigaciones Científicas, in Madrid, told me. "For Spain, the history of al-Andalus has a totally different meaning. After all, what we know as Spain was made in opposition to the Islamic presence on the peninsula. Only recently have people begun to accept that Islam was a part of Spain."

Although many Spanish historians have painted Moorish Spain as something other than paradise for Jews and Christians, for Muslims it remains not only a symbol of vanished greatness but a kind of alternative vision of Islam—one in which all the ills of present-day Islamic societies are reversed. Muslim tourists, including many heads of state, come to Spain to imagine a time when Islam was at the center of art and learning, not on the fringes. "The Alhambra is the No. 1 Islamic monument," Malik A. Ruíz Callejas, the emir of the Islamic community in Spain and the president of Granada's new mosque, told me. "Back when in Paris and London people were being eaten alive by rats, in Córdoba everyone could read and write. The civilization of al-Andalus was probably the most just, most unified, and most tolerant in history, providing the greatest level of security and the highest standard of living."

Imams sometimes invoke the glory of al-Andalus in Friday prayers as a reminder of the price that Muslims paid for turning away from the true faith. When I asked Moneir el-Messery, of the M-30 mosque, if the Madrid bombers could have been motivated by the desire to recapture al-Andalus, he looked up sharply and said, "I can speak of the feeling of all Muslims. It was a part of history. We were here for eight centuries. You can't forget it, ever."

THE FEAR THAT the "Moors" would one day return and reclaim their lost paradise—through either conquest or immigration—is a paranoid theme in Spanish politics. Construction of the mosque in Granada was delayed for twenty-two years because of the intense anxiety surrounding the growing Islamic presence, which sharply increased after 1986, when Spain joined the European Union. Generous EU subsidies ignited an economic boom, drawing thousands of young men from North Africa. Smugglers in high-speed powerboats make nightly drop-offs on the ragged Spanish coastline, and the frequent discovery of corpses washing up on the beaches testifies to the desperation of those who did not quite get to shore.

Muslim immigration is transforming all of Europe. This population is disproportionately young, male, and unemployed. The societies these men have left are typically poor, religious, conservative, and dictatorial; the ones they enter are rich, secular, liberal, and free. For many, the exchange is invigorating, but for others Europe becomes a prison of alienation. A Muslim's experience of immigration can be understood in part by how he views his adopted homeland. Islamic thought broadly divides civilization into *dar al-Islam*, the land of the believers, and *dar al-Kufr,* the land of impiety. France, for instance, is a secular democracy, largely Catholic, but it is now home to approximately five million Muslims. Should it therefore be considered part of the Islamic world? This question is central to the debate about whether Muslims in Europe can integrate into their new communities or must stand apart from them. If France can be considered part of *dar al-Islam,* then Muslims can form alliances and participate in politics, they should have the right to institute Islamic law, and they can send their children to French schools. If it is a part of *dar al-Kufr,* then strict Muslims must not only keep their distance; they must fight against their adopted country.

"The Internet is the key issue," Gilles Kepel, a prominent Arabist and a professor at the Institut d'Études Politiques, in Paris, told me. "It erases the frontiers between the *dar al-Islam* and the *dar al-Kufr.* It allows the propagation of a universal norm, with an Internet Sharia and fatwa system." Now one doesn't have to be in Saudi Arabia or Egypt to live under the rule of Islamic law. "Anyone can seek a ruling from his favorite sheikh in Mecca," Kepel said. "In the old days, one sought a fatwa from the sheikh who had the best knowledge. Now it is sought from the one with the best website."

To a large extent, Kepel argues, the Internet has replaced the Arabic satellite channels as a conduit of information and communication. "One can say that this war against the West started on television," he said, "but, for instance, with the decapitation of the poor hostages in Iraq and Saudi Arabia, those images were propagated via webcams and the Internet. A jihadi subculture has been created that didn't exist before 9/11."

Though the Internet has become an ideological home for many Muslims, for most Arab immigrants Europe has provided comfort and support, while at the same time allowing them the freedom to maintain their Islamic identities. Three Moroccan immigrants died on the trains on March 11. One was a devout thirteen-year-old girl, Sanae Ben Salah, for whom the M-30 mosque was said to have been her "second home." Another, Mohamed Itabien, twenty-seven, was an illegal immigrant who taught Arabic classes at a mosque in Guadalajara. He was the sole source of support for his family, including eleven siblings, most of whom lived in a tiny town in Morocco where there were no telephones. The third, Osama el-Amrati, was a builder who was engaged to a Spanish woman. "Europe has given us opportunities our own countries didn't give us," Mustapha el-M'Rabet, the head of the Moroccan Workers and Immigrants Association, told me in Madrid. "Our children are in school, and we are working. Thousands of families in Morocco can live with the money we get here." When I asked M'Rabet if al-Andalus was part of the lure for Moroccan immigrants, he said, "Nobody with common sense could talk about going back to that. It's madness. It's a disease."

Under Aznar, relations with Morocco deteriorated to the point where, in 2002, the countries broke off diplomatic relations over various problems, including territory disputes, immigration, and the flow of drugs into Europe through Spain. Eventually, the governments returned their ambassadors, without resolving the disputes that had led to the rupture. When twelve suicide bombers struck in Casablanca in May 2003, killing forty-five people, one of their targets was a restaurant called Casa de España.

"Spain is the bridge between the Islamic world and the West," Haizam Amirah Fernández said, when we met in a conference room at Madrid's Real Instituto Elcano shortly after the train bombings. "Think of that other bridge to the east, Turkey. Both have been hit by jihadist terrorists—in the same week." In Istanbul, on March 9, two suicide bombers attacked a Jewish club, killing one person and injuring five others. "The whole idea is to cut off these bridges," Amirah said. "If the goal is to polarize people, Muslims and infidels, that is a way of doing it. Jihadists are the most fervent defenders of the notion of a clash of civilizations."

One evening, I went to a pub with some Spanish cops. "There is this legend that Spain and the Arab world were friends," a senior investigator said. He nodded toward the waitress and the customers at several nearby tables. "Here in the bar are five Arabs sitting next to you. Nobody used to think it was strange. Now people are reacting differently." He paused and said, "They want to smell the jasmine of al-Andalus and pray again in the Granada mosque. Can you imagine the mentality these SOBs have?"

One of the most sobering pieces of information to come out of the investigation of the March 11 bombings is that the planning for the attacks may have begun nearly a year before 9/11. In October 2000, several of the suspects met in Istanbul with Amer Azizi, who had taken the nom de guerre Othman al-Andalusi—Othman of al-Andalus. Azizi later gave the conspirators permission to act in the name of al-Qaeda, although it is unclear whether he authorized money or other assistance—or, indeed, whether al-Qaeda had much support to offer. In June, Italian police released a surveillance tape of one of the alleged planners of the train bombings, an Egyptian housepainter named Rabei Osman Sayed Ahmed, who said that the operation "took me two and a half years." Ahmed had served as an explosives expert in the Egyptian Army. It appears that some kind of attack would have happened even if Spain had not joined the coalition—or if the invasion of Iraq had never occurred.

"The real problem of Spain for al-Qaeda is that we are a neighbor of Arab countries—Morocco and Algeria—and we are a model of economy, democracy, and secularism," Florentino Portero, a political analyst at the Grupo de Estudios Estratégicos, in Madrid, told me. "We support the transformation and Westernization of the Middle East. We defend the transition of Morocco from a monarchy to a constitutional monarchy. We are allies of the enemies of al-Qaeda in the Arab world. This point is not clearly understood by the Spanish people. We are a menace to al-Qaeda just because of who we are."

Captured on Film

———

O
n the one side, it's a tragedy that I have made only two feature
films in thirty years," the Syrian director Ossama Mohammed remarked. "Yet, from the other side, I see it as a miracle."
It was April 2006. We were sitting in the Rawda Café, the center of the
modest intellectual life of Damascus, where television stars, screen-
writers, and poets gathered for leisurely midmorning chats. The clat-
ter of backgammon boards and the smell of apple-flavored tobacco
from *sheesha* pipes filled the room. A man in a black jacket at the next
table, who appeared to be reading a magazine, occasionally leaned
toward our conversation.

"In Syria, we have this huge army of secret police and a complete
absence of legal protections," Mohammed said, in a quiet, angry voice.
"You can go to jail for thirty-five years and nobody will ask about
you." He was fifty-two and broad-chested, with an unruly beard and
wiry gray hair streaming down his back; his eyes were the same color
as his habitual unsmoked cigar. "People here have a sense of the balance of forces. They realize they are not strong enough to resist." He
cautioned, "In Syria, what we keep inside our imagination—what we
don't tell—that is the main reality."

Nearly every Middle Eastern country is governed by an authoritarian regime, but that hasn't kept many of those countries—notably,
Iran and Egypt—from developing surprisingly lively cinematic tra-

ditions. In a quarrelsome, voluble region, Syria is a strangely muted place. I wondered if by examining Syrian movies and talking to Syrian filmmakers, I could glimpse this closely guarded inner world.

Mohammed's films, *Stars in Broad Daylight* (1988) and *Sacrifices* (2002), are merciless indictments of the Baathist dictatorship that has controlled Syria since 1963, when it came to power in a military coup. Both movies received international acclaim, although they were banned at home. Many foreign critics have portrayed Mohammed and other Syrian directors as symbols of artistic victimization, but he defiantly rejects that role. "Do you want me to play the hero?" he asked. "Do you want me to repeat two hundred times each day that my films are forbidden? This is my society. I belong to this world. I am *not* a victim."

Yet a look around the Rawda Café suggests that the creative class in Syria has a lot of time on its hands. One writer I met has a job counting the city's streetlamps. Most of the country's filmmakers, including Mohammed, are employees of the National Film Organization, which manages the production of all Syrian films. Mohammed is paid $250 a month, which is the average government wage. This salary allows filmmakers to pay their rent and spend much of their day idling at the Rawda, which has the atmosphere of a perpetual, brooding salon.

The Syrian government and the filmmakers have developed an awkward dependency upon each other. Ibrahim Hamidi, the Damascus bureau chief for the pan-Arab newspaper *Al-Hayat*, says, "By permitting Ossama Mohammed and others to make movies financed by the government, the regime is harming the filmmakers' credibility, and also trying to contain them. The films get awards abroad, which is good PR for the regime. At the same time, Syrians aren't allowed to see the movies." While filmmakers have the opportunity to test the limits of government censorship, the regime acquires an intimate sense of the mood of the nation's intellectuals. "The people who rule Syria are not stupid," Hamidi said. "They play a very sophisticated game."

In this stifled and paralyzed country, the one-sided interchange between the filmmakers and the Assad regime is practically the only political dialogue available. "I have an obsession with facing authority," Mohammed said. "This society is responsible for creating the dictatorship—it's in our culture, our way of believing and thinking. I am trying to expose the authority inside us and the shadow of political authority in front of our doors."

Stars in Broad Daylight is perhaps the greatest film to come out of Syria. It explores the toxic effect of totalitarianism on ordinary Syrians, as seen through the internal battles of a dysfunctional family. The oldest of three children works for the phone company, where he casually listens in on telephone calls. Brutal, corrupt, and whimsical, he forces his siblings to become engaged to people they despise, in order to expand his landholdings. He encourages his brother to savagely beat their sister's suitor, then makes his sister get involved with a member of the regime, who rapes her. Not coincidentally, the actor playing this monstrous character looks like Hafez al-Assad—the man who ruled Syria for nearly thirty years, until his death in 2000.

I asked Mohammed how the movie came to be made. "Dictatorship is not like this monolith where everyone is the same," he explained. "No. Inside, you find a lot of people want to support you. *Stars* wouldn't exist without three or four Syrian cinematographers who read the script on behalf of the National Film Organization." At the time, the government wanted to film an innocuous script by a different director, but the cinematographers had repeatedly rejected it. Finally, they made a deal, Mohammed recalled. "They said, 'We will give you this film if you give us *Stars*.'"

While Mohammed was working on the script, his brother Ali, an electrical engineer, was imprisoned. Government officials had tricked him by inviting him and several university professors to share their views on reform, then locking them up. The authorities subsequently threatened to send Ali to a prison in Palmyra, a notorious torture chamber, if Mohammed did not tone down his script. Mohammed refused to make any changes. "My relationship with my brother is like this: To salute him, I will make *my* movie. That is how I support him!" Ali was released after four and a half years, just before Mohammed began shooting.

During the filming, crew members began to get scared. "The game was to make love with the fear," Mohammed said. "It was 'Yes, let's put Hafez al-Assad *inside* my movie.' " He cast his fellow director Abdullatif Abdulhamid in the lead role, largely because of his unmistakable resemblance to Assad.

I asked Mohammed how he got away with making such a defiant film. "When you live in a garden of corruption, you learn the skills of bluffing," he said. "Some of my colleagues came and said, 'If this is not a piece of great art, you are going to be fucked.' When I was shooting, I forgot about this, but one day, when I was stuck in traffic, I thought, My God! What am I doing?" He thought that he might be jailed the moment he submitted the final cut. To his surprise, he was not. But his movie was put in cold storage.

It took Mohammed fourteen years to make his second project, *Sacrifices,* which portrays the breakdown of social relations under dictatorship. "It is the story of Syria," he told me. "A huge quantity of time has been lost by holding on to illusions—the illusions of heroism, religion, Arab nationalism—and by not dealing with the Other. The Other is not Israel. It is inside our homes. It is inside everybody." When the script was completed, Mohammed submitted it to the National Film Organization. The scenario, about a dying man with a large family whose members are all competing for his blessing, was lyrical but obscure, and laden with references that government officials found both mysterious and provocative. What, they demanded, was the meaning of the child who places birds inside bottles? Or the baby who floats, like Moses, down a Syrian river in his bassinet?

The film ends with a shot of a giant tree, just after a child crawls into a casket. "The tree is positive, right?" a member of the National Film Organization asked him. "It's the homeland, right?"

"No," Mohammed said. "The tree is the tree."

He certainly didn't make it easy for himself. "You want to know my opinion about Syrian politics?" Mohammed told the committee. "Is it democracy? Absolutely not. Is it dictatorship? Yes. But if you want this country to have a democracy after a hundred years, then this is our work together right now. So don't shit on my film."

One scene, in particular, troubled the director of the National Film Organization. Three boys are taught how to slaughter a cow while reciting verses from the Quran. "All the West is attacking us because, for them, we are killers and extremists," the director told Mohammed. "You don't want to say that." He asked Mohammed to cut the scene.

Mohammed refused, claiming that violence was an essential part of the culture. "You can't be a man unless you learn to kill," he declared. The scene represents the initiation of a new generation into the pathologies of Syrian life.

The two men were at an impasse. Mohammed finally said, "I know a secret about you. When you were young, you jumped from one building to another to meet your girlfriend."

"How do you know this?" the astonished bureaucrat asked.

"Ask the man who jumped what he thinks. Does he like the script?"

"It's amazingly beautiful."

"Please, follow *yourself.* Don't forget who you are."

"Go!" the director of the National Film Organization said. "Do it!"

Four years later, when *Sacrifices* was finally completed, Baath Party officials demanded considerable cuts. Mohammed declined, even though he knew that the film would therefore not be shown in Syria.

Mohammed's brother Ali happened to wander into the Rawda Café while we were talking. I recognized him—a white-haired man with kind green eyes—because he appears in *Sacrifices.* In a startling scene, a pubescent boy is tied to a post after violating the fast during Ramadan. A Quran is tied into the knot of the rope. Ali enters and unties the rope. The image is deeply personal: Mohammed had told me that Ali was the first in his family to deny the authority of religion.

"When I did that scene, Ossama took me aside and asked me to push my anger," Ali said. "So I told him a story. When I was in prison, someone came to take a thirteen-year-old boy to Palmyra prison. He was terrified. He held on to me and pleaded not to let them take him away. This shot is for that boy."

Sacrifices received enthusiastic reviews at its premiere, at the 2002 Cannes Film Festival, although some viewers were put off by Mohammed's elliptical storytelling. Indeed, when I first saw *Sacrifices,* the references seemed so personal that I wondered if this is what happens when a director no longer expects to have an audience—he makes a film that is entirely for himself. Even Syrian intellectuals who have obtained the film on the underground DVD circuit were puzzled by some of the scenes, like the opening shot, which shows a naked boy being lowered into a cave to fetch a chicken, or the sequence in which a boy's pants burst into flames.

Mohammed does not see the hermetic qualities of *Sacrifices* as a weakness. "The kitchen of cinema here is full of poisonous materials," he told me. "But we are lucky as filmmakers to work in this kitchen. Because there is no audience, at least we don't have to worry about the censorship imposed by commercialism." He paused, then said, "Even if there *were* an audience, I would not change my ways."

A FEW BLOCKS AWAY from the Rawda Café is the Syrian Parliament Building, with its requisite portraits of Hafez al-Assad and his son Bashar, who has run the country since his father's death. The parliament happens to stand on the site of Syria's first movie theater, which burned down a month after it was constructed, in 1916. Across the street is the Cham Palace, the only movie theater in the capital that shows current releases. When I went, on a Thursday evening, there was a small audience of families with children to see *Big Momma's House 2,* the Martin Lawrence comedy. Damascus was once home to dozens of first-run theaters, but because moviegoing draws people together in a communal experience, the Baathist regime considers it a dangerous habit. Starting in the 1980s, party thugs began disrupting film audiences; at the same time, the selection of movies officially offered became smaller and smaller, and the theaters, which were forbidden to raise ticket prices, deteriorated. "Two decades ago, there were a hundred and twenty cinemas in Syria," one filmmaker told me. "Now there are only six that are functioning." As the country's cinemas fell into ruin, civil life withered and Syrians increasingly stayed indoors.

Ossama Mohammed fondly recalls the time when Syrians went to the movies regularly. One of nine children, Mohammed grew up in Latakia, a town on the Mediterranean coast. "Before 1963, people could see films the same year they were produced," he said. When *Spartacus,* the 1960 Stanley Kubrick classic, came to town, he said, "I didn't have money to go to the cinema, so I would steal from my brother Ali and invite my friends. Ali discovered this, and he brought a big stick and said, 'For every franc you steal, I will beat you once.' I thought about it, and the next day I stole three francs. It was worth it!"

Mohammed's father was a teacher at an elementary school where corporal punishment was commonplace. "But I am proud that my father didn't do that once," he said. "At school, I was punished hundreds of times. Once, I warned a teacher who was going to beat me. I was used to fighting on the streets. I said, 'If you strike me, I will hit you back.' He didn't believe me. So I beat him up. I was sixteen."

Thrown out of Latakia's schools, Mohammed moved to Damascus to finish high school. The following year, one of his sisters, a doctor, called with some good news. She had saved the life of a government official who was in charge of giving foreign-study scholarships to Syrian students. "Do you want to study in Russia?" she asked Mohammed.

"Study what?"

"Medicine," she proposed.

"No."

"Engineering?"

"No."

"Film?"

Mohammed remembered *Spartacus,* and agreed. In 1974, he enrolled at the renowned Russian State Institute of Cinematography, or VGIK, which had produced many masters of cinema, including Andrei Tarkovsky and Vasily Shukshin. It would also be the incubator of the Syrian film industry. In Moscow, Mohammed met another Syrian, Mohammed Malas, who was in his final year at VGIK, and Malas introduced him to his mentor, Igor Talankin, who accepted Mohammed as a protégé. A third Syrian, Abdullatif Abdulhamid, arrived in Moscow in 1975.

Upon returning home from Russia, the three Syrians attempted to create an indigenous cinema. In 1974, Malas, along with Omar Amiralay, another young filmmaker, founded the Damascus Cinema Club. Amiralay had already angered the regime by depicting the despair of rural peasants in *Everyday Life in a Syrian Village,* a documentary that sharply undercut the government's boasts about agrarian reform. The film was banned. Three years later, Amiralay made *The Chick-*

ens, a critical look at the government's clumsy efforts to stimulate private industry. He focused on a village where the peasants agreed to put everything they owned into the poultry business, even turning their houses into chicken coops. A plague among the chickens forced the villagers into bankruptcy, but they continued to pursue their ill-advised investment. At the end of the film, the clucking of chickens drowns out the speech of the village's doomed capitalists.

Amiralay said of the cinema club, "We showed the kind of films we dreamed of making." Using projectors borrowed from the Soviet cultural center, the club members set up a screening room on the ground floor of an apartment building. The room, which faced a garden, was too cramped for the film to be projected in front of the screen. So they turned to Nazih Shahbandar, an elderly man who had pioneered movie projection in Syria by making all the equipment himself. Shahbandar set up the projector in an adjoining kitchen and projected the image onto a mirror in the garden, which reflected it onto the rear of the screen. In that manner, the cinema club presented the works of Bergman, Fellini, and Godard, along with a handful of Syrian films.

The screenings were followed by impassioned debates, which provided a safe way to discuss the filmmakers' larger predicament. Club members held screenwriting seminars and technical workshops, and published a magazine, *Film.* The French comic actor and director Jacques Tati visited the club, and the Italian writer and director Pier Paolo Pasolini came to speak when he was shooting *Medea* in Aleppo. In 1978, in conjunction with the French journal *Cahiers du Cinéma,* the club sponsored two weeks of "cinema and politics." There were two screenings a day. "We sold out every performance," Amiralay recalled. The critics of *Cahiers du Cinéma* had chosen eighteen films, but when the Syrian government banned more than half of them, the French critic Serge Daney sat on the stage and provided an imaginative narration of what the films would have shown. "It was a screening without an image—an absolutely beautiful happening," Amiralay said.

In 1980, Hafez al-Assad began a series of mass arrests in an attempt to eliminate dissent altogether. Hundreds of dissidents were imprisoned and tortured. When Amiralay discovered that his name was on a list of people to be arrested, he moved to France. Most of the filmmakers who worked for the government, however, stayed and tried to practice their craft in a society that was cowed and broken.

FARES HELOU IS one of Syria's biggest movie and television stars. He is a burly man with tightly curled hair and a heavy, expressive face, and his gentle humor onscreen reminded me of Jack Lemmon. Helou is also known for declaring his negative views of the regime. "I'm loved as an actor, so I'm protected," he said one afternoon at the Rawda Café. Indeed, as we talked, fans approached him for autographs and snapshots. But his friends worried that Helou's career had been damaged by his political stance. "His star-o-meter is going down," one of them told me. "People are afraid to work with him. Maybe he's not as protected as he thinks he is."

Helou fell in love with cinema while studying at Syria's Higher Institute for Theatre Arts; soon after graduating, he got a role in Mohammed Malas's second feature film, *The Night* (1993). Subsequent television roles have made him known throughout the Arab world. (Syrian miniseries are ubiquitous on Arab satellite television.) I asked him if things had changed in Syria since the ascent to power of Bashar al-Assad, who had presented himself to the West as a reformer. "We had the same amount of freedom, or more, in Hafez's time," Helou said. "Hafez, at least, was clear—with any position, you knew exactly the space that was allowed. But after the son came in, the freedom given us was not real; it was a trap. When voices started to be heard presenting new and modern ideas, the regime arrested those voices."

As Helou and I were talking, a young fan in a jean jacket and a checked shirt approached the table. "I love you," he said to Helou in Arabic. "I just want to exchange mobile numbers. I promise I won't abuse it."

To my surprise, Helou offered his number. "What's your name?" he asked the fan.

"My friends call me Stalin," he said. "Because I'm a killer." Stalin had broad shoulders, a long, unbroken eyebrow that stretched across his forehead, and a gold chain around his neck.

Helou gave a dismissive nod, and Stalin retreated to his table.

I asked Helou about Ossama Mohammed's second film, *Sacrifices*.

Helou plays a father who leaves Syria to fight in the 1973 war against
Israel. When he returns home to his family, on a remote mountaintop,
he is caked with mud. In a savagely ironic scene, he gathers the family
to tell his story. The women are beating cotton bolls on the table, and
a cow stands at the front door. Helou's character explains that he was
nearly killed when he was buried by an explosion. It took three days
for his fellow-Arabs to get a bulldozer to dig him out. "There was no
fuel left, it seems," the character says bitterly. Where was the Arabs'
oil when it was needed? he wonders.

Helou said of his character, "The shock of being defeated makes
him cruel. Embracing the illusion of authority makes him think he
was victorious." But, as the film shows, the only legacy of violence is
more violence. Helou's character eventually abuses power in the same
way as the corrupt and incompetent state that sent him into the disastrous war. When he comes home, he forces his children to drink oil.

Stalin suddenly returned to our table. "I have another phone," he
said to Helou, switching to English for my benefit. "I want to give
you the number. Very few people have this. I even take it with me on
operations." He was making it clear that he was with the secret police.

"Is this the first time you've been in this café?" Helou asked him.

"No, I'm *always* here," Stalin said. "We have spoken before. Usually, I'm dressed in a military uniform, so perhaps you don't recognize me."

Stalin asked if Helou was a member of the Baath Party. Helou said
he was not.

"You cannot *not* be a member," Stalin said angrily, grabbing Helou's
hand. "This is a real Baathist handshake! I will pay your dues for you!"

Stalin noticed that I was taking notes on his conversation, and he
began expatiating on American and British aggression in Iraq, and the
interference of human-rights activists in Syrian affairs. "We should be
able to discipline the peasants without outside interference," he said.
"I quote Aristotle to his student, Alexander the Great, who said that
you should treat the Greek people as gentlemen and the people of the
East as slaves." With that, Stalin returned to his table once again.

"He came to deliver a message," Helou said anxiously. "He's telling
me to take it easy—to calm down." His left leg was jiggling furiously.

Minutes later, Stalin returned yet again, this time carrying a cup of coffee and a pack of Gitanes. He had no intention of letting my interview continue. Bizarrely, he pulled yet another telephone from a jacket pocket. "This is my most private number," he said to Helou. He pointed to an arrow on the phone's screen, beside Helou's mobile number. "This arrow goes *through* you," he said, laughing. He squeezed in next to Helou, who had become quiet.

"Do you work for the government?" I asked Stalin.

"Of course—that's why I'm talking to you," he said. "But I am very open. I am not a spee. Do you say spee or spy?"

"Spee."

Stalin said that, like me, he was also a journalist, working for a pro-government magazine. He added that he loved movies—"*Syrian* movies," he said. "I love the movies that are produced by the National Film Organization and the movies made by this man, regardless of the fact that he is not obedient."

Stalin took Helou's hand once more. "I feel the need to beat someone," he said, laughing into Helou's shoulder. "May I beat you?"

I could see that Helou was ready to get out of there. "Welcome to Syria," Stalin said as we left.

"MEET ME IN Salhieh Square in ten minutes," Orwa Nyrabia, a young Syrian filmmaker, said when I called him one afternoon to ask about the market in pirated DVD movies.

A bronze soldier stands in the center of the square atop a column; an actual Syrian flag flaps against his scabbard. "It's Yusuf Azmeh," Nyrabia explained. "He was the minister of defense when the French Army invaded in 1921. He and a group of five hundred riflemen went to meet them because they didn't want to see the country occupied without any resistance. There wasn't a single survivor among them. I love this story. This could be a huge, epic film."

Nyrabia told me he intended to be Syria's first independent producer. Digital equipment has reduced the cost of making films, and satellite television has created a potentially huge market for Arab cinema; he thought it could soon be possible for Syrian directors to create work without government funding, though scripts will still require approval by the General Institute of Cinema.

Nyrabia is a big man with a goatee and close-cropped hair that makes his expressive face all the more imposing. We walked to Media Mart, a store by the square, which had a vast selection of pirated DVDs and computer software. In 2004, President George W. Bush placed Syria under an embargo of American goods, except for food and medicine, because of the country's continued support of terrorism and its failure to control the movement of insurgents into Iraq. Kodak film stock and chemicals were included in the embargo. "It would be a problem for our industry, if we actually *had* an industry," Nyrabia told me as we wandered among the small shops. Although hardware was harder to obtain now, software has always been cheap and illegal. "Piracy has been a great blessing," said Nyrabia. "Because of this, most members of my generation are computer literate." For his business, however, he had decided to pay the market rate for software in order to avoid problems with compatibility. "A lot of guys would laugh at me," he said, noting that professional film-editing software costs several thousand dollars in the West, but "you can buy it in the Damascus market for twenty."

The Media Mart was crammed with recent movies, such as *Capote* and *Sin City*. Nyrabia recalled, "When I was a kid, they had VHS rental stores, but everything was censored. They were all stamped by the Ministry of Culture. Now, nothing is censored." Only pornography— and banned Syrian movies—were absent from the shelves. The Assad government has apparently decided that it can placate its citizens by allowing thousands of American films to circulate, as long as they aren't watched in large groups. As Nyrabia explained, "The regime has decided, 'Let's encourage people to stay home. It's safer.'"

Nyrabia purchased *March of the Penguins* and at my suggestion the Mike Nichols production of *Angels in America*. We wandered outside, past the Cham Palace to a coffeehouse named Aroma, which faces the grounds of the parliament building. The flat roofs of the nearby apartments were topped with satellite dishes pointed west, like flowers inclining toward the afternoon sun. Nyrabia was telling me about a script he had just submitted for review to a committee of the General Institute that he hoped to direct himself. "It's about a family, husband and wife and child, and they pass a shop," Nyrabia said. "We just see the husband's eyes glance at a brown suit. The wife catches this and asks him, 'Should we go in? That suit would look beautiful on you.' But he declines, he's in a hurry. 'Every week, we are always the first ones to arrive at your mother's house,' she says. 'Take twenty minutes for yourself!' But, still, he declines. While they are arguing, their child runs away. But it's about the relationship of the man and the woman, and you tell everything just in the glances and the way they react to each other."

"What did the committee say?"

"They didn't get it. They wanted it to be all about the search for the child. But that would be banal, parents looking everywhere, you know what happens already."

I said that I actually agreed with the committee. His idea seemed strangely inert.

Nyrabia recalled a protest he had joined in December 1990, just before the American bombing of Baghdad, when the Syrian government authorized a demonstration in front of the American Embassy that got out of hand. "It started out peacefully, but it became a monster," Nyrabia said. The embassy was burned, along with the ambassador's residence, the American School, and the British Council. I asked him how he felt now about having been part of such a mob.

"I feel good," he said. "For the first time in my life, I was part of a violent protest, something which is normal all over the world. I believe this is the main problem in Syria. It's a very static society, so I'm happy when I see something dynamic happening. I mean, we don't even have crimes! This is not good. I might sound like an anarchist, but this even applies to the commercial film industry. Most action films in Hollywood couldn't be made here, because we don't have the action to put onto film! And you are forbidden to do movies about corruption, or comedies about the police or the army. Crime or horror films are also not allowed here. Where can you go to come up with a decent project to make a proper blockbuster? You need action thrillers or comedies, and we can't do either."

I pointed out that his own scenario had avoided the obvious action—the parents searching for their missing child. "That's not forbidden, surely," I said. "Maybe it's a problem of your imagination, that you don't allow yourself to think about action."

Nyrabia paused. "I don't know," he said. "Could be."

IN 1992, Omar Amiralay, after making eight films in France, came back to Syria. "I was fed up with Paris," he said, and he sensed that he could go home without being arrested. Also, he had fallen in love with a Damascene woman. "It was a sentimental return," he said.

But Amiralay had a score to settle, too. As a young documentarian, he had been given the chance to make a movie about the damming of the Euphrates River. The result, *Film-Essay on the Euphrates Dam* (1970), was heavily influenced by Soviet documentaries, with a reverent approach to the mighty instruments of labor. He came to see it as a naively Marxist work—"a hymn to the crane" is how he refers to it—that is wholly uncritical of the Baathist regime. "For me, that first film is a deep wound in my heart," Amiralay told me. "I was able to make a career outside of my homeland. I don't regret it, but if they had given me the chance to live in Syria maybe I and my colleagues could have created a better country."

In 2003, he returned to the dam region. "I wanted to make a film of fifteen shots, which are the fifteen reasons I hate the Baath Party. The last reason was that I hate myself, for having been obliged to make a film for them. They spoiled forty years of my life."

Flood begins with a bitter voice-over. Amiralay says, "In 1970, I was a firm advocate of the modernization of my homeland, Syria, so much so that I dedicated my first film to the building of a dam in the Euphrates River, the pride and joy of the Baath Party then in power. Today, I regret this error of my youth."

I asked if *Flood* had ever been shown in Syria. Amiralay shook his head. "But when I finished I decided to give it to some film pirates," he explained. "Two months later, everybody in Damascus had seen it. It was a digital flood."

IN APRIL 2000, the filmmaker Nabil Maleh started the Committee for the Revival of Civil Society, along with a small group of lawyers and intellectuals. Decades earlier, Maleh had directed some of Syria's most insurrectionary movies, including *The Leopard* (1972), a historical film about a revolt against an earlier Syrian regime. Maleh, who was born in 1936, was old enough to recall a Syria with a vigorous press and numerous political parties, as well as a vibrant civic life.

Once his movement got going, allied committees began springing up all over Syria. Hafez al-Assad died that June, which increased expectations that Syria might finally open up. In September, ninety-nine prominent Syrians, including fifteen filmmakers, signed a petition calling for an end to the restrictions on freedom of assembly, opinion, and the press; a general amnesty for all political prisoners; and a decree allowing political exiles abroad to return. The regime responded by releasing six hundred political prisoners.

Encouraged by this, in January 2001, more than a thousand prominent Syrians, some of them living in exile, signed a broader and more daring petition, called the Basic Document, which had been drafted by Maleh's committee. The Basic Document called for an end to Baath Party domination. "Immediately came the crash," Maleh recalled. Bashar al-Assad warned that the advocates of greater openness were outsiders and were undermining the stability of the country. He declared that all social, political, and cultural gatherings had to be approved in advance. A few months later, ten signatories of the Basic Document were imprisoned for "attempting to change the constitution by illegal means." Officials told Maleh that he would never be able to make films again. The government effectively smothered the reform movement, even as it maintained the appearance of liberalizing by releasing elderly political prisoners and allowing the publication of new journals with minimal political content. "The development of civil-society institutions must come at a later stage," Bashar declared.

"We lost the war without ever fighting it," Maleh admitted one evening at dinner in an old house in the Christian quarter of Damascus, now a lovely but generally empty restaurant. I had suggested that political opposition in Damascus often seemed more gestural than real, and that making movies no one could see was therefore a characteristic expression of Syrian dissent. Perhaps the society was so tamed by the regime that no more could be expected of it, but it was also possible that the regime was simply the political expression of a brutal and authoritarian culture.

Maleh had told me about an incident in his childhood, when he was seven years old. "I was with my family in a public park in Damascus," he recalled. "I wanted to use the swing. There were some children already playing there, and they were guarded by a soldier, probably a driver for some big shot. I don't know what I did to provoke it, but the soldier slapped me, knocking me four meters away. I picked up a clod of dirt, threw it at the soldier, and ran away. From that moment, all my life has been connected with a hatred of the uniform and of authority." As an adult, after a protest, Maleh was taken to prison and beaten. "It was part of the fun of the times," he said, in a strangely off-kilter tone.

Before I went to Damascus, the characters in Syrian films had seemed to me full of unmotivated cruelty, but now they were beginning to make sense. In every movie I saw, physical abuse played a role; and the more I talked to the filmmakers, I realized that abuse—and the consequent sense of helplessness and victimhood—had shaped their lives in defining ways.

This anger was palpable in Maleh's films, most poignantly in *The Extras* (1993), in which two lovers meet at a friend's apartment for an assignation. They suppose that they have finally shut out the world that has prevented them from consummating their relationship, but fear prevents them from enjoying their moment alone. The film gets its title from the male character, who plays bit parts in theatrical productions, underscoring Maleh's belief that "we are all extras in this society." The real world intrudes when the secret police enter the apartment, supposedly investigating a blind musician who lives next door. The man tries to prevent the musician's arrest and, in a reverie, imagines dispatching the police with a few judo moves, but his fantasy is broken by a hard slap that knocks him to the floor. He is humiliated and powerless in front of his lover—a devastating turning point in their relationship. "They enter the apartment as lovers," Maleh told me. "They leave as strangers."

I thought of other scenes in Syrian cinema in which physical abuse plays a significant role—for example, in Mohammed's film *Stars,* a character is made permanently deaf by a blow from his father. These scenes, I knew, reflected the filmmakers' experiences. When I asked them about the abuse, however, their responses surprised me. Abdullatif Abdulhamid, whose films often feature punitive fathers, told me about going to see *Hercules* when he was a boy. Afterward, he ran into his family's wheat field with a stick, engaging in mock battle. When he damaged a few stalks, he said, with a smile, "my father beat me." Amiralay, whose father died when he was five, said, "I was beaten only by the slippers of my mother, and for this I am grateful. Such beatings awakened me."

I went to dinner one night in a restaurant with some Syrian artists, and I brought up the subject of physical abuse. "It's common," the middle-aged woman across from me acknowledged. She added, "For me, it was a positive experience."

"What do you mean?"

"I was twenty-six years old," she recalled. "At first, I was hurt. I was living just to please others—for example, my ex-husband and his family. Then I realized that a word from your mouth can make the difference between survival and destruction." She was staring at me; her shining brown eyes seemed strangely untroubled.

"A beating did this for you?"

She nodded. "It was like a revolution. It was like you are not living any more to please others. You suddenly become very brave. I was one step from death, but I was thinking of my children, and I was determined to survive. It was positive for me. This is when I decided to be a creative person."

"So your ex-husband hit you?"

"No," she said quietly, so the other guests wouldn't hear. She took my notepad and wrote, "Raped by the government."

Later, I asked Maleh if Syrian society had always been so abusive. "No," he said. "Violence became a part of the daily practice in the last forty years." The Baathist throttling of democratic expression, he believed, replicated itself in the relationships between authority figures and people without power—women, children, and the poor.

Although the filmmakers often talked about freedom, they revealed a perverse desire to romanticize the artistic constraints of dictatorship. "The most beautiful Soviet films were produced in the era of Stalin," Abdulhamid told me. "When the Soviet Union collapsed and suddenly you could say whatever you wanted, the Russians began producing the most trivial films. Nobody should be forbidden to say what he wants, but it is a phenomenon that dazzles me: when you're suppressed, you *think* better."

"THE ARAB CINEMA HAS few masterpieces—no more than ten,"
Omar Amiralay pronounced one afternoon over cappuccino. Among
them he included two Egyptian films, *Cairo Station,* by Youssef Cha-
hine, and *Fools' Alley,* by Tewfik Saleh. Both films, he observed, were
the directors' first major efforts. "It is a syndrome in Arab cinema that
directors who make a remarkable first film rarely succeed in making
another," he said. There were no Syrian films in his pantheon.

I asked where he placed his friend Ossama Mohammed. "Ossama
is an exception," Amiralay said. "But he hasn't had the liberty to
make an accomplished film, and, of course, he suffers from a lack of
opportunity and experience." Syrian films have the potential to be
great films, he continued, "but they lack the dimension of unity—the
compact structure, the purposeful style, the visual sensibility. Many
of the actors are not sufficiently mature or experienced. I always feel
there is something wrong, as if they were ordinary people who were
simulating acting. And, finally, the narration. We are so obsessed by
daily reality that scriptwriters don't have the courage to invent new
realities from their own imaginations. Because of this, I think they are
making bad documentaries and passing them off as fiction."

One evening, I went to the Old City with a Syrian cameraman,
Samer al-Zayat, for a drink at Café Mar Mar, in a sixteenth-century
building with stone walls and twenty-foot ceilings. We walked into
a roomful of upturned faces illuminated by the familiar flickering
light of a movie. I had stumbled upon the latest incarnation of the
Damascus Cinema Club. I ordered popcorn and a martini (it's a very
congenial club) and watched *Big Fish.* In attendance were many of
Syria's film and television stars, who apparently had enough influence
to keep the underground operation alive. "This is the only venue left
for new artistic movies," Zayat told me. "They advertise by SMS messages on the telephones, and show films every Monday night. Last
week, we watched *Munich.*" Unlike the old days of the cinema club,
however, the audience departed quietly when the film was over.

The week after I left Syria, a government-approved newspaper
announced that the following day Ossama Mohammed's *Sacrifices*
would be given its first public showing, in Homs, a provincial town

in central Syria. Mohammed raced to Homs, only to discover that his film was not being shown after all; instead, a Baathist youth rally was under way. It was a prank. Though he knew that he wouldn't change the situation, he acted out the role of the fearless dissident. "I shouted and made a scene," Mohammed told me. "I said I would call the governor. I really played the game."

Postscript

Many of the people I interviewed in this piece are now in exile, along with millions of other Syrians. Ossama Mohammed is in Paris. Orwa Nyrabia was arrested and imprisoned during the early stage of the civil war, but was freed after an international campaign on his behalf by fellow filmmakers. He now lives in Berlin. In 2013, he produced *Return to Homs,* by Syrian director Talal Derki, a gritty portrait of the resistance inside one of the country's most battered cities. The film won the Grand Jury Prize at Sundance. Nyrabia also served as a producer for Ossama Mohammed's film (with Wiam Simav Bedirxan) *Silvered Water, Syria Self-Portrait,* which premiered at the Cannes Film Festival in 2014. Nabil Maleh died in Dubai in Febrary 2016.

The Master Plan

Even as members of al-Qaeda watched in exultation while the Twin Towers fell and the Pentagon burned on September 11, 2001, they realized that the pendulum of catastrophe was swinging in their direction. Osama bin Laden later boasted that he was the only one in the group's upper hierarchy who had anticipated the magnitude of the wound that al-Qaeda inflicted on America, but he also admitted that he was surprised by the towers' collapse. His goal had been to goad America into invading Afghanistan, an ambition that had caused him to continually raise the stakes—the simultaneous bombings of the U.S. embassies in Kenya and Tanzania in August 1998, followed by the attack on the American warship, the *USS Cole,* in the harbor of Aden, Yemen, in October 2000. Neither of those actions had led the United States to send troops to Afghanistan. After the attacks on New York and Washington, however, it was clear that there would be an overwhelming response. Al-Qaeda members began sending their families home and preparing for war.

Two months later, the Taliban government in Afghanistan, which had given sanctuary to bin Laden, was routed, and the al-Qaeda fighters in Tora Bora were pummeled. Although bin Laden and his chief lieutenants escaped death or capture, nearly 80 percent of al-Qaeda's members in Afghanistan were killed. Moreover, al-Qaeda's cause was repudiated throughout the world, even in Muslim countries, where

the indiscriminate murder of civilians and the use of suicide operatives were denounced as being contrary to Islam. The remnants of the
organization scattered. Al-Qaeda was essentially dead.

From hiding places in Iran, Yemen, Iraq, and the tribal areas of
western Pakistan, al-Qaeda's survivors lamented their failed strategy.
Abu al-Walid al-Masri, a senior leader of al-Qaeda's inner council, later
wrote that al-Qaeda's experience in Afghanistan was "a tragic example
of an Islamic movement managed in an alarmingly meaningless way."
He went on, "Everyone knew that their leader was leading them to
the abyss and even leading the entire country to utter destruction, but
they continued to carry out his orders faithfully and with bitterness."

In June 2002, bin Laden's son Hamzah posted a message on an
al-Qaeda website: "Oh, Father! Where is the escape and when will
we have a home? Oh, Father! I see spheres of danger everywhere I
look. . . . Tell me, Father, something useful about what I see."

"Oh, son!" bin Laden replied. "Suffice to say that I am full of grief
and sighs. . . . I can only see a very steep path ahead. A decade has
gone by in vagrancy and travel, and here we are in our tragedy. Security has gone, but danger remains."

In the view of Abu Musab al-Suri, a Syrian who had been a member of al-Qaeda's inner council and who is a theorist of jihad, the greatest loss was not the destruction of the terrorist organization but the
downfall of the Taliban, which meant that al-Qaeda no longer had a
place to train, organize, and recruit. The expulsion from Afghanistan,
Suri later wrote, was followed by "three meager years which we spent
as fugitives," dodging the international dragnet by "moving between
safe houses and hideouts." In 2002, Suri fled to eastern Iran, where
bin Laden's son Saad and al-Qaeda's security chief, Saif al-Adl, had
also taken refuge. There was a $5 million bounty on his head. In this
moment of exile and defeat, he began to conceive the future of jihad.

ABU MUSAB AL-SURI WAS BORN into a middle-class family in
Aleppo, Syria, in 1958, the year of bin Laden's birth. His real name
is Mustafa Setmariam Nasar. He became involved in politics at the
University of Aleppo, where he studied engineering. Later, he moved
to Jordan, where he joined the Muslim Brotherhood. In 1982, when

Assad decided that the Brotherhood posed a threat to his authority, his troops slaughtered as many as thirty thousand people in the city of Hama, one of the group's strongholds. The ruthlessness of Assad's response shocked Suri. He renounced the Brotherhood, which he held responsible for provoking the destruction of Hama, and took refuge in Europe for several years. In 1985, he moved to Spain, where he married and became a Spanish citizen; two years later, he found his way to Afghanistan, where he met Osama bin Laden.

The two men had a contentious relationship. Although Suri became a member of al-Qaeda's inner council, he grew disillusioned by the fecklessness and the disorganization that characterized al-Qaeda's training camps in Afghanistan. "People come to us with empty heads and leave us with empty heads," he complained. "They have done nothing for Islam. This is because they have not received any ideological or doctrinal training."

In 1992, Suri moved back to Spain, where he helped to establish a terrorist cell that played a part in the planning of September 11. Two years later, he went to England. Red-haired and sturdily built, with a black belt in judo and a reputation for curmudgeonly commentary, he soon became a fixture in the Islamist press in London. He wrote articles for the magazine *Al-Ansar*, which promoted the insurgency in Algeria that resulted in more than a hundred thousand deaths. The magazine's editor was Abu Qatada, a Palestinian cleric who was often characterized as al-Qaeda's spiritual guide in Europe. *Al-Ansar* was, in many ways, the first jihadi think tank; Suri and other strategists suggested tactics for undermining the despotic regimes in the Arab world, and they promoted attacks on the West. American and European intelligence agencies were still blind to the threat that the Islamist movement posed.

Jamal Khashoggi, a prominent Saudi journalist, met Qatada and Suri in the early nineties. They struck him as far more radical than Osama bin Laden; at the time, al-Qaeda was primarily an anti-Communist organization. "Osama was in the moderate camp," Khashoggi told me. He coined the phrase "Salafi jihadis" to describe men, such as Abu Qatada and Suri, who had been influenced by Salafism, the puritanical, fundamentalist strain of Islam, which stressed the notion of continual warfare against unbelievers. "Osama was flirt-

ing with these ideas," Khashoggi said. "He was not the one who orig-
inated the radical thinking that came to characterize al-Qaeda. He
joined these men, rather than the other way around. His organization
became the vehicle for their thinking."

Suri later wrote about bin Laden's conversion to his ideas, which
took place after bin Laden returned to Afghanistan from Sudan, in
1996. Bin Laden was already angry at his own country for letting
American and coalition troops defend the kingdom against Saddam
Hussein's million-man army, rather than relying on bin Laden's own
small core of Arab Afghan veterans. He also held the Americans
responsible for having his Sudanese hosts summarily expel him from
the country, stealing everything he owned. So he was a willing lis-
tener when the Salafi jihadists presented him with their analysis.

They pointed first to the continuing presence of American troops
on the holy soil of the Arabian Peninsula. The corrupt Islamic scholars
lent their authority to the royal family, which in turn sanctioned the
presence of the coalition forces. There were two possible solutions:
either attack the royal family—which might infuriate the Saudi people—or strike at the American presence. "Bin Laden chose the second
option," Suri recalled.

Suri believed that the jihadi movement had nearly been extinguished by the drying up of financial resources, the killing or capture
of many terrorist leaders, the loss of safe havens, and the increasing
international cooperation among police agencies. Accordingly, he saw
the Taliban's takeover of Afghanistan in 1996 as a "golden opportunity," and he went there the following year. He set up a military camp
in Afghanistan, and experimented with chemical weapons. He also
arranged bin Laden's first television interview with CNN. The journalist Peter Bergen, who spent several days in Suri's company while
producing the segment, recalled, "He was tough and really smart.
He seemed like a real intellectual, very conversant with history, and
he had an intense seriousness of purpose. He certainly impressed me
more than bin Laden."

In 1999, Suri sent bin Laden an e-mail message accusing him of
endangering the Taliban regime with his highly theatrical attacks
on American targets and mocking his love of publicity: "I think our
brother has caught the disease of screens, flashes, fans, and applause."

In his writings, Suri rarely mentions al-Qaeda and disavows any direct connection to it, despite having served on its inner council. He prefers to speak more broadly of jihad, which he sees as a social movement, encompassing "all those who bear weapons—individuals, groups, and organizations—and wage jihad on the enemies of Islam." By 2000, he had begun predicting the end of al-Qaeda, whose preeminence he portrayed as merely a stage in the development of the worldwide Islamist uprising. "Al-Qaeda is not an organization, it is not a group, nor do we want it to be," he wrote. "It is a call, a reference, a methodology." Eventually, its leadership would be eliminated, so in the time that remained al-Qaeda's main goal should be to stimulate other groups around the world to join the jihadi movement. Suri's mission was to codify the doctrines that animated Islamist jihad, so that Muslim youths of the future could discover the cause and begin their own spontaneous religious war.

In 2002 Suri, in his hideout in Iran, began writing his defining work, *Call for Worldwide Islamic Resistance*, which is sixteen hundred pages long and was published on the Internet in December 2004. Didactic and repetitive, but also ruthlessly candid, the book dissects the faults of the jihadi movement and lays out a plan for the future of the struggle. The goal, he writes, is "to bring about the largest number of human and material casualties possible for America and its allies." He specifically targets Jews, "Westerners in general," the members of the NATO alliance, Russia, China, atheists, pagans, and hypocrites, as well as "any type of external enemy." At the same time, he perversely blames al-Qaeda for dragging the entire jihadi movement into an unequal battle that it is likely to lose.

In Suri's view, the underground terrorist movement—that is, al-Qaeda and its sleeper cells—is defunct. This approach was "a failure on all fronts," because of its inability to achieve military victory or to rally the Muslim people to its cause. He proposes that the next stage of jihad will be characterized by terrorism created by individuals or small autonomous groups (what he terms "leaderless resistance"), which will wear down the enemy and prepare the ground for the far more ambitious aim of waging war on "open fronts"—an outright struggle for territory. He explains, "Without confrontation in the field and seizing control of the land, we cannot establish a state, which is the strategic goal of the resistance." His ideas would lay the intellectual groundwork for the rise of ISIS.

There are five regions, according to Suri, where jihadis should focus their energies: Afghanistan, Central Asia, Yemen, Morocco, and, especially, Iraq. The American occupation of Iraq, he declares, inaugurated a "historical new period" that almost single-handedly rescued the jihadi movement just when many of its critics thought it was finished.

Suri was captured in Pakistan in November 2005, and is rumored to have been rendered to Syria; however, in 2010, an article with his byline appeared in the online magazine *Inspire,* a publication of the al-Qaeda affiliate in Yemen. It's unclear where he is today.

THE AMERICAN OCCUPATION CREATED a major opportunity for a man named Abu Musab al-Zarqawi, a Bedouin from Jordan. Neither an intellectual nor a strategist, Zarqawi was a convicted criminal who acted largely on brute impulse, but he was also a reckless warrior who gained the respect of the Arab mujahideen when he arrived in Pakistan, in the early nineties. His spiritual guide was a Palestinian sheikh named Abu Muhammad al-Maqdisi, who transformed him from a foot soldier in jihad to a leader who rivaled bin Laden.

Maqdisi and Zarqawi formed an immediate bond, an alliance of the man of thought and the man of action. They spent five years in prison together in Jordan, but in March 1999 Jordan's new king, Abdullah II, granted amnesty to political prisoners. Zarqawi went to Afghanistan, while his defiant mentor chose to stay in Jordan, where he felt that he was doing productive work; however, he was soon back in prison.

Unruly and independent, Zarqawi refused to swear fidelity to bin Laden, instead establishing his own camp in western Afghanistan, populated mainly by Jordanians, Syrians, and Palestinians. He was bluntly critical of al-Qaeda's decision to wage war against America and the West rather than against corrupt Arab dictatorships. After September 11, Zarqawi and his followers were flushed out of Afghanistan by the invasion of the coalition forces. He took refuge in Iran and, eventually, in the Kurdish region of Iraq.

In April 2003, after the U.S. invasion of Iraq, Zarqawi set up a new terror group, al-Tawhid wal Jihad (Monotheism and Jihad). Unlike the senior members of al-Qaeda, Zarqawi was obsessed with fighting the Shiites, "the most evil of mankind," thinking that he would unite the much larger Sunni world into a definitive conquest of what he saw as the great Islamic heresy. That August, shortly after he began his Iraq campaign, he bombed a Shiite mosque, killing 125 Muslim worshippers, including the most popular Shiite politician in the country, Ayatollah Mohammad Bakr al-Hakim, who, had he lived, would probably have become Iraq's first freely elected president. Zarqawi also blew up the UN headquarters in the Canal Hotel in Baghdad, effectively driving the international aid community out of the country. Among the murdered was Sérgio Vieira de Mello, one of the most able and charismatic leaders the UN has ever produced. These deaths, so significant in themselves, were characteristic of Zarqawi's war on the very people who could make Iraq into a functioning society—the teachers, the doctors, the courageous political thinkers.

In a letter to bin Laden in January 2004, which was intercepted by U.S. intelligence, Zarqawi explained that "if we succeed in dragging [the Shia] into the arena of sectarian war it will become possible to awaken the inattentive Sunnis as they feel imminent danger." He said that he would formally pledge allegiance to al-Qaeda if bin Laden endorsed his battle against the Shiites. In his weakened position, bin Laden agreed, telling Zarqawi to go ahead and "use the Shiite card," perhaps because his son Saad and other al-Qaeda figures were being held in Iran, and he vainly hoped that Zarqawi would pressure the Iranians to hand them over.

Zarqawi grabbed the wheel of al-Qaeda at a time when its founders were immobilized, reduced to making the occasional pleading videotape designed to sway the unseen jihadi masses. Zarqawi's ability to act, not just talk, was an affront to the secluded leaders, who were unable to influence the bloody flow of events in Iraq, the terrorist Super Bowl. Deprived of the managerial oversight of bin Laden, an economics major and international businessman, al-Qaeda began to shape itself around Zarqawi's organizational experience, which is to say that it turned into a gang. It was a model easily replicated by would-be jihadis everywhere.

Zarqawi's operatives spread into Europe, where they forged documents and gathered recruits for Iraq. One of his lieutenants in Spain, Amer Azizi, assisted the 9/11 hijackers in Spain and participated in the March 11, 2004, train bombings in Madrid. Zarqawi and his men were putting into action the vision that Abu Musab al-Suri had laid out for them: small, spontaneous groups carrying out individual acts of terror in Europe, while waging an open struggle for territory in Iraq.

Suicide bombings became a trademark of Zarqawi's operation, despite Abu Muhammad al-Maqdisi's condemnation of the practice. Zarqawi soon improvised a more gruesome signature: in May 2004, he was filmed decapitating Nicholas Berg, a young American contractor. The footage was posted on the Internet. Other beheadings followed, along with bombings and assassinations—hundreds of them.

Within radical Islamist circles, Zarqawi's gory executions and attacks on Muslims at prayer became a source of controversy. From prison, Maqdisi chastised his former protégé. "The pure hands of jihad fighters must not be stained by shedding inviolable blood," he wrote in July 2004. "There is no point in vengeful acts that terrify people, provoke the entire world against mujahideen, and prompt the world to fight them." Maqdisi also advised jihadis not to go to Iraq, "because it will be an inferno for them. This is, by God, the biggest catastrophe."

Zarqawi angrily refuted his spiritual mentor's remarks, saying that he took orders only from God; however, he was beginning to realize that his efforts in Iraq were another dead end for jihad. "The space of movement is starting to get smaller," he had written to bin Laden in June. "The grip is starting to be tightened on the holy warriors' necks and, with the spread of soldiers and police, the future is becoming frightening." The headstrong terrorist was begging for help. Finally, bin Laden agreed to let Zarqawi use the al-Qaeda brand as a way of drawing recruits to his cause. In October 2004, Zarqawi announced his new job title: emir of al-Qaeda in Iraq.

Zarqawi launched a murderous campaign unmatched in the history of al-Qaeda. Before he became a member, al-Qaeda had killed some 3,200 people, most of them on 9/11. Zarqawi's forces probably killed twice that number.

In July 2005, Ayman al-Zawahiri, al-Qaeda's chief ideologue and second-in-command, attempted to steer the nihilistic Zarqawi closer to the founders' original course. In a letter, he outlined the next steps for the Iraqi jihad: "The first stage: Expel the Americans from Iraq. The second stage: Establish an Islamic authority or emirate, then develop it and support it until it achieves the level of a caliphate. . . . The third stage: Extend the jihad wave to the secular countries neighboring Iraq. The fourth stage: It may coincide with what came before—the clash with Israel, because Israel was established only to challenge any new Islamic entity." It was a clear and prescient agenda.

Zawahiri also advised Zarqawi to moderate his attacks on Iraqi Shiites and to stop beheading hostages. "We are in a battle," Zawahiri reminded him. "And more than half of this battle is taking place in the battlefield of the media."

Zarqawi did not heed al-Qaeda's requests. As the Iraqi jihad fell into barbarism, al-Qaeda's leaders began advising their followers to go to Sudan or Kashmir, where the chances of victory seemed more promising. Al-Qaeda, meanwhile, was confronting a new problem, which one of its primary thinkers, Abu Bakr Naji, had already anticipated, in an Internet document titled "The Management of Savagery."

NAJI'S IDENTITY IS unknown. Other Islamist writers have said that he was Tunisian, but a Saudi newspaper identified him as Jordanian. William McCants, a fellow at the Brookings Institution and author of *The ISIS Apocalypse: The History, Strategy, and Doomsday Vision of the Islamic State,* has translated Naji's work. He said that "Abu Bakr Naji" might be a collective pseudonym for various theorists of jihad. But, he added, Naji's work has appeared in *Sawt al-Jihad,* the authoritative al-Qaeda Internet magazine, meaning that it reflects the prevailing views of the organization.

Naji's document, published in the spring of 2004, addresses the crisis and the opportunity posed by the tumult in the Arab world. "During our long journey, through victories and defeats, through the blood, severed limbs and skulls, some of the movements have disappeared and some have remained," he writes. "If we meditate on the factor common to the movements which have remained, we find that there is political action in addition to military action." Understanding the politics of the enemy, Naji suggests, is a necessary evil. "We urge that the leaders work to master political science just as they would work to master military science."

Control of the media is especially important in the anarchic period that the jihadi movement has entered, when people are outraged by the carnage. "If we succeed in the management of this savagery, that stage—by the permission of God—will be a bridge to the Islamic state which has been awaited since the fall of the caliphate," he proclaims. "If we fail—we seek refuge with God from that—it does not mean an end of the matter. Rather, this failure will lead to an increase in savagery."

Naji writes in the dry, oddly temperate style that characterizes many al-Qaeda strategy studies. And, like all jihadi theorists, he embeds his analysis in the tradition of Ibn Taymiyya, the thirteenth-century Arab theologian whose ideas undergird the Salafi jihadist tradition. However, Naji is also an attentive reader of Western thinkers; indeed, the thesis of "The Management of Savagery" is drawn from the observation of the Yale historian Paul Kennedy, in his book *The Rise and Fall of the Great Powers* (1987), which is that imperial overreach leads to the downfall of empires.

Naji began writing his study in 1998, when the jihad movement's most promising targets appeared to be Jordan, the countries of North Africa, Nigeria, Saudi Arabia, and Yemen—roughly the same countries that bin Laden later penciled in. Naji recommended that jihadis continually attack the vital economic centers of these countries, such as tourist sites and oil refineries, in order to make the regimes concentrate their forces, leaving their peripheries unprotected. Sensing weakness, Naji predicts, the people will lose confidence in their governments, which will respond with increasingly ineffective and alienating acts of repression. Eventually, the governments will lose control. Savagery will naturally follow, offering Islamists the opportunity to capture the allegiance of a population that is desperate for order. Even though the jihadis will have caused the chaos, that fact will be overlooked as the fighters impose security, provide food and medical treatment, and establish Islamic courts of justice.

After coalition forces overran al-Qaeda compounds in Afghanistan in late 2001, they seized thousands of pages of internal memoranda, records of strategy sessions and ethical debates, and military manuals, but not a single page devoted to the politics of al-Qaeda. Naji briefly addresses whether jihadis are prepared to run a state should they succeed in toppling one. He quotes a colleague who posed the question "Assuming that we get rid of the apostate regimes today, who will take over the ministry of agriculture, trade, economics, etc.?" Beyond the simplistic notion of imposing a caliphate and establishing the rule of Islamic law, the leaders of the organization appear never to have thought about the most basic facts of government. What kind of economic model would they follow? How would they cope with unemployment, so rampant in the Muslim world? Where do they stand on the environment? Health care? The truth, as Naji essentially concedes, is that the radical Islamists have no interest in government; they are interested only in jihad. In his book, Naji breezily answers his friend as follows: "It is not a prerequisite that the mujahid movement has to be prepared especially for agriculture, trade, and industry. . . . As for the one who manages the techniques in each ministry, he can be a paid employee who has no interest in policy and is not a member of the movement or the party. There are many examples of that and a proper explanation would take a long time."

FOUAD HUSSEIN, a radical Jordanian journalist, met Zarqawi and Maqdisi in 1996, when, he writes, "a career of trouble led me to Suwaqah Prison." He had published a series of articles criticizing the Jordanian government, and, in response, the authorities locked him up for a month. Since Zarqawi and Maqdisi were being held at the same jail, Hussein sought out interviews with them; eventually, Zarqawi served him tea while Maqdisi talked politics. Zarqawi mentioned that he had just been released from solitary confinement after more than eight months and had lost his toenails as a result of being tortured. The next week, Zarqawi was sent to solitary again, and his followers staged a riot. Hussein became the negotiator between the prisoners and the warden, who relented—an episode that cemented Hussein's standing among the radical Islamists.

In 2005, Hussein produced what is perhaps the most definitive outline of al-Qaeda's master plan: a book titled *Al-Zarqawi: The Second Generation of al-Qaeda*. Although it is largely a flattering biography of Zarqawi and his movement, Hussein also incorporates the insights of other al-Qaeda members—notably, Saif al-Adl, the security chief.

It is chilling to read this work and realize how some events hewed to al-Qaeda's forecasts. On the basis of interviews with Zarqawi and Adl, Hussein claims that dragging Iran into conflict with the United States was the key to al-Qaeda's strategy. Al-Qaeda, he writes, expects the Americans to go after Iran's principal ally in the region, Syria. The removal of the Assad regime—a longtime goal of jihadis— will allow the country to be infiltrated by al-Qaeda, putting the terrorists within reach, at last, of Israel.

Al-Qaeda's twenty-year plan, begun on September 11, inaugurated a stage that Hussein calls "The Awakening." The ideologues within al-Qaeda believed that "the Islamic nation was in a state of hibernation," because of repeated catastrophes inflicted upon Muslims by the West. By striking America—"the head of the serpent"—al-Qaeda caused the United States to "lose consciousness and act chaotically against those who attacked it. This entitled the party that hit the serpent to lead the Islamic nation." This first stage, says Hussein, ended in 2003, when American troops entered Baghdad.

The second stage, "Eye-Opening," would last until the end of 2006, Hussein writes. Iraq would become the recruiting ground for young men eager to attack America. The electronic jihad on the Internet would propagate al-Qaeda's ideas, and Muslims would be pressed to donate funds to make up for the seizure of terrorist assets by the West. The third stage, "Arising and Standing Up," would last from 2007 to 2010. Al-Qaeda's focus would be on Syria and Turkey, but it would also begin to directly confront Israel, in order to gain more credibility among the Muslim population.

In the fourth stage, lasting until 2013, al-Qaeda would bring about the demise of Arab governments. "The creeping loss of the regimes' power will lead to a steady growth in strength within al-Qaeda," Hussein predicts. Meanwhile, attacks against the Middle East petroleum industry would continue, and America's power would deteriorate through the constant expansion of the circle of confrontation. "By then, al-Qaeda will have completed its electronic capabilities, and it will be time to use them to launch electronic attacks to undermine the U.S. economy."

Then an Islamic caliphate can be declared—the fifth stage of al-Qaeda's grand plan. "At this stage, the Western fist in the Arab region will loosen, and Israel will not be able to carry out preemptive or precautionary strikes," Hussein writes. "The international balance will change." Al-Qaeda and the Islamist movement will attract powerful new economic allies, such as China, and the European Union will fall into disarray.

The sixth phase will be a period of "total confrontation," he predicts. The now established caliphate will form an Islamic army and will instigate a worldwide fight between the "believers" and the "non-believers." Hussein proclaims, "The world will realize the meaning of real terrorism." By 2020, "definitive victory" will have been achieved. Victory, according to the al-Qaeda ideologues, means that "falsehood will come to an end. . . . The Islamic state will lead the human race once again to the shore of safety and the oasis of happiness."

The Spymaster

In May 2007, Director of National Intelligence Michael McConnell, a soft-spoken South Carolinian, learned that Sunni insurgents in central Iraq had captured three U.S. soldiers. As a search team of six thousand American and Iraqi forces combed through Babil province, analysts at the National Security Agency, in Fort Meade, Maryland, began examining communications traffic in Iraq, hoping to pick up conversations among the soldiers' captors. To McConnell's consternation, such surveillance required a warrant—not because the kidnappers were entitled to constitutional protections but because their communications might incidentally pass electronically through U.S. circuits.

The kidnappings could have been just another barely noticed tragedy in a long, bloody war, but at that moment an important political debate was taking place in Washington. Lawmakers were trying to strike a balance between respecting citizens' privacy and helping law enforcement and intelligence officials protect the country against crime, terror, espionage, and treason. McConnell, who had been in office for less than three months when the soldiers were captured, was urging Congress to make a change in the 1978 Foreign Intelligence Surveillance Act, or FISA, which governs the process of eavesdropping on citizens and foreigners inside the United States and requires agencies to obtain a warrant within seventy-two hours after monitoring begins. The act was a response to abuses of the Nixon era, when the U.S. government turned its formidable surveillance powers against peace activists, reporters, religious groups, civil rights workers, politicians, and even a member of the Supreme Court. Over the years, the act had been amended many times, but McConnell believed that FISA—a law written before the age of cell phones, e-mail, and the web—was dangerously outmoded. "If we don't update FISA, the nation is significantly at risk," McConnell told me. He said that federal judges had recently decided, in a series of secret rulings, that any telephone transmission or e-mail that incidentally flowed into U.S. computer systems was potentially subject to judicial oversight. According to McConnell, the capacity of the NSA to monitor foreign-based communications had consequently been reduced by 70 percent. Now, he claimed, the lives of three American soldiers had been thrown onto the scale.

McConnell was the head of the sprawling assemblage of covert agencies known as the "intelligence community"—a term that first appeared in the minutes of a staff meeting of the Intelligence Advisory Committee in 1952. That year, President Truman signed a secret memorandum creating the NSA, which is still the largest of the sixteen intelligence bureaucracies. The Pentagon has a Defense Intelligence Agency, and each military branch has its own intelligence shop. There are three very expensive technical agencies: the NSA, which is responsible for code-breaking, code-making, communications monitoring, and information warfare; the National Geospatial-Intelligence Agency, which makes maps and analyzes surveillance photographs; and the National Reconnaissance Office, which provides satellite imagery. The Central Intelligence Agency is in charge of human intelligence on foreign targets, while the Defense Intelligence Agency conducts similar "humint" operations for the military. Domestic intelligence is handled by the Federal Bureau of Investigation, the Drug Enforcement Administration, and divisions of the Department of Homeland Security. The State Department has its own intelligence-analysis bureau, as do the Energy and Treasury Departments. The intelligence community employs more than a hundred thousand people, including tens of thousands of private contractors. And its official budget, which in 2007 was $43.5 billion, omits the military's intelligence operations, which, if included, would probably push the total annual cost past $50 billion—more than the government spends on energy, scientific research, or the federal court and prison systems.

To call the disparate intelligence bureaucracies a community suggests that they share a collegial spirit, but throughout their history these organizations have been brutally competitive, undermining one another and even hoarding vital information. Since the establishment of the CIA, in 1947, the fractious intelligence community has botched many of the major tasks assigned to it. Its failures include the Bay of Pigs invasion, the unforeseen collapse of the Soviet Union, the inability to prevent the September 11 attacks, and the catastrophic assessment that Iraq, under Saddam Hussein, possessed weapons of mass destruction. There have been successes—in 2006, American intelligence helped lead to the arrest in England of twenty-four conspirators who were plotting to blow up at least ten transatlantic airliners—but they don't outweigh the damage caused by bungled operations and misguided analysis. "We have such a huge infrastructure that adds so little to our understanding and frequently gets us in trouble," says Richard Clarke, who served as the counterterrorism coordinator under President Clinton and, until 2003, as a special advisor on the National Security Council in the Bush administration. "You're left with the impression that it wouldn't make any difference if they didn't exist."

Over the past sixty years, frustrated presidents and lawmakers have commissioned more than forty studies of the nation's intelligence organizations, to determine how to rearrange, reform, or even, in some cases, abolish them. Most of these studies have concluded that the rivalries and conflicting missions of the warring agencies could be resolved only by placing a single figure in charge. Yet until September 11, there was no political will to do so. Finally, in 2004, after the 9/11 Commission recommended the appointment of a powerful overseer, Congress passed the Intelligence Reform and Terrorism Prevention Act, which created the Office of the Director of National Intelligence, or ODNI. Dissenting lawmakers complained that the new office would simply add another tier of bureaucrats to an already congested roster. Indeed, although the 9/11 Commission suggested that the ODNI needed no more than a few hundred employees, it quickly expanded to some fifteen hundred. The CIA fiercely opposed the establishment of the new office, the leader of which became the official head of the intelligence community. Now the agency reports to the DNI, just as the intelligence branch of the Coast Guard does.

In April 2005, Congress confirmed John Negroponte, then the U.S. ambassador in Iraq, as the office's first director. General Michael Hayden, the head of the NSA, became his deputy. But Negroponte lasted only two years in the job before returning to the State Department, where he clearly felt more at home, and Hayden left to lead the CIA. There were few candidates eager to replace Negroponte in the last two years of an embattled, lame-duck administration.

The president turned to Mike McConnell, a retired admiral who had directed the NSA from 1992 to 1996 but was not well known outside the intelligence community. Sixty-three years old at the time, with pale, thin, sandy hair, blue eyes, and skin as pink as a baby's, McConnell was part of the featureless parade of management consultants and security experts who work for federal contractors based in northern Virginia, near CIA headquarters. His friends describe him as quick-minded and crafty, with an unusual ability to synthesize large amounts of information, regularly lugging two briefcases home each night. Like many retired spooks, he was reaping the benefits of his government experience and his top-secret clearance, finally making real money—$2 million a year as a senior vice president of Booz Allen Hamilton—and looking toward a comfortable retirement, perhaps in a cabin in the Carolinas, where he could build birdhouses (he and his wife, Terry, are members of a society whose purpose is to protect the Eastern bluebird) and listen to soft rock and rhythm and blues. He claims to be a terrific dancer.

McConnell had previously been offered the DNI job and turned it down. One of the major limitations of the post was that 80 percent of the intelligence budget was controlled by the secretary of defense, and in September 2006, that was Donald Rumsfeld, whose contempt for the CIA and other civilian intelligence agencies was well known. Two months later, however, Rumsfeld resigned, and Robert M. Gates replaced him. Vice President Dick Cheney approached McConnell again, over Christmas, and he asked for time to think about it.

He called Gates. The two men had known each other since the first Gulf War, when Gates worked in the White House as deputy national security adviser and McConnell was the intelligence officer for the Joint Chiefs of Staff. Gates, a former CIA director, had been offered the DNI job before Negroponte, and also turned it down. "Mike had a lot of the same concerns I had with the 2004 act, in terms of the ability to get things done," Gates told me. "Under the legislation, the DNI had the responsibility for executing the intelligence budget and assuring that everybody in the community obeyed the law, but he didn't have the authority to fire anybody." The community that both men had spent decades serving was in tumult. Morale was low, especially after the WMD disgrace, when many Americans blamed the intelligence community for dragging the country into an unnecessary conflict. A number of experienced officers had walked away in shame and frustration. Moreover, the nation that had launched a war in Iraq because of faulty intelligence was now losing the battle, in part because it was so poorly prepared to understand the enemy. Al-Qaeda, which the CIA and the military thought they had vanquished in Afghanistan, was reconstituting itself there, as well as in Pakistan, Iraq, Somalia, and North Africa. Meanwhile, North Korea had exploded a low-yield nuclear bomb and China was emerging as a rival to American supremacy. The need for reliable intelligence was arguably greater than it had been during the Cold War, when the enemy was easy to find, if hard to destroy; now the enemy might be a small group of lightly armed men who could be anywhere, and whose capacity to cause great harm had been convincingly demonstrated.

Gates informed McConnell that he had recommended McConnell's old friend Lieutenant General James Clapper to be under secretary of defense for intelligence. "I thought that, between Hayden, McConnell, Clapper, and myself, we could reach an agreement on some of the issues that hadn't been resolved by the legislation," Gates recalled. If McConnell and Clapper took office, each of the major agencies would be led by a military man. This unique alignment, Gates and McConnell believed, would offer the best chance that the intelligence community would ever have to reform itself. Unsurprisingly, the model they had in mind was the American armed forces.

All four men were insiders who understood the culture of intelligence gathering. "There hadn't been this kind of alignment of stars in the more than forty years of my experience in the intelligence community," Gates said. The question was whether they could be sufficiently objective and forceful to reshape a subterranean branch of government that had failed so deeply in its mission.

McConnell accepted the post and in February 2007, he was sworn in. Clapper's wife gave McConnell and her husband clocks that counted down to the last second of the Bush administration, on January 20, 2009. That was the amount of time, McConnell believed, that he had to lead a revolution.

"I DON'T KNOW much about you," I admitted to McConnell when we met for the first of a series of discussions in Washington. Despite his long career, there was little in the public record about his background.

"That's a good thing," he said. "I'm a spy."

He told me that he was born in Greenville, South Carolina, in 1943. "Working class. My father grew up in a mill village. In the Depression, he worked sixty hours [a week] for six bucks. His view of the world was that wasn't right. So he decided to become a union organizer." McConnell's father campaigned against child labor and was an outspoken proponent of civil rights. "He pushed back against everything," McConnell recalled. "When I was ten, maybe thirteen years old, he described to me bureaucratic behavior and people being afraid of change. He said that people never accept change willingly. I remember it as clear as day, thinking, Change will never frighten me."

McConnell's parents were poor—"They had, basically, nothing"— so he got a student loan and a job and went to North Greenville Junior College, where he was elected student body president; he then transferred to Furman University, a private college, living in a closet in the gym during his first semester while he managed the basketball team. In his senior year, he married his childhood sweetheart, Suzanne Gideon, in the first of two marriages. It was 1965, during the Vietnam War.

"Where I grew up, in South Carolina, there's a war, you're supposed to go," McConnell said. He joined the navy and, in August 1967, went to Vietnam, spending a year on a boat patrolling the Mekong River. The lesson he learned from Vietnam was "Be careful what you get into." He went on, "During the latter stages of Vietnam, soldiers were fragging their own officers, and drugs were rampant. The military was a shambles." Like the agencies of the intelligence community, the military's various branches undermined rather than helped one another. As McConnell put it, "The navy has its own ground force, its own air force, and its own ships. So the view of the navy is: Why do we need anybody else?"

A new generation of leaders at the Pentagon, McConnell said, decided that the military needed to be reformed. "Guys like Colin Powell, they just made a decision—'This is our army, we're taking it back.' And they did. What that led to was an all-volunteer force, the most professional army in history." In 1986 the Goldwater-Nichols Act restructured the military, despite resistance from the leaders of the uniformed branches. The law established the secretary of defense as the top decision-maker and awarded battlefield commanders more control. The 1991 Gulf War, with its coordinated use of overwhelming power, provided a stunning example of the restructured armed forces. McConnell recalled, "Every service chief stood up and said, 'This is the greatest thing to happen to the United States military.'"

The 2004 intelligence legislation was not nearly as comprehensive as Goldwater-Nichols, but McConnell came into office with a slate of reforms he called the 100-Day Plan, modeled on the streamlined military command. He proposed a "culture of collaboration," which would require agencies to work together. The cost of one agency hiding intelligence from others was made dismally clear in the June 2005 inspector general report on the performance of the CIA before 9/11. It revealed that in March 2000 between fifty and sixty individuals within the agency had known that two future al-Qaeda hijackers had infiltrated America, but nobody at the CIA had informed the FBI until it was too late to find them.

In August, just before the congressional recess, members of the House and the Senate were frantically seeking a compromise on a FISA-reform bill. McConnell explained one day over lunch at his office, "When the law was passed, in seventy-eight, almost all international communication was wireless," meaning that it relied mainly on satellites. "Today, ninety percent goes through a glass pipe"—a fiber-optic cable. "So it went from almost all wireless to almost all wire." He put down his sandwich and walked over to a world map on

his wall. "Terrorist on a cell phone, right here"—he pointed at Iraq—
"talking to a tower, happens all the time, no warrant. Tower goes up
to a microwave tower, no warrant. Goes up to a satellite, back to the
ground station, no warrant. Now, let us suppose that it goes up to
a satellite, and in the process it does this"—his finger darted to the
U.S. before angling back to Pakistan. "Gotta have a warrant! So it was
crazy."

The changes to FISA that McConnell proposed were minor, in his
view. "Three things we wanted," he told me, in characteristic bulletin
language. "First, we had to have a situation where it doesn't require
us to get a warrant for a foreign person in a foreign country. Second
point, we need the cooperation of the private sector. The private sector
is being sued for allegedly cooperating with the government." He was
referring to reports that even before 9/11, many of America's major
telecommunications companies had diverted virtually all records of
telephone and e-mail traffic from their routers into NSA data banks,
where it could be stored and examined. McConnell wanted liability
protection not only for the companies' future cooperation but for
their past actions as well. McConnell's third point was uncontrover-
sial: he wanted a warrant to be required whenever a person in the U.S.
was the object of surveillance. However, the reform bill before Congress, which Democrats in both houses had rejected, did not shield
Americans—travelers, soldiers, exchange students, diplomats—who
happened to be outside the United States.

As the vote on the legislation approached, the Bush administration
let it be known that threats from al-Qaeda had increased in number,
also claiming that there had even been signs of a plot to attack Congress. Many lawmakers felt manipulated and suspicious. In a meeting
with McConnell, I said, "According to Senator Harry Reid, the legislation 'authorizes warrantless searches and surveillance of American
phone calls, e-mails, homes, offices, and—'"

"Totally untrue!" McConnell exclaimed. "I'm telling you, if you're
in the United States you have to have a warrant. Authorized by the
court. Period!" Critics argued, however, that the proposed law left a
loophole. If the attorney general and the DNI decided that a foreign
target was a subject of interest, the law permitted them to conduct
surveillance on any Americans who might be in touch with that per-

son, to break into their homes, to open their mail, to examine their medical records—all without a warrant. Legislators worried that the law would permit the intelligence community to "reverse-target" Americans who happened to be making international calls but who had nothing to do with terrorism.

"That's a violation of the Constitution," McConnell said. "We can't do that, wouldn't do that." Naturally, some innocent Americans would be overheard, he conceded. "What do you do about it? It's called 'minimize.' Courts reviewed it—it works. You get an inadvertent collection? When you recognize what it is, you destroy it. Exception: let's suppose it was terrorism or crime. In that case, as a community, it is our obligation to report it. But to claim that this community is monitoring the e-mail and telephone calls of millions of Americans, and that we're doing reverse-targeting, is clearly absurd."

McConnell admitted that Congress had reason to be wary of the intelligence community's intentions. "In the forties, fifties, sixties, seventies—every president used either law enforcement or intel to conduct activities in the interest of national security by tapping telephones of Americans," he said. FISA had been a useful corrective. He summed up the law's intent as follows: "You intel guys go off and do your foreign-intel mission, but if you ever do it in this country you gotta have a warrant, okay?" Six weeks after 9/11, Congress passed the USA Patriot Act. The FBI was given expanded authority to issue "national security letters," a form of subpoena entitling the bureau to pry into the private transactions of American citizens and visitors who were not the subject of a criminal investigation and might not even have been suspected of being terrorists or spies. There was no judicial oversight. Unlike a FISA warrant, a national security letter does not permit the government to eavesdrop on phone calls or read e-mails, but it does allow the examination of phone records, bank accounts, web searches, and credit-card purchases. The FBI is required to prove a specific national security need before serving such letters, but a recent Justice Department audit had uncovered dozens of cases in which bureau officials appeared to have violated this rule. I asked McConnell how the new FISA law would be different. How could Americans be sure that the intelligence community wouldn't commit even more intimate invasions of privacy?

"A national security letter was a whole new tool," he explained. "Now, did the FBI have the structure and experience and time to learn, the way you do in the FISA world? In fact they did not. It was used in a sloppy way." He said that the FISA system, by contrast, was governed by a strict protocol that had been in place for decades. (A special FISA court in Washington, established in 1978, confidentially weighs all requests for FISA warrants. It has rarely turned down such requests.)

On August 1, McConnell and his staff stayed up all night preparing their position on FISA for lawmakers. Despite his long government service, McConnell had never been enmeshed in a partisan legislative debate, and his inexperience showed. The next afternoon, top Democratic leaders gathered in the office of Nancy Pelosi, the Speaker of the House, and placed a call to McConnell. The Democrats presented him with their proposal, which stated, among other things, that if Congress was going to allow the president to conduct warrantless surveillance against foreign targets the power had to be limited to matters of terrorism. McConnell responded that this would hamper the ability of the intelligence community to collect information about dangerous foreign powers such as Iran and North Korea. He also rejected language in the bill requiring the attorney general and the FISA court to establish guidelines for which kinds of contact between a targeted foreigner and a U.S. person merited a warrant; he called the idea a "poison pill." The Democrats ceded both points. He pledged to get back to the leaders half an hour later, with a new draft of their bill that reflected his concerns.

When McConnell didn't call back, the Democrats telephoned his office. His assistant told them that he was talking to the White House. McConnell finally called back at around seven. He apologized, saying that he had been on the phone with "the other side" and that he could no longer abide by their compromise. He told the Democrats, "I've spent forty years of my life in this business, and I've been shot at during war. I've never felt so much pressure in my life."

On Friday, August 3, in a furious scramble, the Democrats and the Republicans pushed rival bills to the floor. McConnell happened to be on Capitol Hill, explaining some of the technical language to the senators, and was surprised to discover that the Senate was about to vote. "At that point, I had seen neither version," he said. Each side claimed to be sponsoring "McConnell's bill." McConnell wrote a note officially rejecting the Democratic version, saying that it "creates significant uncertainty."

The Republican bill, called the Protect America Act, passed that night. The next day, the House, desperate to adjourn, passed the legislation, which was designated a placeholder that would expire in six months, allowing lawmakers to deliberate more fully after their break.

"Then all the press stuff started," McConnell said. " 'The White House rolled McConnell!' 'The naive admiral learns a hard political lesson.' I guess the part that bothered me a bit was the rhetoric coming off the Hill, impugning my integrity, saying I was less than honest." When asked if he had bowed to the White House, McConnell said, "Nothing could be further from the truth."

SIX MORNINGS a week, at 6:00 a.m., a dark armored Suburban arrives at McConnell's home in northern Virginia and takes him to the White House. On the way, he reads summaries of operational and intelligence traffic from the past twenty-four hours. The presidential briefing starts between seven thirty and eight and rarely lasts longer than an hour. In addition to Bush and Cheney, the core group includes Joshua Bolten, Bush's chief of staff, and Stephen Hadley, the national security advisor. By nine thirty, McConnell is back in the Suburban, headed to Bolling Air Force Base. His temporary office is in the Defense Intelligence Agency building there, a chilly steel-and-glass structure with a Scud missile erected beside the elevator bank and a pair of Saddam Hussein's gold-plated automatic weapons displayed in the lobby. His office is spare, except for a photograph of his children and a few treasured artifacts—a Yemeni dagger and a blue vase from the People's Liberation Army of China. Through the large windows, one can see planes landing at Washington's National Airport and marines running around a track. He frequently leaves the office to testify before Congress, or flies off for a speech. He usually arrives home around eight. "My wife gets about fifteen minutes a day," he said. "She's not a happy camper. Now, I'm not complaining. This is a demanding job, but I love doing it."

McConnell often spoke admiringly of General Colin Powell, who, as chairman of the Joint Chiefs of Staff in 1990, hired McConnell, then a navy captain, to be his intelligence officer. "I was impressed by his reputation and by his interview," Powell told me. McConnell was well versed in technical intelligence, but not in other important areas, such as ground warfare. That didn't seem like such a liability at the time. "It was going to be a quiet summer, so I hired him," Powell said, laughing. Four days later, Saddam Hussein's troops invaded Kuwait.

The government was desperate to determine whether Iraqi troops were merely on a maneuver or were poised for invasion. Cheney, then the secretary of defense, was demanding a verdict, and the intelligence community was typically reluctant to render one. Twenty-two hours before the invasion, McConnell correctly judged that Saddam intended to move into Kuwait. His willingness to take a stand earned Cheney's admiration. Soon after the onset of Desert Storm, the American-led effort that repelled the Iraqi invasion, Powell had so much confidence in the navy man's grasp of army maneuvers that he charged McConnell with delivering daily press briefings. "He got so good that he started being parodied by *Saturday Night Live*," Powell recalled. "That's when I knew we'd made a good decision."

In 1992, both Powell and Cheney sponsored McConnell's candidacy to become the head of the NSA, even though McConnell had been promoted to a one-star admiral only nine months earlier. By law, the NSA position requires three stars; thanks to his powerful patrons, McConnell received two additional ones.

When McConnell took over the NSA, the Cold War had just ended and Congress had decided to extract a "peace dividend" from the intelligence community. New hiring came to a near-halt just as the security challenges became far more diverse. There was a surfeit of Russian linguists but scarcely anyone who, for instance, could speak Serbo-Croatian, during the breakup of the former Yugoslavia, or the Creole dialect of Haiti, when the Clinton administration sent troops there to restore order. The agency had to hire Haitian gardeners in

Washington and put them to work listening to intercepts at NSA headquarters.

There was, however, an even greater challenge for the NSA than hiring new linguists. The Internet and e-mail were radically expanding the abilities of terrorists and rogue states to communicate. "When I went there in ninety-two, the Internet existed—it was called Arpanet—but the World Wide Web did not," McConnell recalled. "Then the web made the Internet accessible for everybody. My world exploded."

ONE AFTERNOON, as McConnell and I were walking back to his office from the cafeteria, we passed the security room, where a pair of guards monitored half a dozen screens displaying video of the building's grounds. The setup was, by Hollywood standards, disappointingly low-tech. I asked McConnell if he'd seen *The Bourne Ultimatum*, in which Matt Damon's character is pursued by CIA officers with instant global access to surveillance cameras, banking transactions, and passport controls. "Yeah, we can't do that," McConnell admitted. "That's all horse pucky."

The intelligence community lags significantly behind private industry in the development and use of innovative technology. "There have been breakthroughs," General Clapper, the defense undersecretary, told me, citing the use of cell phones and computers on the battlefield, although he acknowledged that al-Qaeda has also made creative use of those technologies. By comparison, during the Second World War the U.S. government developed advanced radar and jet engines, and invented the atomic bomb.

After the 2004 reforms, which mandated greater information sharing, the community turned to private industry for help in creating the National Counterterrorism Center, which is at an undisclosed location in northern Virginia. An engineer from Walt Disney Imagineering, the theme-park developer, designed it. "Even the chairs in the lunchroom are the same ones we had at the Disney Studios," a former Disney executive, who now works at the center, told me. "The only difference is these chairs don't have the mouse ears." She was one of several former Disney employees who signed up for government service after 9/11. The fantasy worlds that Disney creates have a surprising amount in common with the ideal universe envisaged by the intelligence community, in which environments are carefully controlled and people are closely observed, and no one seems to mind.

The center has a futuristic videoconference room, featuring a shape-changing table with pop-up computer consoles. Three times a day, analysts gather around it to discuss the "threat matrix." The heart of the building is the operations center, where analysts from various agencies are illuminated by the lights of multiple computer monitors. When I was there, Fox News was playing on a huge television screen at the front of the room.

Disney Imagineering also provided the ODNI's first science and technology director, Eric Haseltine, who joined the NSA after September 11. He was dismayed by the lumbering pace of innovation, the absence of collaboration, and the lack of thought about how new products might be employed. Much of the intelligence community is technophobic and hamstrung by security concerns. Many offices didn't even have Internet connections. "Insufficient attention was being paid to the end user," Haseltine said. "At Disney, we had to make technology work for a four-year-old and a grandmother instantly, and be fun."

Haseltine and his successor, Steve Nixon, set up an intelligence version of DARPA, the Defense Advanced Research Projects Agency, which was created in 1958, after the Soviet launch of Sputnik, and led to the development of the Internet, the Global Positioning System (GPS), night-vision goggles, Predator drones, and stealth aircraft. (After 9/11, DARPA also gave birth to Total Information Awareness, a program designed to sort through vast sets of data about individuals, including Americans, in order to identify potential terrorists. Congress killed the program in 2003, but many of its capabilities—including its data-mining software—were passed along to other departments, in particular to the NSA.) Like DARPA, the ODNI version sponsors radical innovation—"game-changing breakthroughs," as Nixon put it. The most significant product of this effort so far is Argus, a program that monitors foreign news reports and other open sources looking for evidence of bird die-offs, crop failures, an unusual number of death notices—anything that could provide an early warning of an epidemic, nuclear accident, or environmental catastrophe. The program, which began in 2004, spotted the appearance of avian flu in 2006 and an outbreak of Ebola in Angola a year later. Argus monitors more than a million web pages in twenty-eight languages and in nearly every country in the world—except the United States, where it was assumed that such scrutiny would stir concerns about domestic spying.

The Defense Department detected three million unauthorized probes of its computer networks every day in 2007; the State Department fended off two million. Sometimes, these turned into full-scale attacks, such as an assault that spring on the Pentagon that required fifteen hundred computers to be taken off-line. Russian spying had not decreased at all since the end of the Cold War, McConnell said; and there was an immense challenge posed by the Chinese. Ed Giorgio, a security consultant who worked at the NSA under McConnell, and who is the only person to have been both the nation's chief code breaker and its chief code maker, explained, "There are forty thousand Chinese hackers who are collecting intelligence off U.S. information systems and those of our partners. How many of them can read English? Almost every one of them. If you ask how many intelligence-gathering people are doing similar things in Mike's vast empire, the answer would be tiny. And you won't find any who understand Mandarin. We should never get into a hacking war with the Chinese."

"Have we gotten meaningful information through torture?" I asked McConnell.

"We don't torture," he responded automatically.

"Okay, through aggressive interrogation techniques."

"'Aggressive' is your word," he said. "Have we gotten meaningful information? You betcha. Tons! Does it save lives? Tons! We've gotten incredible information. Khalid Sheikh Mohammed. K.S.M. No. 3. Go pull his testimony. A lot of what we know about al-Qaeda and what we shut down came out of that." (The reliability of the confession of Mohammed, who was waterboarded 183 times, has been widely questioned.) McConnell peered over his glasses. "And this was a test for Mike McConnell. When Abu Ghraib happened, my view was that we had lost the moral high ground."

McConnell had not yet returned to government when the Abu

Ghraib scandal broke, but after becoming director of national intelligence he received the secret protocol that the White House had devised to govern future interrogations. Shortly after Attorney General Alberto Gonzales came into office, in February 2005, he issued an opinion endorsing the most brutal interrogation techniques that the CIA had ever used. According to *The New York Times*, the agency had learned some of these methods from Egyptian and Saudi intelligence officials; others were drawn from old Soviet techniques. Besides waterboarding, an act of simulated drowning that was used in the Spanish Inquisition, the methods included stripping a suspect naked and placing him in a cold cell; manacling him in a painful posture; subjecting him to deafening rock music; and slapping his head. Any one of these abusive techniques would likely violate the international legal standards banning torture, such as the Geneva Conventions. The CIA had used "special methods of questioning" on about thirty people, McConnell learned.

"I had to sign off on that program," McConnell told me. "The president said we don't torture anyone, but I had to convince myself by going through the whole process." He pored over the procedures that had been secretly authorized by the Bush administration. "I sat down with the doctors and the medical personnel who oversee the process," he said. "Our policies are not torture."

I asked how he defined torture.

"There's a history of people making claims that it's not torture if you don't force the failure of a major organ," McConnell said, referring to the infamous 2002 memo by John Yoo, a Justice Department lawyer, who argued that an interrogation technique was torture only when it was as painful as organ failure or resulted in death. "My view is, that's kind of absurd. It's pretty simple. Is it excruciatingly painful to the point of forcing someone to say something because of the pain?" McConnell leaned forward confidentially. "Now, how descriptive do I want to be with you? I don't want to tell you everything, and why is that? Look, these guys talk because, among other things, they're scared."

McConnell asserted that it was not difficult to evaluate the truthfulness of a confession, even a coerced one. "We can tell in minutes if they are lying," he claimed. "One, you know a lot. And you know when someone is giving you information that is not connecting up to what you know. You also know when to use a polygraph."

McConnell refused to specify what new methods had been approved for the CIA. "There are techniques to get the information, and when they get the information it has saved lives," he said vaguely. "We have people walking around in this country that are alive today because this process happened."

Couldn't the information be obtained through other means?

"No," McConnell said. "You can say that absolutely." He again cited the case of Khalid Sheikh Mohammed. "He would not have talked to us in a hundred years. Tough guy. Absolutely committed. He had this mental image of himself as a warrior and a martyr. No way he would talk to us."

I mentioned McConnell's hero, General Powell, whose disastrous speech to the United Nations, in February 2003, made the case to the world for invading Iraq—a case founded on faulty intelligence. Part of Powell's presentation was based on the testimony of Ibn al-Sheikh al-Libi, an al-Qaeda operative who was captured by Pakistani forces in December 2001. The Pakistanis turned him over to the Americans. According to Jack Cloonan, a former FBI agent involved in the interrogation, Libi was providing useful and accurate intelligence until the CIA took custody of him. The agency placed him inside a plywood box and sent him to Egypt to be tortured. (An agency spokesman said, "The CIA does not transport individuals anywhere to be tortured." Michael Scheuer, who is the former head of the CIA's Alec Station, devoted to tracking down Osama bin Laden, told my *New Yorker* colleague Jane Mayer that Egypt was favored as a rendition destination because you could send a list of questions in the morning and get the answers in the afternoon.) Libi told his interrogators that the Iraqi military had trained two al-Qaeda associates in chemical and biological warfare. This was the basis of Colin Powell's claim that Saddam had weapons of mass destruction and was working with al-Qaeda. Neither assertion was true. How could we ever trust information obtained under torture when such methods had already led us into a catastrophic war?

"Now, wait a minute," McConnell said. "You allege torture. I don't know. Maybe it was. I don't know." He wasn't in government at the time.

I asked what personal experiences informed his views.

"What do you mean?"

"Have you ever been through the SERE program?" I was referring to the military's Survival, Evasion, Resistance and Escape protocol.

McConnell nodded. "I've been tortured," he said.

"Tell me about it."

"It was preparing for Vietnam. You had to go through jungle training, get slapped around, knocked down, put in a box, physically abused," he said. "That's to prepare you for what the enemy might do to you." McConnell was tossed into a covered pit with a snake. "They beat us up reasonably well," he said. However, he always knew that he was not going to die.

Waterboarding was not a part of the training when McConnell went through SERE, although it sometimes has been. "You know what waterboarding is?" he asked. "You lay somebody on this table, or put them in an inclined position, and put a washcloth over their face, and you just drip water right here." He pointed to his nostrils. "Try it! What happens is, water will go up your nose. And so you will get the sensation of potentially drowning. That's all waterboarding is."

I asked if he considered that torture.

McConnell refused to answer directly, but he said, "My own definition of torture is something that would cause excruciating pain."

Did waterboarding fit that description?

Referring to his teenage days as a lifeguard, he said, "I know one thing. I'm a water-safety instructor, but I cannot swim without covering my nose. I don't know if it's some deviated septum or mucous membrane, but water just rushes in." For him, therefore, "waterboarding would be excruciating. If I had water draining into my nose, oh God, I just can't imagine how painful! Whether it's torture by anybody else's definition, for me it would be torture."

I queried McConnell again, later, about his views on waterboarding, since this exchange seemed to suggest that he personally condemned it. He rejected that interpretation. "You can do waterboarding lots of different ways," he said. "I assume you can get to the point that a person is actually drowning." That would certainly be torture, he said. The definition didn't seem very different from John Yoo's. The reason that he couldn't be more specific, McConnell said, was that "if it ever is determined to be torture, there will be a huge penalty to be paid for anyone engaging in it."

IN EARLY SEPTEMBER 2007, German authorities arrested three Islamic radicals who were allegedly planning terrorist strikes against an American military base and the Frankfurt airport. In a hearing of the Senate Homeland Security and Governmental Affairs Committee, on September 10, Senator Joseph Lieberman asked McConnell if the temporary FISA legislation that Congress had just passed contributed to the arrests of those men. "Yes, sir, it did," McConnell replied, explaining that by monitoring the communications of the underground cell, the United States learned that the men had already obtained explosive liquids. "The German authorities decided to move," he said.

In fact, the information about the German cell had been obtained under the previous FISA law. McConnell conceded the point two days later, after an article in the *Times* questioned his claim.

Later that month, McConnell appeared before congressional committees, seeking to make the provisional Protect America Act a permanent law. He underscored the need for FISA reform by citing the example of the three kidnapped American soldiers in Iraq. (Though it was not known at the time, the soldiers had already been killed after extensive torture. Their bodies were later recovered.) In a hearing of the House Intelligence Committee, McConnell asserted that bureaucratic delays caused by requesting a FISA warrant had slowed the search in the critical moments after the soldiers' capture. This argument made a deep impression on the legislators. Representative Heather Wilson, of New Mexico, said to McConnell, "We had U.S. soldiers who were captured in Iraq by insurgents and . . . we weren't able to listen to their communications. Is that correct?" She asked, "If it was your kid, is that good enough?"

I asked McConnell about the relevance of the soldiers' kidnapping, since the FISA law allowed a three-day grace period after the start of monitoring to obtain a warrant. "When people hear that story, they say, 'Well, don't you have emergency authority?'" McConnell responded. "Sure we do. But the emergency authority still has to go through a process. Somebody's gotta approve it."

He refused to be more specific about what, if anything, had prevented the intelligence community from monitoring the kidnappers immediately. "If you understand it, and you write it down, then the bad guys understand it," he said cryptically. "I've told you that this debate, this debate is going to cost American lives." He tapped the table for emphasis. "This debate is going to cost American lives!"

McConnell returned for another hearing on September 25. Many Democrats remained angry with him over his retreat from the compromise bill during the August FISA debate. "You gave assurances that were not fulfilled, and made agreements that were not kept," Senator Jay Rockefeller, of West Virginia, had written him during the summer recess. Senator Sheldon Whitehouse, of Rhode Island, echoed these complaints. "The stampede worked," he wrote in a note. "You won. But you did so at a substantial price, one that will be paid in rancor, suspicion, and distrust."

Such emotions were very much in evidence as McConnell sat at the witness table in a wood-paneled hearing room. The glowering face of Senator Patrick Leahy, of Vermont, loomed over the dais. Before administering the oath to McConnell, he chided, "I hope we'll not hear any more irresponsible rhetoric about congressional inquiries risking American lives."

Many Democrats clearly regretted passing the temporary FISA bill. Leahy, in his introduction, said that the act "provides no meaningful check by the FISA court, or by the Congress for that matter." Shortly after McConnell began his opening statement, Leahy testily cut him off. He mentioned McConnell's mistaken testimony about the relevance of the Protect America Act to the recent arrests in Germany. "Now, I'm just wondering, why did you testify to something that was false?" McConnell's ears turned bright red. He said that he had been referring to FISA in general, not the new reforms.

Leahy referred to an attorney in his home state who was representing a client detained at the American-run prison in Guantánamo Bay, Cuba. "He's worried that his calls regarding his client are being monitored by the government," Leahy said. "He makes calls overseas, including to Afghanistan, on behalf of his client. . . . You can see why people worry."

That month, McConnell's office was forced to make another embarrassing disclosure. Silvestre Reyes, the House Intelligence Committee chairman, demanded that the ODNI release a time line of the kidnapping of the American soldiers in Iraq. McConnell had earlier testified that it took "somewhere in the neighborhood of twelve hours" to get the attorney general to authorize an emergency FISA wiretap on insurgents.

The ODNI's time line showed that the soldiers were kidnapped south of Baghdad on May 12. Over the next two days, intelligence officials picked up signals that they believed were coming from the kidnappers, and they received FISA authorization to target the communications of insurgents. The record shows that the intelligence community had immediately assigned all available assets to search for the missing soldiers.

Then, on May 15, at 10:00 a.m., leaders from several key intelligence agencies met to discuss other options for "enhanced" surveillance. (McConnell would not disclose what form of additional monitoring was being explored.) By 1:00 p.m., the NSA had determined that all the requirements for an emergency FISA authorization had been met. But intelligence officials and lawyers continued to debate minute legal issues for four more hours. At 5:15 p.m., hours after the NSA had made its determination, and three days after the soldiers had disappeared, Justice Department lawyers delayed the process further by deciding that they needed to obtain direct authorization from Attorney General Gonzales, who was in Texas making a speech. Gonzales finally called back, at 7:18 p.m., and within twenty minutes the enhanced surveillance began. Internal wrangling between the Justice Department and the intelligence community retarded the intensified monitoring of the insurgents and exposed the confusion over the limits of American law when applied to a desperate situation in a foreign country and underscored the need for legal clarity.

Despite his missteps, McConnell had so far succeeded in winning every important point in the FISA debate. The bills that were under consideration awarded the intelligence community nearly as much authority as it enjoyed under the president's secret wiretapping program, although with somewhat more supervision and with the stipulation that warrants be obtained to monitor Americans inside the country. The battle harmed McConnell's reputation, however. "It is convenient to say, 'McConnell was a bad guy, McConnell broke faith'—it's easy to say that because they lost!" McConnell said. "We went to the mat, and they lost."

McConnell forced a debate upon the country that it was reluctant to have. In agreeing to reform FISA along the lines that he proposed, Congress acknowledged that technology had created new tools for terrorists and made a salad out of existing laws that distinguished between foreign and domestic intelligence. Instantaneous global communications, cell phones, the free flow of commercial data, an untethered Internet, and the unprecedented ease of travel have erased the once rigid distinction between what is native and what is foreign. American law needed to reflect these changes. But the reforms leave it up to the intelligence community to decide whether to monitor an American's international communications without a warrant and what to do with that knowledge. Moreover, by giving immunity to telecommunications companies for future actions, the legislation pressures them to turn over to the government any and all communication records, whenever they are asked for.

Unfortunately, intelligence officials have a poor record of safeguarding civil liberties within the country, nor do Americans have any obvious recourse if they learn that they have been spied upon.

When McConnell and I first met, he defended the intelligence community's vast power to monitor the international phone calls and e-mails of American citizens. To many, the program seemed to violate the spirit of FISA, because Americans were clearly involved in the conversations. McConnell didn't see it that way. "There's no spying on Americans," he had told me. "The issue was if a known bad guy, somebody associated with al-Qaeda, calls into the United States, the president authorized the community to monitor that call. If you have a different political point of view, you turn that into 'spying on Americans.'"

"Let me make a disclosure," I said. "I have been monitored." I told him that while I was researching *The Looming Tower*, a book about al-Qaeda, the FBI had come to my house, in Austin, to ask about some calls that I had made from my home office. I also said that a contact in the intelligence community had read to me a summary of a telephone conversation that I had from my home with a source in Egypt.

"I'm not surprised at that," McConnell said. "Because you were getting a phone call from some telephone number that's associated with some known outfit—okay, that's monitored. In my view, it should be."

Actually, I had placed the call.

On another occasion, at McConnell's prompting I described more fully what had happened. After I published a profile of Ayman al-Zawahiri, the deputy of bin Laden, in *The New Yorker*, in February 2002, I was asked by one of his relatives, a respected architect in Cairo who had been a useful source, if I could learn whether all of Zawahiri's children were dead. An FBI source told me that they were, and that there was no reason the family shouldn't know that. I relayed the news to the architect. (The FBI official turned out to be wrong.) Following that, a different source in the intelligence community told me that a summary of my conversation was archived in an internal database. I was surprised, because the FISA law stated that my part of the conversation should have been "minimized"—redacted or rendered anonymous—because I am an American citizen.

"He's a terrorist, or he's associated with terrorists," McConnell said of my Egyptian contact. "Now, if I'm targeting, I'm looking at his number. If he places a call, I listen. If he gets called, I listen. I don't know who is going to call him, but once I got it, I gotta deal with it. Turns out it is Larry Wright. You would have been reported as 'U.S. Person 1.' You would never have been identified, except if the FBI learns that this unidentified U.S. person is talking to a known terrorist. Then the FBI would go in and request the identity of U.S. 1. The NSA would have to go through a process to determine if the request was legitimate. So here's what I think—I'm guessing. You called a bad guy, the system listened, tried to sort it out, and they did an intel report because it had foreign-intelligence value. That's our mission."

I then told him about the FBI officials who visited my house. "They were members of the Joint Terrorism Task Force," I said. They wanted to know about phone calls made to a solicitor in England who represented several jihadis I had interviewed for my book.

"Now if you ever became a target for surveillance, they would go get a warrant and tap your telephone," McConnell said. "But they would have to have probable cause to do that."

"What bothers me is that my daughter's name came up in this," I said. The agents had told me they believed that she was the one making the calls. That was ridiculous, but it placed her on the F.B.I.'s link chart as an al-Qaeda connection. "Her name is not on any of our phones," I continued. "So how did her name arise?"

"I don't know," McConnell admitted. "Maybe you mentioned her name."

"That troubles me," I said.

"It may be troublesome, it may not be," McConnell said. "You don't know."

IN 2005 the intelligence community informed President Bush that the greatest danger in the Middle East came from Iran. A National Intelligence Estimate (NIE) on the subject declared that Iran intended to build a nuclear weapon. Some of that information came from a purloined laptop containing drawings of an implosion device and information about the history of the Iranian nuclear effort. But there was little supporting evidence, and the president was frustrated that reliable intelligence was so difficult to obtain. Soon afterward, the CIA created the Iran Operations Division. There was already an Iran mission manager in the ODNI, whose job was to coordinate all the available resources in the community.

Those efforts were being folded into a new NIE on Iran, which had been demanded by Congress; the report, expected in the spring of 2007, was mysteriously delayed. In mid-November, McConnell said that he did not intend to declassify any part of the NIE. On occasion, the key judgments of NIE reports have been made public, though they are generally kept secret so that analysts can present their findings with candor. "But here's the real reason," McConnell said. "If I have to inform the public, I am informing the adversary." He used the example of code breakers in the Second World War. "On Nebraska Avenue, where the Department of Homeland Security is located now, there was a girls' school. The nation recruited many young women gifted in science and math to that girls' school. They were brought in and told, 'If you ever tell anybody what you are doing, you will go to prison for the rest of your life.'" The women operated the machinery that deciphered the German naval code, shaving months off the war. "Now, that is secrecy in its most powerful form," McConnell said. "Changed the course of history, I would argue, for the good."

Secrecy imposes its own risks, however. In 1991, Daniel Patrick Moynihan, who was a distinguished social scientist before becoming a U.S. senator from New York, sought to understand why the American intelligence community had failed to anticipate the collapse of the Soviet Union. Examining the history of the Cold War, Moynihan saw a series of misguided adventures steered by incorrect or poorly understood intelligence—from the purported "missile gap" that never existed to the confident assumption that the Cuban people would rise up against Fidel Castro following an American-sponsored invasion. In such instances, the community supported its findings with National Intelligence Estimates or authoritative studies that led American policymakers astray. Having served on the Senate Intelligence Committee, Moynihan had seen how the community hoarded secrets and overvalued them to the point of excluding common sense. He spoke of a "culture of secrecy" that inevitably gave rise to conspiracy thinking and loyalty tests, and he recommended that the CIA be shut down.

McConnell strongly disputed Moynihan's analysis. Moreover, he told me that he intended to prosecute anyone who leaks classified information, such as the Iran NIE. That has rarely been done in the past, largely because a trial would have the unwanted consequence of exposing secret sources and methods. "I think we ought to step up and pay the price of going through an investigation, an indictment, and a trial—and, hopefully, from my point of view, a conviction," he said.

Like many reporters, I've received classified information in the past; it was often full of errors. "Because it was secret, it had never been tested," I said. "The secrecy was actually self-destructive."

"I disagree with that completely," McConnell said. "There's as much misinformation and trash in the system on the outside as there is on the inside." Many newspaper articles about him, he noted, contained errors of fact and of interpretation. "So it doesn't surprise me that you would see a classified document that had some incorrect information in it."

"You'd want to prosecute a guy that leaked something to me?"

"Absolutely," McConnell said. "He ought to be put in the slammer."

"You'd want to prosecute me as well?"

"Depending on what you did with it."

And yet, three weeks after our discussion, McConnell abruptly decided to declassify the key judgments of the NIE, which was titled "Iran: Nuclear Intentions and Capabilities." Among the revelations was that Iran had decided in the fall of 2003 to halt a secret program to design nuclear weapons. This finding reversed the 2005 assessment that had portrayed the Iranian regime as determined to build a nuclear arsenal. If the former document had supported the Bush administration's aggressive posture toward Iran, the new one introduced a confounding note of uncertainty. "We assess with moderate confidence [that] Tehran had not restarted its nuclear weapons program as of mid-2007," the NIE stated, in the probabilistic language of intelligence, "but we do not know whether it currently intends to develop nuclear weapons."

The report came at a time when the Bush administration was gathering international support at the United Nations to strengthen sanctions against the Iranian regime. John Bolton, the former U.S. ambassador to the UN, told the German magazine *Der Spiegel* that the NIE was "politics disguised as intelligence," and that the release of the document amounted to a "quasi-putsch" by the intelligence community. Many Democratic political figures in Washington, however, welcomed McConnell's decision. "The key judgments show that the intelligence community has learned its lessons from the Iraq debacle," Senator Rockefeller stated. "This demonstrates a new willingness to question assumptions internally, and a level of independence from political leadership that was lacking in the recent past."

I asked McConnell what had changed his mind.

"The fear that, if we didn't release it, it would leak, and the administration at that point would be accused of hiding information," he said. He had a personal conflict as well: the new information was at odds with his own testimony about Iran before Congress, and with remarks that he had made in a background press briefing. He knew how that might look if he kept the intelligence classified and it later came out.

McConnell told me that the NIE had been nearly completed when, in July, new information caused the intelligence community to reevaluate its findings. Iranian nuclear officials were overheard complaining about the suspension of the military program. Analysis of photographs taken during a 2005 visit to Iran's uranium-enrichment plant, in Natanz, suggested that it was not designed for the high level of enrichment required to make nuclear weapons.

"We had to stop and consider the new information, run it to ground, compare it to hundreds of sources of data," McConnell said. "Does it correlate? Is it misinformation? Is this a counterintelligence plan?" He compared the process to a trial: the data are evaluated in terms of the level of confidence the community places in their veracity. "We also examine what's missing," McConnell continued. "What are the gaps? What would let us know more?" From July to late November, Iran analysts vetted the information. "Every source is challenged," McConnell said. "We do alternative analysis. We take a set of smart people and say, 'All right, your mission is to figure out why we got this wrong. What could be an alternative?' We finish that, we have a Red Team. Red Team will attack and see if there are weaknesses. Did we challenge our hypotheses in the right way? Did we put too much emphasis on some evidence?" All this was done in the reflected glare of the failures of the past. "This community is consumed with not repeating the mistakes that were made in 2002," McConnell said, referring to the flawed intelligence that led to the Iraq War. "I will tell you, the tradecraft and the professionalism that went into this NIE was probably the best we have ever known."

Even as the intelligence community was digesting the new information, the administration continued its belligerent rhetoric toward Iran. In October 2007, Vice President Cheney warned, "We will not allow Iran to have a nuclear weapon," and President Bush invoked the specter of a Third World War if Iran continued its supposed secret weapons program. Bush later said that McConnell had told him in August that there was new intelligence about Iran: "He didn't tell me what the information was. He did tell me it was going to take a while to analyze." Later, Dana Perino, the White House press secretary, admitted that the president was also told in the August meeting that Iran might have halted its nuclear weapons program. "The president could have been more precise in that language," Perino told reporters. "But the president was being truthful."

McConnell still wondered why, if Iran had a nuclear weapons program up until the fall of 2003, it suddenly placed it on hold. He said, "They're still pursuing fissile material, they're still building and testing and weaponizing missiles, so why did they do it?" He pointed to the invasion of Iraq earlier that same year. "Although we don't have senior Iranian officials telling us, 'We did this because we were worried about where you crazy Westerners were going to go with this invasion,' I believe, as an analyst, that certainly had some bearing on the decision."

On Wednesday, November 28, 2007, McConnell went to the White House for the daily briefing and shared the NIE's key judgments with President Bush. He took with him the three principal analysts who had done the assessment. Cheney was also present, as were members of the National Security Council. "We handed the president the key judgments to read, which he skimmed through," McConnell said. "You could see him thinking about what this meant, how do we manage this information."

The new NIE refuted a previous assessment and inevitably raised the question of whether this one was any more reliable. McConnell also worried that the effect of the release would be to diminish the serious threat that he believes Iran still poses. "What's the difference between being on hold and not being on hold?" he asked rhetorically. "The Supreme Leader could say, 'Turn it back on.'"

When we last spoke, I asked McConnell if he believed that by releasing the key judgments of the NIE, he had compromised sources and methods, which was the reason he had given previously for withholding the document. "Our job is to steal the secrets of foreign governments, or foreign terrorist organizations, and so the more they know about the effectiveness of our tradecraft the more difficult it's going to be for us," he said. "I think putting it out was the right thing, but as the leader of this community, I've got to tell you, we're going to need better information in the future. We've got to go back and verify, 'Did they re-start it?' For the community I represent, I just made our life a lot harder."

The clock on his desk showed that he had four hundred and two days, fifteen hours, seventeen minutes, and forty-five seconds left.

Postscript

McConnell retired on January 27, 2009, and returned to private industry as a vice chairman at Booz Allen Hamilton. He was succeeded as director of national intelligence, briefly, by Dennis C. Blair, and then by General James Clapper.

The *Senate Intelligence Committee Report on Torture* broadly disputes the claims McConnell made to me about the effectiveness of "enhanced interrogation techniques." The report split the senate committee along partisan lines, with Democrats endorsing its conclusions and Republicans unanimously opposing them. The report alleges that these techniques played no part in gaining accurate information or detainee cooperation in the counterterrorism successes that the CIA attributed to them; moreover, the agency lied to or hid information from Congress, the White House, and the intelligence community, as well as the American people. The report specifically cited the director of national intelligence as being misled by the agency: "The ODNI was provided with inaccurate and incomplete information about the program, preventing the director of national intelligence from effectively carrying out the director's statutory responsibility to serve as the principal advisor to the president on intelligence matters."

In a rebuttal to the report, CIA director John Brennan admitted that there were instances in which the agency misrepresented the effectiveness of the program. The agency's response notes that "it is unknowable whether, without enhanced interrogation techniques, C.I.A. or non-C.I.A. interrogators could have acquired the same information from those detainees."

The Rebellion Within

I n May 2008, a fax arrived at the London office of the Arabic newspaper *Asharq al-Awsat* from a shadowy figure in the radical Islamist movement who went by many names. Born Sayyid Imam al-Sharif, he was a former leader of the Egyptian terrorist group al-Jihad, and known to those in the underground mainly as Dr. Fadl. Members of al-Jihad became part of the original core of al-Qaeda; among them was Ayman al-Zawahiri, Osama bin Laden's chief lieutenant. Fadl was one of the first members of al-Qaeda's top council. Twenty years before, he had written two of the most important books in modern Islamist discourse; al-Qaeda used them to indoctrinate recruits and justify killing. Now Fadl was announcing a new book, rejecting al-Qaeda's violence. "We are prohibited from committing aggression, even if the enemies of Islam do that," Fadl wrote in his fax, which was sent from Tora Prison, in Egypt.

Fadl's fax confirmed rumors that imprisoned leaders of al-Jihad were part of a trend of former terrorists renouncing violence. His defection posed a terrible threat to the radical Islamists, because he directly challenged their authority. "There is a form of obedience that is greater than the obedience accorded to any leader, namely, obedience to God and His Messenger," Fadl wrote, claiming that hundreds of Egyptian jihadists from various factions had endorsed his position.

Two months after Fadl's fax appeared, Zawahiri issued a handsomely produced video on behalf of al-Qaeda. "Do they now have fax machines in Egyptian jail cells?" he chided. "I wonder if they're connected to the same line as the electric-shock machines." This sarcastic dismissal was perhaps intended to dampen anxiety about Fadl's manifesto—which was to be published serially, in newspapers in Egypt and Kuwait—among al-Qaeda insiders. Fadl's previous work, after all, had laid the intellectual foundation for al-Qaeda's murderous acts. In Cairo, I met with Gamal Sultan, an Islamist writer and a publisher there. He said of Fadl, "Nobody can challenge the legitimacy of this person. His writings could have far-reaching effects not only in Egypt but on leaders outside it." Usama Ayub, a former member of Egypt's Islamist community, who is now the director of the Islamic Center in Münster, Germany, told me, "A lot of people base their work on Fadl's writings, so he's very important. When Dr. Fadl speaks, everyone should listen."

THE ROOTS OF this ideological war within al-Qaeda go back forty years, to 1968, when two precocious teenagers met at Cairo University's medical school. Zawahiri, a student there, was then seventeen, but he was already involved in clandestine Islamist activity. Although he was not a natural leader, he had an eye for other ambitious, frustrated youths who believed that destiny was whispering in their ear.

So it was not surprising that he was drawn to a tall, solitary classmate named Sayyid Imam al-Sharif. Admired for his brilliance and his tenacity, Imam was expected to become either a great surgeon or a leading cleric. (The name "al-Sharif" denotes the family's descent from the Prophet Muhammad.) His father, a headmaster in Beni Suef, a town seventy-five miles south of Cairo, was religiously conservative, and his son followed suit. He fasted twice a week and, each morning after dawn prayers, studied the Quran, which he had memorized by the time he finished sixth grade. When he was fifteen, the Egyptian government enrolled him in a boarding school for exceptional students, in Cairo. Three years later, he entered medical school and began preparing for a career as a plastic surgeon, specializing in burn injuries.

Both Zawahiri and Imam were pious and high-minded, prideful, and rigid in their views. They tended to look at matters of the spirit in the same way they regarded the laws of nature—as a series of immutable rules, handed down by God. This mind-set was typical of the engineers and technocrats who disproportionately made up the extremist branch of Salafism, a school of thought intent on returning Islam to the idealized early days of the religion.

Imam learned that Zawahiri belonged to a subterranean world. "I knew from another student that Ayman was part of an Islamic group," he later told a reporter for *Al-Hayat,* a pan-Arabic newspaper. The organization came to be called al-Jihad. Its discussions centered on the idea that real Islam no longer existed, because Egypt's rulers had turned away from Sharia and were steering believers toward secular modernity. The young members of al-Jihad decided that they had to act.

In doing so, these men were placing their lives, as well as their families, in terrible jeopardy. Egypt's military government, then led by Gamal Abdel Nasser, had a vast network of informers and secret police. The prisons were brimming with Islamist detainees, locked away in dungeons where torture was routine. Despite this repressive atmosphere, an increasing number of disillusioned Egyptians were turning to the mosque for political answers.

In 1977, Zawahiri asked Imam to join his group, presenting himself as a mere delegate of the organization. Imam understood that his agreement was conditional upon meeting the Islamic scholars who Zawahiri insisted were heading the group; clerical authority was essential to validate the drastic deeds these men were contemplating. The meeting never happened. "Ayman was a charlatan who used secrecy as a pretext," Imam said. "I discovered that Ayman himself was the emir of this group, and that it didn't have any sheikhs."

In 1981, soldiers affiliated with al-Jihad assassinated the president of Egypt, Anwar Sadat, who had signed a peace treaty with Israel two years earlier. Sadat's successor, Hosni Mubarak, rounded up thousands of Islamists, including Zawahiri, who was charged with smuggling weapons.

During the next three years, Zawahiri and Imam, who had once been so profoundly alike, began to diverge. Prison hardened Zawahiri; torture sharpened his appetite for revenge. He was humiliated

and disgraced by the fact that he had given up the names of his con-
federates. He abandoned the ideological purity of his youth. Imam, by
contrast, had not been forced to face the limits of his belief. Leaving
his real identity behind, Imam slipped out of Egypt and made his way
to Peshawar, Pakistan, where the Afghan resistance against the Soviet
occupation of Afghanistan was based. He took the name Dr. Fadl. It
was common for those who joined the jihad to take a nom de guerre.
He adopted the persona of the revolutionary intellectual, in the tradition of Leon Trotsky and Che Guevara. Instead of engaging in combat, Fadl worked as a surgeon for the injured fighters and became a
spiritual guide to the jihad.

When Zawahiri finished serving his sentence in 1984, he also fled
Egypt. He was soon reunited in Peshawar with Fadl, who had become
the director of a Red Crescent hospital there. Their relationship had
turned edgy and competitive, and besides, Fadl held a low opinion of
Zawahiri's abilities as a surgeon. "He asked me to stand with him and
teach him how to perform operations," Fadl told *Al-Hayat*. "I taught
him until he could perform them on his own. Were it not for that, he
would have been exposed, as he had contracted for a job for which he
was unqualified."

In the mid-eighties, Fadl became al-Jihad's emir. (Fadl claimed in
Al-Hayat that this was untrue, saying that his role was merely one of
offering "Sharia guidance.") Zawahiri, whose reputation had been
stained by his prison confessions, was left to handle tactical operations, deferring to Fadl's superior learning in Islamic jurisprudence.
Kamal Helbawy, a former spokesman for the Muslim Brotherhood,
was also in Peshawar, and remembers Fadl as a "haughty, dominating presence," who frequently lambasted Muslims who didn't believe
in the same doctrines. Fadl is "not a social man—he's very isolated,"
according to Hani al-Sibai, an Islamist attorney who knew both men.
"Ayman was the one in front, but the real leader was Dr. Fadl."

Fadl resented the attention that Zawahiri received. (In the interview with *Al-Hayat*, Fadl said that Zawahiri was "enamored of the
media and a show-off.") And yet he let Zawahiri take the public role
and give voice to ideas and doctrines that came from his own mind,
not Zawahiri's. This dynamic eventually became the source of an
acrimonious dispute between the two men.

IN PESHAWAR, Fadl devoted himself to formalizing the rules of holy war. The jihadis needed a text that would school them in the proper way to fight battles whose real objective was not victory over the Soviets but martyrdom and eternal salvation. "The Essential Guide for Preparation" appeared in 1988, as the Afghan jihad was winding down. It quickly became the central text in the jihadis' training.

The guide begins with the premise that jihad is the natural state of Islam. Muslims must always be in conflict with nonbelievers, Fadl asserts, resorting to peace only in moments of abject weakness. Because jihad is, above all, a religious exercise, there are divine rewards to be gained. He who gives money for jihad will be compensated in Heaven, but not as much as the person who acts. The greatest prize goes to the martyr. Every able-bodied believer is obligated to engage in jihad, since most Muslim countries are ruled by infidels who must be forcibly removed in order to bring about an Islamic state. "The way to bring an end to the rulers' unbelief is armed rebellion," the guide states. Some Arab governments regarded the book as so dangerous that anyone caught with a copy was subject to arrest.

On August 11, 1988, Dr. Fadl attended a meeting in Peshawar with several senior leaders of al-Jihad, along with Abdullah Azzam, a Palestinian who oversaw the recruitment of Arabs to the cause. They were joined by a protégé of Azzam's, a young Saudi named Osama bin Laden. The Soviets had already announced their intention to withdraw from Afghanistan, and the prospect of victory awakened many old dreams among these men. They were not the same dreams, however. The leaders of al-Jihad, especially Zawahiri, wanted to use their well-trained warriors to overthrow the Egyptian government. Azzam longed to turn the attention of the Arab mujahideen to Palestine. Neither had the money or the resources to pursue such goals. Bin Laden, on the other hand, was rich, and he had his own vision: to create an all-Arab foreign legion that would pursue the retreating Soviets into Central Asia and also fight against the Marxist government that was then in control of South Yemen. According to Montasser al-Zayyat, an Islamist lawyer in Cairo who is Zawahiri's biographer, it was Dr. Fadl who advocated supporting bin Laden with members of al-Jihad. Combining the Saudi's money with the Egyptians' expertise, the men who met that day formed a new group, called al-Qaeda. Fadl was part of its inner circle. "For years after the launching of al-Qaeda, they would do nothing without consulting me," he boasted to *Al-Hayat.*

In 1992, three years after the Soviet withdrawal from Afghanistan, Zawahiri and most members of al-Jihad relocated to Sudan, where bin Laden had set up operations. Zawahiri urged Fadl and his family to join them there. Fadl, who was completing what he considered his masterwork, *The Compendium of the Pursuit of Divine Knowledge,* agreed to go. "Zawahiri picked us up from the Khartoum airport and took us to our flat," Fadl's son Ismail al-Sharif told me. "Zawahiri said, 'You don't need to work, we will pay your salary. We just want you to finish your book.'"

From Sudan, members of al-Jihad watched enviously as a much larger organization, the Islamic Group, waged open warfare on the Egyptian state. Both groups wished for the overthrow of the secular government and the institution of a theocracy, but they differed in their methods. Al-Jihad was organized as a network of clandestine cells, centered in Cairo; Zawahiri's plan was to take over the country by means of a military coup. The Islamic Group was a broad, aboveground movement that was determined to launch a social revolution by enforcing austere Islamic values. They ransacked video stores, music recitals, cinemas, and liquor stores. They demanded that women dress in *hijab,* and rampaged against Egypt's Coptic minority, bombing its churches. They attacked a regional headquarters of the state security service, cutting off the head of the commander and killing a large number of policemen. Blood on the ground soon became the measure of the Islamic Group's success, and it was all the more exhilarating because the murder was done in the name of God.

In 1990, the spokesman for the Islamic Group was shot dead in the street in Cairo. There was little doubt that the government was behind the killing, and soon afterward the Islamic Group announced its intention to respond with a terror campaign. Dozens of police officers were murdered. Intellectuals were also on its hit list, including Naguib Mahfouz, the Nobel Prize–winning novelist, who was stabbed in the neck. (He survived.) Next, the Islamic Group targeted the tourist industry, declaring that it corrupted Egyptian society by bringing "alien customs and morals which offend Islam." Members of the group attacked tourists with homemade bombs on buses and trains, and fired on cruise ships that plied the Nile. The economy swooned. During the nineties, more than twelve hundred people were killed in terror attacks in Egypt. The minister of the interior, Abdul Halim Moussa, responded to this insult by declaring, "I don't want prisoners. I want bodies."

The exiled members of al-Jihad jealously decided that they needed to enter the fray. Fadl disagreed; despite his advocacy of endless warfare against unjust rulers, he contended that the Egyptian government was too powerful and that the insurgency would fail. He also complained that al-Jihad was undertaking operations only to emulate the Islamic Group. "This is senseless activity that will bring no benefit," he warned. His point was quickly proved when the Egyptian security services captured a computer containing the names of Zawahiri's followers, nearly a thousand of whom were arrested. In retaliation, Zawahiri authorized a suicide bombing that targeted Hasan al-Alfi, the interior minister, in August 1993. Alfi survived the attack with a broken arm. Two months later, al-Jihad attempted to kill Egypt's prime minister, Atef Sidqi, in a bombing. The prime minister was not hurt, but the explosion killed a twelve-year-old schoolgirl.

Embarrassed by these failures, members of al-Jihad demanded that their leader resign. Many were surprised to discover that the emir was Fadl. He willingly gave up the post, and Zawahiri soon became the leader of al-Jihad in name as well as in fact.

IN 1994, Fadl moved to Yemen, where he resumed his medical practice and tried to put the work of jihad behind him. Before he left, however, he gave a copy of his finished manuscript to Zawahiri, saying that it could be used to raise money. Few books in recent history have done as much damage.

Fadl wrote the book under yet another pseudonym, Abdul Qader bin Abdul Aziz, in part because the name was not Egyptian and would further mask his identity. Given Fadl's critique of al-Jihad's violent operations as "senseless," the intransigent and bloodthirsty document that Fadl gave to Zawahiri must have come as a thrilling surprise.

The Compendium of the Pursuit of Divine Knowledge, which is more than a thousand pages long, starts with the assertion that salvation is available only to the perfect Muslim. Even an exemplary believer can wander off the path to Paradise with a single misstep. Fadl contends that the rulers of Egypt and other Arab countries are apostates of Islam. "The infidel's rule, his prayers, and the prayers of those who pray behind him are invalid," Fadl decrees. "His blood is legal." He declares that Muslims have a duty to wage jihad against such leaders; those who submit to an infidel ruler are themselves infidels, and doomed to damnation. The same punishment awaits those who participate in democratic elections. "I say to Muslims in all candor that secular, nationalist democracy opposes your religion and your doctrine, and in submitting to it you leave God's book behind," he writes. Those who labor in government, the police, and the courts are infidels, as is anyone who works for peaceful change; religious war, not political reform, is the sole mandate. Even devout believers walk a tightrope over the abyss. "A man may enter the faith in many ways, yet be expelled from it by just one deed," Fadl cautions. Anyone who believes otherwise is a heretic and deserves to be slaughtered.

Fadl also expands upon the heresy of *takfir*—the excommunication of one Muslim by another. To deny the faith of a believer—without persuasive evidence—is a grievous injustice. The Prophet Muhammad is said to have remarked, "When a man calls his brother an infidel, we can be sure that one of them is indeed an infidel." Fadl defines Islam so narrowly, however, that nearly everyone falls outside the sacred boundaries. The *Compendium* gave al-Qaeda and its allies a warrant to murder all who stood in their way. Zawahiri was ecstatic. Zawahiri exclaimed, "This book is a victory from Almighty God."

When Fadl moved to Yemen, he considered his work in revolutionary Islam to be complete. Fadl cut off all contact with bin Laden, complaining that the terrorist leader "doesn't listen to the advice of others, he listens only to himself." Fadl moved his two wives, four sons, and two daughters to the mountain town of Ibb. He called himself Dr. Abdul Aziz al-Sharif. On holidays, the family took walks around the town. Otherwise, he spent his spare time reading. "He didn't care to watch television, except for the news," Ismail al-Sharif told me. "He didn't like to make friends, because he was a fugitive. He thinks having too many relations is a waste of time."

While awaiting a work permit from Yemen's government, Fadl volunteered his services at a local hospital. His skills quickly became evident. "People were coming from all over the country," his son told me. The fact that Fadl was working without pay in such a primitive facility—rather than opening a practice in a gleaming modern clinic in Kuwait or Europe—drew unwelcome attention. He had the profile of a man with something to hide.

While in Ibb, Fadl learned that his book had been bowdlerized. His original manuscript contained a barbed critique of the jihadi movement, naming specific organizations and individuals whose actions he disdained. Those sections of the book had been removed. Other parts were significantly altered. Even the title had been changed, to *Guide to the Path of Righteousness for Jihad and Belief.* The thought that a less-qualified writer had taken liberties with his masterpiece sent him into a fury. Who might that be? A member of al-Jihad who had come to Yemen for a job broke the news. "He informed me that Zawahiri alone was the one who committed these perversions," Fadl said.

In 1995, a sheepish Zawahiri traveled to Yemen to appeal to Fadl for forgiveness. By this time, Zawahiri had suspended his operations in Egypt, and his organization was floundering. Now his former emir refused to see him. "I do not know anyone in the history of Islam prior to Ayman al-Zawahiri who engaged in such lying, cheating, forgery, and betrayal of trust by transgressing against someone else's book," the inflamed author told *Al-Hayat.* Zawahiri and Fadl have not spoken since, but their war of words was only beginning.

MEANWHILE, a furtive conversation was taking place among the imprisoned leaders of the Islamic Group, including one of its founders, Karam Zuhdy. "We started growing older," Zuhdy says. "We started examining the evidence. We began to read books and reconsider." Just opening the subject for discussion was extremely threatening, not only for members of the organization but for groups that had an interest in prolonging the clash with Egypt's government. Zuhdy points in particular to the Muslim Brotherhood. "Instead of supporting us, they wanted us to continue the violence," he says. "We faced very strong opposition inside prison, outside prison, and outside Egypt."

In 1997, rumors of a possible deal between the Islamic Group and the Egyptian government reached Zawahiri, who was then hiding in an al-Qaeda safe house in Kandahar, Afghanistan. Montasser al-Zayyat, the Islamist lawyer, was brokering talks between the parties. Zayyat has often served as an emissary between the Islamists and the security apparatus, a role that makes him both universally distrusted and invaluable. In his biography of Zawahiri, *The Road to al-Qaeda: The Story of Bin Laden's Right-Hand Man,* Zayyat reports that Zawahiri called him in March of that year, when Zayyat arrived in London on business. Zawahiri was furious about the nonviolence initiative. "Why are you making the brothers angry?" he demanded. Zayyat responded that jihad did not have to be restricted to an armed approach. Zawahiri urged Zayyat to change his mind, even promising that he could secure political asylum for him in London. "I politely rejected his offer," Zayyat writes.

The talks between the Islamic Group and the government remained secret until July, when one of the imprisoned leaders, who was on trial in a military court, stood up and announced to stunned observers the organization's intention to cease all violent activity. Incensed, Zawahiri wrote a letter addressed to the group's imprisoned leaders. "God only knows the grief I felt when I heard about this initiative and the negative impact it has caused," he wrote. "If we are going to stop now, why did we start in the first place?"

To Zawahiri's annoyance, imprisoned members of al-Jihad, his own organization, also began to express an interest in joining the nonviolence initiative. "The leadership started to change its views," said Abdel Moneim Moneeb, who, in 1993, was charged with being a member of al-Jihad. Although Moneeb was never convicted, he spent fourteen years in an Egyptian prison. "At one point, you might mention this idea, and all the voices would drown you out. Later, it became possible." Independent thinking on the subject of violence was not easy when as many as thirty men were crammed into cells that were about nine feet by fifteen. Except for a few smuggled radios, the prisoners were largely deprived of sources of outside information.

They occupied themselves with endless theological debates and glum speculation about where they had gone wrong. Eventually, though, these discussions prompted the imprisoned leaders of al-Jihad to open their own secret channel with the government.

Zawahiri became increasingly isolated within his own movement. He believed that violence was the only fuel that kept the radical Islamist organizations running; they had no future without terror. Together with several leaders of the Islamic Group who were living outside Egypt, he plotted a way to raise the stakes and permanently wreck the attempts at reform. On November 17, 1997, just four months after the announcement of the nonviolence initiative, six young men entered the magnificent ruins of Queen Hatshepsut's temple, near Luxor. Hundreds of tourists were strolling through the grounds. For forty-five minutes, the killers shot randomly. A flyer was stuffed inside a mutilated body, taking credit on behalf of the Islamic Group. Sixty-two people died. It was the worst terrorist incident in Egypt's bloody political history.

If Zawahiri and the exiled members of the Islamic Group hoped that this action would undermine the nonviolence initiative, they miscalculated. The Islamic Group's imprisoned leaders wrote a series of books and pamphlets, collectively known as "the revisions," in which they formally explained their new thinking. "We wanted to relay our experience to young people to protect them from falling into the same mistakes we did," Zuhdy told me. In 1999, the Islamic Group called for an end to all armed action, not only in Egypt but also against America. "The Islamic Group does not believe in the creed of killing by nationality," one of its representatives later explained.

BEFORE 9/11, the Egyptian government had quietly permitted the Islamic Group's leaders to carry their discussions about renouncing violence to members in other prisons around the country. After the attacks, state security decided to call more attention to these debates. Makram Mohamed Ahmed, who was close to the minister of the interior and was then the editor of *Al Musawar,* a government weekly, was permitted to cover some of the discussions. "There were three generations in prison," he said. "They were in despair." Many of these

Islamists had fantasized that they would be hailed as heroes by their society; instead, they were isolated and rejected. Now Karam Zuhdy and other imprisoned leaders were asking the radicals to accept that they had been deluded from the beginning. "We began going from prison to prison," Ahmed recalled. "Those boys would see their leaders giving them the new conception of the revisions." Ahmed recalls that many of the prisoners were angry. "They would say, 'You've been deceiving us for eighteen years! Why didn't you say this before?'"

Despite such objections, the twenty thousand imprisoned members of the Islamic Group largely accepted the leaders' new position. Ahmed says that he was initially skeptical of the prisoners' apparent repentance, which looked like a ploy for better treatment; however, several of the participants in the discussions had already been sentenced to death and were wearing the red clothing that identifies a prisoner as a condemned man. They had nothing to gain. Ahmed says that one of these prisoners told him, "I'm not offering these revisions for Mubarak! I don't care about this government. What is important is that I killed people—Copts, innocent persons—and before I meet God I should declare my sins." Then the man burst into tears.

The moral dimensions of the prisoners' predicament unfolded as they explored the ramifications of the revisions. What about the brother who was killed while carrying out an attack that we now realize was against Islam? Is he a martyr? If not, how do we console his family? One of the leaders proposed that if the brother who died was sincere, although genuinely deceived, he would still gain his heavenly reward; however, because "everyone knows there is no advantage to violence, and that it is religiously incorrect," from now on those who commit such actions were doomed. What about correcting the sins of other Muslims? The Islamic Group had a reputation in Egypt for acting as a kind of moral police force, often quite savagely—for instance, throwing acid in the faces of women wearing makeup. "We used to blame the people and say, 'The people are cowards,'" one of the leaders admitted. "None of us thought of saying that the violence we employed was abhorrent to them."

These emotional discussions were widely covered in the Egyptian press. Zuhdy publicly apologized to the Egyptian people for the Islamic Group's violent deeds, beginning with the murder of Sadat, whom he called a martyr. The Egyptian government responded to the nonviolence initiative by releasing 12,500 members of the Islamic Group. Many of them had never been charged with a crime, much less tried and sentenced. Some were shattered by their confinement. "Imagine what twenty years of prison can do," Zuhdy said.

The prisoners returned to a society that was far more religious than the one they had left. They must have been heartened to see most Egyptian women, who once enjoyed Western fashions, now wearing the *hijab,* or completely hidden behind facial veils. Many more Egyptian men had prayer marks on their foreheads. Imams had become celebrities, their sermons blaring from televisions and radios. These newly released men might fairly have believed that they had achieved a great social victory through their actions and their sacrifice.

And yet the brutal indifference of the Egyptian government toward its people was unchanged. As the Islamists emerged from prison, new detainees took their place—protesters, liberals, bloggers, candidates for political office. Wealth was increasingly concentrated in the hands of the already rich; meanwhile, the price of food was shooting up so quickly that people were going hungry. Within a few months of being released, hundreds of the Islamists petitioned, unsuccessfully, to be let back into prison.

From the Egyptian government's point of view, the deal with the Islamic Group has proved to be an unparalleled success. According to Makram Mohamed Ahmed, the former editor of *Al Musawar,* who witnessed the prison debates, there have been only two instances where members showed signs of returning to their former violent ways, and in both cases they were betrayed by informers in their own group. "Prison or time may have defeated them," Montasser al-Zayyat, the lawyer, says of the Islamic Group. "Some would call it a collapse."

DR. FADL WAS PRACTICING surgery in Ibb when the 9/11 attacks took place. "We heard the reports first on BBC Radio," his son Ismail al-Sharif recalls. After his shift ended, Fadl returned home and watched the television coverage with his family. They asked him who he thought was responsible. "This action is from al-Qaeda, because there is no other group in the world that will kill themselves in a plane," he responded.

On October 28, 2001, two Yemeni intelligence officers came to Fadl's clinic to ask him some questions. He put them off. The director of the hospital persuaded Fadl to turn himself in, saying that he would pull some strings to protect him. Fadl was held in Ibb for a week before being transferred to government detention in the capital, Sana'a. The speaker of the parliament and other prominent Yemeni politicians agitated unsuccessfully for his release.

In Fadl's opinion, al-Qaeda had committed "group suicide" by striking America, which was bound to retaliate severely. Indeed, nearly 80 percent of al-Qaeda's members in Afghanistan were killed in the final months of 2001. "My father was very sad for the killing of Abu Hafs al-Masri, the military leader of al-Qaeda," Ismail al-Sharif told *Al-Jarida*. "My father said that, with the death of Abu Hafs, al-Qaeda is finished, because the rest is a group of zeroes."

At first, Yemeni authorities weren't sure what to do with the celebrated jihadi philosopher. There were many Yemenis, even in the intelligence agencies, who sympathized with al-Qaeda. Fadl was offered the opportunity to escape to any country he wanted. Fadl said that he would go to Sudan. But the promised release was postponed. The following year, the offer was changed: either Fadl could seek political asylum or Egyptian authorities would come and get him. Fadl applied for asylum, but before he received a response he disappeared.

According to a 2005 report by Human Rights Watch, which was following his case, Fadl was taken from his cell and smuggled onto a plane to Cairo. For more than two years, Fadl—who had been tried and convicted in absentia on terrorism charges—was secretly held by Egyptian authorities. He was eventually transferred to the Scorpion, a facility inside Tora Prison where major political figures are held. It was clear that he was getting special treatment. His son says that he has a private room with a bath and a small kitchen, adding, "He has a refrigerator and a television, and the newspaper comes every day." Fadl passes the time reading and trying not to gain weight. (The Egyptian authorities rejected multiple requests to speak with Fadl in prison.)

There may be many inducements for Dr. Fadl's revisions, torture among them, but his smoldering resentment of Zawahiri's literary crimes was obviously a factor. Fadl claimed in *Al-Hayat* that his differences with Zawahiri were "objective," not personal. "He was a burden to me on the educational, professional, jurisprudential, and sometimes personal levels," Fadl complained. "He was ungrateful for the kindness I had shown him and bit the hand that I had extended to him. What I got for my efforts was deception, betrayal, lies, and thuggery."

The first segment of Dr. Fadl's new book appeared in the newspapers *Al-Masri al-Youm* and *Al-Jarida,* in November 2007, on the tenth anniversary of the Luxor massacre. Titled "Rationalizing Jihad in Egypt and the World," it attempted to reconcile Fadl's well-known bloodthirsty views with his sweeping modifications. A majority of the al-Jihad members in prison signed Fadl's manuscript—hoping, no doubt, to follow their Islamic Group colleagues out the prison door.

Hisham Kassem, a human rights activist and a publisher in Cairo, told me that the newspapers that published Fadl's work "bought it from the Ministry of the Interior for a hundred and fifty thousand Egyptian pounds." The circumstances of the publication added to the general suspicion that the government had supervised the revisions, if not actually written them. Perhaps to counter that impression, Mohammad Salah, the Cairo bureau chief of *Al-Hayat,* was allowed into Tora Prison to interview Fadl. In the resulting six-part series, Fadl defended the work as his own and left no doubt of his personal grudge against Zawahiri. Whatever the motivations behind the writing of the book, its publication amounted to a major assault on radical Islamist theology, from the man who had originally formulated much of that thinking.

The premise that opens "Rationalizing Jihad" is "There is nothing that invokes the anger of God and His wrath like the unwarranted spilling of blood and wrecking of property." Fadl then establishes a new set of rules for jihad, which essentially define most forms of terrorism as illegal under Islamic law and restrict the possibility of holy war to extremely rare circumstances. His argument may seem arcane, even to most Muslims, but to men who had risked their lives in order to carry out what they saw as the authentic precepts of their religion, every word assaulted their worldview and brought into question their chances for salvation.

In order to declare jihad, Fadl writes, one must observe certain requirements. One must have a place of refuge. There should be adequate financial resources to wage the campaign. Fadl castigates Muslims who resort to theft or kidnapping to finance jihad: "There is no such thing in Islam as ends justifying the means." Family members must be provided for. "There are those who strike and then escape, leaving their families, dependents, and other Muslims to suffer the consequences," Fadl points out. "This is in no way religion or jihad. It is not manliness." Finally, the enemy should be properly identified in order to prevent harm to innocents. "Those who have not followed these principles have committed the gravest of sins," Fadl writes.

To wage jihad, one must first gain permission from one's parents and creditors. The potential warrior also needs the blessing of a qualified imam or sheikh; he can't simply respond to the summons of a charismatic leader acting in the name of Islam. "Oh, you young people, do not be deceived by the heroes of the Internet, the leaders of the microphones, who are launching statements inciting the youth while living under the protection of intelligence services, or of a tribe, or in a distant cave or under political asylum in an infidel country," Fadl warns. "They have thrown many others before you into the infernos, graves, and prisons."

Even if a person is fit and capable, jihad may not be required of him, Fadl says, pointing out that God also praises those who choose to isolate themselves from unbelievers rather than fight them. Nor is jihad required if the enemy is twice as powerful as the Muslims; in such an unequal contest, Fadl writes, "God permitted peace treaties and cease-fires with the infidels, either in exchange for money or without it—all of this in order to protect the Muslims, in contrast with those who push them into peril." In what sounds like a deliberate swipe at Zawahiri, he remarks, "Those who have triggered clashes and pressed their brothers into unequal military confrontations are specialists neither in fatwas nor in military affairs. . . . Just as those who practice medicine without background should provide compensation for the damage they have done, the same goes for those who issue fatwas without being qualified to do so."

Despite his previous call for jihad against unjust Muslim rulers, Fadl now says that such rulers can be fought only if they are unbelievers, and even then only to the extent that the battle will improve the situation of Muslims. Obviously, that has not been the case in Egypt or most other Islamic countries, where increased repression has been the usual result of armed insurgency. Fadl quotes the Prophet Muhammad advising Muslims to be patient with their flawed leaders: "Those who rebel against the Sultan shall die a pagan death."

Fadl repeatedly emphasizes that it is forbidden to kill civilians—including Christians and Jews—unless they are actively attacking Muslims. "There is nothing in the Sharia about killing Jews and the Nazarenes, referred to by some as the Crusaders," Fadl observes. "They are the neighbors of the Muslims . . . and being kind to one's neighbors is a religious duty." Indiscriminate bombing—"such as blowing up of hotels, buildings, and public transportation"—is not permitted, because innocents will surely die. "If vice is mixed with virtue, all becomes sinful," he writes. "There is no legal reason for harming people in any way."

The prohibition against killing applies even to foreigners inside Muslim countries, since many of them may be Muslims. "You cannot decide who is a Muslim or who is an unbeliever or who should be killed based on the color of his skin or hair or the language he speaks or because he wears Western fashion," Fadl writes. "These are not proper indications for who is a Muslim and who is not." As for foreigners who are non-Muslims, they may have been invited into the country for work, which is a kind of treaty. What's more, there are many Muslims living in foreign lands considered inimical to Islam, and yet those Muslims are treated fairly; therefore, Muslims should reciprocate in their own countries. To Muslims living in non-Islamic countries, Fadl sternly writes, "I say it is not honorable to reside with people—even if they were nonbelievers and not part of a treaty, if they gave you permission to enter their homes and live with them, and if they gave you security for yourself and your money, and if they gave you the opportunity to work or study, or they granted you political asylum with a decent life and other acts of kindness—and then betray them, through killing and destruction. This was not in the manners and practices of the Prophet."

Fadl does not condemn all jihadist activity, however. "Jihad in Afghanistan will lead to the creation of an Islamic state with the triumph of the Taliban, God willing," he declares. The jihads in Iraq and Palestine are more problematic. As Fadl sees it, "If it were not for the jihad in Palestine, the Jews would have crept toward the neighboring countries a long time ago." Even so, he writes, "the Palestinian cause has, for some time, been a grape leaf used by the bankrupt leaders to cover their own faults."

Fadl addresses the bloody division between Sunnis and Shiites that is at the heart of Islam: "Harming those who are affiliated with Islam but have a different creed is forbidden." He quotes Ibn Taymiyya, one of the revered scholars of early Islam, who is also bin Laden's favorite authority: "A Muslim's blood and money are safeguarded even if his creed is different."

Fadl still asserts that "terrorizing the enemy is a legitimate duty"; however, he points out, "legitimate terror" has many constraints. Al-Qaeda's terrorist attacks in America, London, and Madrid were wrong, because they were based on nationality, a form of indiscriminate slaughter forbidden by Islam. In his *Al-Hayat* interview, Fadl labels 9/11 "a catastrophe for Muslims," because al-Qaeda's actions "caused the death of tens of thousands of Muslims—Arabs, Afghans, Pakistanis and others."

Fadl's most original argument is his assertion that the hijackers of 9/11 "betrayed the enemy," because they had been given U.S. visas, which are a contract of protection. "The followers of bin Laden entered the United States with his knowledge, and on his orders double-crossed its population, killing and destroying," Fadl continues. "The Prophet—God's prayer and peace be upon him—said, 'On the Day of Judgment, every double-crosser will have a banner up his anus proportionate to his treachery.'"

At one point, Fadl observes, "People hate America, and the Islamist movements feel their hatred and their impotence. Ramming America has become the shortest road to fame and leadership among the Arabs and Muslims. But what good is it if you destroy one of your enemy's buildings, and he destroys one of your countries? What good is it if you kill one of his people, and he kills a thousand of yours? . . . That, in short, is my evaluation of 9/11."

IF THE SECURITY SERVICES in Egypt, in tandem with the al-Azhar scholars, had undertaken to write a refutation of al-Qaeda's doctrine, it would likely have resembled the book that Dr. Fadl produced; and, indeed, that may have been exactly what occurred. And yet, with so many leaders of al-Jihad endorsing the work, it seemed clear that the organization in Egypt itself was now dead. Terrorism might continue in some form, but the historic violent factions were finished, departing amid public exclamations of repentance for the futility and sinfulness of their actions.

As the Muslim world awaited Zawahiri's inevitable response, the press and the clergy were surprisingly muted. One reason was that Fadl's revisions raised doubts about political activity that many Muslims do not regard as terror—for instance, the resistance movements in Palestine and elsewhere that oppose Israel and the presence of American troops in Muslim countries. "In this region, we must distinguish between violence against national governments and that of the resistance—in Iraq, in Lebanon, in Palestine," Essam el-Erian, the spokesman of the Muslim Brotherhood, told me. "We cannot call this resistance 'violence.'" Nevertheless, such movements were inevitably drawn into the debate surrounding Fadl's book.

A number of Muslim clerics struggled to answer Dr. Fadl's broad critique of political bloodshed. Many had issued fatwas endorsing the very actions that Fadl now declared to be unjustified. Their responses were often surprising. For instance, Sheikh Hamid al-Ali, an influential Salafi cleric in Kuwait, whom the U.S. Treasury has described as an al-Qaeda facilitator and fund-raiser, declared on a website that he welcomed the rejection of violence as a means of fostering change in the Arab world. Sheikh Ali's fatwas have sometimes been linked to al-Qaeda actions. (Notoriously, months before 9/11, he authorized flying aircraft into targets during suicide operations.) He observed that although the Arab regimes have a natural self-interest in encouraging nonviolence, that shouldn't cause readers to spurn Fadl's argument. "I believe it is a big mistake to let this important intellectual transformation be nullified by political suspicion," Ali said. The decision of radical Islamist groups to adopt a peaceful path does not necessarily mean, however, that they can evolve into political parties. "We have to admit that we do not have in our land a true political process worthy of the name," Ali argued. "What we have are regimes that play a game in which they use whatever will guarantee their continued existence."

On the other hand, Sheikh Abu Basir al-Tartusi, a Syrian Islamist living in London, railed against the "numbness and discouragement" of Fadl's message in telling Muslims that they are too weak to engage in jihad or overthrow their oppressive rulers. "More than half of the Quran and hundreds of the Prophet's sayings call for jihad and fighting those unjust tyrants," Tartusi exclaimed on a jihadist website. "What do you want us to do with his huge quantity of Sharia provisions, and how do you want us to understand and interpret them? Where is the benefit in deserting jihad against those tyrants? Because of them, the nation lost its religion, glory, honor, dignity, land, resources, and every precious thing!" Jihadist publications were filled with condemnations of Fadl's revisions. Hani el-Sibai, the Islamist attorney, is a Zawahiri loyalist who runs a political website in London; he said of Fadl, "Do you think any Islamic group will listen to him? No. They are in the middle of a war."

Even so, the fact that al-Qaeda followers and sympathizers were paying so much attention to Fadl's manuscript made it imperative that Zawahiri offer a definitive refutation. Since al-Qaeda's violent ideology rested so much on Fadl's foundation, Zawahiri would have to find a way to discredit the author without destroying the authority of his own organization. It was a tricky task.

In February 2008, Zawahiri announced in a video that he had finished a "letter" responding to Fadl's book. "The Islam presented by that document is the one that America and the West wants and is pleased with: an Islam without jihad," Zawahiri said. "Because I consider this document to be an insult to the Muslim nation, I chose for the rebuttal the name 'The Exoneration,' in order to express the nation's innocence of this insult." This public response to internal dissent was unprecedented.

The "letter," which finally appeared on the Internet the following month, was nearly two hundred pages long. "This message I present to the reader today is among the most difficult I have ever written in my life," Zawahiri admits in his introduction. Although the text is laden with footnotes and lengthy citations from Islamic scholars, Zawahiri's strategy is apparent from the beginning. Whereas Fadl's book is a trenchant attack on the immoral roots of al-Qaeda's theology, Zawahiri navigates his argument toward the familiar shores of the "Zionist-Crusader" conspiracy. Zawahiri claims that Fadl wrote his book "in the spirit of the Minister of the Interior." He characterizes it as a desperate attempt by the enemies of Islam—America, the West, Jews, the apostate rulers of the Muslim world—to "stand in the way of the fierce wave of jihadi revivalism that is shaking the Islamic world." Mistakes have been made, he concedes. "I neither condone the killing of innocent people nor claim that jihad is free of error," he writes. "Muslim leaders during the time of the Prophet made mistakes, but the jihad did not stop. . . . I'm warning those Islamist groups who welcome the document that they are giving the government the knife with which it can slaughter them."

In presenting al-Qaeda's defense, Zawahiri displays the moral relativism that underlies the organization. "Keep in mind that we have the right to do to the infidels what they have done to us," he writes. "We bomb them as they bomb us, even if we kill someone who is not permitted to be killed." He compares 9/11 to the 1998 American bombing of a pharmaceutical plant in Sudan, in retaliation for al-Qaeda's destruction of two American embassies in East Africa. (The U.S. mistakenly believed that the plant was producing chemical weapons.) "I see no difference between the two operations, except that the money used to build the factory was Muslim money and the workers who died in the factory's rubble"—actually, a single night watchman—"were Muslims, while the money that was spent on the buildings that those hijackers destroyed was infidel money and the people who died in the explosion were infidels." When Zawahiri questions the sanctity of a visa, which Fadl equates with a mutual contract of safe passage, he consults an English dictionary and finds in the definition of "visa" no mention of a guarantee of protection. "Even if the contract is based on international agreements, we are not bound by these agreements," Zawahiri claims, citing two radical clerics who support his view. In any case, America doesn't feel bound to protect Muslims; for instance, he claims, it is torturing people in its military prisons in Guantánamo

Bay, Cuba. "The U.S. gives itself the right to take any Muslim without respect to his visa," Zawahiri writes. "If the U.S. and Westerners don't respect visas, why should we?"

Zawahiri clumsily dodges many of the most penetrating of Fadl's arguments. "The writer speaks of violations of the Sharia, such as killing people because of their nationality, skin color, hair color, or denomination," he complains in a characteristic passage. "This is another example of making accusations without evidence. No one ever talked about killing people because of their skin color or hair color. I demand the writer produce specific incidents with specific dates."

Zawahiri makes some telling psychological points; for instance, he says that the imprisoned Fadl is projecting his own weakness on the mujahideen, who have grown stronger since Fadl deserted them, fifteen years earlier. "The Islamic mujahid movement was not defeated, by the grace of God; indeed, because of its patience, steadfastness, and thoughtfulness, it is headed toward victory," he writes. He cites the strikes on 9/11 and the ongoing battles in Iraq, Afghanistan, and Somalia, which he says are wearing America down.

To dispute Fadl's assertion that Muslims living in non-Islamic countries are treated fairly, Zawahiri points out that in some Western countries Muslim girls are forbidden to wear the *hijab* to school. Muslim men are prevented from marrying more than one wife, and from beating their wives, as allowed by some interpretations of Sharia. Muslims are barred from donating money to certain Islamic causes, although money is freely and openly raised for Israel. He cites the 2005 cartoon controversy in Denmark and the celebrity of the author Salman Rushdie as examples of Western countries exalting those who denigrate Islam. He says that some Western laws prohibiting anti-Semitic remarks would forbid Muslims to recite certain passages in the Quran dealing with the treachery of the Jews.

Writing about the treatment of tourists, Zawahiri says, "The mujahideen don't kidnap people randomly"—they purposely kidnap or harm tourists to send a message to their home countries. "We don't attack Brazilian tourists in Finland, or those from Vietnam in Venezuela," he writes. No doubt Muslims may be killed occasionally, but if that happens it's a pardonable mistake. "The majority of scholars say that it is permissible to strike at infidels, even if Muslims are among them," Zawahiri contends. He cites a well-known verse in the Quran to support, among other things, the practice of kidnapping: "When the sacred months are drawn away, slay the idolaters wherever you find them, and take them, and confine them, and lie in wait for them at every place of ambush."

As for 9/11, Zawahiri writes, "The mujahideen didn't attack the West in its home country with suicide attacks in order to break treaties, or out of a desire to spill blood, or because they were half-mad, or because they suffer from frustration and failure, as many imagine. They attacked it because they were forced to defend their community and their sacred religion from centuries of aggression. They had no means other than suicide attacks to defend themselves."

Zawahiri's argument demonstrates why Islam is so vulnerable to radicalization. It is a religion that was born in conflict, and in its long history it has developed a reservoir of opinions and precedents that are supposed to govern the behavior of Muslims toward their enemies. Some of Zawahiri's commentary may seem comically academic, as in this citation in support of the need for Muslims to prepare for jihad: "Imam Ahmad said: 'We heard from Harun bin Ma'ruf, citing Abu Wahab, who quoted Amru bin al-Harith citing Abu Ali Tamamah bin Shafi that he heard Uqbah bin Amir saying, "I heard the Prophet say from the pulpit: 'Against them make ready your strength.'"' Strength refers to shooting arrows and other projectiles from instruments of war." Such proofs of the rightfulness of jihad, or taking captives, or slaughtering the enemy are easily found in the commentaries of scholars, the rulings of Sharia courts, the volumes of the Prophet's sayings, and the Quran itself. Crude interpretations of Islamic texts can lead men like Zawahiri to conclude that murder should be celebrated. They come to believe that religion is science. They see their actions as logical, righteous, and mandatory. In this fashion, a surgeon is transformed from a healer into a killer, but only if the candle of individual conscience has been extinguished.

SEVERAL TIMES IN his lengthy response, Zawahiri complains of double standards when critics attack al-Qaeda's tactics but ignore similar actions on the part of Palestinian organizations. He notes that Fadl ridicules the fighting within al-Qaeda. "Why don't you ask Hamas the same thing?" Zawahiri demands. "Isn't this a clear contradiction?" At another point, Zawahiri concedes the failure of al-Jihad to overthrow the Egyptian government, then adds, "Neither has the eighty-year-old jihad kicked the occupier out of Palestine." He goes on to point out that Palestinian missiles also indiscriminately kill children and the elderly, even Arabs, but no one holds the Palestinians to the same ethical standards as al-Qaeda.

Zawahiri has watched al-Qaeda's popularity decline in places where it formerly enjoyed great support. In Pakistan, where hundreds have been killed by al-Qaeda suicide bombers—including, perhaps, former prime minister Benazir Bhutto—public opinion has turned against bin Laden and his companions. An Algerian terror organization, the Salafist Group for Preaching and Combat, formally affiliated itself with al-Qaeda in September 2006 and began a series of suicide bombings that have alienated the Algerian people, long weary of the horrors that Islamist radicals have inflicted on their country. Even members of al-Qaeda admit that their cause has been harmed by indiscriminate violence. In February 2008, Abu Turab al-Jazairi, an al-Qaeda commander in northern Iraq, whose nom de guerre suggests that he is Algerian, gave an interview to *Al-Arab*, a Qatari daily. "The attacks in Algeria sparked animated debate here in Iraq," he said. "By God, had they told me they were planning to harm the Algerian President and his family, I would say, 'Blessings be upon them!' But explosions in the street, blood knee-deep, the killing of soldiers whose wages are not even enough for them to eat at third-rate restaurants . . . and calling this jihad? By God, it's sheer idiocy!" In Saudi Arabia, Sheikh Salman al-Oadah, a cleric whom bin Laden had praised in the past, appeared on an Arabic television network in 2007 and read an open letter to the al-Qaeda leader. He asked, "Brother Osama, how much blood has been spilled? How many innocent children, women, and old people have been killed, maimed, and expelled from their homes in the name of al-Qaeda?" These critiques echoed some of the concerns of the influential Palestinian cleric Sheikh Abu Muhammad al-Maqdisi. "Mujahideen should refrain from acts that target civilians, churches, or other places of worship, including Shiite sites," Maqdisi wrote in 2004. "The hands of the jihad warriors must remain clean."

In order to stanch the flow of criticism, Zawahiri boldly initiated a virtual town hall meeting, soliciting questions in an online forum. In the spring of 2008, he released two lengthy audio responses to nearly a hundred of the nine hundred often testy queries that were posed. The first one came from a man who identified himself sardonically as the Geography Teacher. "Excuse me, Mr. Zawahiri, but who is it who is killing, with Your Excellency's permission, the innocents in Baghdad, Morocco, and Algeria? Do you consider the killing of women and children to be jihad?" Then he demanded, "Why have you not—to this day—carried out any strike in Israel? Or is it easier to kill Muslims in the markets? Maybe you should study geography, because your maps show only the Muslim states." Zawahiri protested that al-Qaeda had not killed innocents. "In fact, we fight those who kill innocents. Those who kill innocents are the Americans, the Jews, the Russians, and the French and their agents." As for al-Qaeda's failure to attack Israel, despite bin Laden's constant exploitation of the issue, Zawahiri asks, "Why does the questioner focus on how al-Qaeda in particular must strike Israel, while he didn't request that jihadist organizations in Palestine come to the aid of their brothers in Chechnya, Afghanistan, and Iraq?"

The murder of innocents emerged as the most prominent issue in the exchanges. An Algerian university student sarcastically congratulated Zawahiri for killing sixty Muslims in Algeria on a holy feast day. What was their sin? the student wanted to know. "Those who were killed on the eleventh of December in Algeria are not from the innocents," Zawahiri claimed. "They are from the Crusader unbelievers and the government troops who defend them. Our brothers in al-Qaeda in the Islamic Maghreb"—North Africa—"are more truthful, more just, and more righteous than the lying sons of France." A Saudi wondered how Muslims could justify supporting al-Qaeda, given its long history of indiscriminate murder. "Are there other ways and means in which the objectives of jihad can be achieved without killing people?" he asked. "Please do not use as a pretext what the Americans or others are doing. Muslims are supposed to be an example to the world in tolerance and lofty goals, not to become a gang whose only concern is revenge." But Zawahiri was unable to rise to the questioner's ethical challenge. He replied, "If a criminal were to storm into your house, attack your family and kill them, steal your property, and burn down your house, then turns to attack the homes of your neighbors, will you treat him tolerantly so that you will not become a gang whose only concern is revenge?"

Zawahiri even had to defend himself for helping to spread the myth that the Israelis carried out the attacks of 9/11. He placed the blame for this rumor on Hezbollah, the Lebanese Shiite organization, which aired the notion on its television station, Al Manar. Zawahiri said indignantly, "The objective behind this lie is to deny that the Sunnis have heroes who harm America as no one has harmed it throughout its history."

Many of the questions dealt with Dr. Fadl, beginning with why Zawahiri had altered without permission Fadl's encyclopedia of jihadist philosophy, *The Compendium of the Pursuit of Divine Knowledge.* Zawahiri claimed that the writing of the book was a joint effort, because al-Jihad had financed it. He had to edit the book because it was full of theological errors. "We neither forged anything nor meddled with anything," Zawahiri said. Later, he added, "I ask those who are firm in their covenant not to pay attention to this propaganda war that the United States is launching in its prisons, which are situated in our countries." Fadl's revisions, Zawahiri warned, "place restrictions on jihadist action which, if implemented, would destroy jihad completely."

ONE AFTERNOON IN CAIRO, I visited Kamal Habib, a key leader of the first generation of al-Jihad, who is now a political scientist and analyst. His writing has gained him an audience of former radicals who, like him, have sought a path back to moderation. We met in the cafeteria of the Journalists' Syndicate, in downtown Cairo. Habib is an energetic political theorist, unbroken by ten years in prison, despite having been tortured. (His arms are marked with scars from cigarette burns.) "We now have before us two schools of thought," Habib told me. "The old school, which was expressed by al-Jihad and its spinoff, al-Qaeda, is the one that was led by Ayman al-Zawahiri, Sheikh Maqdisi, Zarqawi. The new school, which Dr. Fadl has given expression to, represents a battle of faith. It's deeper than just ideology." He went on, "The general mood of Islamist movements in the seventies was intransigence. Now the general mood is toward harmony and coexistence. The distance between the two is a measure of their experience." Ironically, Dr. Fadl's thinking gave birth to both schools. "As long as a person lives in a world of jihad, the old vision will control his thinking," Habib suggested. "When he's in battle, he doesn't wonder if he's wrong or he's right. When he's arrested, he has time to wonder."

"Dr. Fadl's revisions and Zawahiri's response show that the movement is disintegrating," Karam Zuhdy, the Islamic Group leader, told me one afternoon in his modest apartment in Alexandria. He is a striking figure, fifty-six years old, with blond hair and black eyebrows. His daughter, who is four, wrapped herself around his leg as an old black-and-white Egyptian movie played silently on a television. Such movies provide a glimpse of a more tolerant and hopeful time, before Egypt took its dark turn into revolution and Islamist violence. I asked Zuhdy how his country might have been different if he and his colleagues had never chosen the bloody path. "It would have been a lot better now," he admitted. "Our opting for violence encouraged al-Jihad to emerge." He even suggested that had the Islamists not murdered Sadat in 1981, there would be peace today between the Palestinians and the Israelis. He quoted the Prophet Muhammad: "Only what benefits people stays on the earth."

"It's very easy to start violence," Zuhdy said. "Peace is much more difficult."

Captives

I n southwest Israel, at the border of Egypt and the Gaza Strip, there is a small crossing station not far from the kibbutz of Kerem Shalom. A guard tower looms over the flat, scrubby buffer zone. Gaza never extends more than seven miles in width, and the guards in the tower above the featureless plain can see the Mediterranean Sea to the north. The main street in Gaza, Salah El-Deen Road, runs along the entire twenty-five-mile span of the territory, and on a clear night the guards can watch a car make the slow journey from the ruins of Yasir Arafat International Airport, near the Egyptian border, toward the lights of Gaza City, on the Strip's northeastern side. Observation balloons hover just outside Gaza, and pilotless drones freely cross its airspace. Israeli patrols tightly enforce a three-mile limit in the Mediterranean and fire on boats that approach the line. Between the sea and the security fence that surrounds the 140 square miles of Gaza live a million and a half Palestinians.

Every opportunity for peace in the Middle East has been led to slaughter, so it's not surprising that in the early-morning hours at this isolated desert crossing, on June 25, 2006, another moment of promise would meet the butcher. It had been a tumultuous month already. Hamas, which had convincingly won Palestine's parliamentary elections earlier that year, was waging civil war with its more moderate rival, Fatah. Armed factions ruled the streets. Then, on June 9, a tentative truce between Hamas and Israel ended after an explosion near Gaza City, apparently caused by an Israeli artillery shell, killed seven members of a Palestinian family who were picnicking on the beach. (The Israelis denied responsibility.) Hamas fired fifteen rockets into Israel the next day. The Israelis then launched air strikes into Gaza, killing eight militants and fourteen civilians, including five children.

Amid this strife, Mahmoud Abbas—the head of Fatah, and the president of the Palestinian Authority, the governing body established by the Oslo peace accords of 1993—put forward a bold idea. The people of Palestine, he declared, should be given the chance to vote on a referendum for a two-state solution to its conflict with Israel. Perhaps it was a cynical political maneuver, as the leaders of Hamas believed. The fundamental platform of Hamas was its refusal to accept Israel's right to exist, yet polls showed that Palestinians overwhelmingly supported the concept of two states. A referendum would be not only a rebuke to Hamas; it also would be a signal to Israel—and to the rest of the world—that Palestinians were determined to make peace. Abbas set the referendum for July.

Then, as muezzins were calling the Muslims to prayer just before dawn on June 25, eight Palestinian commandos crawled out of a tunnel into a grove of trees beside the Kerem Shalom crossing. A new moon was in the sky, making it the darkest night of the month. With mortar fire and anti-tank missiles providing cover, the commandos, some of them disguised in Israeli military uniforms, split into three teams. One team attacked an empty armored personnel carrier, which had been parked at the crossing as a decoy. Another team hit the observation tower. The two Israelis in the tower were injured, but not before they killed two of the attackers.

The third team shot a rocket-propelled grenade into a Merkava tank that was parked on a berm facing the security fence. The explosion shook the tank; then its rear hatch opened and three soldiers tried to flee. Two of them were shot and killed, but a third, lightly wounded, was captured. The attackers raced back into Gaza with their prize: a lanky teenager named Gilad Shalit.

Within days, the Israel Defense Forces, or IDF, had bombed the only power station in Gaza, cutting off electricity to tens of thousands of people. The borders were shut down as Israeli troops searched residential areas for Shalit, rounding up males older than sixteen. On June 29, Israeli officials arrested sixty-four senior Palestinian officials, including a third of the Palestinian cabinet and twenty members of parliament. At least four hundred Gazans were killed over the next several months, including eighty-eight children. The Israelis lost six soldiers and four civilians. Israeli authorities promised not to leave the Strip until they recovered Shalit, but by November he still had not been found, and both sides declared a cease-fire. Nothing had been resolved. Another explosion was sure to come. Certainly, no one was talking about peace initiatives any longer, and that may well have been the goal of those who captured Shalit.

FROM THE ISRAELI PERSPECTIVE, the Gaza problem was supposed to have been solved in August 2005, when Ariel Sharon, then the prime minister, closed down the Jewish settlements on the Strip and withdrew Israeli forces. The international community and the Israeli left wing applauded the move. But almost immediately, mortar and rocket attacks from the Strip multiplied. Five months later, Hamas won its parliament victory. "We dismantled the settlements, and then we sat back and said, 'Let's have a new beginning.' What we got was rockets and Gilad Shalit," Ari Shavit, a prominent columnist for the Israeli newspaper *Haaretz*, told me in 2009, three years after Shalit's capture. "People became very angry, and Shalit becomes an icon of that frustration."

We were sitting in Restobar, a noisy café in downtown Jerusalem. Nearby, Shalit's parents and supporters maintained a tent; from this makeshift office, they lobbied for Israel to release hundreds of Palestinian prisoners and detainees in exchange for Shalit's freedom. Shalit had just graduated from high school when he began his compulsory military service. His father, Noam, has described him as "a shy boy with a nervous smile and a studious disposition," who loved basketball and excelled in physics. His plight was driving Israel slightly mad. There were demonstrations, bumper stickers, and petition drives demanding his freedom. On websites and in newspapers, counters chronicled how long Shalit had been in captivity. Many voters wrote in Shalit's name in the last presidential election. "Israel is obsessed with Gilad Shalit in a way that no other nation in history has been obsessed with a prisoner of war," Shavit said.

In practice, lopsided prisoner exchanges have long been a part of Israel's history. In 1985, for instance, Israel traded more than a thousand prisoners for three soldiers captured in Lebanon. Some of those released went on to become terrorist leaders. One of them was Sheikh Ahmed Yassin, the quadriplegic schoolteacher who became the spiritual leader of Hamas, which was founded three years later. Attacks by the Hamas military wing inside Israel began in earnest in the early 1990s.

In Restobar, Shavit pointed to a spot a few feet away. "In March 2002 there was a beautiful twenty-five-year-old girl dead on the floor, right there," he said. A suicide bomber had targeted the café, which was then called Café Moment. That month alone, Palestinians killed eighty-three Israeli civilians. The entire country was in a panic, "like London during the Blitz," Shavit said. He was living nearby at the time, and at ten thirty on the night of March 9 he heard the bomb explode. He rushed out of his apartment to the scene. "I think I never ran so fast."

The restaurant was "oddly glowing," he said. He saw mutilated bodies scattered on the sidewalk. People had been blown across the street. The survivors were screaming or moaning, but inside the café it was eerily quiet. The dead girl was lying near the doorway. Inside, at the bar, three young men were sitting upright on the stools, but they were all dead. "It was as if they were still drinking their beers," Shavit recalled, "a party frozen by death." Eleven Israelis died, and more than fifty were injured. Hamas proclaimed it a "brave attack" intended to "avenge the Israeli massacres against our people."

Hamas, which was founded in Gaza, has come to embody the fears that many Israelis hold about the Palestinians. Its charter declares, "There is no solution to the Palestinian problem except by jihad." The document, which is in many respects absurd and reflects the intellectual isolation and conspiracy-fed atmosphere in Gaza at the time, cites the *Protocols of the Elders of Zion,* the infamous anti-Semitic forgery, and links Zionism to the Freemasons, the Lions Club, and "other spying groups" that aim "to violate consciences, to defeat virtues, and to annihilate Islam." In 2007, after Hamas solidified its control of Gaza, the Israeli government declared Gaza a "hostile entity" and began enforcing a blockade on a population that was already impoverished, isolated, and traumatized by years of occupation. Gaza became "Hamastan" in the Israeli newspapers. But Hamas was not weakened by the blockade. Instead, the collective punishment strengthened its argument that Israel's real goal was to eliminate the Palestinians.

On June 25, 2007, several days after Hamas took over in Gaza, the captors of Gilad Shalit released an audio recording to prove that he was still alive. "It has been a year since I was captured and my health is deteriorating," he said. "I am in need of prolonged hospitalization." He urged the Israeli government to accept Hamas's demands for his release: "Just as I have a mother and father, the thousands of Palestinian prisoners also have mothers and fathers—and their children must be returned to them." Hamas said that it would not free Shalit until Israel released 1,400 individuals, 450 of whom have been convicted of terrorist killings, including the men who planned the Café Moment bombing. The most precious commodity in all of the Gaza Strip was its only Jew.

GAZA IS A SEA of children. The average woman there has 5.1 offspring, one of the highest birth rates in the world. More than half the population is eighteen or younger, and they are crammed into a ghetto with very little for children to do. The Israeli blockade included a ban on toys, so the only playthings available were smuggled, at a premium, through tunnels from Egypt. Music is rare, except at weddings. The movie theaters were burned down by Islamists in the early 1980s. Many of Gaza's sports facilities have been destroyed by Israeli bombings, including the headquarters for the Palestinian Olympic team. There's a zoo, where donkeys have been painted to look like zebras.

Only one television station was broadcasting from Gaza, al-Aqsa—a Hamas-backed channel that gained notice for a children's show called *Pioneers for Tomorrow*. It sought to shape the thinking of Gaza's children and help them cope with the repeated traumas of their lives. The host was a young woman named Saraa. Her cohosts had a rather unfortunate history. There was Farfour the mouse, who was beaten to death by an Israeli interrogator. Then came Nahoul the bumblebee, who died trying to cross into Egypt for medical treatment. "The soldiers of the Pioneers of Tomorrow will grow up," Saraa exclaimed after the rabbit, Assud, succumbed to an Israeli bomb. "Oh, Palestine, we will liberate your soil, God willing. We liberate it from the filth of the Zionists. We will purify it with the soldiers of the Pioneers of Tomorrow." The message of the show was that life is brief and tragic and counts for little, except for the eternal struggle. Gaza's children were being groomed to die.

The main diversion for children was the beach, and after noon prayers on Fridays the shore was massed with families. Unlike the topaz waters off Tel Aviv, here the sea was murky, a consequence of twenty million gallons of raw and partially treated sewage dumped offshore every day. The main water-treatment plant was broken, and because of the blockade the spare parts that would fix it were unavailable. Fishermen with nets waded into the surf as kids romped in the stinking waves.

Israeli authorities maintained a list of about three dozen items that they permitted into Gaza, but the list was closely kept and subject to change. Almost no construction materials—such as cement, glass, steel, or plastic pipe—were allowed in, on the excuse that such items could also be used for building rockets or bunkers. Meanwhile, Hamas rocket builders and bomb makers smuggled everything they needed through the secret tunnels, as international aid organizations had to account for every brick or sack of flour.

Operation Cast Lead—a three-week-long Israeli attack on Gaza, which began in December 2008—left Gaza in ruins. "Half a year after the conflict, we don't have a single bag of cement and not a pane of glass," John Ging, the director of the United Nations Relief and Works Agency (UNRWA) for Palestinian refugees, told me. Humanitarian supplies that had been struck from Israel's list of approved items were piling up in large storage warehouses outside the Kerem Shalom crossing, and international aid worth billions of dollars awaited delivery. "For the last two school years, Israeli officials have withheld paper for textbooks because, hypothetically, the paper might be hijacked by Hamas to print seditious materials," Ging complained. When John Kerry, then the chairman of the Senate Foreign Relations Committee, visited Gaza in February 2009, he asked why pasta wasn't allowed in. Soon, macaroni was passing through the checkpoints, but jam was taken off the list. According to *Haaretz,* the IDF calculated that a hundred and six truckloads of humanitarian relief were needed every day to sustain life for a million and a half people, but the number of trucks coming into Gaza fell as low as thirty-seven. Israeli government officials told international aid officials that the aim is "no prosperity, no development, no humanitarian crisis."

VISITORS ENTER GAZA at its northeastern end, through the Erez Crossing—a high-security, barnlike building that is rarely congested, since scarcely any Palestinians are allowed to exit and so few foreigners care to visit. In 2004, the first female suicide bomber for Hamas, Reem Riyashi, a twenty-two-year-old mother of two children, blew herself up there, killing four Israelis. Since then, security cameras and remote-controlled gates have largely replaced the Israeli staff.

In Gaza, the rocky hills of Jerusalem have been ironed into a sandy plain sparsely adorned with oleander and cactus, as in South Texas. The area near Erez used to be the region's industrial zone. Israeli forces concentrated much of their fire, and their wrath, on this area. Until Operation Cast Lead, there were several concrete plants, a flour mill, and an ice cream factory, but they were all bombed or bulldozed, and the mixing trucks for the concrete were toppled. Houses and mosques and shops lay in rubble; entire neighborhoods were demolished.

The eight refugee camps in Gaza form a society that is even more isolated that the larger gulag of the Strip. More than 70 percent of Gazans are descendants of the two hundred thousand people who fled to the Strip in 1948, when the State of Israel was established. "I lived eighteen years of my life in a refugee camp," Ahmed Yousuf, the deputy foreign minister, told me. "It was one square kilometer. We just knew the sky above us and the earth below." Eventually, Yousuf was able to gain the rare opportunity to go to the West for his training (he attended the University of Missouri). "I thought at one time that Gaza was the center of the world, but when I left Gaza, I found no Gaza on the map."

The boundaries of the modern Strip were determined after the

1949 armistice between Egypt and Israel. Gaza marked the final redoubt of the Egyptian Army, and the armistice left a ribbon of coastal land, between three and seven miles wide, in Egypt's reluctant control. British authorities, who had once administered Gaza as part of their mandate over Palestine, considered Gaza *res nullius*—nobody's property. The Egyptians administered the territory until the 1967 war, when Israel captured the entire Sinai. The issue of Gaza came up repeatedly during the 1978 peace negotiations at Camp David between Israeli prime minister Menachem Begin and Egyptian president Anwar Sadat. "I myself suggested many times to Sadat, 'Take Gaza! Take Gaza!'" Aharon Barak, a former Israeli supreme court justice, who was one of Begin's main advisers, told me. "He said, 'I don't want Gaza.'" Israel and Egypt agreed to try to set up a Palestinian entity that would rule Gaza, but it was clear that neither party wanted responsibility for the Strip, so it remained in limbo, little more than a notional part of a Palestinian entity that might never come into existence.

Gaza's status as a ward of someone else's state changed abruptly with the 2006 elections. Fatah, long the dominant force in the two Palestinian territories, had been expected to win easily, but this underestimated popular resentment against a party that was famously crooked, incompetent, and so careless that it ran several candidates for identical offices. On the ballot, Hamas called itself the List of Change and Reform, although voters knew whom they were voting for. Polls had predicted that Hamas would receive about 30 percent of the vote; instead, it won a decisive majority in the Palestinian Legislative Council.

International organizations declared that in order for Hamas to be accepted it would have to recognize the State of Israel, renounce violence, and respect extant diplomatic agreements. Hamas rebuffed those conditions, triggering a drastic cutoff of aid. Israel was further shaken when Ariel Sharon, the prime minister, suffered a debilitating stroke and fell into a coma. His replacement, Ehud Olmert, declared that the Palestinian government was becoming a "terrorist authority" and that the Israelis would have no contact with it.

Fatah refused to step aside and let Hamas govern. For months, there were large demonstrations by both factions in the West Bank and Gaza, along with kidnappings, gun battles, and assassinations. In March 2007, King Abdullah of Saudi Arabia arranged a peace accord, but it was merely a prelude to open civil war in Gaza, three months later. During six bloody days in June, Hamas swept aside the American-trained Fatah security force and took over the government that it had been elected to lead the previous year. These clashes left a bitter residue. "In Gaza Strip, we are crowded into a very small space," Yehia Rabah, a member of Fatah and a former ambassador to Yemen, told me. "Hate doesn't dissolve easily. We see each other every day."

Although the new prime minister of Gaza, Ismail Haniyeh, emphasized that Hamas had no intention of making Gaza an Islamic state, it seized the judiciary, appointing Islamist judges who imposed Sharia on the court system. "The whole place is becoming a mosque," a young female reporter, Asma al-Ghoul, told me. She had recently been hassled on the beach by self-appointed morality police, even though she was wearing jeans and a long-sleeved shirt. An economist, Omar Shaban, said, "The siege has left Hamas with no competition. Secular people are punished. The future is frightening."

ON A SEARINGLY HOT July day, I visited a Hamas summer camp. Hundreds of young boys in green caps shouted slogans before several top party officials, who were seated under an awning in the courtyard of the school where the camp was taking place. One by one the leaders stood to make speeches, exhorting the children with their flushed faces to struggle and sacrifice. I had come to meet with some of the men involved with the Shalit negotiations—in particular, Khalil el-Hayya, one of the early leaders of Hamas.

As it happened, I had food poisoning. I wished I had paid more attention to the waiter the night before, as I was ordering dinner. After my earlier examination of the polluted Gaza coastline, I had ruled out eating fish. I decided to try the steak, which would have been smuggled through the tunnels. "Would you like that well done, or *very* well done?" the waiter had asked. At four in the morning, I understood his caution.

Finally the droning speeches ended, the children dispersed, and Hayya and I retreated to a classroom to talk. A former professor of

Islamic law, Hayya sported a graying beard and a prayer mark high on his forehead below his retreating hairline. He seemed serene and almost jolly, despite the constant threat of assassination, perhaps from one of the Israeli drones patrolling the sky.

There was a semicircle of folding chairs set up in the classroom, where Hayya and I sat, along with a dozen other Hamas leaders who came to watch the interview. I felt like Oprah—a nauseous and dehydrated Oprah. A ceiling fan barely stirred the broiling air. It was so humid I thought it might rain in the room.

I asked Hayya about the population explosion. The Israelis feel threatened by what they often call a "demographic time bomb." Hayya laughed and said that there was nothing sinister about the enormous number of children. "We just love to reproduce," he said. He has six living children himself; an Israeli bomb, which had been aimed at him, had killed a seventh.

Five minutes into the interview, I realized I was going to faint.

As Hayya was assuring me that Hamas stands for "the Islam of tolerance and justice and equality," I suddenly found myself on the floor of the classroom. Two men dragged a very sketchy mattress into the circle of chairs and covered it with prayer mats. I crawled onto the mattress and continued the interview, surrounded by the dusty boots of Hamas.

Later, I reflected on this moment, thinking how reduced I sometimes feel as an American in the Middle East—how feckless are my good intentions, my attempts at understanding people whose hatred for each other is as unchanging as the sunrise. These concerned men who were holding my hand and asking if I wanted water or a soda, anything to make me feel better, they were the same ones who were holding Gilad Shalit.

THE NEXT MORNING, I visited a mosque where about forty teenage boys were attending a day camp devoted to memorizing the Quran. The Islamic holy book contains more than six thousand verses—it's about the same length as the New Testament—and this summer twenty thousand boys and girls had undertaken the challenge, in camps across the Strip. At the mosque, a small crowd was waiting for the prime minister, who was rumored to be coming to talk to the boys. Because the Israelis had targeted Haniyeh for assassination (they have fired missiles into his office and his home), he's constantly on the move. I was told that his visit to the mosque was my best chance to meet him.

While the boys rocked back and forth on the carpet, reciting in low voices, I was introduced to an elderly refugee and a former member of the Palestinian Legislative Council. Bald and freckled, with a white mustache, he gave his name as Abu Majid. He was urged to tell me his story. "On 15 May, 1948, I was twenty-two years old," he said. Israel had formally declared itself an independent nation the day before, triggering the invasion by five Arab armies bent on destroying the Zionists. Egypt moved forces into the Negev Desert, approaching Beersheba, where Majid lived. "The Egyptian Army asked youngsters like me to help with logistics," he said.

After one battle with the Israelis, Abu Majid and a friend dragged several wounded soldiers inside a bunker. A dozen people were already hiding there. That night, Israeli troops discovered the shelter and ordered everyone out. "There were four old men over seventy, one of whom had a wife who was sixty or sixty-five," Abu Majid said. A younger, dark-skinned woman had two boys and a girl. Upon leaving the shelter, with their hands raised, they were all shot. "I don't know why I'm alive," Abu Majid said. "The blood came on me. I was one of three who God saved. We were seven days in the desert of Negev before we reached the villages around Hebron." He had family there. His parents, believing him dead, had erected a mourning tent and were receiving condolences when a friend brought news that their son was alive. His brother slaughtered a sheep in celebration. As he told me his story, Abu Majid wept, the tears streaming into his mustache.

I wondered: Did this really happen? Israeli troops shooting down wounded soldiers and civilians who had surrendered, including elderly women and children? I checked Benny Morris's definitive history: *1948: The First Arab-Israeli War,* in which he noted that the fall of Beersheba was marked by many atrocities on the part of Israeli forces. "A number of civilians were executed after being stripped of valuables," he writes. The survivors were expelled—into Gaza.

After two hours of waiting for Haniyeh to arrive at the mosque, some members of the audience gave up. Suddenly, the room began to stir. "He's coming after all," a neighbor assured me. Several television reporters appeared, followed by a small convoy, and then Haniyeh strode in, waving at his supporters. He was forty-seven, squarely built, with a round face and cautious green eyes that floated above a trim white beard. He was dressed in a stark white gallabiya and a skullcap, which added to his ministerial air. A former dean of Islamic University, in Gaza City, Haniyeh grew up in one of the local refugee camps. In 1989, after the first intifada, he spent three years in an Israeli prison. Then, in a decision that Israel deeply regrets, Haniyeh and four hundred other activists were expelled to South Lebanon, where they formed an enduring alliance with Hezbollah.

By Hamas standards, Haniyeh was a moderate. He had spoken of negotiating a long-term truce with Israel. That placed him at odds with many of the party's top officials. Khaled Meshal, the overall leader of Hamas, was living in exile in Damascus, Syria; a hard-liner, he was more likely to initiate radical, destabilizing actions—such as capturing Gilad Shalit. A council, dominated by representatives of its underground military wing, governed the party. Because so many Hamas members have been assassinated, the movement operated as an unsteady collective. Even prominent party members didn't always know who was in control. Haniyeh's authority was further undermined by the fact that Mahmoud Abbas, the Palestinian president, dismissed him as prime minister of Gaza in June 2007, after the Hamas takeover, and appointed Salam Fayyad, a Fatah loyalist, in his place. Hamas refused to recognize the move, and Haniyeh continued to govern Gaza while Abbas and Fayyad ran the West Bank, under Israeli occupation.

There were talks under way in Cairo to explore the creation of a unity government between Hamas and Fatah, and to make a deal for Gilad Shalit. The Israeli papers were full of expectation about an imminent prisoner swap, but Noam Shalit, Gilad's father, told me that the reports were "ridiculous." He was pessimistic about the prospects for a deal anytime soon. "Hamas ignores every aspect of international conventions," he said. "They would like hard-core killers released. I feel very bad about that." He added that his son's abduction had become "a bottleneck" that had brought all negotiations to a stand-still.

At the mosque, Haniyeh addressed the campers on the importance of reciting the Quran. "There are two kinds of people," he advised them. "Those who know the Quran is right and who follow it, and those who turn their backs on the Quran." When he finished speaking, Haniyeh kissed each child who had memorized a third of the Quran, and awarded him fifty Israeli shekels.

Afterward, amid a crush of petitioners, I asked Haniyeh whether the Cairo talks had made any progress. "It's just one step in breaking the siege of Gaza," he said, adding that he hoped the talks would allow reconstruction to begin. I asked if he had had contact with the Obama administration. Khaled Meshal had responded positively to Obama's June address to the Muslim world, welcoming the "new language toward Hamas" and calling for open dialogue. Haniyeh didn't answer directly. He said that Washington had no veto power over the choice of the Palestinian people but added, "We are ready to deal." He also said that he would step down from his post if he became an obstacle to peace. "The most important thing is the unity of the Palestinian people. We are willing to do whatever it takes," he said, as the guards shouldered me aside.

I made note of his comments, but wondered what chance he had to make peace if he couldn't even make a deal to release one captured soldier.

I WALKED OUTSIDE, among shuttered shops. "The term 'economy' is no longer valid in the Gaza Strip," Omar Shaban, the economist, told me. In 1994, the poverty rate in Gaza was 16 percent (in the United States at the time, it was 14.5). But by 1996 the Israelis had virtually shut out Palestinian labor, and the second intifada, four years later, put an end to tourism in Gaza. Before then, Shaban said, more than ten thousand people a month were visiting the territory, many of them Israelis who had come to enjoy Gaza's beaches and seafood. Most remaining economic activity abruptly halted in 2007, with the Israeli blockade of Gaza. Two years later, according to the UN, about 70 percent of Gazans were living on less than a dollar a day, and 75 percent

relied on international food assistance. Unemployment was practically universal, except for people working for international organizations, or trading in the black market. According to the International
Committee of the Red Cross, 96 percent of Gaza's industrial sector
collapsed after Operation Cast Lead.

Ever since the Hamas takeover, Egypt, Gaza's nominal ally, has
cooperated with the Israelis in enforcing the blockade. The authorities in Cairo have their own reasons for sequestering Gaza. Hamas is
a spinoff of the Muslim Brotherhood, and the Egyptian government
of Hosni Mubarak worried about contagion. The wall that defines
the Gaza Strip along the Israeli border simply turns the corner upon
reaching Egypt.

In January 2008, Hamas improvised a radical solution to Egypt's
restrictions by blowing holes in the security fence surrounding Rafah,
the southernmost town in Gaza. Over the next eleven days, hundreds
of thousands of Gazans streamed into the Sinai with shopping lists.
The Egyptian police formed a cordon that kept Gazans from straying
too far into the country. The shops along the border were soon empty.
The Gazans went home and the Egyptians sealed up the wall again.

Although the West Bank is only twenty-five miles from the Gaza
Strip, it feels in many respects even more distant than other parts
of the world. The Israelis began requiring special permits for travel
between the two halves of Palestine in 1988. When Taher al-Nunu,
the chief spokesman for Prime Minister Haniyeh, was working in the
Foreign Ministry, he was allowed to travel around the world, but like
many Gazans, he's never been to the West Bank. "I was in China,
Istanbul, and Indonesia, but I didn't go to Nablus, Ramallah, and
Qalqilya," he said.

I began to see Gaza as, I suspect, many Gazans do: a floating island,
a dystopian Atlantis, drifting farther away from contact with any other
society. Omar Shaban told me that twenty years before, he could easily drive to Tel Aviv for dinner, and more than a hundred thousand
Palestinians traveled into Israel every day for work. "The Palestinian
economy was structured to work with the Israeli economy," he said.
"Most Palestinians knew Hebrew. There were real friendships." Now,
he said, "two-thirds of Gaza youth under thirty have never been out-

side the Strip. How can they psychologically think of peace? You can fight someone you don't know, but you can't make peace with him."

A NERVOUS-LOOKING YOUNG MAN was pacing on the side of the narrow coastal road outside Gaza City, just past the ruins of the presidential palace, which had been destroyed during Operation Cast Lead. My driver stopped for him, and he got into the backseat without a word, indicating that we should continue driving south. It was a Friday afternoon, after prayers, and the beaches were crowded.

Since the Hamas takeover, there have been many warnings that al-Qaeda has infiltrated Gaza. In the summer of 2007, Mahmoud Abbas accused Hamas of "shielding" jihadists. "Through its bloody conduct, Hamas has become very close to al-Qaeda," he said. I had heard about several splinter groups in Gaza that were seen as al-Qaeda affiliates. After extensive negotiations, I was able to arrange a meeting with a representative of one of them. The man in the backseat would guide us there.

We drove past the site of a former Jewish settlement. Across the road were the remains of the greenhouses that the settlers had left behind, intact, with the understanding that Gaza farmers would take them over. The greenhouses were meant to become an important part of the agricultural economy. Gaza's main exports were strawberries, cherry tomatoes, and carnations, destined mainly for Israel and Europe. But then the Israelis clamped the borders shut and the fruit rotted. The carnations were fed to livestock. Now the greenhouses are nothing more than bare frames, their tattered plastic roofing fluttering in the sea breeze.

Our guide pointed to a rise ahead, where a lookout stood guard over another stretch of public beach. We turned in to a sandy drive and parked behind a row of palm-frond cabanas. The lookout ducked into a Port-a-Potty and emerged with an AK-47 and a 9-mm pistol. Like the guide, he was quiet and unsmiling. He wore jeans and a plaid shirt. He led me to one of the cabanas, where a heavy man in a blue suit was waiting. The man said that I should call him Abu Mohammed. He politely offered tea.

Abu Mohammed claimed to represent four armed groups that have joined a jihadi coalition. (There was such an alliance, called the Popular Resistance Committees.) "When I speak, I speak for all of them," he told me. "We consider Osama bin Laden our spiritual father." He said his group followed the same ideology as al-Qaeda, but there was no direct connection. "The siege around Gaza has disconnected us from the outside world," he said. "None of us can travel." In Gaza, he estimated, there were about four hundred armed fighters in cells like his, down from as many as fifteen hundred before the Hamas takeover. When Fatah ran the Strip, it was easier for subversives to operate, he said, but now "Hamas is in full control, and their power is very tight." Hamas, he explained, wanted to dictate when violence occurred in Gaza and tried to keep the al-Qaeda sympathizers like him penned in.

As we talked, the lookout with the machine gun dragged in a table, and a tea boy arrived, carrying a tray and glasses. It was sweltering inside the hut. Abu Mohammed took off his jacket; his shirt was soaked through. He had a quiet voice and often stared into space as he spoke. He said that he was a former political science student who had been jailed first by the Israelis and later by Hamas officials. He gestured to his suit jacket, now in his lap. During his second internment, "Hamas brought in a moderate sheikh with a suit and a tie and the smell of roses to discuss the way we look," he said, in a wry tone. "If I want to dress like my comrades in Afghanistan and Iraq"—wearing the shalwar kameez, the uniform favored by jihadi veterans—"that's prohibited." Finally his jailers released him with a warning: "Don't do anything against our cease-fire!" He complained, "We feel we're under a microscope. If an Internet café or a beauty salon is burned, immediately they come round up the people they know. If Hamas suspects I am behind all this troublemaking, they will hang me by both hands and both feet for thirty days—that's the minimum."

I asked what his main complaint was against Hamas.

"We thought Hamas was going to apply Islamic law here, but they are not," he said. He spoke of the "fancy restaurants on the beach" and said that Hamas tolerated uncovered women there. "They have a much more moderate way of life, and we cannot deal with that."

When I mentioned Gilad Shalit, Abu Mohammed smiled and said,

"I cannot talk about this, but a member of our group participated." (Three factions claimed responsibility for the abduction: the armed wing of Hamas, the Popular Resistance Committees, and the Army of Islam.) Mohammed said that the participant's name was Mohammad Farwaneh, and that he had been killed during the operation. Hamas had exclusive control of Shalit. Mohammed said of the arrangement, "We respect this, because of the higher interest of the exchange of prisoners." Recently, he said, his group had tried to carry off another abduction, but had failed.

I asked him what drew young men into his movement. "First, we have a clear ideology," he said. "Some come because they like our style, and they don't want to live by the rules. Those we don't usually put our money on—when they're tortured, we're finished. Some come from Hamas and feel that they were not treated fairly." Others, like him, thought that Hamas was not following true Islam. Abu Mohammed said that most of the recruits were fellow refugees, but "many are locals from hard-line families—those who believe there is no middle road."

Joint operations with Hamas, such as the Shalit abduction, had ended. "We have no meetings at all with Hamas," Abu Mohammed said. "It's almost as if they want to finish us." He met my eyes at last. "We know how strong they are and how supported they are on the street, but we can't live underground forever."

Six weeks after this conversation, a group of radical Islamists, calling themselves the Soldiers of the Followers of God, stood on the steps of a mosque near the Egyptian border and declared Gaza to be an Islamic emirate. That afternoon, members of the Hamas military wing and the Gaza police surrounded the mosque, demanding that the radicals give themselves up. A shoot-out erupted, continuing into the night. At least twenty-four people were killed, including the group's leader, Sheikh Abdul Latif Mousa. A hundred people were wounded. I have not been able to determine if Abu Mohammed was a casualty. One of the Hamas fatalities was Abu Jibril Shimali, a commander of its armed wing. Israelis blamed him for orchestrating the capture of Gilad Shalit.

JUST OUTSIDE RAFAH, the smuggling capital of Gaza, there is a bill-board with a portrait of Shalit, behind bars, juxtaposed with a photograph of a masked Hamas fighter. The Arabic text declares, "Your prisoner will not have safety and security until our prisoners have safety and security." In a place where commercial advertising scarcely exists, the billboard looked at first like another ubiquitous martyr poster.

Shalit's pale features and meek expression haunt the imagination of Gazans. A powerful sense of identification had arisen between the shy soldier and the people whose government was holding him hostage, but the similarity rankled many. Like Shalit, Gazans were confined and abandoned; unlike him, no one cared. "Everybody talks about Shalit as if he's a holy man," Ahmed Yousuf, the deputy foreign minister, complained. "The whole world is showing such concern about a soldier who is still young and unmarried." Meanwhile, Israel was holding more than seven thousand Palestinians, nearly nine hundred of them from Gaza, who, like Shalit, were cut off from their families and are sometimes held without charge. "People say, 'What's the difference between their Shalit and our Shalits?'" Yousuf remarked. "We are *all* Shalits."

I spoke to Osama Mozini, a professor of education at Islamic University, who was overseeing the Shalit negotiations for the government. A barrel-chested man with a stiff beard, he spent five years in an Israeli prison and was arrested three times by the Palestinian Authority because of Hamas activities. I asked him why he could not be more flexible in his negotiations for Shalit. Israel was plainly eager to make a deal that would involve the release of hundreds of Palestinians, many of them convicted of bloody crimes. Mozini bridled at the implication that the Palestinian prisoners were murderers and Shalit was not. "This one who has been abducted is an Israeli soldier who was on the border throwing shells that were killing Palestinians," he said. "We did not take him from the market or from his family. We took him from a military tank on the Gaza border."

The IDF wouldn't say whether Shalit had been involved in military actions against Gaza, but the tanks that lined the border did lob shells into the territory, causing many random casualties. While I was there, a teenage girl was killed, and her young brother injured, in such an incident. The Israelis maintained a buffer zone along the border about half a mile deep, which placed at least 30 percent of the Strip's arable land off limits. Every mile along the perimeter there were remotely controlled machine-gun emplacements, called "Spot and Strike," which were operated by an all-female crew, using joysticks to pull the triggers at a remote Israeli base. "Nearly every week, there are reported cases of farmers being shot at," Mohammed Ali Abu Najela, an Oxfam researcher, told me. He said that Gazans understood the rule to be this: "If I can see you, I will shoot you."

Mozini claimed that Gazans whose relatives were being held in Israel were not pressuring him to make a deal for Shalit. "They are backing us up," he said. "Everybody is asking us to stand firm to get our prisoners back, because this is our only chance."

Mozini began reciting the names of Gazan prisoners who had received sentences of more than a thousand years. Hassan Salameh, a Hamas operative, was serving forty-eight consecutive life sentences for recruiting suicide bombers. Walid Anjes helped plan the bombing at Café Moment and two other devastating attacks. He had twenty-six life sentences. Mozini mentioned a prisoner named Abdel Hadi Suleiman Ghneim: "He was riding in a bus. All he did was grab the steering wheel and take it over a cliff." He laughed. "Sixteen people were dead and many wounded—even Ghneim was wounded!" Ghneim received a life sentence for every person who died on the bus. These punishments struck Mozini as ludicrous. He assured me that Israel had "no choice" but to comply with Hamas's terms.

I WENT TO RAFAH to examine the tunnels that have created a subterranean economy in Gaza. Everything that went in or out of the Strip, except the three dozen or so commodities that Israel permitted to enter the territory, traveled through a hole in the ground. That included gas, cows, weapons, money, drugs, cars (which were disassembled for the trip), and people. There were hundreds of such tunnels, and they became a primary target for the Israeli Air Force during Operation Cast Lead. When I got there a few months later, tunnel diggers were still repairing the damage—practically the only reconstruction work I saw in Gaza. A long, ragged row of tents ran about fifty yards from the Egyptian border amid great mounds of sand, and shirtless men worked their claims. Across the border was a village that had once been a part of greater Rafah before the security fence divided the town. The workers aimed the tunnels at different buildings across the border, where collaborators would have hollowed out a bathroom floor or a spot under a bed. Most of the smuggling was done at night, honoring the conceit that the excavations were secret, even though an Egyptian police station nearby had a clear view of the tunnelers' tents. Occasionally, the Egyptians cracked down, blowing up or flooding the passageways. Tunnels also collapsed, especially after bombings, which destabilized the soil. But tunneling was one of the few functioning industries in Gaza, accounting for some thirty-five thousand jobs before Israel's December attacks.

In the tunnel I visited, three men were on the surface and twenty were underground. A motorized pulley extracted buckets of sand. It can take three months to break through to the other side. The tunnel operator, a young man with a big smile and bright calcium deposits on his teeth, slyly introduced himself as Abu Hussein. The other men laughed: it's a pet name in Gaza for Barack Hussein Obama. The operator charged clients a thousand dollars to ship a ton of raw materials through the tunnel, or fifty dollars for a bag of forty kilos. He said that tunnelers frequently bump into one another underground: "It's like Swiss cheese." It was through such a tunnel that the captors of Gilad Shalit crossed into Israeli territory.

Old Soviet-designed GRAD rockets, manufactured in North Korea and China, and knockoff missiles from Iran also made their way through the underground passageways, which was one reason that Israel felt the urgency to act. These weapons had a much greater range than homemade rockets. From the northern end of Gaza, the GRADs could reach Ashkelon, seven miles away, a city of more than a hundred thousand people.

According to the IDF, between 2000 and 2008 some twelve thousand rockets and mortars were fired into Israel; sometimes as many as sixty or eighty rockets a day were launched, but because they are so inaccurate the number of Israeli casualties was relatively modest: fewer than thirty deaths. Still, the anxiety and fury stirred up by the fusillade placed the government of Ehud Olmert under extreme pressure in the run-up to the Israeli elections, in February 2009. Across the Israeli border in Sderot, the police station displayed the exploded carcasses of hundreds of rockets that have landed in the area. Barack Obama had visited there as a candidate, in July 2008. "No country would accept missiles landing on the heads of its citizens," he said. "If missiles were falling where my two daughters sleep, I would do everything in order to stop that." Despite Obama's assurances, the Israeli government decided to get the war over before the Bush administration left power.

The stated goal for Operation Cast Lead was to "destroy the terrorist infrastructure," but there were larger aims. "We cannot allow Gaza to remain under Hamas control," Tzipi Livni, the foreign minister at the time, said. Six months before the operation began, Israel and Hamas had agreed to a truce, but neither side really believed in the possibility of peace. Each had become so dehumanized in the eyes of the other that there was actual pleasure in contemplating the catastrophe about to fall on Gaza. The Israeli deputy defense minister, Matan Vilnai, invoked the Holocaust, warning that Gazans were "bringing upon themselves a greater Shoah, because we will use all our strength in every way we deem appropriate." Meantime, Fathi Hamad, a member of the Palestinian parliament, boasted that it was Hamas policy to use civilians as human shields. "We desire death as you desire life," he said, speaking for all Gazans, half of whom are children, who were trapped inside the Strip.

On December 19, 2008, the six-month truce between Hamas and Israel formally expired. Israel was willing to extend it, but Hamas refused. Haniyeh complained that Israel had failed to ease the blockade, as the agreement had stipulated, and so Hamas rockets began flying again. By then, Gaza had run out of allies. Yossi Alpher, an Israeli political analyst and former Mossad officer, was in Europe when the invasion began. "I was having a good stiff drink with a Saudi colleague," he recalled. "He told me, 'This time, do it right.'"

A FEW WEEKS BEFORE Operation Cast Lead began, Colonel Herzi Halevi, the commander of the Thirty-fifth Paratroop Brigade for the IDF, was flying over the Strip in a helicopter when he saw three rockets rise out of the Jabalia refugee camp. "I saw the rainbow of smoke, and then fifty to sixty seconds later you see it goes into Sderot," he told me. "It's eleven o'clock in the morning. Children are in school. Whether they live or die is a question of whether they are lucky or not. This is something that no other country can accept."

Halevi, now a brigadier general, is tall and lean, and has a reputation for being an even-tempered, sometimes aloof commander. Like many Israelis, he had come to the conclusion that Gazans deserved what they were going to get. "I had a feeling that on the other side of the fence, in the Gaza Strip, we didn't find a leadership, or even the sound of people in Gaza saying something different except fighting, shooting rockets, and kidnapping." His long career has taught him that in dealing with terrorism, "if you are not decisive enough, it is not going to be effective." He had spent much of his career in Sayeret Matkal, an elite hostage-rescue unit. It is likely that rescuing Gilad Shalit was another goal of the operation, although the IDF wouldn't comment on that. "I told my soldiers that was not our mission," Halevi told me. "Our mission was to take care that we do not become another Gilad Shalit."

On the morning of December 27, 2008, a training exercise was under way at the police academy in Gaza City. Scores of police officers were in a courtyard. Across the street, children were getting out of school. A pair of Israeli F-16s screamed overhead, part of the first wave of aircraft aimed at police stations, command centers, and Hamas training camps. Explosions engulfed the courtyard. In less than five minutes, dozens of people were killed, and hundreds were wounded.

At the school, many of the students were injured. As parents frantically searched for their children, another wave of aircraft raced over the Strip, targeting the militants, who were expected to respond by launching retaliatory rockets. Indeed, one Israeli was killed that day by a Hamas rocket; according to the UN, the death toll in Gaza reached 280, with 900 wounded. It was one of the deadliest days of conflict between Israel and its neighbors since 1967.

An Arabic teacher, who asked not to be identified, carried to al-Shifa hospital one of his students—a fourteen-year-old boy with shards of glass blown into his back and leg. That night, the teacher and his family stayed in their house. "The bombing started again—it felt like an earthquake, our home was shaking," he recalled. He was afraid that the windows would shatter, so he removed them. The weather was freezing and the utilities in his home had been shut off. The next day, he went foraging for food and fuel. A mosque near his house had been destroyed. Also nearby was Beit Lehia Elementary School, which the UNRWA had turned into an emergency shelter for fifteen hundred people. It had just been hit by white-phosphorus artillery shells. Such munitions are usually employed to produce smoke screens, but they are also powerful incendiaries, and their use in civilian areas is considered a war crime. "The smoke was very white, and when it comes on the ground it doesn't explode—it just burns," the teacher recalled. The tentacles of fire that enveloped the school reminded him of a giant octopus. Two children burned to death.

From the beginning, there was a dispute about who among the dead and wounded qualified as a "civilian." Some police officers in Gaza had been recruited from the military wing of Hamas, but the Israelis regarded all police as Hamas apparatchiks. In several instances, armed drones killed children who were on rooftops. Were they "spotters," as the Israelis speculated, or children at play, as human-rights workers in Gaza contended? Such questions demonstrate the difficulty that any urban conflict poses in separating actual combatants from innocent civilians. They also underscore the biases that had taken root in each camp: the Israeli belief that Hamas terrorists and the Gazan people were one and the same; the Gazan tendency to support any act of resistance against the Israelis, no matter how self-defeating it might be.

The air operation lasted for more than a week. Gaza's main prison was struck, with prisoners still in their cells. Drones crisscrossed the Strip, using high-resolution cameras for precisely targeted missile strikes. Despite the accuracy of such weapons, Israeli and Palestinian human-rights groups reported that eighty-seven civilians were killed by drone strikes, including twelve people who were waiting for a UN bus.

On December 30, the Air Force began demolishing government buildings and cultural institutions. "The Israeli authorities said they were going to destroy the infrastructure of terror," John Ging, the UNRWA director, told me. But they also attacked what he called "the infrastructure of peace," such as the American International School in Gaza, the premier educational institution in the Strip. "It had been attacked on two occasions by the extremists," Ging said. "They did not succeed in destroying it. It took an F-16 for that." The caretaker of the school was killed in the attack. The ministries of finance and foreign affairs, the presidential palace, and the parliament were also struck. "These are the buildings of democracy," Ging said. "We in the international community have been building these for a decade, for a future state of Palestine, and they now lie in ruins." Over a six-hour period, several buildings in the UNRWA compound housing the agency's food and fuel supplies were shelled repeatedly, despite numerous calls from UN officials protesting the onslaught.

Meanwhile, Hamas rockets continued flying into Israel. One hit a construction site in Ashkelon, killing a Bedouin construction worker and injuring sixteen colleagues. A mother of four died when a rocket exploded near her car in the center of Ashdod. Another rocket landed in Beersheba, twenty-five miles from the Gaza border, injuring six Israeli citizens, including a seven-year-old boy. At Bar Zilai Hospital in Sderot, a rocket landed nearby. "Maybe God prevented the hospital from being hit," the director, Shimon Scharf, told me. Then a GRAD rocket struck a mall in the city. "Twenty minutes later, I had eighty-five patients in the ER," Scharf said. "The next day, one hundred thirty." Four or five of them, he said, were "real casualties," including a woman who had shrapnel in her face. The remainder suffered from what Dr. Scharf diagnosed as post-traumatic stress.

The Israeli military adopted painstaking efforts to spare civilian lives in Gaza. Two and a half million leaflets were dropped into areas that were about to come under attack, urging noncombatants to "move to city centers." But Gaza is essentially a cage, and the city centers also came under attack. Intelligence officers called residents whose houses were going to be targeted, urging them to flee. The Israeli Air Force dropped "roof knockers"—small, noisemaking shells—on top of some houses to warn the residents to escape before the real bomb fell on them.

During the eight days of bombings, the Strip's water and electrical facilities were hit, and many mosques were destroyed. The Israelis assert that mosques served as arms depots for the resistance, and that

Hamas placed its own citizens at risk by launching attacks from civilian areas.

All the while, ground troops stood by on the perimeter of Gaza. None of the goals of the operation had been achieved: every day, there were rocket and mortar attacks from the Strip, Hamas remained in control, and Gilad Shalit was still missing. Hamas officials even baited the Israelis, saying, "We are waiting for you to enter Gaza—to kill you or make you into Shalits." That prospect was very much in the minds of some military leaders. The Israeli press reported that soldiers were ordered to kill themselves if they were captured. "No matter what happens, no one will be kidnapped," a company commander told his troops, according to the Tel Aviv newspaper *Yediot Ahronot*. "We will not have Gilad Shalit 2."

A ground invasion began on January 3. According to Amnesty International, some Israeli troops were encouraged to fire at "anything that moved." A number of soldiers spoke to a human-rights group called Breaking the Silence about the behavior of Israeli forces during Operation Cast Lead. One said that his orders were "You see a house, a window? Shoot at the window. You don't see a terrorist there? Fire at the window. . . . In urban warfare, anyone is your enemy. No innocents." Another soldier said, "The goal was to carry out an operation with the least possible casualties for the army, without its even asking itself what the price would be for the other side." A military rabbi told soldiers, "No pity, God protects you, everything you do is sanctified," and "This is a holy war."

The ground troops attacked Gaza simultaneously from the north and the east. The soldiers expected fierce resistance, but the border areas were spookily empty. Some units spent a week in the Strip without seeing a single Arab. Halevi led the paratroopers into the northeastern zone. The first night, he occupied a small town, El Atatra. "This is what I found," he told me later, in his office on a military base near Tel Aviv. He unfurled a map, drawn by Hamas fighters, showing where snipers were to be stationed, tunnels had been dug, and improvised explosive devices had been planted. "They took a civilian neighborhood and turned it into a military camp," Halevi observed. He showed me photographs of arms caches that his soldiers had uncovered in mosques, and of houses that had been booby-trapped.

"This is the house of one of the Hamas officers in El Atatra," he said, projecting a photograph of a dummy standing beside a dark staircase. "The dummy is to make us think he is a soldier. Behind him was an IED. There was also a tunnel. The idea was that our soldiers see the dummy, they run to shoot him, and the IED explodes. Then the terrorists come out of the tunnel and kidnap our soldiers."

Human Rights Watch reported eleven instances of Israeli troops shooting civilians carrying white flags, including five women and four children—one of many incidents that human-rights groups say may constitute war crimes. According to Halevi, Hamas fighters had stationed weapons in various houses so that they could fire on the Israelis. When the troops approached, the fighters came outside unarmed, carrying a white flag. Maintaining this guise, they ran over to another arms cache and resumed firing.

Halevi also accused Hamas of using human shields: "If you launch a rocket and two seconds later hold a child in your hands in order to protect yourself from our helicopters, *you* are committing a war crime." (Amnesty International has reported that it found "no evidence that Hamas or other Palestinian fighters directed the movement of civilians to shield military objectives from attacks.")

Halevi told me, "The easiest thing would have been to attack from the air with cannons—just erase the town. We didn't even think about that." He said his unit took extra risks in order to avoid civilian casualties. One of his officers was killed. "To speak about us like the tribes in Darfur or Bosnia that really exercise war crimes, this is something I can't understand," he said.

Most of Israel's immediate military goals were achieved within hours of the ground invasion. What followed was the systematic destruction of Gaza's infrastructure. Al Quds hospital, where many of the wounded were being treated, was shelled, under the mistaken belief that a Hamas headquarters was in the building. Meanwhile, tanks fired on houses, mosques, and schools. The Israeli Navy strafed buildings along the coast and the intelligence headquarters in Gaza City. Armored bulldozers took down houses and factories. Israel's deputy prime minister, Eli Yishai, later said, "Even if the rockets fall in open air, or to the sea, we should hit their infrastructure and destroy one hundred homes for every rocket fired." Houses that weren't destroyed were sometimes vandalized. Halevi had to send several soldiers back to Israel for ethical violations. "We told them, 'We don't want you, you have a level of morality we don't accept.'" But most of the damage was officially tolerated, if not encouraged. According to various international agencies, 14 percent of the buildings in Gaza were partially or completely destroyed, including 21,000 homes, 700 factories and businesses, 16 hospitals, 38 primary health-care centers, and 280 schools.

Thirteen Israelis died, including nine soldiers—four of them from friendly fire—and four civilians, who were killed by rockets. (Israeli civilian casualties were kept to a minimum because many residents near the border fled the area, and those who remained hid inside fortified bunkers.) Hamas claims that only forty-eight fighters were lost during the entire operation. The toll on Gaza civilians was far higher. According to Amnesty International, 1,400 Gazans died, including 300 children; 5,000 were wounded. Israel claims that only 1,166 Palestinians died, 295 of them civilians.

Because the Israeli military forbade international observers and journalists to enter Gaza during the operation, the scale of the destruction was largely hidden from view. One voice in Gaza that became familiar to Israeli television viewers was that of Ezzeldeen Abu al-Aish, a Palestinian gynecologist and peace activist who had trained and practiced in Israel. He often spoke to Israel's Channel 10, giving reports, in Hebrew, about the medical crisis in the Gaza hospitals. On January 16, the day before the war ended, a tank shell went through a bedroom window of his fourth-floor apartment in Jabalia, killing two of his teenage daughters and a niece, and seriously injuring another daughter and several relatives. His oldest daughter ran into the room to see what had happened, only to be struck dead by a second tank shell.

Moments later, he rang the Channel 10 newsman Shlomi Eldar on his cell phone, in the middle of a broadcast. Eldar answered on air, and the anguished wails of Abu al-Aish on the other end of the line jolted many Israelis. "No one can get to us," the doctor cried, begging for help to get his injured family to a hospital. "My God. . . . Shlomi, can't anyone help us?" Eldar persuaded the Israeli Army to let ambulances through to rescue the survivors.

The IDF initially claimed that Palestinian rockets had struck the building, and then, after that was disproved, that the Israeli tank was responding to "suspicious" figures on the third floor. Later still, the IDF admitted that the tank had fired the two shells that killed the girls.

"We have proven to Hamas that we have changed the equation," Tzipi Livni said on January 12, five days before Israel declared a unilateral cease-fire and started to pull out of the Strip. "Israel is not a country upon which you fire missiles and it does not respond. It is a country that when you fire on its citizens it responds by going wild."

The morning that the Israelis began their withdrawal, Hamas launched five more missiles at Sderot, then declared its own cease-fire. Khaled Meshal, who was in Damascus, far from the action, claimed victory for Hamas.

IN JUNE 2009, five months after Operation Cast Lead, Hamas sponsored a workshop in Gaza City titled "How to Talk to Israel." Two dozen people attended, most of them academics or journalists. "What Israel knows about Hamas is that Hamas wants to eliminate them," one of the panelists observed. Governing imposes new responsibilities, he said, but since coming to power "Hamas has not changed its speech." A member of the audience said that Hamas had not even decided what to call Israel, pointing out that some speakers had used the term "Israeli entity" and others had called it the "Zionist entity." "You can't say to our own public you are going to throw Israel into the sea and then talk another way to the outside world—you have to have one speech," the audience member said. "We address moderates in Israel with words, and then we also sent rockets to them. We should be responsible but also clear in what we want. The world is not going to wait for us forever."

Many Gazans I spoke to were introspective about Israel's crushing retaliation. A Palestinian aid worker saw the invasion in geopolitical terms. "The war has a double meaning for the whole world, but especially for Iran," he said. "This is how it will be for anyone who would think to play with Israel." Eman Mohammed, a young photographer, told me that she was shocked by the indifference of the Arab world, compared to the West. "Look at the U.S. and Britain, sending convoys of aid," she said. "Maybe we needed this war to look at things in a different way." The sight of buildings being destroyed in Gaza made her more sympathetic to the reaction of America to 9/11. "I thought Osama bin Laden was a hero, but he's not. He's just a corrupted man taking us all to hell."

The teacher in Gaza told me that many children have been reluctant to return to class, because that's where they were when the bombs began to fall. (The Ministry of Education and Higher Education has reported that 164 pupils and 12 teachers were killed during the operation.) Some of the children have become extremely aggressive, forming gangs. "They don't listen, they don't care what you're saying," the teacher told me. Others are mute, but "as soon as they hear a loud sound they start screaming."

The boy he carried to the hospital has become one of the disruptive ones. Before the war, the boy was good at his lessons. "Now he has a dark future," the teacher said. "If he doesn't continue his learning, he is not going to be able to go to the university. He will lose his opportunity to be an effective member of the community. Soon, you will see him on the street."

Ahmed Yousuf warned me, "If there's not a solution in the near future, things will go out of control. At every level, you find people suffering from a siege mentality. They don't know which direction to take. There's no guidance from the world community or from our local leaders. We have lost the wise men among the Palestinians."

Hamas became more firmly entrenched in Gaza than it was before the invasion, and quickly began rearming with high-quality weapons, many of them supplied or paid for by Iran. The Israelis watched in frustration. "I tell you, we will come again," General Halevi said, "in better shape, because we have learned our lessons."

Soon after the troops returned to Israel, Haim Ramon, then the vice-premier, declared that "Israel is facing a serious humanitarian crisis, and it is called Gilad Shalit." He added, "Until he is returned home, not only will we not allow more cargo to reach the residents of Gaza, we will even diminish it." In July, the incoming prime minister, Benjamin Netanyahu, echoed this position.

On October 2, 2009, Hamas released a proof-of-life video of Gilad

Shalit, in exchange for the release of twenty female Palestinian prisoners. Shalit appeared gaunt but healthy. Three months earlier, Shalit's father, Noam, testifying before a UN committee, had made the case that his son's abduction and the refusal of his captors to allow the International Red Cross to determine if he is alive and well were war crimes. He used the forum as an opportunity to address the people of Gaza. "Your leaders are fighting to return your sons and daughters from captivity," he said. "This is an understandable desire." But, he added, "the fate of an entire prison population cannot depend on the ransom of one young man. . . . You know that the injustice done to my son was the trigger for war. You also know that the release of my son is the key to peace.

"I know that you are short of food," he went on. "Some of your loved ones have been killed—women and children, young and innocent. . . . As a parent speaking to a multitude of parents, I ask you to understand my family's anguish."

POSTSCRIPT

On October 18, 2011, five years after his capture, Shalit was finally exchanged for 1,027 Palestinian and Israeli Arab prisoners. Collectively, they had been responsible for the deaths of 569 Israelis. According to reports, dozens of them have returned to paramilitary activity.

Shalit became a sports reporter for *Yediot Achronot,* Israel's largest daily newspaper.

In July 2014, Israel launched another military operation into Gaza, with the goal of reducing Hamas rocket attacks and destroying the tunnel network. More than two thousand Gazans were killed in the month-long war, most of them civilians, according to human-rights groups; Israel reported sixty-six soldiers killed, as well as five Israeli civilians and one Thai worker.

Five Hostages

F ive American families, each harboring a grave secret, took their
seats around a vast dining table at the home of David Bradley,
a Washington, DC, entrepreneur who owns the media com-
pany that publishes *The Atlantic*. It was May 13, 2014, and in the garden beyond the French doors, where magnolias and dogwoods were
in bloom, a tent had been erected for an event that Bradley's wife,
Katherine, was hosting the following evening. The Bradleys' gracious
Georgian town house, on Embassy Row, is one of the city's salons:
reporters and politicians cross paths at off-the-record dinners there
with Supreme Court justices, software billionaires, and heads of state.

These families weren't accustomed to great wealth or influence,
however. Indeed, most of them had never been to Washington before.
Until recently, they had not known of one another, or of the unexpected benefactor who had brought them together. They were the parents of five Americans who had been kidnapped in Syria. The Federal
Bureau of Investigation had warned the families not to talk publicly
about their missing children—and the captors had threatened to kill
their hostages if word leaked out—so each family had been going to
work and to church month after month and reassuring colleagues and
neighbors and relatives that nothing was wrong, only to come home
and face new threats and ransom demands. After hiding the truth for
so long, the families were heartened to learn that others were going

through the same ordeal, and they hoped that by working together they might bring their children home.

Bradley, sixty-two at the time, was pale and nearly bald, with a ring of vivid white hair. He has a priestly presence: meek, soft-spoken, hands clasped in his lap, but his courtly demeanor disguises considerable ambition and persistence. His publishing company, Atlantic Media, had amassed half a dozen titles, from *National Journal* to *Quartz.*

Bradley was drawn into the families' tragedy because he had helped to free hostages once before. In 2011, soldiers loyal to the government of Colonel Muammar Qaddafi captured Clare Gillis, a freelancer who had contributed a few stories to *The Atlantic's* website, in Libya, along with two other reporters. (A fourth reporter was killed.) Bradley had been surprised to learn that the U.S. government was not involved in negotiating the return of the hostages. Even though Gillis was not an *Atlantic* employee, Bradley had felt an obligation to help her. He assembled a small team, drawn mostly from his staff, to track her down. On a whiteboard, Bradley drew several concentric circles. The smallest represented people in charge of the hostages, such as guards and wardens; a wider circle included military officers and junior members of the Qaddafi administration; wider still was the circle of senior Libyan officials, including Qaddafi and his family. The largest circle contained any people Bradley or his staffers could think of who might have a connection to those in the smaller rings. Bradley called this a network-analysis chart. The idea was that someone would know someone who knew someone who could locate Gillis. The team pinpointed about a hundred people to approach. One led to an American woman, Jacqueline Frazier, who had once lived in Tripoli, serving as the personal assistant to one of Qaddafi's sons. Frazier volunteered to return to Libya, and she persuaded her contacts in the government to release the reporters, after forty-four days of captivity. It hadn't been that hard to gain Gillis her freedom. But where would she be had no one tried? The success of that earlier venture in Libya emboldened Bradley to try his luck once more, this time in the even more chaotic killing fields of Syria.

At the dinner in Washington, Bradley urged the families to serve themselves before the main course—chicken potpie—got cold. When everyone was seated, he suggested going around the table, with each family telling the others about their missing child.

Jim

One of the reporters who had accompanied Gillis out of the Libyan prison in 2011 was a thirty-seven-year-old freelancer named James Foley. Bradley had never met Foley, but he received a thank-you note after the release. A second note arrived a couple of weeks later, in which Foley said that he hadn't fully understood how much he owed to Bradley and his team. Bradley was touched that Foley had taken the extra trouble, and he presented the second letter to his children as a model of grace. A year later, Foley was kidnapped again, in Syria, on Thanksgiving Day 2012.

Foley's parents, John and Diane, live in a small town in New Hampshire. John practices internal medicine, and Diane worked as a nurse practitioner until she quit to focus on obtaining her son's freedom. Three of the five mothers at Bradley's gathering happened to be nurses. Diane had already experienced the journey through gray government offices that the others were about to endure. Her anger and weariness were evident, and some of the parents found her off-putting. But to others her steeliness was inspiring. "She could run General Motors," one of the mothers said. Diane became the families' de facto leader.

As Diane spoke about her son, she mentioned themes that the others recognized in their own children's stories—courage and idealism chief among them. Jim had been an altar boy in an observant Catholic family, the oldest of five children, growing up in "Norman Rockwell country," as Diane described it. After graduating from Marquette University, Foley joined Teach For America and spent three years instructing eighth-graders in history and social studies and coaching basketball in a run-down Latino neighborhood in Phoenix. He spent two years in Iraq, working for a USAID development project and embedding as a correspondent with the Indiana National Guard. In 2011 he went to Afghanistan as a reporter for the military paper *Stars and Stripes.*

Foley was tall and striking, with his mother's long face and dark features and his father's jutting Irish chin. Women were drawn to his wide, gap-toothed smile and welcoming eyes. He struck up conversations effortlessly, even in Syria, despite having rudimentary Arabic. He'd pass out cigarettes, trusting in the goodwill of strangers, while children trailed after him in the streets.

After Foley was freed in the first kidnapping, his relatives joked about hiding his passport. Most of Foley's work had appeared in GlobalPost, an online news service founded by Philip Balboni. Balboni had offered Foley a desk job in Boston, but after a few months he longed to be back in the field. He returned to Libya in October 2011, during the fall of the Qaddafi regime, and the following March he was part of the first wave of Western reporters to enter Syria. The country quickly became a graveyard for correspondents, including Marie Colvin, of the London *Sunday Times,* and Anthony Shadid, of *The New York Times.* But the war was heating up, and the migratory troop of war reporters set up camp on the Turkish border. Clare Gillis arrived, as did many of Foley's colleagues from previous wars.

Those who knew Foley noticed that he had become more introspective. He showed a vulnerability that left him unable to manage the feelings stirred up by war. Like many of the reporters, he was fiercely opposed to violence but helplessly drawn to conflict. One of his friends was a young photographer named Nicole Tung, whom he had known in Libya. The two of them spent a week in Aleppo in July 2012, working on a story about Dar al-Shifa Hospital. Jim had been very affected by what he had seen: people dying because of the lack of medical supplies; the heroism of doctors in the face of the savagery of the regime, which dropped barrel bombs on bread lines. Just as Jim and Nicole were coming out of an interview, a government jet roared overhead and bombed the apartments on the block. People began streaming out of the buildings, covered in dust and ash. Jim dutifully filmed the dead and injured, but the emotional distance that the lens often provided failed to block the emotions he felt. It was no longer enough for him to bear witness to the trauma that was unfolding in Syria—he had to do something. He set up an online fund-raising campaign that brought in ten thousand dollars for a used ambulance in Austria that he had shipped to the hospital in Aleppo. Jim and Nicole were there when it was delivered. A few months later, the government bombed the hospital. The ambulance was destroyed.

When Diane didn't hear from Jim on Thanksgiving, she was worried: he always called on holidays. The next day, the phone did ring. It was Clare Gillis. Diane knew immediately that she wasn't calling to chat.

"I felt shock," Diane recalled to me.

"Anger," John added. "Why do we have to go through this again?"

It wasn't immediately clear how alarmed Foley's friends and family should be. After all, he had survived the previous kidnapping. It had become an anecdote—confirmation of his bravado. But it was disquieting that there had been no word from his captors. Where was the ransom demand?

The Foleys believed that the Syrian government was holding their son, and in January 2013 they publicly called for his release. Bradley wrote a note to Diane offering to help once again. Initially, she thought it unnecessary. Philip Balboni had hired Kroll, the investigations and security-consulting firm, and the FBI was also on the case, so the Foleys felt that they were in good hands. By spring, however, their opinion had changed, including their assessment of officials at the bureau.

"They kept telling us to do nothing," Diane said.

"And trust them," John added.

"And telling us that our kid was their highest priority. Which we didn't believe."

In April 2013, Diane asked Bradley if he could put together another team.

Bradley enlisted his general counsel and chief of staff, Aretae Wyler, along with a few others in his office. He also contacted Wendy Kopp, the head of Teach For America, requesting volunteers. This new team, now numbering more than a dozen people, began creating another network-analysis chart.

The FBI and Kroll shared the Foleys' view that Jim had been taken by the regime. It was logical: Shiite gangs affiliated with Bashar al-Assad, Syria's president, had kidnapped other reporters, reportedly including Austin Tice, a photojournalist from Houston. Sources claimed that the Syrian Air Force Intelligence Directorate was holding Westerners in a Damascus prison. That seemed better than the alternative. Syria was in tumult; more than a thousand armed groups roamed the shattered country. Assad's regime was brutal, but at least it was a government, with interests and alliances that could facilitate a deal. Moreover, U.S. law forbade paying ransoms to terrorists.

Bradley's team sought out diplomats and journalists who had fixers in the region. They were looking for members of Assad's inner circle. Some Syrians living in exile had maintained ties to influential figures, and these elites would have been educated in American schools. Bradley's team also approached Russian supporters of Assad. But the sources consistently reported that the regime did not have Foley. Bradley recalled, "By summertime, I was of the view that, if this was my child, I'd be looking in the north." That was ISIS territory now—a long way from Norman Rockwell country.

Theo

"Who *is* this man?" Nancy Curtis had asked upon being told to get in touch with David Bradley. "Why does he want to help us?" She was skeptical by nature and not inclined to ask for favors. A museum administrator in Cambridge, Massachusetts, Curtis was the picture of a New England intellectual: wry and doughty, her white hair chopped into an unruly pageboy. But by the time she attended the dinner, her suspicions about Bradley had faded, and it was deeply comforting to be among people with the same secret. As Curtis learned about the other children, however, she was distressed to realize that the hostages themselves also carried secrets—ones that could get them killed. That was certainly true of her son.

Peter Theophilus Padnos had a doctorate in comparative literature from the University of Massachusetts at Amherst, and he spoke French, German, and Russian. He had been working as a bicycle mechanic in 2004 when he abruptly decided to move to Yemen and study Arabic. It was a year into the second Iraq War, and Americans were intensely unpopular in the region. Padnos had a little nest egg from the sale of his first book, about teaching poetry to prisoners, called *My Life Had Stood a Loaded Gun*. The title came from an Emily Dickinson poem. That was Theo: erudite but interested in criminals and other outliers, always drawn to extremity.

Yemen fascinated him. He'd never lived in a society where everybody believed in God. He studied at one of the world's most radical mosques, Dar al-Hadith, where al-Qaeda members had reportedly trained, and wrote a memoir about his experiences, *Undercover Muslim*, an unsparing account of the dead-end lives of the students and the propaganda of the imams. At the mosque, Padnos had declared allegiance to Islam in front of witnesses, and so his book seemed tantamount to apostasy—a mortal sin to radical Islamists.

After the book came out, Padnos formally changed his name to Theo Curtis, in order to continue traveling in Muslim countries, but he never bothered to change certain revealing personal details, such as his Facebook page. In the conspiratorial circles that Padnos often passed through, he had the profile of a spy, if not a very careful one.

In October 2012, he traveled to Antakya, a Turkish border town that served as the informal headquarters of the press corps covering the Syrian conflict. The site of ancient Antioch had long been a tourist stop for Christian pilgrims. Now it was overrun with refugees, spies, and jihadis. To the east, across a mountain range, was Syria, where a hundred thousand people had already perished.

About fifty journalists were covering Syria at the time; the battle for Aleppo was under way and the war seemed to be nearing resolution. The wire services were still there, and occasionally the networks sent in a team, but most of the journalists were freelancers. They drank in the same bars and slept on one another's couches and sat in the same cafés in the morning, hiring fixers and making plans for their next trip across the border. They had little money and no security, but they were writing history. Islam was at war with itself, the map of the Middle East was being redrawn, and the freelancers had the story largely to themselves.

Padnos was forty-four, a decade or two older than most of his colleagues. He spent a few days at a ten-dollar-a-night hotel, then rented an apartment with a Tunisian fishmonger. He soon met three young men who claimed to be providing supplies to the Free Syrian Army. At the time, reporters still regularly crossed into Syria: Foley wasn't kidnapped until a month later. The three men and Padnos went to the border and squeezed through a hole in a barbed-wire fence. Padnos hadn't told anyone where he was going. Few people even knew that he had been in Antakya.

Nancy Curtis was puzzled when her son stopped writing. He was helping her buy a woodstove for a vacation house that she owned in Vermont, and they had been communicating daily. After three days, she finally got an e-mail. The subject line said, "Hey." There was no message.

Curtis called her cousin Viva Hardigg. "Something calamitous has happened," Curtis said. Hardigg immediately believed her. She enlisted two other cousins: Amy Rosen, who was the chairman of the board of the KIPP charter schools in Newark; and Betsy Sullivan, an editor at the *Cleveland Plain Dealer*. Rosen had served on Amtrak's board of directors and knew her way around Washington; Sullivan brought the experience of having been detained by the Bosnian Serb Army while reporting on that conflict. Curtis, Hardigg, Sullivan, and Rosen became known as the All-Girl Team.

Curtis contacted the International Committee of the Red Cross, which often visits prisons to assess human-rights violations. She was hoping to learn that the Syrian government was holding her son. The woman she talked to had no information about that, but shared some news. "I shouldn't be telling you this," she said, "but there's another family in New England you ought to call." She gave her Diane Foley's number.

At the time, U.S. government policy was to keep information about hostages strictly secret, for privacy reasons, but Diane and Nancy were each immensely relieved to learn of another family searching for a son in Syria. They traded information about avenues they had explored and people they had approached—workers for non-governmental organizations (NGOs), State Department officials, FBI agents—and they rebuked themselves for failing to set up emergency contacts for their sons, and for not getting their digital passwords. As each learned more about the other's son, she saw how much the men had in common. What good friends they'll be when this is all over, they often said.

One night in May 2013, Amy Rosen was invited to a dinner that was part of *The Atlantic*'s Ideas Forum in New York. She intended just to drop by for a drink, but she stuck around when she realized that she was seated next to David Bradley. Rosen had met him socially before. She confided in him about Padnos and the failure of the All-Girl Team to find him. Bradley described his theory of concentric circles, but admitted that his team still hadn't located Foley. They decided to combine efforts.

The first break in the kidnappings occurred on July 29, 2013, when an American photojournalist, Matt Schrier, escaped from his cell in Syria, after seven months of captivity, and crossed into Turkey. He told C. J. Chivers, of the *Times*, that in January he had been placed in a cell with another American, who was filthy and had a ragged beard. The American said that his captors had accused him of working for the CIA. For months, the men were tortured—sometimes by a twelve-year-old who beat them and shocked them with Tasers. They were forced to make videotaped confessions, wearing orange jumpsuits that mimicked the prisoner uniforms worn at the U.S. internment camp in Guantánamo Bay, Cuba.

Schrier recalled that he and his cellmate had gouged a hole in the wire mesh on one window. Schrier said that he was able to squeeze through, but said his cellmate was larger and couldn't break free. Although the *Times* didn't name the other American, Nancy received a call from officials at the State Department two days after Schrier's escape. We have proof of life on Theo, they said.

Steven

Shirley Sotloff felt that she was in a movie, watching people act out roles. Even the Bradleys' beautiful home, with servers carrying silver trays, resembled a set. It certainly didn't seem real when David Bradley said that Secretary of State John Kerry had been at this same table the previous week, and the king of Jordan before that.

Her husband, Art, observed the furnishings in the Bradleys' house with an appreciative professional eye. His business was organizing home shows—exhibitions offering furnishing ideas. He noticed the hand-carved dining set, the chandelier with actual candles, the pale-yellow fabric covering the dining room walls.

The Sotloffs, who were from Pinecrest, Florida, a Miami suburb, brought with them Barak Barfi, a researcher for the New America Foundation. He was the best friend of their son, Steven, a journalist who had been held in Syria for nine months. Barfi, brilliant and assertive, was controversial among the families. He clearly felt that he should lead the group, since he spoke fluent Arabic and was by far the most knowledgeable among them about the Middle East. On August 4, 2013, it was Barfi who notified Art that Steven was missing. Art didn't tell Shirley. He didn't want to worry her in case Steven suddenly showed up, but after four days Shirley suspected something. Art poured himself a Scotch and gave her the news.

Steven had lived in the Middle East for many years, but hadn't done much to disguise that he was Jewish; it could be discovered by a Google search or a look at his Facebook page. He had a defiant nonchalance that had posed problems for him in the past. He was such a difficult student that Shirley and Art had sent him to a treatment center for troubled boys and then to the Kimball Union Academy, an elite boarding school in New Hampshire. Sarcastic and argumentative, but with a ready and infectious laugh, Steve had the reputation of being an underachiever. Then in his junior year he resurrected the school paper the *Kimball Union,* which had gone defunct because of lack of funding. Steven and another student raised the money to resuscitate and completely revamp it, winning a collegiate journalism award for their effort. He had found his calling.

In 2005, Steven entered the Interdisciplinary Center Herzliya, an Israeli college, where he played rugby and joined the debate society. He also took Israeli citizenship. He wanted to become a reporter, and wrote to Barfi, then a producer for ABC News affiliates, asking for advice about studying Arabic abroad. Barfi, who was ten years older than Steven, became his mentor. "He was a young, chubby kid," Barfi recalled. "I told him, 'You can go to Egypt, which has a good teaching infrastructure, but you'll be overexposed to Western influences. You could go to Syria, where you won't be so exposed to the West but will be pursued by security people all the time. The best place is Yemen. There are no Westerners, the state is weak, and you'll be pretty much left alone.'" Steven took his counsel. In Sana'a, he posed as a Chechen American from a secular Muslim family. "I 'converted' in my first week, so I wouldn't have to deal with all that rubbish," he wrote to a friend, "lol."

The Arab Spring began in 2010, and aspiring journalists like Sotloff swarmed into the region. Soon he was freelancing for the *Christian Science Monitor, Foreign Policy,* and *Time.* He was in Tahrir Square the day President Hosni Mubarak stepped down, in 2011, and in Libya the following year, where he first met Jim Foley. For *Time* he provided crucial coverage of the attack on the U.S. compound in Benghazi, where four Americans were killed, including the ambassador. He wrote about the flow of arms from Libya to Syria, and in December of that year he reported from Aleppo. During that period, when American foreign policy depended on information arising from these zones of conflict, Sotloff never made enough money to have to file a tax return.

Many publications began pulling back their staff from areas of conflict, which only increased their reliance on freelancers, who had none of the institutional support that the great news organizations bring with them. "It's the freelancer's conundrum," Jim Foley told *Newsweek* in 2012. "I think it's just the basic laws of competition; you need to have something the staffers don't, but in a conflict zone that means you take bigger risks: Go in sooner, stay longer, get closer." After Clare Gillis was captured in Libya, Bradley and his editorial board decided they could not accept or commission freelance work in war zones, unless the journalist had previous experience, a thorough security plan, insurance, and appropriate equipment. Of course, there were scarcely any freelancers who could supply such assurances. "I've been here over a week and no one wants freelance because of the kidnappings," Steven complained to a friend in October 2012, while he was in northern Syria. "I've been sleeping at a front, hiding from tanks the past few nights, drinking rain water."

The journalists in Antakya maintained a secret Facebook site that functioned as a message board for reporters and aid workers planning to enter Syria. The news was that Turkish airports and train stations were filling up with foreign fighters who were flocking to the conflict—"beirdos," Jim Foley called them. No one knew what to make of this new element.

Some members of the site began speculating that spotters on the border were selling information about reporters to Islamists. In December 2012, criminals associated with the Free Syrian Army abducted Richard Engel, an NBC correspondent, and five members of his crew. Two aid workers, an Italian and a British man, were taken in March 2013; a Danish photographer in May; four French journalists and a German tourist in June. About seventy Syrian reporters had been killed in 2012 and 2013. Because the media observed a blackout on abductions, more reporters kept arriving, not fully aware of the dangers they faced.

Many journalists who were in Antakya at the time now speak of having maintained a willful ignorance, even as the risks became obvious. They talked among themselves about the dangers but kept crossing the border, sustained by the adventure, the significance of the story, and the exhilaration of survival. "It's easy to feel invincible, even with death all around," Sotloff wrote to Janine di Giovanni, the Middle East editor for *Newsweek*. "It's like, This is my movie, sucker— I'm not gonna die."

Peter

David Bradley burst out laughing when Paula and Ed Kassig showed up for dinner that night. Earlier, when Bradley issued the invitation, Ed had nervously asked if there was a dress code. "Black tie, of course," Bradley had said. Ed arrived in a short-sleeved tattersall shirt with a black tie that he'd cadged from the concierge at the hotel. It became a running joke between them.

At the dinner, Ed and Paula tried to sort out who was who. Some of the other families had brought along an adviser. Barfi, who came with the Sotloffs, had been folded into Bradley's team, as had Jim Foley's former girlfriend, April Goble, who runs the KIPP schools in Chicago. Several members of Bradley's staff were also present. "But you knew the other parents right away," Ed observed.

Paula and Ed lived in Indianapolis. She was a public health nurse; he taught high school biology. He was in the classroom on October 1, 2013, when his phone began vibrating. His flip phone was so old that his pitying students could scarcely recognize it. Sometimes, when he left it sitting on his desk, he returned to find coins beside it.

Ed's phone indicated that he'd received an international call. He assumed that it was his son, Peter, who was doing humanitarian work in Turkey, and sometimes crossing into Syria. Ed thought that if it was important, Peter would call back. The school day ended and Ed went outside, where buses were loading, and there was the usual commotion of the kids leaving. His phone rang again. Ed answered, thinking it was Peter, but it was someone else—a friend of Peter's—who was trying to explain something, but Ed couldn't hear clearly, because of the racket. It was homecoming weekend, and as Ed moved to a quieter spot, a marching band burst through the doors. Ed couldn't break away; the drum line seemed to be deliberately trailing him. The one word that registered through the din was "detained."

Unlike the other families, Ed and Paula received a message from ISIS right away. "It was almost cordial," Paula recalled. "'We have your son. We are treating him as a guest.'" A second, more ominous note followed. "You say he is an aid worker. We know that all Westerners who say they are EMTs or aid workers are just spies and just sent over as part of the war between the West and the East." The captors asked for a hundred million, but didn't specify dollars or euros. They also demanded the release of all Muslim prisoners worldwide. "Like that was something we were going to be able to do," Paula said.

ISIS warned that Peter would be killed if word of the kidnapping leaked out, so the Kassigs bore the additional weight of fearing that their friends might guess what was going on. People were always asking about Peter's welfare. "I hope he's not in Syria!" people said probingly, and Ed would respond, "Don't worry, he's not." He was playing with words: technically, he figured, Peter was in the Islamic State.

Like Theo Padnos and Steven Sotloff, Peter Kassig also had something to hide. He had served in Iraq in the Army Rangers. He left with an honorable medical discharge after only four months at war, and friends weren't sure what had happened. He returned to Indianapolis and trained to be an emergency medical technician, then studied political science at Butler University, but he was restless and looking for direction. He got married, but the union quickly dissolved. Kassig was a "driven soul," his parents acknowledge, and highly unpredictable. During his senior year, he told Ed and Paula that he was spending spring break camping in the Smoky Mountains. A week later, he called them from Beirut, where he was working in a refugee camp, watching people die in front of him. In a few hours, he said, his return flight was scheduled to leave, but he couldn't abandon them. He finally knew what he was going to do with the rest of his life.

A CNN reporter later filmed him in a hospital bandaging wounded Syrian refugees. He still wore his hair in a military-style buzz cut, and his arms were covered with tattoos. "This is what I was put here to do," he told the reporter. "I guess I am just a hopeless romantic, and I am an idealist, and I believe in hopeless causes."

In 2012 Kassig established his own NGO, called Special Emergency Response and Assistance. His goal was to provide food and blankets and medical supplies where they were most needed. He enlisted Ed and Paula to raise money at their Methodist church. In Turkey, he taught emergency care to reporters and photographers on the border. One of his friends coined a verb, "to Kassig," which meant "to selflessly put oneself in harm's way in order to help others in need, all the while looking suave and sexy."

Kassig had been friends with Steven Sotloff, and joined the effort to find him. "We have to be ruthlessly efficient and professional in securing information and his eventual safe release," he wrote to a friend. "Someone we know knows where Steven is and who has him. This can go 1 of 2 ways, either we do right and get our beloved friend back, or this goes south and he gets hurt or worse." But two months passed without any significant leads.

Shortly before Kassig was abducted, he admitted in a call to his parents that he was "a little more worried about this trip." He had promised to deliver medical supplies to Deir ez-Zor, the largest city in eastern Syria, where his medical expertise was desperately needed. The city once had about five hundred doctors; now there were only five. Factions and allegiances were shifting, Peter told his parents. Ed and Paula didn't know exactly what he meant, but it sounded ominous.

Soon after Kassig entered Syria, he called a coworker. He said that he'd been stopped at a roadblock and told to report to an ISIS commander. If you don't hear from me in several hours, Kassig said, institute the emergency protocol. That was when Ed got the call.

Later, a European hostage who had been held with Steven Sotloff told Ed and Paula about the day Peter was put in their cell. "Steve!" Peter cried. "I finally found you!"

Kayla

Carl Mueller was working in his body shop in Prescott, Arizona, when he got a call from a man he'd never met, Barak Barfi, who said that he knew about the abduction of his daughter, Kayla. Carl froze. He and his wife, Marsha, had stopped seeing friends because people were always asking about Kayla, and they didn't want to lie.

Kayla was well known and admired in Prescott. In high school, she received a presidential medal for public service, and she won a five-hundred-dollar prize for her local philanthropic efforts. She gave the money to charity. At Northern Arizona University, she founded a branch of Amnesty International and a service organization for veterans while also working for peace groups and teaching anger management in the county jail. Despite all this activity, she graduated in two years, impatient to get out into the world.

In India, she worked with orphans; in Tibet, she taught English to refugees. Kayla had grown up a Baptist, but she was fascinated by different religions. She was devoted to the teachings of the Zen master Thich Nhat Hanh, and for a time considered becoming a nun in his Buddhist community in France. But Kayla was an activist by nature. In Israel, she worked with African refugees, and in Palestine she stood outside houses scheduled to be bulldozed by the Israeli military. "Let me live on both sides of the wall before I act," she wrote in her diary. In the fall of 2010, she came home, suffering from typhoid and parasites, and recuperated for a year while volunteering at an AIDS clinic—which she took over—and working at a women's shelter at night. She hoped to join the Peace Corps; she had been told that if she became fluent in French she would be sent to Africa, so she took a job as an au pair in France. Before she left, she cut off her ponytail to donate to Locks of Love, which provides hairpieces for children with cancer. She made Marsha promise to send it.

Given the scale of suffering in Syria, it wasn't surprising that Kayla would be drawn there. She was abducted the same day as Sotloff, just before her twenty-fifth birthday.

Kayla had been missing for a few months when Barfi called Carl to say that a wealthy man in Washington, DC, wanted to help the Muellers and others in the same situation. Carl and Marsha had been dreading that the news of Kayla's abduction would get out and the kidnappers would follow through on their threat. Now somebody knew. What kind of name was Barak Barfi? Was he one of the terrorists? Carl went behind his shop, knelt down, and prayed.

Of all the families, the Muellers were the most isolated. Even at the Bradleys' home, Carl and Marsha were anxious. The FBI had assured them that Kayla would probably be safe, because she was a woman. Was it wise to get her case mixed up with others? Although Marsha quickly felt a sense of solidarity with the other mothers, Carl remained mistrustful. To him, Bradley seemed like something out of a comic-book fantasy: a person with vast resources who could summon powerful people at will. And, given that Bradley was the publisher of *The Atlantic,* Carl wondered: Was this just an elaborate way of getting a story?

Less than a month before the dinner, four French journalists had been released by ISIS, apparently ransomed by the French government, along with five members of Doctors Without Borders. One of the journalists told Carl that Kayla had been held in another cell at the prison, and that he'd often heard her speaking French to one of the Doctors Without Borders prisoners, but in recent months Kayla had been in solitary. Sometimes the men were able to leave notes for her in the toilet. The day the French journalists were freed, the guards brought Kayla to them, so they could confirm that she was alive. She gave the journalists a letter to take to her parents, which Marsha read aloud at the Bradleys' dinner table.

"Everyone, if you are receiving this letter it means I am still detained," the letter begins. It was written in tiny script on paper ripped out of a spiral notebook, and full of abbreviations. "Please know that I am in a safe location, completely unharmed + healthy (put on weight in fact); I have been treated w/the utmost respect + kindness." She had wanted to write "a well thought out letter" but had been given the opportunity only at the last minute. "Just the thought of you all sends me into a fit of tears," she wrote. "If you could say I have 'suffered' at all throughout this whole experience it is only in knowing how much suffering I have put you all through; I will never ask you to forgive me as I do not deserve forgiveness."

Kayla listed some things she thought of with special fondness: her little niece, her first family camping trip. She fantasized about how much she'd love the reunion at the airport when they finally met again. The letter ended forcefully: "I DO NOT want the negotiations for my release to be your duty, if there is any other option take it. All my everything, Kayla."

The other parents were moved by Kayla's letter and by the picture Carl painted of their daughter, who seemed like a cross between a barefooted sprite and a Buddhist saint. He called her Special K. Of course, all the hostages were remarkable people, and their finest qualities had led them to Syria. "If anything bound us together, it was our children, and their courage and compassion," John Foley recalled.

Earlier, Philip Balboni, the GlobalPost founder, had asked how many parents wanted the U.S. military to attempt a rescue. Not a single hand went up. It seemed too dangerous. Now Bradley suggested that the families consider publicizing the kidnappings. The Foleys agreed with Bradley that going to the media might put pressure on the U.S. government and, possibly, the hostage-takers. The Sotloffs were willing to consider this, but the Kassigs were so opposed that the idea was tabled. How could you know if ISIS was bluffing with its threat to kill the hostages?

The families tried to select one member of the team to deal with ransom demands collectively. But who could be trusted with the lives of their children? Barfi desperately wanted this responsibility, but some parents were wary. He was aggressive, and perhaps he was too heartbroken by Sotloff's abduction to think clearly. The Kassigs had brought along an adviser—Peter's partner in his NGO—and they nominated him instead. A power struggle among the family advocates followed, which resulted in no one being chosen for the role. Barfi was bitter. "Either I should have been more restrained or I should have gotten on top of the table and said, 'Your kids are in dire danger,'" he recalled. "They decided to go with unanimity. I said, 'That's like the Arab League—you'll never get anything done. You need a leader.'"

The families signed a statement authorizing Bradley to receive updates about the hostages from the FBI and other government agencies. The families left the dinner feeling hopeful and relieved: Bradley was a powerful champion, and now they had one another. Art Sotloff impulsively hugged Bradley, who recoiled slightly. He has a formal manner, and the families quickly concluded that he doesn't like to be touched.

Before everyone left, Bradley expressed the hope that they would soon meet again—with their children, in the same lovely room.

THE NEXT AFTERNOON, the families met in the West Wing of the White House with Lisa Monaco, the homeland security adviser to President Barack Obama, and members of the National Security Council. The families had written a letter to Obama. Calling themselves Parents of American Hostages in Syria, they asked Obama to give them a clear idea of what could be done. ISIS seemed to be proceeding in an orderly manner in releasing European hostages, first the Spanish and then the French; an Italian journalist was freed several days after the White House meeting. The released Europeans spoke of enduring torture and starvation. They heard frequent gunfire—presumably the sound of Syrian and Iraqi prisoners being executed. Some of the Westerners were more abused than others, but the treatment was always capricious and sadistic. These accounts dismayed the families, yet they also were fortified by the intelligence they had gained from the Europeans about their children's lives in captivity.

"This is a moment of opportunity," the group letter to the president said. "We have knowledge of the groups that are holding our children; we have knowledge of their location and the motives of their captors; we have examples of successful releases facilitated by foreign governments." At the meeting, the families asked that Obama appoint someone to coordinate among the White House, the FBI, and the State Department, providing the timely information they needed to make life-and-death decisions.

Officials at the White House meeting expressed sympathy and concern, but were vague about what the government might do to help. On this and two other occasions, Colonel Mark Mitchell, the director of counterterrorism at the National Security Council, bluntly warned the families that they risked prosecution if they paid terrorists or tried to persuade an allied power to do so. "I'd rather be in prison myself and have Jimmy home," John Foley said afterward. Nancy Curtis shrugged it off: "I'm seventy-six years old. Let them put me in jail."

The fact that the European hostages were safely home underscored the ineffectiveness of American policy. Didier François, a released hostage, told me that although French officials publicly deny paying ransoms, "they do negotiate, because every French citizen taken is an attack on French sovereignty." François added, "It doesn't mean we surrender to all the demands of the captors. It doesn't mean we change our foreign policy." The German magazine *Focus* reported that the French government paid ransoms totaling 18 million euros for the four journalists. François called this sum "ridiculous." He explained that captors always start high, but skillful diplomacy can moderate their demands. He added, "As long as it doesn't change the situation on the ground, why should we *not* get our people out?"

The U.S. government's position was that the Europeans imperil everybody by paying off terrorists. In a 2012 speech, David Cohen, then the undersecretary for terrorism and financial intelligence at the Treasury Department, said, "Ransom payments lead to future kidnappings, and future kidnappings lead to additional ransom payments. It all builds the capacity of terrorist organizations to conduct attacks." The U.S. government estimated that between 2008 and 2014, radical Islamist groups collected more than $200 million in ransom payments, which allowed those groups to spread. ISIS might not exist in its present rampant form without the funds that kidnapping provided.

The families themselves had mixed feelings about ransoms. The Foleys were already seeking pledges (and eventually obtained nearly $1 million worth). The Kassigs stayed up late worrying over the morality of giving money to a terrorist group—yet their only child's life was at stake, and ISIS was already rich. "If we had been able to come up with any ransom, it would have been much smaller than what they were getting daily from the oil fields," Paula observed. Carl Mueller felt that the government was putting its precious policy ahead of their daughter's life; Marsha, however, didn't want ISIS to receive another cent and didn't think that Kayla would either. Although the Sotloffs were considering a ransom, Barfi privately thought the practice misguided. "You're funding terrorism," Barfi said. "What happens if ISIS uses the money to fund an attack?"

This was the stated logic behind U.S. policy, and yet the government has paid ransoms to criminal organizations, such as drug cartels. Every Federal Reserve branch in the United States maintains a stash of bills to be used to pay ransoms. Corporations routinely take out ransom insurance for employees stationed abroad, and the FBI even facilitates such payments. It's only when the kidnappers are part of an acknowledged terrorist group that payments become illegal.

Hovering silently over this wrenching discussion was the fact of Bradley's fortune. He was already bankrolling the team that was trying to free the hostages; he was absorbing the families' travel expenses; he was flying to foreign destinations himself. His generosity was without question but not, apparently, without limits. Prudent and conservative by temperament, he had forbidden his staff to discuss ransoms. Carl Mueller hinted that he was willing to sell his house, but Bradley didn't bite. The risk of prosecution that made Bradley wary of ransoms posed an obstacle to other potential donors as well. And there was an additional complication: if Bradley was known to be involved, the ransom demands would inevitably increase.

Art Sotloff was incensed by the repeated threats of prosecution. He and Shirley had received the same outlandish ransom demand as the Foleys and the Kassigs—100 million euros. The U.S. government could refuse to help them, but why should it stand in their way if they turned to other sources? At one government meeting, Art excused himself to go to the men's room, and an FBI agent escorted him down the hall. The agent confided that no American had ever been prosecuted for paying a ransom. The families were confounded by the mixed messages; moreover, if the government actually did prosecute them, wouldn't these very agents have to testify against them?

In any case, because of international sanctions, it was exceedingly difficult to send any money to Syria, much less millions of dollars. In September 2013, Nancy Curtis had tried to wire eight thousand dollars to a fixer in Aleppo, who had heard a rumor that an American hostage had been condemned to death by a Sharia court. The source was willing to investigate further, but wanted payment. Curtis tried to use Western Union to send the money to an intermediary in Beirut, but when she had to describe the purpose of the transfer, she was refused. The All-Girl Team then divided the sum among themselves. Viva Hardigg, Curtis's cousin, took her children to the bank, and while the kids begged for lollipops the teller put the wire transfer through.

The Aleppo fixer reported hearing that the American hostage had been killed. The All-Girl Team decided not to tell Nancy Curtis.

Then, several months later, she received a Skype call from someone who claimed to be in touch with Padnos's kidnappers. The intermediary asked for proof-of-life questions that only Padnos could answer. Curtis and the All-Girl Team came up with such questions as "Where is your car?" (In the barn.) The correct answers came back the following day. Padnos was alive.

Apparently the intermediary was also able to relay messages from Padnos. One of them was "Sorry, Mom, I should have listened to you."

Curtis had previously dealt with intermediaries, and their demands had ranged between three million and five million euros. Those conversations never went anywhere. Were the intermediaries really in contact with her son? All the families had to contend with scammers who claimed to represent the hostage-takers. The Kassigs were approached by somebody they called Bitcoin Man, who described in detail how to transmit money through the Internet. Curtis had already calculated that she could raise $200,000 in cash, and perhaps twice that if she sold her vacation house in Vermont. But if she had to sell her house in Cambridge, too, how would she live? Would there be anything left for her daughter and her family? Was it right to throw everything she had into a murky deal with terrorists?

This intermediary demanded 15 million euros to release Padnos—triple what had been originally proposed but a fraction of what was being asked for Foley, Sotloff, and Kassig. The price for Kayla Mueller was 5 million euros. On the advice of the FBI, Curtis countered with fifty thousand dollars. The idea was to get the captors to think realistically about what the family could pay.

On May 31, 2014, while this negotiation was under way, the U.S. suddenly exchanged five Taliban leaders held in Guantánamo for a sergeant in the U.S. Army, Bowe Bergdahl. President Obama justified the swap by noting that military prisoners are routinely traded at the end of a conflict. Evidently he believed that American involvement in Afghanistan had reached such a point. Some of the families felt deceived—they'd just been told that ransoms and prisoner exchanges were out of bounds. They were also alarmed by the public furor that followed the Bergdahl swap. It seemed certain to make the captors more intransigent and the U.S. government even less willing to act on the families' behalf.

Fortunately, the parents still had Bradley's team on their side. But none of them realized how little time they had left.

DAVID BRADLEY GREW UP as a Christian Scientist, believing that God created man as a perfect being. Disease, death, pain, and evil were imaginary afflictions that could be prayed away. Although Bradley no longer saw himself as especially religious, many tenets of the faith had left their mark on him. "I remain deeply sympathetic to Christian Science, but, as to evil, I've changed my mind," he said. "There is evil in the world."

Katherine Bradley observed that her husband had "a fundamental quality of faithfulness, which is not the same thing as faith." Most of the Bradleys' charities concentrated on education and poverty in the U.S. Her husband didn't seek out additional projects, she said, but when a need arose, he had a hard time turning away. She shared a story from the Philippines, where Bradley went on a Fulbright scholarship in 1977. Ferdinand Marcos then ruled the country. Bradley, who had just received an MBA from Harvard, was there studying whether multinational corporations prefer to operate under authoritarian governments. (They do.) He subsequently set up a child-protection unit at a Manila hospital. Every year, he returns to the city to visit the matriarch he stayed with as a student, who was a hundred and three on his most recent trip. "The Philippines just came into his life," Katherine said. "He attached and never let go."

Growing up in Bethesda, Maryland, just outside Washington, DC, Bradley developed a longing for power. At thirteen, he imagined becoming the Republican junior senator from Maryland by the age of thirty. When he was twenty, he worked as an intern in the Nixon White House, just as the Watergate scandal was unfolding. He then enrolled at Georgetown law school. Deciding that he needed an income to support a political career, he took a year off to start a policy research firm, the Advisory Board Company, then spun off a division of it, the Corporate Executive Board. Most of his business was in health-care consulting. His office was in the living room of his mother's apartment in the Watergate. Twenty years later, he took one of the businesses public; two years after that, he sold the second.

These deals made him about $300 million richer. He now owns one of the buildings in the Watergate complex.

By the time Bradley made his fortune, he had reluctantly abandoned his political dreams. Although he desired power, he cherished humility. He was not someone who could turn heads while entering a room. He speaks in a near whisper, the result of nerve damage to his vocal cords. His elaborately deferential manner can make him seem aloof or strange, even enigmatic. Such qualities are ill-suited for a political life, and his shortcomings became especially apparent when he compared himself to his next-door neighbor on Embassy Row—an attractive young senator who seemed to be the embodiment of the man Bradley had sought to be. But eventually the life of that senator, John Edwards, took a wrong turn, and the house next door now served as the Hungarian Embassy. Bradley's search for influence found other outlets: in wealth, media, and philanthropy.

In directing the families' efforts, Bradley was in some respects usurping the role of several federal agencies, and yet the families had largely lost faith in their government. The State Department appointed Carrie Greene, in the Office of Overseas Citizens Services, to be a liaison with the families. She seemed impatient with their independent investigations. "You really shouldn't be talking to these terrorists," she warned. "It's against the law." Viva Hardigg responded, "Excuse me, Carrie, but we are well acquainted with U.S. laws, and if someone you love is being held by terrorists, with whom else should you talk?" Greene ended her e-mails with "Please enjoy your day!"

When Peter Kassig was kidnapped, his parents got a call from a State Department official. Paula recalled, "She basically said, 'We know your son has been taken in Syria. We don't have an embassy in Syria. We don't have people on the ground in Syria. We don't have a diplomatic relationship with them, so we can't do anything to help you.'" In May 2014, the families had a joint meeting with Daniel Rubinstein, a special envoy appointed to handle affairs in Syria. "He was nice, but when we asked how to contact him we were told not to e-mail or phone him," Diane Foley said. In order to talk with him on the phone, the families had to travel to a local FBI office, so an agent could dial Rubinstein's number for them. When the Foleys drove to the Boston office for this purpose, they learned that the phone line they were using wasn't even secure. So what was the point? They concluded that the only reason for the protocol was to allow local agents to monitor them.

At least three FBI agents were assigned to each family: one supervising agent, one for "victim assistance," and one for hostage negotiation. Nancy Curtis describes one of her agents as "professional, compassionate, and committed." But none of the other families believed that the bureau was aggressive enough. "The FBI called me once a week from Washington, every Tuesday between three thirty and four o'clock, without fail, just to see if I had information for *them*," Art Sotloff said. "Not to give *me* information. After three or four phone calls, I just let them go to voice mail."

THE FBI IS AUTHORIZED to investigate the kidnapping of American citizens. The bureau has long experience with the crime domestically, but is poorly equipped to handle foreign cases in which the motivation for the abduction is political. Bradley's team scheduled a meeting for Nancy Curtis and the chief FBI hostage negotiator. The agent insisted that the bureau had jurisdiction over kidnappings; but then the State Department, which has no expertise in criminal investigations, informed Curtis that it was in charge. Bradley's team then set up a meeting with Robert Ford, the last U.S. ambassador to Syria. Ford said that although the FBI does have jurisdiction, the State Department has an understanding of Syrian culture and the region that the bureau lacks. Curtis left these meetings frustrated and confused. Not only was there a turf war; it was obvious that the agencies weren't sharing information. State essentially backed down, leaving the fate of the hostages in the hands of the FBI.

To the FBI, it's natural that it should lead the kidnapping cases wherever they occur. The bureau, a senior FBI official explained, pursues three related goals in a kidnapping investigation: "the safe return of the hostage, collection of intelligence about the captor network, and the eventual prosecution of the perpetrators."

Although FBI agents felt that Bradley and his team were acting nobly, they considered them amateurs entering a sensitive and dangerous environment, with American lives in the balance. The bureau does not like its playing field to be crowded with competitors. Bradley's team gave the FBI any leads it turned up, but the bureau made it clear that this was not a partnership. "We're happy to take their information," the FBI official told me, but noted that the relationship could not be fully reciprocal: Bradley, his team members, and the families lacked the security clearances that would allow them to look at all the data that the FBI was collecting. The official admitted, however, that "in some of these cases the lack of information passed to the families was simply because there *was* a lack of information."

At certain key points, the FBI forcefully shut down an investigative path that members of the Bradley team were following, usually with the explanation that they had to "deconflict" their effort with one that, presumably, the bureau was conducting on its own. "Swords get crossed," the FBI official noted. But people close to the scene saw little evidence that the bureau was investigating with urgency. After Jim Foley's abduction in November 2012, it took two weeks for the FBI to dispatch a pair of agents to Antakya to interview his friends. To be fair, the bureau requires permission from the Turkish government to conduct investigations. As in most other foreign countries where the bureau works, it is forbidden to go undercover there, and it has to get clearance from the CIA before cultivating sources.

In Antakya, the FBI agents who showed up seemed woefully out of place and inexperienced—"fish out of water," as Nicole Tung put it. Tung and Clare Gillis, the freelancer who had been abducted with Foley in Libya, worried that Foley was a low priority for the United States. The journalists on the ground believe that the bureau never interviewed any of the fixers who had been captured with the hostages and then released. (The journalists knew these fixers well.) In any case, that was the last that the journalists saw of the FBI. The Bradley team eventually contacted more than 150 people. Only a handful of them said that they had spoken to the U.S. government.

According to a former federal official, there was a mistaken interpretation of U.S. policy against ransoms: it was taken to mean no negotiating at all, and that even talking to the hostage-takers was forbidden. Neither the White House nor the National Security Council stepped in to clarify the matter, leaving the investigation essentially paralyzed.

The CIA, which collects intelligence abroad, apparently gathered little of use about the hostages. Robert Ford told Bradley's team that the agency had no assets closer to Syria than Gaziantep, Turkey, thirty miles from the border. Although Bradley's team and some of the reporters in Antakya identified sites where the hostages were likely being held, there was no drone surveillance until late in the crisis, and even then only one drone was made available—for part of the day. "The president wouldn't authorize it," Barfi said. "He didn't want to get into Syria."

While Bradley lacked the government's resources, he had impressive connections, and he didn't feel constrained by protocol. Several of the families worried that information on the hostages' social media sites could be used against them—Sotloff's Israeli citizenship, Padnos's book on Islam, Kassig's army experience in Iraq—but the FBI said that it could not gain access to the hostages' accounts because of privacy concerns. Bradley called Sheryl Sandberg, the chief operating officer of Facebook; Dick Costolo, then the CEO of Twitter; and Brad Smith, the general counsel of Microsoft, and they were immediately willing to work with the families to help.

BRADLEY PRIDES HIMSELF on his ability to discover and enlist what he calls "extreme talent." Soon after he acquired *The Atlantic*, he successfully lured away Jeffrey Goldberg, a writer then working for *The New Yorker*. Bradley's blandishments included going to Goldberg's house with a trailer full of ponies for his children to ride. In an era when many magazines were retrenching or folding, it was extraordinary for a publisher to court a journalist so lavishly, and the story spread through the trade. Barak Barfi heard about the Goldberg pony gambit in Turkey.

"Why are you doing this?" Goldberg asked Bradley when he heard about the team he had assembled. After all, Bradley was not the attorney general or the secretary of defense. Bradley responded, "When I wake in the morning, I could study online advertising patterns—or I could try in some way to save the lives of Americans who are held by fanatics. When I looked at the options in front of me, it was obvious what was the best use of my time."

Goldberg believed that Bradley's obsession with hostages began with the death of Michael Kelly, the first journalist Bradley hired to edit *The Atlantic*. As Goldberg puts it, Kelly was "hysterically rude and bitingly funny"—qualities that Bradley admired but certainly didn't share. Kelly and Bradley became close. Kelly was the first reporter to be killed in the Iraq War, in April 2003. After burying Kelly, Bradley realized, "I had trouble letting one of my colleagues do something I couldn't do." The next year, he traveled to Baghdad, where William Langewiesche was reporting for *The Atlantic*. At the time, Abu Musab al-Zarqawi, the leader of al-Qaeda in Iraq—the precursor of ISIS—was beheading Westerners and posting videos on the Internet. Bradley was genuinely frightened. At the hotel where he was staying, he was told to shove the dresser and an extra bed against the door. Despite such precautions, a journalist was kidnapped from that hotel a few weeks later.

BRADLEY KEPT ADDING people to the team, paying their travel expenses, and often a salary as well. He installed two young researchers in cubicles in the Watergate office. He recruited a former Syrian diplomat, now known as Noor Azar, who had gone into exile after the revolution. Meanwhile, April Goble, Foley's ex-girlfriend, worked with eleven volunteers from Teach For America, looking for inroads into the Syrian regime.

Bradley also discovered a West Coast lawyer who had moved to Kandahar, Afghanistan, to study insurgencies. "She traveled around on a motorcycle with an assault rifle around her shoulders," Bradley said. "Her job was interviewing potential Taliban recruits and giving reports to NGOs." Because the lawyer still works in the region, she asked me to refer to her as Mary Hardy. Bradley's dazzled staff called her the Blond Bombshell.

Bradley sent Hardy to Antakya in June 2013. Foley and Padnos were the only ones taken at the time. Antakya struck her as "a typical bad border town." The place was filled with intelligence agents, Turkish and otherwise. Jihadists and smugglers and young freelancers had taken over the tourist hotels. Because only Foley's name had been made public, Hardy recalls, she was besieged by people offering to sell her information about him: "The town was awash in 'Foley's alive, Foley's dead, Foley's in Damascus, Foley's coming out tomorrow. Just get in my van and I can take you to see him.'"

Hardy sought out more experienced journalists and aid workers in the area. They had fixers who spoke Arabic and could get the phone numbers of ISIS commanders and the GPS coordinates of their various headquarters. Hardy learned that the people who had abducted Padnos and Matt Schrier were using Schrier's PayPal account to order such items as sunglasses; the items were delivered to a shop owner on the Turkish border who was known for providing fake identifications. Hardy believed that a gang connected to the shop owner had abducted Padnos. She obtained photographs of the shop owner and the gang members and sent all this information to the FBI, along with images of a prison in Aleppo. She suspected—correctly—that Padnos had been held there. The FBI ordered her to shut down her operation. It's unclear whether the bureau had already acquired similar intelligence on its own.

Hardy concluded that the gang who had kidnapped Padnos had sold him to the highest bidder. Foley's case was more complicated. He had been taken with John Cantlie, a British journalist; they were good friends, although Cantlie had a reputation for recklessness. Once, in Libya, Clare Gillis told me, Cantlie invited her and Foley to chase down a story in a particularly dicey area. Gillis declined, but Foley went ahead. (To her relief, they returned unscathed.)

In Turkey, Hardy met a British security contractor who had seen Cantlie just before he disappeared. Cantlie had been making boorish jokes in front of a group of Syrians, and his countryman reprimanded him for his cultural insensitivity. Cantlie laughed it off. He had been kidnapped once before in Syria, in July 2012, by British jihadists. They shot him in the arm when he tried to escape. A week later, he was liberated by the Free Syrian Army. Not long after, he returned to Syria with an assignment to make a documentary about his captivity. He intended to go to the site where he had been abducted—a foolhardy trip, but actual assignments were precious. He apparently enlisted Foley to be his videographer. Within days, they had been captured.

Mary Hardy had developed a theory about staying safe in dangerous places: "One third is good management—how many people do I have working with me, and how many bad guys are out there? The second third is local goodwill. And the last third is good luck." She faulted Cantlie and Foley on all three counts. They had been spotted filing their stories in an Internet café, speaking English: bad management. Cantlie's crude humor: a strike against goodwill. And both men had been taken before—so their luck had plainly run out.

"If you go into that environment, you have to do some soul-searching," Hardy says. "The macho thing is 'I am willing to take the risk.' But it's not just you and your freedom you're risking." A conflict journalist should acknowledge that he is also placing his institution at risk. He is asking his friends and his family to potentially stop everything while they pursue his freedom. And he is tacitly demanding that his government risk soldiers' lives if a rescue attempt is made. Not every journalist, Hardy observed, cares to be encumbered by such considerations, but "at least that's an interesting conversation to have at the bar."

On June 10, 2014, ISIS forces overran Mosul, Iraq's second-largest city. Sleeper cells had carried out assassinations that left the city leaderless, and the Iraqi Army quickly dissolved under assault. Because so few journalists remained on the ground to document events, the news came as a shock. The very next day, Tikrit fell. On June 29, ISIS announced the formation of a new caliphate. In Mosul, ISIS's leader, Abu Bakr al-Baghdadi, climbed the minbar of the Great Mosque of al-Nuri and boldly declared himself the new caliph, demanding the fealty of Muslims everywhere. Henceforth, the territory held by ISIS would be called the Islamic State. Despite the disparagement of many mainline imams, thousands of new fighters answered Baghdadi's call, animated by the vision of a restored Islamic empire and exhilarated by the savagery practiced by his followers.

Fifty thousand Yazidis, an ancient monotheistic community north of Mosul, fled when ISIS announced plans to exterminate them. The U.S. felt rising international pressure to stop an impending genocide. Simultaneously, ISIS forces swept toward the Kurdish capital of Erbil, where American advisers and diplomats were stationed. The families of the hostages were caught in a vise: any American action to halt ISIS's advance would likely trigger retaliation against their children, but their plight was still a secret, so little political effort was being exerted on their behalf.

The White House certainly realized that intervening against ISIS could affect the fortunes of the hostages. "It weighed on everyone's mind," Ben Rhodes, a deputy national security adviser, told me. But, he added, "not to take action in confronting the potential genocide against the Yazidis would be both a failure in terms of enabling the slaughter to go forward and also would suggest our own foreign policy can be held in check by the presence of hostages." That, he said, would be "the ultimate form of empowering the hostage-taker."

Meanwhile, the ransom demand for Padnos rose to 22 million euros. In July, a video of Padnos surfaced in several American embassies, through intermediaries. He was seated on the floor, wrists bound, with a gun pointed at his head. "My life is in very, very, very grave danger," Padnos said. "They've given me three days—three days to live." The video had apparently been made two days earlier.

Bradley had previously met with Ali Soufan, a former FBI agent whose skillful interrogation of al-Qaeda members had led to the identification of the 9/11 hijackers. Soufan, who is Lebanese American, has since founded a security company, the Soufan Group, with offices in New York and Doha. Soufan's heart sank as he learned of the hostages' plight. He doubted that the U.S. had assets on the ground, and he was well acquainted with the limitations of the American intelligence community. There was only one direction to turn. "Let's go to Qatar," he told Bradley.

Late on July 10, Bradley and Soufan were in the lobby of the St. Regis hotel in Doha, waiting to meet Ghanem Khalifa al-Kubaisi, the head of the Qatari intelligence service. Qatar is a conservative Wahhabi society, but it plays a confounding role in the region, hosting both the Al Jazeera network and an American airbase, for instance. Many rebel groups in Syria depend on Qatari support, but the country also provides an underground channel of communication between radical Islamists and the West. Six weeks earlier, Qatar had arranged the exchange of the Taliban prisoners for Bowe Bergdahl.

It was Ramadan, the fasting month, when Soufan and Bradley arrived—a complicated time to approach government officials. Moreover, Qatari intelligence was preoccupied by the military operation that Israel had just launched in Gaza. That very evening, Kubaisi was briefing the emir. After midnight, Soufan got a call from Kubaisi's chief of staff saying that his boss couldn't meet that night. "You have to," Soufan told him. "We're leaving at three in the morning."

Kubaisi showed up at 1:30 a.m. Bradley had expected him to be a hard-boiled veteran, but he was young and soft-spoken, with warm, lively eyes. Bradley presented flyers with photographs of the captives and details about the kidnappings. Kubaisi leafed through them without much hope. "You cannot predict with these groups," he said. "They are so irrational." Yet he paused upon seeing the Padnos flyer. "I think we can help on this one," he said. Alone among the five hostages, Padnos was being held by Jabhat al-Nusra, an al-Qaeda affiliate that had broken away from ISIS in February 2014. The two factions had been battling each other since then. Although Qatar maintained influence with al-Nusra, sending an operative into Aleppo was extremely dangerous, and the three-day deadline for Padnos had already passed. Kubaisi realized he would have to act fast if there was any hope of saving Padnos. He told Bradley, "I will do it—for the mother."

IN JUNE 2014, one of the remaining European hostages, Daniel Rye Ottosen, a Danish photographer, was freed. The Danish government refused to pay a ransom, but the family reportedly scraped together three and a half million euros. Ottosen's captors allowed him to carry letters from the other hostages, except Foley. In the final months of captivity, Foley and Ottosen had been chained together, and Ottosen memorized a message from Foley to his family. One of his first calls after being freed was to recite the letter to Diane Foley. "I remember going to the mall with Dad, a very long bike ride with Mom," the message begins. "Dreams of family and friends take me away and happiness fills my heart." Foley downplays the abuse, saying that he has "weak and strong days." He adds, "We are so grateful when anyone is freed, but of course yearn for our own freedom." He mentions each of his three brothers and his sister, Katie, expressing hope that he will attend her wedding one day. "Grammy, please take your medicine," he says. "Stay strong, because I am going to need your help to reclaim my life."

Diane and a few of the other parents talked to some of the freed European hostages. The Europeans were guarded in those conversations, but they spoke frankly to Barfi and Bradley, and in interviews that they later gave to the press. They said that among their guards was a group of British Muslims, whom the captives called the Beatles. The ones they called George and John were especially sadistic. The Beatles paid particular attention to Foley, because he and John Cantlie had tried to escape. Foley had made it out of his cell, but when Cantlie couldn't break free of his chains Foley surrendered. "I couldn't leave John on his own," he told the others. They were beaten savagely, and waterboarded on one occasion. Later, Foley incurred the guards' anger because he requested extra rations and more frequent trips to the toilets for the weakest captives. He gave his mattress to another prisoner and slept on the stone floor. He never complained about abuse. "They didn't like the fact he would not submit," Didier François, the French hostage, told me. "He tried to establish some balance of forces with the guards—some breathing space."

Foley organized informal lectures among the captives. Kassig told stories about hunting and fishing with his father. François described covering the war in Chechnya. Cantlie explained how to pilot a plane. Foley lectured on American literature and his captivity in Libya. The others depended on Foley to keep their spirits buoyed. "This guy, he was a man," Nicolas Hénin, another French hostage, later told *L'Express*. "He remained upright, dignified." He added, "When I see his mother's reaction, I recognize her son. They are made of the same metal."

On August 7, 2014, President Obama authorized limited air strikes on ISIS in order to relieve the Yazidis and block the jihadi advance on Erbil. "Earlier this week, one Iraqi in the area cried to the world, 'There is no one coming to help,'" Obama said in a televised address. "Well, today America is coming to help."

Five days later, the Foley family received an awkwardly spelled e-mail, asking, "how long with the hseep follow the blind sheppard?" It was addressed to "the American government and their sheep-like citizens," and it continued:

You were given many chances to negotiate the release of your people via cash transactions as other governments have accepted. . . .
however you proved very quickly to us that this is not what you
are interested in. . . .

Now you return to bomb the Muslims of Iraq once again, this
time resorting to Arial attacks and "proxy armies," all the while
cowardly shying away from a face-to-face confrontation!

Today our swords are unsheathed towards you, government
and citizens alike! and we will not sotp untill we quench our
thirst for your blood. . . .

The first of which being the blood of the American citizen,
James Foley!

A week later, Diane got a call from a distraught reporter from the
Associated Press. Diane could barely understand her. "She was sob-
bing," Diane said. "She asked if I had seen the Internet." The reporter
wouldn't elaborate. But within a short time the theatrically staged
execution of Diane Foley's son was all over the news. No one called
her from the FBI or the State Department. She contacted her primary
FBI agent, but he didn't respond. The Foleys' parish priest, however,
rushed to their house. "I'll never forget it," Father Paul Gousse told
the magazine *St. Anthony Messenger*. "Diane came and hugged me and
said, 'Father, please pray for me that I don't become bitter. I don't want
to hate.'"

When Nancy Curtis heard about Foley, she collapsed onto the
kitchen floor. For the first time since the ordeal began, her spirit was
broken. The Bradleys were at their house in the south of France when
the phone rang. David was incredulous. "I had never thought that ISIS
would kill Jim," he admitted. "The next morning, the implications hit
me. For the first time in eighteen months, our search for Jim was over.
And we had failed Jim's family."

Bradley called April Goble, in Chicago, and told her of Foley's
death. She went outside and sat under a tree. She called Diane, who
kept saying that her son was now free. Meanwhile, dozens of Goble's
and Foley's friends filled Goble's house. It got so crowded that some
people slept on the roof that night.

The next day, the Foleys got a call from the president. He was

vacationing on Martha's Vineyard. Diane remarked that Jim had campaigned for Obama. "He expected you to come get him," she said.

"Well, we tried," Obama replied. The president was sharing a
secret: the U.S. military had launched a raid to rescue the hostages
the previous month, on July 3. The FBI had finally interviewed two
of the freed European journalists, who provided detailed descriptions
of the industrial building where they and twenty-one other foreigners
had been imprisoned. U.S. officials determined that the building was
outside Raqqa, the designated capital of the Islamic State. Evidently,
the rescue team had arrived three days too late. There was a firefight,
in which two ISIS members were killed and an American soldier was
shot in the leg. But it was all for naught: no prisoners remained at the
facility.

The video of Foley's execution begins with Obama making his
announcement of air strikes against ISIS. Then Foley is seen on his
knees in a stretch of desert, wearing an orange jumpsuit that billows
in the breeze. His head is shaved. He looks strong and not frightened.
He reads out a statement denouncing the American bombing campaign, saying that his death certificate was signed that day. Then a
masked figure in black brandishes a knife. "We're no longer a part of
an insurgency," he says, in a North London accent. "We are an Islamic
army and a state that has been accepted by a large number of Muslims worldwide. So, effectively, any aggression toward the Islamic
State is an aggression toward Muslims." He grabs Foley's head and
slashes his neck. The next shot is of Foley's bloody head resting on
his back, against his handcuffed wrists, his plastic sandals askew in
the sand. Then the executioner is shown with another kneeling hostage, dressed in orange with his head shaved. The executioner points
the knife at the camera: "The life of this American citizen, Obama,
depends on your next decision."

It is Steven Sotloff.

GHANEM AL-KUBAISI HAD SENT an operative into Syria to see
what it would take to free Theo Padnos. The operative talked his way
into an extremist base but the jihadis accused him of being a spy and
threatened to kill him. The frantic emissary finally persuaded them

that he really represented the Qatari government, which had suddenly taken an active interest in the life of this one American.

The Qataris had repeatedly been told that the U.S. didn't pay ransoms to terrorists, but it was unclear how else Padnos could be saved. The All-Girl Team wondered why it was the American government's business if Padnos's family arranged for another government to rescue him. But under U.S. law, conspiring to enrich an al-Qaeda affiliate such as al-Nusra was considered material support of terrorism. Kubaisi understood the constraints, and he is vague about what he proposed, saying only that he exercised influence on al-Nusra through other rebel groups in the area. Certainly, al-Nusra had many reasons to placate Qatar, one of the Gulf's strategic powers.

On August 24, Bradley received a text from Kubaisi. "Done," he wrote, along with a thumbs-up emoji.

Ali Soufan had arranged for the handoff to take place in the Golan Heights, on the Israeli border, but the FBI and a dozen American officials were mistakenly waiting for him in Jordan. Bradley had to call and redirect them. As Padnos was being transported to the demilitarized zone, the FBI team was driving all night to get in place to receive him.

The terrorists dropped Padnos off at a UN observation post. A doctor tenderly examined his brutalized body. Then Padnos crossed into Israel, where the American officials had just arrived. At a seaside hotel in Tel Aviv, he finally got to call Nancy: "Mom, I'm in this five-star hotel! And I'm drinking a beer! And there are women here!" It was his first phone call in two years.

An FBI agent instructed him to stay in his room. The moment she left, Padnos headed out to the beach. The Mediterranean was gorgeous. There was a paddleball court and a jogging trail. Padnos strolled down to a youth hostel. Two Canadian guys were sitting outside, and they looked friendly. Padnos impulsively walked up to them and said that he'd just been freed by al-Qaeda. They offered him a drink. The next morning, the FBI agent found Padnos with his new friends passed out on the floor of his hotel room.

The word was out that there were other hostages, and although only a few journalists knew their names, such information was almost impossible to bottle up. The parents of Foley, Padnos, and Sotloff were instantly besieged by the press. Bradley asked Emily Lenzner, the communications director of Atlantic Media, to try to keep imperiling details out of the press. Lenzner had to plug one hole after another. She dissuaded a *Washington Post* reporter from running a story; Ed Kassig says that the reporter told him, "I'm going to publish. This is too big for you." A Miami television station interviewed some of Sotloff's friends, and one of them innocently commented on how much Sotloff's Jewish faith had meant to him. After Lenzner intervened, the reference was snipped from the story. But the wall of secrecy was breaking down. The *Times* reported that an American woman was among the ISIS hostages. Editors at *The Atlantic*—a few floors below Bradley's office at the Watergate—wondered how they were supposed to cover a major news event involving their employer.

Bradley summoned the Sotloffs, the Kassigs, and the Muellers to Washington, in the hope of devising a new strategy. They arrived on Sunday, August 24—the very day of Padnos's release. It felt at once ominous and hopeful to see their circle of families abruptly diminished, one by murder and the other by freedom.

Bradley wanted his involvement to remain secret, so they met in the conference room of a law firm. He introduced the families to Nasser Weddady, an activist who was born in Mauritania and grew up in Syria. Bradley described him as a social media specialist. Weddady proposed that the three mothers make a video, beseeching Baghdadi to spare their children. "The fact that the government and the families have remained silent for so long has allowed ISIS to totally control the process and to dehumanize the hostages," he contended. "My idea is to reverse that trend."

The mothers decided against a joint video. Instead, they would each make one individually. Sotloff had been placed next on ISIS's kill list, so Shirley Sotloff would release her video at once. Paula Kassig and Marsha Mueller would film similar appeals but wait to release them.

Weddady was soon at odds with Barak Barfi over the tone and the content of Shirley's statement. Barfi urged her to cover her hair, but Weddady thought it was patronizing and smacked of Orientalism. Barfi had combed through the Quran and Islamic history, trying to find useful precedents for a hostage release. Passages in the

Quran discuss prisoners of war, but their meaning is ambiguous. For instance, in 624 A.D., the Prophet Muhammad captured seventy prisoners during the Battle of Badr. His closest advisers debated ransoming or killing them. Two were executed. Other prisoners were released, including one who was not a Muslim: the husband of the Prophet's daughter Zainab. After she had sent a necklace to her father, he granted clemency to her husband. "The necklace was symbolic, of course," Weddady observes. But if the story were cited in a video "it could be misconstrued as if we were inviting a ransom—and that was a no-go zone."

The more that Barfi argued for including theological references and historical parallels, the angrier Weddady became. He and Barfi had differing conceptions of the video's audience. Barfi was addressing ISIS's leadership; Weddady was aiming his message at the Muslim world, in order to undermine ISIS's authority and appeal. Despite his frustration, Weddady could appreciate Barfi's desperation. They were Steven Sotloff's only hope.

Shirley was numb. The other mothers tried to support her, but they were also struggling to maintain their composure. As the men commiserated with Art Sotloff, Ed Kassig and Carl Mueller talked about how painful it had been to keep the abductions a secret. Art remarked that once Steven's name was out, his friends rushed to support him. Ed and Carl almost envied him.

Marsha Mueller retreated into writing in her journal. She told Weddady that she hoped to give it to Kayla one day, so she would know what had happened in her absence. This detail struck him with unexpected emotional force. The scale of the tragedy in Syria and Iraq was so vast, and this was just a piece of it. Millions of people had been displaced, and hundreds of thousands were dead, and yet the children of these parents had willingly placed their lives in jeopardy. "They went on their own into one of the most dangerous places in the world with the intention of helping the weak and downtrodden, who were being crushed by dictatorship and terrorism," Weddady told me. "They came to the rescue. That's why I see them as heroes."

While Weddady and Barfi fought about Shirley's script, Noor Azar—the former Syrian diplomat on Bradley's team—helped Paula Kassig create hers. The Kassigs wanted the captors to know that their son lamented the suffering of Syrians and wished to help them achieve freedom. Ed talked about how the Kassigs came from a long line of teachers. As a nurse, Paula planned to characterize her son as a caretaker. Azar told them that their approach was all wrong. ISIS doesn't care about freedom, she said. The militants think it's a Western notion that has been imposed on the Muslim world. They wouldn't be moved by the family's humanitarian legacy. ISIS was filled with foreign fighters who opposed many Syrian insurgent groups. The whole idea of nationality was anathema to them. Azar persuaded the Kassigs to highlight Peter's spirituality.

Meanwhile, Shirley was struggling. "I was still in a movie that had gone bad," she said. She read one script after another into the camera, but her emotional affect was wooden. She had trouble pronouncing some names and stumbled over Quranic references. She invoked Baghdadi's authority as the caliph to grant Steven amnesty, "and to follow the example set by the Rashidun Caliphs, who I have learned were the most just Muslim rulers, under whom People of the Book, like Steve, were protected." Weddady bridled at this language. "Putting a Jewish woman on TV lecturing to Muslims about Islam is a disaster," he contended. The video struck him as academic and labored, and Shirley appeared hypnotized. Bradley agreed that it should be reshot the next day.

That night, Bradley invited the families and his team to his house for dinner once again. The Kassigs were exhausted and declined. On Embassy Row, the mood had decidedly darkened from the evening in May when the dogwoods were in bloom. Sensing this, Bradley opened the floor to any idea, however crazy. Azar proposed urging the Syrian regime to do a prisoner swap with ISIS. Bradley worried that Assad would demand something in return—something that Bradley couldn't deliver, such as spare parts for airplanes. Nor did he believe that the American government would grant such a concession.

Bradley was always hard to read, even by his staff. Aretae Wyler, Bradley's general counsel, thought that the video idea was a "Hail Mary pass," but her boss seemed determined to keep pessimism from capsizing the process. We can't just sit around and do nothing, he said. Throughout dinner, he sketched possible action plans on a legal pad. Weddady would go to Egypt to enlist the aid of some radical sheikhs.

Bradley would go to Kurdistan and meet with its head of intelligence. He would plead with the king of Jordan for help. He would return to Qatar. He even aired the notion of hiring a private army to attempt a rescue.

Shirley injected a note of hope. She kept saying, "I know Steve's alive, he's going to survive, I just know it." She said that he got his strength from her parents, who had survived Auschwitz.

THE NEXT MORNING, the Muellers were close to panic. Without revealing Kayla's name, Brian Ross, of ABC, had reported the details of her capture. Other journalists who had kept quiet about Kayla were angry with Emily Lenzner, because they believed, falsely, that she had cooperated with Ross. She begged the reporters to restrain themselves: the lives of three Americans were still on the line.

Bradley's team was cracking under the tension. As Weddady and Barfi shouted at each other over Shirley's script, Wyler took Weddady's laptop, sat on the floor beside Shirley, and quietly coached her to deliver the speech.

"I am sending this message to you, Abu Bakr al-Baghdadi al-Quraishi al-Husayni, the caliph of the Islamic State," Shirley says in the final version. Her hair is uncovered. Her fatigue is evident, but she delivers the message potently:

> My son Steven is in your hands. Steven is a journalist who traveled to the Middle East to cover the suffering of Muslims at the hand of tyrants. Steven is a loyal and generous son, brother, and grandson. He is an honorable man and has always tried to help the weak.
>
> We have not seen Steven for over a year and we miss him very much. We want to see him home safe and sound, and to hug him.
>
> Since Steven's capture, I have learned a lot about Islam. I've learned that Islam teaches that no individual should be held responsible for the sins of others. Steven has no control over the actions of the U.S. government. He is an innocent journalist.
>
> I've also learned that you, the caliph, can grant amnesty. I ask you to please release my child. . . .

I want what every mother wants—to live to see her children's children. I plead with you to grant me this.

Shirley's video was released on August 27, and was instantly picked up by news organizations, especially Arabic satellite stations. As expected, ISIS followers on social media derided her plea, calling her Sheikha Shirley, but many other Muslims reacted with sympathy. Still, the overwhelming reaction that Weddady had hoped for did not happen. ISIS's grisly video had made a far bigger impact: the shot of Foley kneeling in the sand before his execution was indelible. The intent of the killing was to prod the U.S. into open war with the Islamic State, a challenge that many Americans now welcomed. In 2013, Americans heavily opposed air strikes in Syria. Now a majority favored them—an immediate, measurable consequence of the killing. For the families of the remaining hostages, there was another omen of their waning hopes: after Foley's execution, a Reuters poll found that 62 percent of Americans opposed paying ransoms for hostages.

Six days after Shirley's video appeared, Art Sotloff was heading out to drop off dry cleaning when a news bulletin flashed on his phone: "Second American Hostage Killed." No one had called him. He returned home to tell Shirley. At the same time, Wyler went into Bradley's office and told him. She found him staring, ashen-faced, at his computer. He and Katherine flew to Miami to sit shiva with the Sotloffs.

"Everyone has two lives," Steve had observed in a smuggled message; "the second one begins when you realize you only have one."

AFTER THIS DEVASTATING BLOW, Bradley decided that his team needed a lift. Each of the meals in the Bradleys' pale yellow room had marked another milestone in the hostage saga, so Bradley invited Theo Padnos to dinner. The team members finally got to meet one of the people they had worked so hard to rescue. Padnos talked about beatings, solitary confinement, exposure to cold; his captors had even buried him alive for half an hour. One nearly fatal assault left him disoriented for days. When he first returned home, he ate and slept little, and wanted to be mainly in the company of women and children. His family worried about him: his thoughts could get scattered, his emotions swinging from elation to fits of weeping.

At the dinner, Bradley asked Padnos what he had learned about evil. Bradley had been dwelling on this question. He remarked that the jihadis in Syria embodied "the purest strain of evil and malice and violence I have ever seen in my life."

"No, David, it's not like that," Padnos said. Many of the young people guarding him had acted on principle when they "rejected the West," but in doing so they had been drawn into a wildly adolescent jihadi culture. Padnos had watched children playing with grenades. If someone was making tea, a kid might place a bullet on the burner, causing it to explode. For twenty of the twenty-two months he was held, Padnos saw women only three times—and always for just a few seconds. The fighters were as isolated from women as he was. Even the married men seemed uninterested in being with their wives. And yet they all wanted to marry American women, dropping hints that Padnos might hook them up.

When his captors tortured him, they called it an "investigation." They prayed before each session. Padnos—a student of jihadi religion—came to believe that his tormentors saw their job as a religious duty. They were trying to align people with the Quran and the sayings of the Prophet. Torturing people may be morally distasteful, but stepping outside the bounds of conventional behavior was essential in order to comply with the literal demands of the religion. The Quran and the Hadith are filled with admonitions about war and punishment. "Fighting is prescribed for you and ye dislike it. But it is possible that ye dislike a thing which is good for you, and that ye love a thing which is bad for you. But Allah knoweth, and ye know not," says one famous verse. Another says: "I will cast terror into the hearts of those who disbelieve. Therefore strike off their heads and strike off every fingertip of them." The captors forced children to learn how to brutalize helpless prisoners, including Padnos, but in the jihadi mind-set, this was a sacred task. "I think the purpose of the torture is to reconcile Muslims with the literal meaning of the Quran, and the ancient—they would say 'eternal'—values of Islam," Padnos observed.

Toward the end of his confinement, Padnos was taken to a villa.

On a television, Al Jazeera was airing an image of a man in an orange jumpsuit in the desert. Text on the screen identified him as an American hostage. It was James Foley. Until then, Padnos hadn't known that other Americans were being held. His captors handed him the remote, but when he changed the channel there was Foley again.

AFTER SOTLOFF WAS MURDERED, the black-clad killer, now universally known as Jihadi John, presented the next victim. David Haines, a British citizen, had spent sixteen years as an aid worker. He had been working for a humanitarian group in a Syrian refugee camp when he was kidnapped, with an Italian colleague, in March 2013. Until the European hostages were ransomed that spring, Bradley's team was unaware that there were British hostages other than John Cantlie. Like the United States, the United Kingdom forbids ransom payments, and the Foreign Office had barred the families from discussing the abductions.

Haines was beheaded, and an execution video was released on September 13, 2014. Another British man, a cabdriver named Alan Henning, who had spent his savings on buying a used ambulance to help Syrian refugees, was placed next in line. Peter Kassig was still not named. Until David Haines was killed, the executions had been ordered by nationality. Bradley took hope from this violation of protocol: perhaps there was still time to bargain for Kassig's life.

A few days later, the Kassigs and the Muellers returned to Washington, to meet Obama. The president had just announced that the bombing campaign against ISIS was expanding into parts of Syria. He knew that the families were angry. Art Sotloff had refused to accept a condolence call from him. At the White House, Obama expressed his sympathy to the two remaining hostage families. But they felt he didn't offer any indication that the government could help. "He said if one of his daughters were taken he would do everything he could to get her home," Carl Mueller recalled. "Marsha took that to mean that we should go out and get the money. I didn't think that at all. The government continued to block our efforts."

In September 2014, ISIS made a surprising adjustment in its propaganda campaign, releasing the first of a series of videos in which John

Cantlie offers news commentary on behalf of the Islamic State. In the first video, Cantlie wears the orange jumpsuit that signals his likely execution. "I want to take this opportunity to convey some facts that you can verify," he says, striking a tone of reasonableness. He sits at a wooden desk against a black background, as on *Charlie Rose*. He notes that he was captured two years earlier. "Many things have changed, including the expansion of the Islamic State to include large areas of eastern Syria and western Iraq," he observes. He says that in subsequent videos he will explain the motivations of the Islamic State, and how Western media outlets—"the very organizations I used to work for"—distort the truth.

It was macabre to watch a man under threat of death attesting to the legitimacy of his captors' goals; the video itself was a form of psychological torture. The apparent goal of the Cantlie videos was to divide Western opinion and, perhaps, to appeal to Muslims offended by the slaughter of hostages. Indeed, Cantlie soon developed a fan base on social media.

On October 3, Henning's death was confirmed, and this time Kassig was named as the next to die. Ed and Paula had seen reporters camped out on the Sotloffs' lawn for the deathwatch. They established two safe houses and filled their car with enough food and water to last a week, in order to escape the press horde. But an odd thing happened. Journalist friends of Peter's from the Turkish border began arriving in Indianapolis to help. "They spent the entire day at our dining room table, shooting e-mails, every one of them doing everything they could to bring Peter home," Ed recalls. Jodi Perras—a former AP reporter who taught Sunday school with Paula—volunteered to be the Kassigs' spokesperson. "We were watching social media," Perras recalls. "The theme ISIS was trying to push was 'Here's an Army Ranger who fought in Iraq and deserves to die.' And we were pushing the counternarrative of a humanitarian who was helping the Syrian people and who, in fact, had converted to Islam."

Peter Kassig had been interested in Islam long before his capture. He had read the Quran while working in Palestinian camps in Lebanon. On a trip into Syria to supply Deir ez-Zor, he spent hours discussing religion with a sheikh, and when he returned he told friends that he had stopped drinking. He fasted during Ramadan. After his capture, a Syrian cellmate taught him how to pray, and he adopted the name Abdul Rahman, which means "servant of the merciful God."

Indianapolis has a large Muslim population, including Syrian exiles. The Islamic Society of North America has its headquarters nearby. A friend called Ed and Paula and asked if they would meet some local Syrians who had gathered at an interfaith center. Ed and Paula said yes. As Paula was looking at the building directory for the room number, Ed heard the sound of weeping. "It's this way," he said.

The Muslims were moved by Peter's commitment to Syria, and they and the Islamic organizations joined the campaign to pressure ISIS to spare Peter's life, holding prayer vigils in universities and mosques. Paula and Ed made their own video. "I'm a schoolteacher, and my wife is a nurse who works with refugees," Ed says into the camera, with Paula sitting beside him, her hair covered. "Our son is Abdul Rahman, formerly known as Peter." Muslims who had worked with Peter in Syria added testimonials. More surprisingly, an al-Qaeda commander tweeted that Peter had saved his life at a Syrian field hospital, performing "a successful surgical operation" while under bombardment from the Assad regime. The commander called Peter a "humanitarian activist." Jodi Perras kept up a stream of videos, tweets, and testimonials from Kassig's friends and Muslim supporters. She felt that she was personally waging the war on terror through her MacBook Air.

Two days after Peter's name was revealed, the Kassigs released a letter that he'd written, given to them by one of the freed European hostages. "I figured it was time to say a few things that need saying before I have to go," Peter writes. He says that he is underweight but not starved. "I'm a tough kid and still young so that helps." He had cried a lot in his first few months, "but a little less now":

> They tell us you have abandoned us and/or don't care but of course we know you are doing everything you can and more. Don't worry Dad, if I do go down, I won't go thinking anything but what I know to be true. That you and mom love me more than the moon & the stars.
>
> I am obviously pretty scared to die but the hardest part is not knowing, wondering, hoping, and wondering if I should even

hope at all. . . . If I do die, I figure that at least you and I can seek refuge and comfort in knowing that I went out as a result of trying to alleviate suffering and helping those in need.

He added that he prayed every day, although he was in a "dogmatically complicated situation here." The Europeans who were incarcerated with Kassig attest to his genuine faith, but ISIS follows an apocalyptic creed that challenges the beliefs of even orthodox Muslims.

Stanley Cohen, a New York attorney who has defended members of terrorist groups, including some in Hamas and Hezbollah, read Kassig's letter in the press. According to *The Guardian,* Cohen enlisted several radical Islamists to try to persuade ISIS to free Kassig, by arguing that doing so could prompt the release of Muslim prisoners in Guantánamo. Cohen enlisted a Palestinian imam living in Jordan, Abu Muhammad al-Maqdisi, who is revered among jihadis, in his effort, but before Maqdisi could act, the Jordanian government arrested him for promoting terrorist organizations.

The executions had been taking place every two weeks, but for six weeks there was a pause. Finally, on November 16, a new ISIS video appeared. Its theatrics are markedly different from those of previous execution videos. The ceremony begins with the simultaneous beheading of about twenty hostages, many of them Syrian Air Force pilots. Then, in a separate scene, Jihadi John appears with Peter Kassig's head at his feet. There is no body. "Here we are, burying the first American crusader in Dabiq, eagerly waiting for the remainder of your armies to arrive," Jihadi John says. Dabiq, a town in northern Syria, is where ISIS followers believe an apocalyptic battle between Muslims and Christians will take place.

After the video aired, there was speculation that Kassig had died in a bombing, or had been shot. (He appears to have a wound above one eye.) He apparently did not make a statement denouncing American policy. Former Army Rangers wondered if Kassig was honoring their creed, which concludes, "Under no circumstances will I ever embarrass my country."

Another significant detail of this video is that neither John Cantlie nor Kayla Mueller is named as the next victim.

The first memorial service for Peter was held at the Al Huda mosque, outside Indianapolis. An imam from Damascus led the prayers. "There were people from almost every continent," Ed recalled. Among them were many of Peter's friends, who then showed up at the Kassigs' home that night. "We had people sleeping in our camper, we had people draped across couches, on the floor," Ed said. "At about three in the morning, they made a circle and everybody went around and told Peter's story. And I really got to know my son, the man, that night."

As expected, President Obama called with condolences. He was on *Air Force One,* returning from Asia, and his voice sounded tired. Ed told him, "You've got one last chance to make this right. Save Kayla."

THE TWO SYRIANS WHO were working on David Bradley's team had to bear the additional emotional weight of watching their home-land being destroyed. They had felt helpless about the Syrian conflict until Bradley had infused them with his entrepreneurial spirit and sense of possibility. "At last, I could do something," Nasser Weddady said. Bradley sent him to Istanbul, where he recruited a tribal sheikh who had influence in Syria. Bradley himself then flew to Istanbul to meet the sheikh; that's where he was when he got the news of Kassig's murder.

Noor Azar, the former Syrian diplomat, was born in Raqqa, and still has relatives there. She had also been excited when she joined Bradley's team; at the same time, she was shocked by the U.S. gov-ernment's inaction. Syrians grow up knowing that their government doesn't value their lives, she says, but their image of the United States is informed by countless movies of Americans being rescued by the police or the FBI or the army. "When did it happen that the policy became more important than the actual U.S. citizen?" she asked. "Or was it always a myth?"

Although Azar never met Jim Foley, she looked at so many photo-graphs and videos of him that she felt she had come to know him. His brutal death hit her hard. She went to two therapists. Despite having migraines, she kept coming into the office to work on the other hos-tage cases. But she was afraid to look at a picture of Kayla.

Azar tried to find Kayla's jailers, who were assumed to be women. Through Skype and Facebook, she narrowed her search to five female Europeans. She even got in touch with one of their husbands, who gave her permission to talk to his wife. When Azar relayed her findings to the FBI, the bureau told her to stop her investigation. "Contact with ISIS is breaking the law," she was told, which was not accurate. Azar felt doubly threatened, because her visa status in the United States was uncertain. Though the FBI claimed to be pursuing its own inquiry, Azar was doubtful that it could succeed. "I don't think they have a woman who has the accent of Raqqa," she told me.

The Bradley team always held out more hope for Kayla than for the others. It helped that she was a woman, and her ransom demand— five million euros, plus prisoners—was relatively low, closer to what the European governments had reportedly paid. The Muellers tried to solicit private donations, but they were rebuffed by wealthy people who, like Bradley, feared prosecution. "They would always say they were so sorry," Marsha said. Bradley was privately considering paying the ransom himself, provided that the prisoner demand could be dropped. "If it were my child, I would pay, whether it was against the law or not," he said. "But since it was not my child, I decided it was not my place. It was a sixty-forty decision."

There had been a threat, in July, that Kayla would be killed in thirty days if the ransom wasn't paid. But August 14, her birthday, passed with her still alive. The tone of the demands for Kayla softened. The Muellers sensed that the captors really did want to release her, and yet their demands expanded to include both the release of a female al-Qaeda prisoner held in the United States and a halt to the bombing of ISIS positions. The FBI crafted replies to each message that Carl and Marsha received. "They were writing the communications, and we'd just hit 'send,'" Carl said. The agency focused on lowering the expectations of the captors, and never made a proper counteroffer.

Meanwhile, in Qatar, Ghanem al-Kubaisi summoned one of his operatives in Syria. He wanted a message passed to ISIS: "We hear you're going to kill Kayla. Before you do, let us know. We might be interested." Kubaisi heard back that the hostage-takers did not yet intend to kill her.

Didier François, the French journalist, sometimes heard Kayla asking her jailers for fruit or sanitary napkins. The male hostages wondered who she was. Then, when François and the other French journalists were released, they were given five minutes with Kayla. "She had a beautiful inner strength," Nicolas Hénin, one of the French hostages, recalled. "She was looking beautiful. She was strong—I mean, to the point that Jihadi John believed she converted to Islam. And she said, 'Oh, I just want to correct you: I did not convert.' And I mean, no one would dare to contradict him, but she did." Jihadi John remarked to the other prisoners, "She's stronger than you. She doesn't pretend."

In October 2014, a pair of Yazidi sisters—the elder was fourteen—turned up at a U.S. Special Operations command center in Iraqi Kurdistan. They had been taken as slaves by Abu Sayyaf, a senior ISIS commander, along with Kayla Mueller, but had escaped. The Yazidi girls knew Kayla well enough to describe to American interrogators a tattoo of an owl feather that Kayla had on her torso. They said that Kayla worried that her obvious Western appearance would draw attention, so she stayed behind so that the Yazidi girls could have a better chance of escape. She was also taking care of another hostage, who was older and may have been wounded by shrapnel.

Two months later, Navy SEALs attempted to rescue two hostages—an American photojournalist, Luke Somers, and a South African teacher, Pierre Korkie—in Yemen, where al-Qaeda in the Arabian Peninsula was holding them. During the raid, the captors killed both hostages. President Obama said that he authorized the raid because the captors had threatened to kill Somers within seventy-two hours; the South African, however, had been ransomed and was about to be freed. Carl and Marsha Mueller had previously told the White House that they supported a raid to save Kayla, but now they stressed that they wished to be consulted before such an attempt. "We had David and his team—we had people in Qatar and London and here working on things," Carl reasoned. "We didn't want to have a plan in place and then have Kayla killed."

Bradley had been working his diplomatic contacts, and one day he got a call from the chief of staff for Qatar's foreign minister, claiming good news: "Kayla has converted and is married. She is happily living with a family and doesn't want to come home."

"You don't believe that, do you?" Bradley said. He couldn't imagine that Kayla would not want to see her parents.

"Is that what you'd like me to communicate to the foreign minister?" the chief of staff asked.

"Exactly."

Kubaisi and Ali Soufan suspected that the story of Kayla's marriage was a negotiating tactic—a way out for ISIS, which could say, "We don't have her. Go talk to her husband." It might also provide the U.S. government or private individuals with a way to dodge the ransom problem. On the other hand, there was another rumor that Kayla was no longer a hostage; she was with the Kurds, fighting against ISIS. None of these stories rang true.

Suddenly, an opportunity arose. In December 2014, news broke that Lebanese authorities had arrested Baghdadi's alleged former wife and one of his children, who were trying to slip into Syria using false identification. There was a discussion of a prisoner exchange involving captured Lebanese soldiers for Baghdadi's relatives. Soufan flew to Doha, where he and Kubaisi discussed the possibility of adding Kayla's name to the list of prisoners to be swapped. An excited Soufan called Bradley and said that the Muellers should come to Qatar right away.

Carl and Marsha packed their best clothes, asked their son to pick up their dog, and rushed to the Phoenix airport. They arrived in Qatar nearly twenty hours later, shortly before midnight. Several government officials were waiting for them, along with Soufan, whom they hadn't met before. They all got into Mercedes sedans and drove into Doha. The whole city seemed to be under construction. Carl felt that he was transported into the twenty-second century.

Soufan had not explained what prompted his summons, and now the opportunity to do so had already passed: that very day, the Qatari foreign minister had canceled talks about the prisoner exchange after one of the Lebanese soldiers was killed by jihadis. But Soufan felt that Carl and Marsha could still take advantage of being in Qatar. He introduced them to Kubaisi, who wept as he heard Kayla's story and learned of her humanitarian deeds. Privately, he hoped that one day he would escort Kayla home.

The Muellers were staying in a five-star hotel jammed with business people attending an economic convention. The next morning, when Carl went downstairs for breakfast, he was seized with paranoia. Everywhere he turned were Arabs in traditional dress. "I was beside myself," he said. "Who were these people? Were they going to kidnap me? We went back to the room and tried to take a nap."

That morning, the Muellers met with Kubaisi's deputy director, Abdullah al-Assiri. The Qataris seemed puzzled by America's reluctance to pay ransoms. "I don't know anything about this," Carl said. "I'm an auto-body man." That struck a chord with Assiri, who took Carl to his cousin's house to show off an impressive car collection. They talked about drag racing, a passion of Carl's. Assiri persuaded Carl and Marsha to stay a few more days, to get to know the country. They were moved to another five-star hotel. Carl noticed the Lamborghinis and the Aston Martins parked outside. "It impressed on me the kind of people we were in with," he says. When they entered their immense suite, the television displayed a message: "Welcome! General al-Kubaisi." Carl finally felt that the government was taking care of him—only it wasn't his government.

WARS ARE A BEACON to idealists and adventurers and thugs, but also to a kind of tourist, who is drawn to conflict for obscure personal reasons. Experienced reporters usually keep their distance from such people, because their naïveté not only gets them in trouble; it can get others killed. Such a tragic chain of events began in the summer of 2014, when Haruna Yukawa, a forty-two-year-old Japanese citizen who called himself a security consultant, crossed the Syrian border.

The first person he put in jeopardy was a man he deeply admired, Kenji Goto, a Japanese journalist and pacifist. They had met in Syria in the spring of 2014, when Yukawa passed through a camp of the Free Syrian Army, where Goto was reporting. That August, Yukawa was taken into captivity by ISIS. Goto apparently felt obliged to try to free his inexperienced countryman. The two Japanese turned up again in January 2015, kneeling at the feet of Jihadi John, who demanded $200 million dollars within seventy-two hours. It was the same amount that Japan's prime minister, Shinzo Abe, had pledged in the fight against ISIS. When the deadline expired, Yukawa was beheaded.

On a video, Goto read a statement saying that ISIS wanted to exchange him for an Iraqi woman, Sajida Mubarak Atrous al-Rishawi, who had participated in the 2005 hotel suicide bombings in Amman, which killed more than fifty people. (Rishawi's suicide belt failed to detonate.) It is one of the most notorious terrorist events in Jordan's history. The swap didn't happen. Goto was killed.

There was a hostage the Jordanians were willing to exchange for Rishawi, however: Moaz al-Kasasbeh, a pilot in the Jordanian Air Force, whose F-16 had crashed near Raqqa on Christmas Eve. The Jordanians asked for proof of life before initiating an exchange. ISIS could not provide it. On February 3, the group released a video of Kasasbeh being burned alive inside a cage. Rishawi was hanged in revenge the next day.

These deaths were a prelude to one more.

WHEN CARL MUELLER GOT the news, he called the sheriff. The local police had already made plans, in the event of Kayla's death, to seal off the road that leads to the Muellers' house in the red granite hills outside Prescott.

On February 6, 2015, ISIS tweeted that Kayla had been killed in a bombing by the Jordanian Air Force. The U.S. and Jordanian governments denied this, although the building where she was supposedly killed—a weapons-storage facility—had been struck before by coalition aircraft. Carl and Marsha asked Kayla's captors to provide proof of her death. ISIS sent them several photographs of her corpse. In their note, the captors called Kayla "our sister."

It was two days after the hanging of Rishawi in Jordan, and most people on Bradley's team suspected that Kayla had actually been murdered in reprisal. Carl and Marsha agreed. (Lisa Monaco, the homeland security adviser, suggested to me that Kayla had died in a bombing of unknown provenance. "We have no information that it was one of ours," she said. "Nor was there any information to support the claims that it was a Jordanian plane.")

"You must share the same deep sadness and sense of defeat that Kayla's execution brings to me," Bradley wrote to his team. "While there was Kayla still to save, it was possible to look forward after Jim, then Steve, then Peter's death. But, now, it's hard to look any direction but back, at the string of defeats and unending pain created at the hands of ISIS. I don't have anything good to say here. It feels like evil won."

MARSHA MUELLER'S SISTERS CAME to Arizona for a visit and Marsha took them into Kayla's room. In the closet, there is a trunk filled with dozens of diaries. Carl was slowly going through them. When Marsha placed something on one of the closet shelves, a bag fell down. It contained Kayla's ponytail, which she had left for Marsha to give to Locks of Love.

On Jim Foley's birthday, October 18—two months after he was killed—a memorial service was held at his church, in New Hampshire. Theo Padnos attended, and afterward he asked Katherine Bradley, "Why did your husband save me?" She responded, "Because Jim Foley wrote him a second thank-you letter."

The Foleys sent the Sotloffs a magnolia sapling, which Art planted in his backyard, next to a towering palm tree that he and Steven had grown from a coconut when Steven was a boy. Sometimes Art sits beside the magnolia and has conversations with Steven. "Why'd you do that?" he asks. One night he thought that he heard Shirley listening to television. She was online, watching Steven's execution. Art said, "They don't really show it." Shirley responded, "You see his neck, you see his foot move."

Ed Kassig told me, "I have friends who say we'll get back to doing stuff the way we used to do. That's gone. Now we're looking for a new normal, and where that will be, frankly, I don't know."

HUNDREDS OF AMERICANS ARE kidnapped abroad every year, most of them taken by drug cartels and other criminal elements. Joshua Boyle and Caitlin Coleman, a married couple, disappeared in Afghanistan in 2012 and are presumed to be held by the Haqqani network. Austin Tice, the photojournalist from Houston, went missing in Syria in August 2012, several months before Jim Foley was taken. He is thought to be held by the Syrian government. There may be others, but the White House refused to specify how many Americans are being held by foreign terrorist organizations.

Political kidnappings pose a dilemma for U.S. presidents. Americans in captivity can, in a sense, hold the entire country hostage. Jimmy Carter's presidency was destroyed by the Iranian hostage crisis. In part because Ronald Reagan was so personally invested in the plight of American families who had relatives held in Lebanon, members of his administration authorized the secret sale of arms to Iran, leading to the Iran-Contra scandal. Since then, administrations have kept presidents from getting too close to such situations. Obama's predicament was particularly delicate: he had the choice of protecting thousands of Yazidis and Kurds at the risk of a few American lives. It was a gamble that he lost, although it might not have made any difference in the fates of Foley, Sotloff, and Kassig.

After the Americans were executed, the U.S. government initiated a policy review, led by the White House and coordinated by Lieutenant General Bennet Sacolick, the director for strategic operational planning at the National Counterterrorism Center.

Sacolick commanded the Delta Force during the second Iraq War. One of his jobs was rescuing hostages. "We never had one killed," he told me. His personal view is: "If I ever get taken, I want those guys to rescue me." As an Army man, he added, "It's got to be the Green Berets."

For the policy review, two dozen American hostage families were interviewed about their experiences with the government. That led to the creation of a "hostage recovery fusion cell," headed by the FBI, with deputies from State and Defense. These officials would report to a new division of the National Security Council: the Hostage Response Group. The goal is to fold the expertise of various agencies into a single government unit that will be represented at a high level in the White House. "What we saw in our review was that our hostage policy and the mechanisms in government for engaging with the families were constructed for a different era," Lisa Monaco told me. Third-party efforts, like that of Bradley's team, will have a greater voice, and efforts will be made to share information more freely. "Nothing is going to be satisfactory to parents unless they get their kids back," Monaco said. "But we gotta do better."

The no-ransom policy was never up for review. "The U.S. government will not pay ransoms or make concessions, but it's not going to abandon families when they make private, independent decisions about engaging or negotiating with hostage-takers," Monaco said. "What guides us is a focus on the families' safety and security—are they in jeopardy, are they going to be defrauded?"

I asked Ben Rhodes, the deputy national security advisor, what he thought the government's responsibility was when Americans are kidnapped abroad. "We have two obligations," he said. "One is we warn our citizens beforehand about places where they may face greater risk. We also have a responsibility to any American citizen to do what we can to get them home."

Whatever diplomacy the State Department engaged in, it was ineffectual, although Secretary John Kerry made numerous calls, some of them at Bradley's request. Bradley's team, along with the journalists on the Turkish border, repeatedly produced leads that the FBI failed to pursue. When Padnos came home, he was surprised to discover that his iPhone, which had been confiscated by his captors, could be remotely followed. He can still track the phone's location through various apps that his captors are using. Jim Foley had also carried an iPhone; April Goble had given it to him. A year after his kidnapping, she asked an FBI agent if he was following the phone. "Have you got the serial number?" the agent asked. Even without using the Find My iPhone app, intelligence agencies can locate mobile phones, and can eavesdrop on conversations while the phones are turned off.

The July 2014 raid on the Raqqa facility may have been a masterpiece of coordination, as General Sacolick called it, but it came too late. The intelligence community was slow to contribute drones and other tools that might have helped the military act more quickly. (The White House told *The Wall Street Journal* that the military's sole request for drone surveillance came just before the Raqqa raid.) The government's greatest failure, however, was its handling of five American families under extraordinary duress. Bradley's team did not succeed in bringing four of those children home, but it did give the families hope and comfort.

BRADLEY HAS BEEN TRYING to learn from his experience. When hostages are taken, U.S. government officials often consider the families and their advocates a distraction; yet such people frequently have resources and networks at hand, and they bring a commitment that is unequaled. "Washington might benefit from positively encouraging this public-private partnership," Bradley observed. "The majesty of the American government—plus all its protocols and procedures—can make for slow going. Whereas the rest of us can pick up the phone to call, say, a just-released Italian hostage, the government must labor through diplomatic channels. I don't envy them."

Marsha and Carl Mueller think that the U.S. government was leading them on by asking them to send so many e-mails to Kayla's captors. "What is so hard for us is that we had a way to get her home through negotiation, but it was used to stall in hopes of finding these people and getting them," Marsha said. After Kayla's death, representatives from the FBI and the State Department asked the Muellers to sanction a reward for information leading to the capture of Kayla's kidnappers. The reward would be between five million and seven million dollars—about the same as the ransom demand. Carl and Marsha declined.

On May 16, 2015, seven months after learning of Kayla Mueller's presence in the Abu Sayyaf household, the Delta Force conducted a raid that killed Abu Sayyaf and about a dozen fighters. The raiders also captured Abu Sayyaf's wife, Umm Sayyaf. American intelligence learned that she was selling female captives as slaves. The Yazidi sisters who had escaped told American intelligence that the leader of ISIS, Abu Bakr al-Baghdadi, would often come to the Sayyaf house, where he tortured and repeatedly raped Kayla, claiming that she was his wife. He also raped one of the Yazidi girls. He forced them to watch the beheading of James Foley and said the same would happen to them if they failed to convert to Islam.

Theo Padnos sometimes feels burdened by the fact that he remains alive. He is still in touch with his captors, who he thinks might have been able to intercede with ISIS to free the other hostages. Often, when he was in captivity, he imagined being in a bicycle race in which he'd dropped out of the pack, forcing him to finish on his own. "Which brings me to Kayla Mueller," he wrote in a blog post. "She seems to have been in a mood similar to mine during her captivity. I'm sure she also spent a lot of time in private, telepathic conversations with her family." Padnos quoted from her letter:

> None of us could have known it would be this long but know I am also fighting from my side in the ways I am able + I have a lot of fight left inside of me. I am not breaking down + I will not give in no matter how long it takes.

"I'm gonna stop for a moment and talk to you directly, Kayla," Padnos wrote. "If you happen to be reading this, which I think is just maybe possible, I want to tell you: I'm so sorry we let you down. I just cannot imagine how we could have done this. Sweetheart, take care of yourself. O.K.?"

Epilogue

Terror, as a strategy, rarely succeeds, except in one respect: it creates repression on the part of the state or the occupying power. This is an expected and longed-for goal of terrorists, who seek to counter the state's vast military advantage by forcing it to overreact, generating popular support for their cause. Fighting terror is an expensive and clumsy enterprise. Great powers have often been humbled by small, highly motivated groups that are willing to kill and willing to die, as France learned in Algeria and Britain in Palestine. Osama bin Laden was deliberately provoking the United States in his attacks on the American embassies in East Africa in 1998, the USS *Cole* in Yemen in 2000, and mainland America on 9/11. He wanted the United States to invade Afghanistan, believing that America would suffer the same fate as the Soviet Union, which simply dissolved after its withdrawal in 1988. Bin Laden took credit for that. He imagined that America would bankrupt itself and alienate Muslims everywhere in its pursuit of the "war on terror." Eventually the United States would also become disunited states, thus opening the road for Islam to regain its rightful place as the world's only superpower.

Bin Laden miscalculated, but he didn't entirely fail. Even though the core organization of al-Qaeda has been devastated by American and allied strikes, bin Laden's progeny have spread through the Middle East, Africa, and South Asia, controlling far more territory in the aggregate than at any time before 9/11. Moreover, the goals of al-Qaeda's savage offspring have expanded far beyond what the founder envisioned; they seek a civil war within Islam, the annihilation of the Shiites, and the conquest of all peoples who do not believe in their literalist reading of their religion. All of that is seen as a prelude for the end of time.

IT'S COMMON to suggest that dealing with root causes of terrorism is the best and maybe only way to bring it to an end, but there is very little evidence to support that notion—or, indeed, what those root causes are. Poverty doesn't necessarily lead to acts of terror. Nor does tyranny, nor do wars, corruption, a lack of education or opportunity, physical abuse, ethnic hatred, food insecurity, political instability, gender apartheid, a feeble civil society, a muzzled press, nor an absence of democracy. Not one of these factors by itself is sufficient to say that here at last is the reason that idealistic young people line up for the opportunity to behead their opponents or blow themselves up in a fruit market. But each of them is a tributary in a mighty river that floods the Middle East, a river that we can call Despair.

Yes, there is an absolute relationship between poverty, education, and violence, but it often works in the reverse of what is commonly assumed. Palestinians who are involved in terror organizations, such as Hamas and Hezbollah, tend to have better educations, are more likely to be employed, and have higher incomes than the general population. The worst violence in the occupied territories often occurs in times of relative prosperity. Game theorists have discovered that improving economies may actually lead to increased acts of terror, perhaps because the targets are richer. And as for the absence of democracy, America's experience in overthrowing tyrants in Iraq and Libya and attempting to bring pluralistic rule to the Middle East should be a sufficient caution about applying such remedies in the future.

And yet all terrorist groups eventually die out. Audrey Kurth Cronin, a professor of public policy at George Mason University and the author of an insightful book, *How Terrorism Ends,* studied 475 groups that met her elemental definition of terrorist organizations: they deliberately targeted noncombatants in a series of attacks. She found that the average life span of such groups was eight years. Al-Qaeda, having been founded in 1988, has far outlasted its life expectancy, although religiously based terror groups tend to be more durable than average. One such group, the Hindu Thugs, lasted six hundred years.

Professor Cronin outlines six ways terrorist organizations come to an end.

The first is the elimination of the charismatic figure usually at the head of such groups. This worked exceptionally well with the 1992 capture of Abimael Guzmán, the leader of Peru's Sendero Luminoso (the Shining Path), one of the most lethal groups of the twentieth century: nearly seventy thousand people were killed in the struggle between Guzmán's organization and the Peruvian government. Similarly, the arrest of Shoko Asahara, the blind yogi who founded the Japanese doomsday cult Aum Shinrikyo (Supreme Truth), which was responsible for the sarin gas attacks on Tokyo subways in 1995, effectively ended an organization that could have been more dangerous than al-Qaeda, given the skill and ambition of its membership. On the other hand, the targeting of Palestinian terror chieftains by Israel failed to reduce violence and actually boosted recruitment by those groups.

The killing of bin Laden by American Special Forces in 2011 has had a mixed legacy. His successor, Ayman al-Zawahiri, enjoys none of the magnetism that bin Laden exerted on his followers; and even though 75 percent of the core al-Qaeda organization has been killed by drone attacks or raids, it is still capable of inspiring kindred groups to follow its example.

Terror sometimes ends in negotiations—in other words, terrorists enter a legitimate political process. No one likes to talk to terrorists, nor do terrorists like to talk, which is why there are so few examples of successful compromises that lead to the end of violence. The Good Friday Agreement of April 10, 1998, effectively did so, by compelling the paramilitary groups in Northern Ireland to surrender their weapons and commit to peaceful and democratic means of resolving differences. The conflict between the Colombian government and the narcotrafficking mafia FARC (the Revolutionary Armed Forces of Colombia), which has cost nearly a quarter-million lives over half a century, may be another example, if the agreement announced in September 2015 endures.

It is the nature of organizations, even ones based on terror, to adjust their mission if circumstances undermine their reason for existence. When bin Laden created al-Qaeda, he envisioned it as an anticommunist Muslim foreign legion, a potential ally of the West, just as the mujahideen in Afghanistan had been in their war against the Soviets. Even before bin Laden's death, al-Qaeda had turned into an anti-Western, Islamist fantasy, with unrealizable utopian goals. The core al-Qaeda organization wouldn't know how to negotiate because it doesn't know what it wants.

It's a myth that terrorism never succeeds, although Professor Cronin found that only about 5 percent of the groups she studied achieved their goals. Most of them were movements associated with the so-called wars of liberation against colonial powers, as in Ireland, Cyprus, Vietnam, and Algeria. The prototype of the successful terrorist organization is Irgun, the Jewish group headed by Menachem Begin in the British Mandate of Palestine. Begin improvised many of the theatrical, headline-grabbing actions that demoralized the British public and led to the government's decision to turn over control of Palestine to the United Nations in 1948. That same year, Begin's irregulars attacked a peaceful Palestinian village, Deir Yassin. His men went house to house, hurling hand grenades through the windows and shooting villagers who attempted to flee. Within two months of Deir Yassin, about 350,000 Palestinians had fled or been chased into neighboring countries, a total that would eventually reach as many as 750,000. Irgun's success would spawn many imitators, notably among those same Palestinian refugees.

Ukhonto we Sizwe (Spear of the Nation), the armed wing of the African National Congress, was directly fashioned after Irgun, according to its cofounder Nelson Mandela, in order to wage a terrorist campaign against the white apartheid regime in South Africa. Beginning with acts of sabotage against the government, the campaign eventually turned to bombings of bars, banks, supermarkets, and stadiums, as well as torture and murder. The ANC renounced violence in 1990, when it entered negotiations with the governing white party, and then came to power four years later. Terrorism was not the central element in eliminating apartheid, but it was certainly a contributor.

When American soldiers entered Afghanistan after 9/11, they found a copy of Begin's memoir *The Revolt* in the library of an al-Qaeda training camp. Bruce Hoffman, the director of the Center for Security Studies at Georgetown University, and the dean of counterterrorism scholarship, speculates that bin Laden was studying Begin's transition from terrorist leader to statesman (Begin later became Israel's prime minister and won the Nobel Peace Prize following the signing of the Camp David Accords in 1979).

Most terror organizations simply end in failure. Internal schisms may cause the group to implode. Sometimes the ideological rationale behind the movement becomes irrelevant, as happened with Marxist-based terror organizations after the fall of the Soviet Union. Any remnant of popular support can wither in the face of widespread revulsion if the terror crosses an emotional line. That was the cause of the collapse of the Islamic Group in Egypt after the 1997 Luxor massacre. Similarly, many of bin Laden's inner circle decried 9/11 as a catastrophe for their group, observing that instead of driving the West out of the Middle East, al-Qaeda attacks prompted two wars that drew the United States and other Western powers much more deeply into the region.

Repression is the way that governments routinely attempt to stamp out terror organizations, but it requires a rapacity and persistence that democratic countries find difficult to justify or sustain. A combination of repression and internal division brought an end to Zawahiri's al-Jihad group in Egypt. Russia crushed the Chechen separatist movement, which gave up armed resistance in 2009; however, hundreds of Chechens have joined the Islamist ranks in Syria, and may pose a real threat to Russia if and when they return. When Israel invaded Lebanon in 1982 in order to root out the Palestinian Liberation Organization, Prime Minister Menachem Begin thought that the operation would last forty-eight hours; in fact, it continued for eighteen years. Israel finally succeeded in expelling the PLO, but the political vacuum was filled by Hezbollah, which was formed with Iranian assistance in reaction to the invasion. Hezbollah now controls Lebanon.

The last of Professor Cronin's categories for how terrorist groups end is reorientation—that is, the transition of the group from terror into something else, usually crime. But volatile organizations can move in multiple directions. The Philippine Islamist group Abu Sayyaf began as a separatist organization, became a criminal enterprise, and has since pledged allegiance to the Islamic State.

Judging the future of al-Qaeda through the lenses of these six categories, we can say that decapitation has had an effect, although it has not proved fatal. Negotiation will not be a factor with the core organization. Success is out of reach, and failure is a real possibility, especially with the rise of vigorous competitors. Repression, in the form of military action, will continue to erode the ability of al-Qaeda to act. Reorientation is unlikely.

ISIS, OR THE ISLAMIC STATE, has been a different organization since its beginning, in 1999, when a thuggish but charismatic Jordanian ex-convict, Abu Musab al-Zarqawi, arrived in Kandahar, Afghanistan, seeking to join al-Qaeda. Bin Laden didn't accept him at the time; however, he did underwrite a training camp for Zarqawi, who recruited mostly from Jordan, the Palestinian territories, Syria, and Lebanon. This region is known in Arabic as al-Sham, loosely translated into English as the Levant. Thus the organization that Zarqawi later founded would come to be called either the Islamic State in al-Sham (ISIS) or in the Levant (ISIL).

Judged by Professor Cronin's schemata, one possible end to ISIS terrorism is success. Zarqawi was killed in 2006 by an American air strike, and yet his organization survived the loss of its leader. It is already the richest terror group in history, raking in revenue from taxes, oil, ransoms, the black market in antiquities, and even traffic fines and the sale of fishing licenses. It is not even proper now to call it a terrorist group; it is a proto-state that uses terror not just to conquer but to rule. And yet, a state requires governance, which Islamists have never done well, and the actual control of territory, which opens the door to conventional warfare, where terrorists are at a decided disadvantage.

Bin Laden never saw Iraq as a prosperous place to wage jihad, because the population is 65 percent Shiite. Although al-Qaeda is an entirely Sunni organization, bin Laden had no interest in creating a civil war inside Islam. That was exactly what attracted Zarqawi, believing that slaughtering other Muslims was the only way of purifying the religion. "Someone may say that, in this matter, we are being hasty and rash," by leading Muslims into a fratricidal battle "that will be revolting and in which blood will be spilled," Zarqawi admitted in a letter to bin Laden. "This is exactly what we want."

Both bin Laden and Zarqawi dreamed of the restoration of the caliphate, which they expected would bring back the golden age of Islam, when it reached from Morocco to southern China, ruled over Spain, and went as far as the gates of Vienna. But for bin Laden, the caliphate lay far over the horizon; his first priority was to unite the Muslims in the struggle against the West. By contrast, Zarqawi's goals were to set Muslims against each other, acquire territory, and declare the caliphate as soon as possible.

The U.S. invasion of Iraq in 2003 let loose a flood of end-time thinking among Muslims. As in Christianity and Judaism, more-educated believers tend to hold themselves somewhat apart from such beliefs. This was certainly true of the elite leaders of al-Qaeda, for whom the apocalypse was a distant, if longed-for, inevitability. The Iraq War changed that, setting loose a cascade of prophecies that threw the Sunni world into panic and confusion, but also thrilled those who imagined a glorious final act. Zarqawi, a man of the streets and the jail cell, gave focus to the radicalized Muslims, who were reminded of the sayings of the Prophet that in the end-time believers are supposed to gather in Syria and Iraq to await the Day of Judgment. According to prophecy, Jesus will return to fight with the Muslims against the Jews, who will be led by the Antichrist, called the Deceiving Messiah in Islam. That final battle will take place in Dabiq, a small Syrian village near the Turkish border. Zarqawi and his successors were in a hurry to establish the caliphate to prepare for that fateful hour. "We will not lay down this flag until we present it to Jesus, the son of Maryam, and the last of us fights the Deceiver," an ISIS spokesman declared in 2013.

"Titanic upheavals convulse the region in the very places mentioned by the prophecies," William McCants notes in his excellent study of jihadi thinking, *The ISIS Apocalypse*. "Sunnis and Shi'a are at war, both appealing to their own versions of prophecies to justify their politics." He concludes: "This is not Bin Laden's apocalypse."

The conflict that the Islamic State has provoked will ultimately bring about its destruction, but not without much more havoc and heartache. It is the belief of the leaders of that organization that chaos, conflict, and despair are their allies, and to some extent I agree with them. I have a theory, not verified by scholarship, that it is a feature of human nature to want to equalize one's inner and outer worlds. A child brought up in an abusive family is more likely to become abusive as an adult. Imagine the effect of the trauma and barbarism that has been visited on the Middle East and North Africa at large; surely, out of such environments emerge individuals who want to extend the chaos and make the rest of the world resemble the emotional state they are experiencing. This would account for at least some of the lure of the Islamic State for shattered young people with few prospects of a fulfilling life. But it also reflects on the idealists, such as James Foley, Steven Sotloff, Peter Kassig, and Kayla Mueller, who enjoyed an abundance of love and security in their own lives, and devoted themselves to trying to extend those blessings to those who have not. It is to them this book is dedicated.

AT THIS WRITING, nearly five million Syrians have fled their country, half into Turkey. About a million are in Lebanon, where they account for one out of four residents in that fragile country. Nearly 700,000 are in Jordan. This does not count the eight million Syrians who have been driven from their homes but still remain in their homeland. Half of the population has been uprooted. They join refugees from other areas of conflict—Afghanistan, Iraq, Sudan, Congo, Myanmar, Somalia—who make up the masses trying to enter Europe every day. Many perish trying, a testament to their desperation.

Refugees are different from other immigrants. They typically arrive with nothing more than they can carry, except for an immense burden of trauma. They will provide a reservoir of young workers, badly needed in Europe, and a degree of cultural diversity that may enliven European societies, but if neglected or made to feel unwelcome, they may form a resentful underclass that will become a dangerous repository for radicalism. One can look at France for an example of a society that has failed to integrate its Muslim population, largely a residue of its colonial experience in North Africa. The U.S. State Department estimates that 10 percent of the French population is Muslim (French census forbids taking religion into account), and yet Muslims account for approximately 70 percent of the prisoners in France. What a stark measure of the alienation that Muslims feel!

America has been comparatively fortunate with its Muslim population, which enjoys about the same income, is about as likely to go to college or graduate school, and is less likely to go to prison than the average American. Moreover, America has largely benefited from great streams of refugees in recent history. In 1975, at the end of the Vietnam War, the United States evacuated 130,000 Vietnamese, many of them military officers and political leaders. That was followed by the wave of "boat people" in 1979, when hundreds of thousands fled, many to the United States. There are now more than a million Vietnamese in the United States, enjoying a higher average income than the general American population. Again, in 1980, there was the Mariel boatlift, when the Cuban government briefly allowed its citizens to emigrate. Between April and October, 125,000 people arrived in Florida, mostly by boat to Key West and Miami. They included several thousand violent criminals and mentally unstable people that President Fidel Castro had mischievously tossed into the mix. Half of the immigrants settled in Miami, where they were quickly absorbed into the local economy. Among them, unsurprisingly, were several murderers and a number of gang members, but there were also a future Pulitzer Prize author, a soap opera star, and a major-league ballplayer. The lesson seems to be that America does a good job of absorbing large numbers of refugees, even with very difficult populations, but there are also significant risks. And yet, if the world does little, and fails to deal with this historic tide of refugees, there will be woeful consequences for decades to come.

ONE DAY IN 1965, I took a date to the airport. I was a senior in high school in Dallas, Texas, and didn't have enough allowance to go to the movies. Love Field, as it is actually called, was a common destination for cheap dates. An American Airlines jetliner had just arrived from some exotic locale—Paris, we supposed—and my girlfriend and I walked out on the tarmac and climbed the ramp into the plane. The flight attendants were cleaning up as we sat in the first-class cabin; one of them actually gave us a snack. After that, we went into the FAA tower. "Come on in, kids!" a flight controller said as I cracked open the unlocked door. We sat on stools and watched the landing lights of the incoming flights, like fireflies in the summer night.

That America is gone. Terrorism killed it. That America is not remembered or even imagined by younger people who have never experienced such freedom, and who have no way of calculating the many sacrifices of liberty that have been made in the name of the war on terror.

This age of terror will end one day, but whether our society can restore the feeling of freedom that once was our birthright is hard to predict. The security state that has grown up since 9/11 has trans-formed our culture; and yes, we have needed the protection. We are often reminded that we must "never forget" what happened on that fateful day. But if we fail to keep in mind the country we were before 9/11, we may never steer in that direction again. In that case, the terrorists really will have won.

INDEX

A NOTE ABOUT THE AUTHOR

Lawrence Wright is a staff writer for *The New Yorker* and the author of eight previous books of nonfiction, including *In the New World, Remembering Satan, The Looming Tower, Going Clear, Thirteen Days in September,* and one novel, *God's Favorite.* His books have received many prizes and honors, including a Pulitzer Prize for *The Looming Tower.* He is also a playwright and screenwriter. He and his wife are longtime residents of Austin, Texas.

A NOTE ON THE TYPE

This book was set in Monotype Dante, a typeface designed by Giovanni Mardersteig (1892–1977). Conceived as a private type for the Officina Bodoni in Verona, Italy, Dante was originally cut only for hand composition by Charles Malin, the famous Parisian punch cutter, between 1946 and 1952. Its first use was in an edition of Boccaccio's *Trattatello in laude di Dante* that appeared in 1954. The Monotype Corporation's version of Dante followed in 1957. Although modeled on the Aldine type used for Pietro Cardinal Bembo's treatise *De Aetna* in 1495, Dante is a thoroughly modern interpretation of the venerable face.

Composed by North Market Street Graphics,
Lancaster, Pennsylvania

Printed and bound by Berryville Graphics,
Berryville, Virginia

Designed by Cassandra J. Pappas